Rome and the Mediterranean 2

The Edinburgh History of Ancient Rome
General Editor: J. S. Richardson

Early Roman Italy to 290 BC: The Origins of Rome and the Rise of the Republic
Guy Bradley

Rome and the Mediterranean 290 to 146 BC: The Imperial Republic
Nathan Rosenstein

The End of the Roman Republic 146 to 44 BC: Conquest and Crisis
Catherine Steel

Augustan Rome 44 BC to AD 14: The Restoration of the Republic and the Establishment of the Empire
J. S. Richardson

Imperial Rome AD 14 to 192: The First Two Centuries
Jonathan Edmondson

Imperial Rome AD 193 to 284: The Critical Century
Clifford Ando

Imperial Rome AD 284 to 363: The New Empire
Jill Harries

From Rome to Byzantium AD 363 to 565: The Transformation of Ancient Rome
A. D. Lee

Rome and the Mediterranean 290 to 146 BC

The Imperial Republic

Nathan Rosenstein

EDINBURGH
University Press

© Nathan Rosenstein, 2012

Edinburgh University Press Ltd
22 George Square, Edinburgh EH8 9LF

www.euppublishing.com

Typeset in Sabon
by Norman Tilley Graphics Ltd, Northampton,
and printed and bound in Great Britain
by CPI Group (UK) Ltd, Croydon, CR0 4YY

A CIP record for this book is available from the
British Library

ISBN 978 0 7486 2321 1 (hardback)
ISBN 978 0 7486 2322 8 (paperback)
ISBN 978 0 7486 2999 2 (webready PDF)
ISBN 978 0 7486 5081 1 (epub)
ISBN 978 0 7486 5080 4 (Amazon ebook)

Published with the support of the Edinburgh University
Scholarly Publishing Initiatives Fund.

Contents

Illustrations

Tables

Acknowledgements

This book has taken me an unconscionably long time to finish, and I am grateful to John Richardson and the editorial staff at the University of Edinburgh Press for their patience and forbearance. However, I have been thinking and writing about various aspects of Roman history during the middle Republic for an even longer time, and I am grateful to Prof. Richardson for offering me the opportunity to bring a greater measure of coherence to those thoughts and in the process come to understand a good deal more than when I began. The College of Humanities at the Ohio State University generously granted me a quarter's leave which enabled me to advance the writing of the manuscript considerably. Ann Kuttner, Seth Bernard, and Stephan Zink all provided valuable guidance on Roman houses at the eleventh hour. The staff at the American Numismatic Society and Art Resource were wonderfully efficient in securing several of the images for the volume, and I am grateful to Jona Lendering of www.livius.org for allowing me to reproduce his photograph of the bust of Pyrrhus, and to Lisa Fentress for permission to reproduce her plan of the House of Diana. My students here at OSU, both undergraduate and graduate, have been a constant source of stimulation for thinking about the middle Republic. One of them, Peter van der Puy, provided invaluable help as my research assistant during the final stages of the project. I am as always indebted to my wife, Anne Jewel, and my daughter, Zoë, for their tolerance of this enterprise, as of so many others, over so many years. This book is dedicated to the memory of my father, who always wanted me to write one like it.

Series editor's preface

Rome, the city and its empire, stands at the centre of the history of Europe, of the Mediterranean, and of lands which we now call the Middle East. Its influence through the ages which followed its transformation into the Byzantine Empire down to modern times can be seen across the world. This series is designed to present for students and all who are interested in the history of western civilisation the changing shape of the entity that was Rome, through its earliest years, the development and extension of the Republic, the shift into the Augustan Empire, the development of the imperial state which grew from that, and the differing patterns of that state which emerged in east and west in the fourth to sixth centuries. It covers not only the political and military history of that shifting and complex society but also the contributions of the economic and social history of the Roman world to that change and growth and the intellectual contexts of these developments. The team of contributors, all scholars at the forefront of research in archaeology and history in the English-speaking world, present in the eight volumes of the series an accessible and challenging account of Rome across a millennium and a half of its expansion and transformation. Each book stands on its own as a picture of the period it covers and together the series aims to answer the fundamental question: what was Rome, and how did a small city in central Italy become one of the most powerful and significant entities in the history of the world?

John Richardson, General Editor

Abbreviations

Primary sources

App.		Appian
	B Civ.	*Bella civilia* (*The civil wars*)
	Celt.	*The Celtic wars*
	Hann.	*The Hannibalic war*
	Hisp.	*The Spanish wars*
	Ill.	*The Illyrian wars*
	Mac.	*The Macedonian wars*
	Pun.	*The Punic wars*
	Sam.	*The Samnite wars*
Asc.		Asconius
Cic.		Cicero
	Brut.	*Epistulae ad Brutum* (*Letters to Brutus*)
	De or.	*De oratore* (*On the orator*)
	Fin.	*De finibus bonorum et malorum* (*On the ends of good and evil*)
	Font.	*Pro Fonteio*
	Leg. agr.	*De lege agraria* (*On the agrarian law*)
	Nat. D.	*De natura deorum* (*On the nature of the gods*)
	Off.	*De officiis* (*On duties*)
	Sen.	*De senectute* (*On old age*)
	Tusc.	*Tusculanae disputationes* (*Tusculan disputations*)
CIL		*Corpus Inscriptionum Latinarum*
Crawford, *RS*		*Roman Statutes*, 2 vols, M. Crawford (ed.)
Dio Cass.		Dio Cassius
Diod. Sic.		Diodorus Siculus
Dion. Hal.		Dionysius of Halicarnassus
Front. *Str.*		Frontinus, *Strategmata* (*Strategies*)
Gell. *NA*		Aulus Gellius, *Noctes Atticae* (*Attic nights*)

Hor. *Carm.*		Horace, *Carmina* (*Poems*)
ILLRP		*Inscriptiones Latinae Liberae Rei Publicae*, A. Degrassi (ed.)
Just.		Justinus
Livy, *Per.*		Livy, *Periochae* (Summaries of the lost books)
Livy, *Oxy. per.*		Livy, *Oxyrhyncheae periochae* (Summaries found at Oxyrhynchus)
*ORF*⁴		*Oratorum Romanorum Fragmenta*, 4th edn, H. Malcovati (ed.)
Oros.		Orosius
Paus.		Pausanias
Plaut. *Men.*		Plautus, *Menaechmi*
Pliny, *HN*		Pliny the Elder, *Naturalis historia* (*Natural history*)
Plut.		Plutarch
	Aem.	*Life of Aemilius Paullus*
	Cat. Mai.	*Life of Cato the Elder*
	Flam.	*Life of Flamininus*
	Marc.	*Life of Marcellus*
	Pyrrh.	*Life of Pyrrhus*
Polyb.		Polybius
ROL		*Remains of Old Latin*, E. H. Warmington (ed.)
Sall.		Sallust
	Cat.	*Bellum Catilinae* (*The war with Catiline*)
*Syll.*³		*Sylloge Inscriptionum Graecarum*, 3rd edn, W. Dittenberger (ed.)
Val. Max.		Valerius Maximus
Vell. Pat.		Velleius Paterculus
Zonar.		Zonaras

Secondary sources

CQ	*Classical Quarterly*
GRBS	*Greek, Roman and Byzantine Studies*
JHS	*Journal of Hellenic Studies*
JRA	*Journal of Roman Archaeology*
JRS	*Journal of Roman Studies*
PCPS	*Proceedings of the Cambridge Philological Society*

Rh. Mus.	*Rheinisches Museum für Philologie*
TAPA	*Transactions of the American Philological Association*

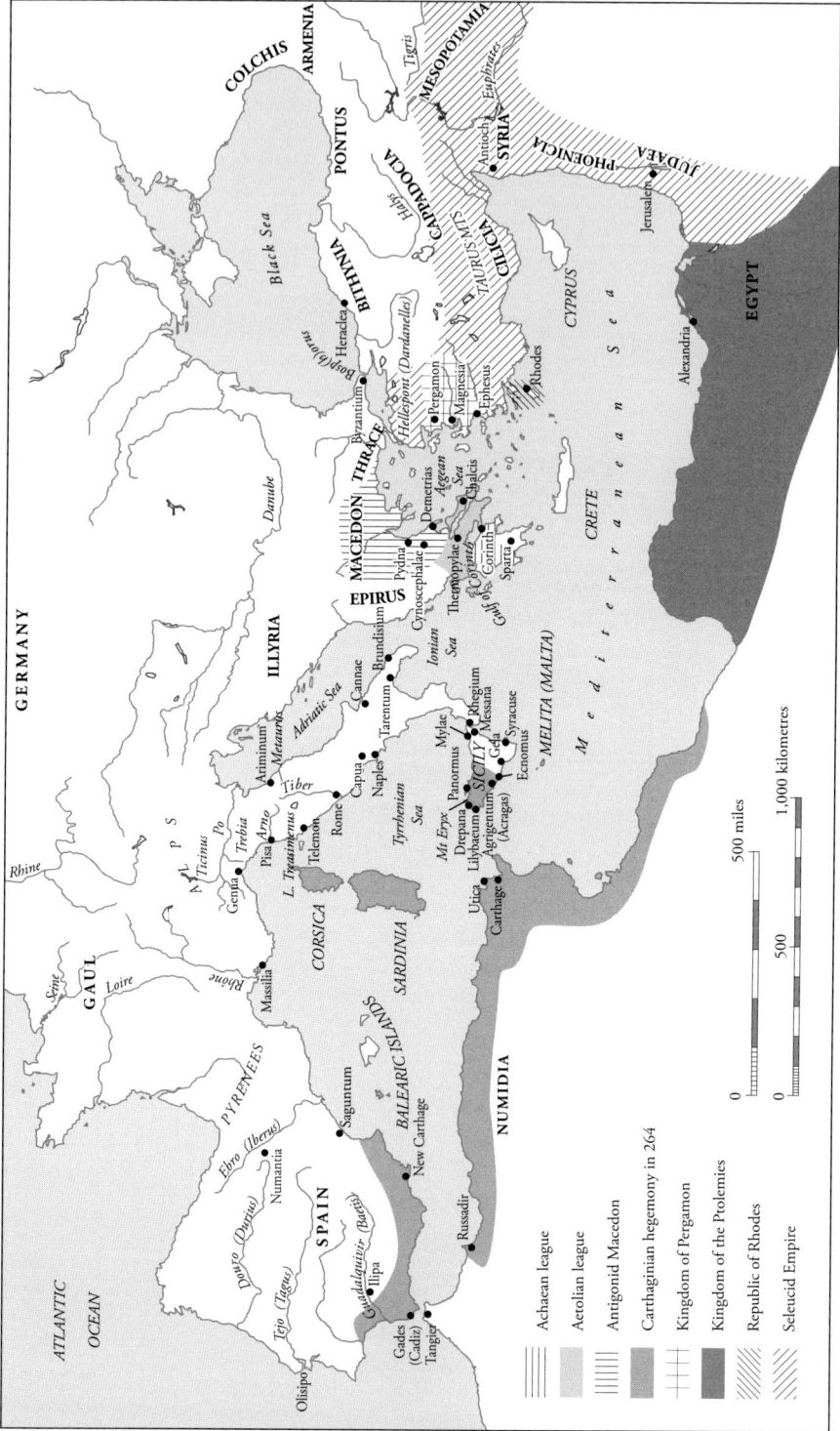

Map 1 The Mediterranean in the third century BC

Aquileia

GALLIA
CISALPINA

Ateste
Po

LIGURIA

Genua

Dalminium

Ariminium

Pisa
Arno

ETRURIA
Arretium
Tiber

UMBRIA

Sena Gallica
Sentinum
Firmum

Issa

CORSICA

Telemon
Cosa
Vulci
Volsinii
Narnia
Faleri
Sutrium
Nepet
Carsioli
Caere
Rome
Ostia
Signia
Norba
Antium
Setia
Circei (Monte Circeo)
Terracina
Minturnae
Sinuessa
Cumae

Arnus
Clanis

VESTINI
Hadria
Alba Fucens
Corfinium
MARSI
PAELIGNI
MARRUCINI
FRENTANI
SAMNIUM
Aesernia
Liris
Fregellae
Suessa
Cales Beneventum
HIRPINI
Saticula
Capua
Neapolis
(Naples)
Paestum
(Posidonia)

Luceria
Ausculum
Aufidus
Cannae
APULIA
Venusia

Brundisium
CALABRIA
Tarentum

LUCANIA

Heraclea

SARDINIA

T y r r h e n i a n
S e a

Thurii

Croton
Lacinian
Promontory

I o n i a n
S e a

BRUTTIUM

Lipara Is.
Messana
Locri
Rhegium

AEGATES
ISLANDS
Drepana
Panormus
▲ Mt. Eryx
Lilybaeum
SICILY

Agrigentum
(Acragas)
Syracuse

Uticia
Carthage
AFRICA
Zama (?)
Nepheris
Great
Plains

M e d i t e r r a n e a n   S e a

MELITA
(MALTA)

DALMATIA

A d r i a t i c   S e a

Map 2 Italy c. 250 BC

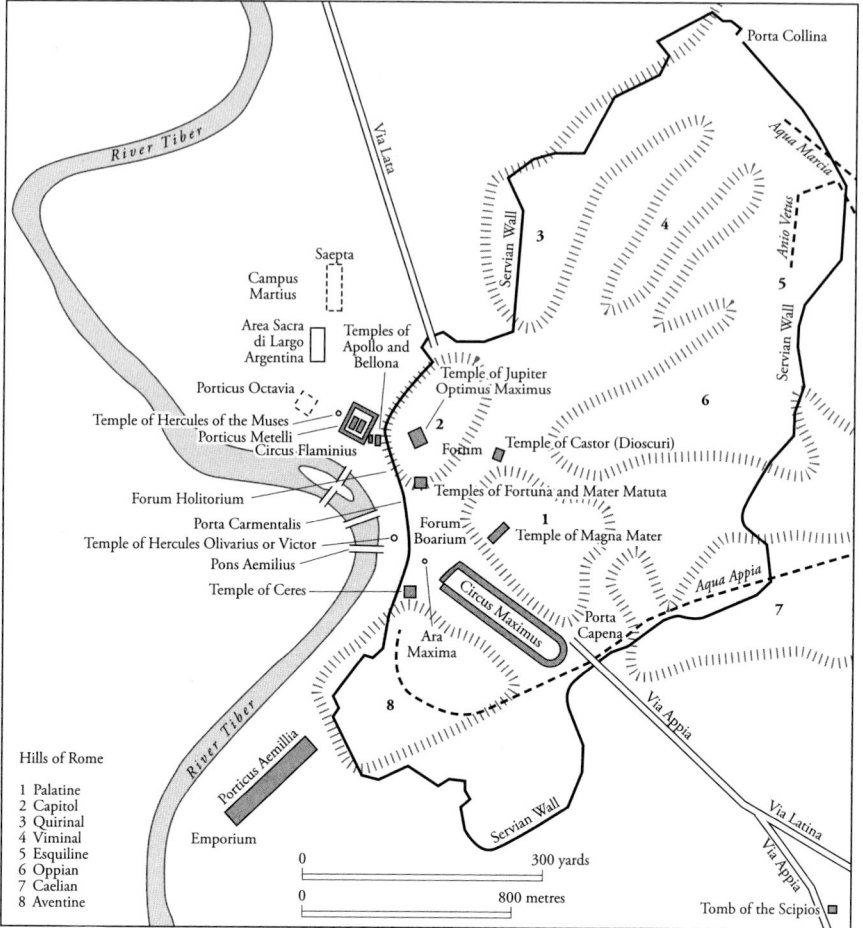

Map 3 Rome c. 150 BC

Text labels within the map:

Porta Collina

River Tiber

Via Lata

Aqua Marcia

Servian Wall

3

4

Anio Vetus

Servian Wall

5

Saepta

Campus
Martius

6

Area Sacra
di Largo
Argentina

Temples of
Apollo and
Bellona

Temple of Jupiter
Optimus Maximus

Porticus Octavia

2

Temple of Hercules of the Muses

Forum

Temple of Castor (Dioscuri)

Porticus Metelli

Circus Flaminius

Temples of Fortuna and Mater Matuta

Forum Holitorium

1

Porta Carmentalis

Forum
Boarium

Temple of Magna Mater

Temple of Hercules Olivarius or Victor

Aqua Appia

Pons Aemilius

7

Temple of Ceres

Circus Maximus

Porta
Capena

Ara
Maxima

Via Appia

8

River Tiber

Porticus Aemilia

Servian Wall

Via Latina

Emporium

Via Appia

Hills of Rome

1 Palatine
2 Capitol
3 Quirinal
4 Viminal
5 Esquiline
6 Oppian
7 Caelian
8 Aventine

0		300 yards

0		800 metres

Tomb of the Scipios

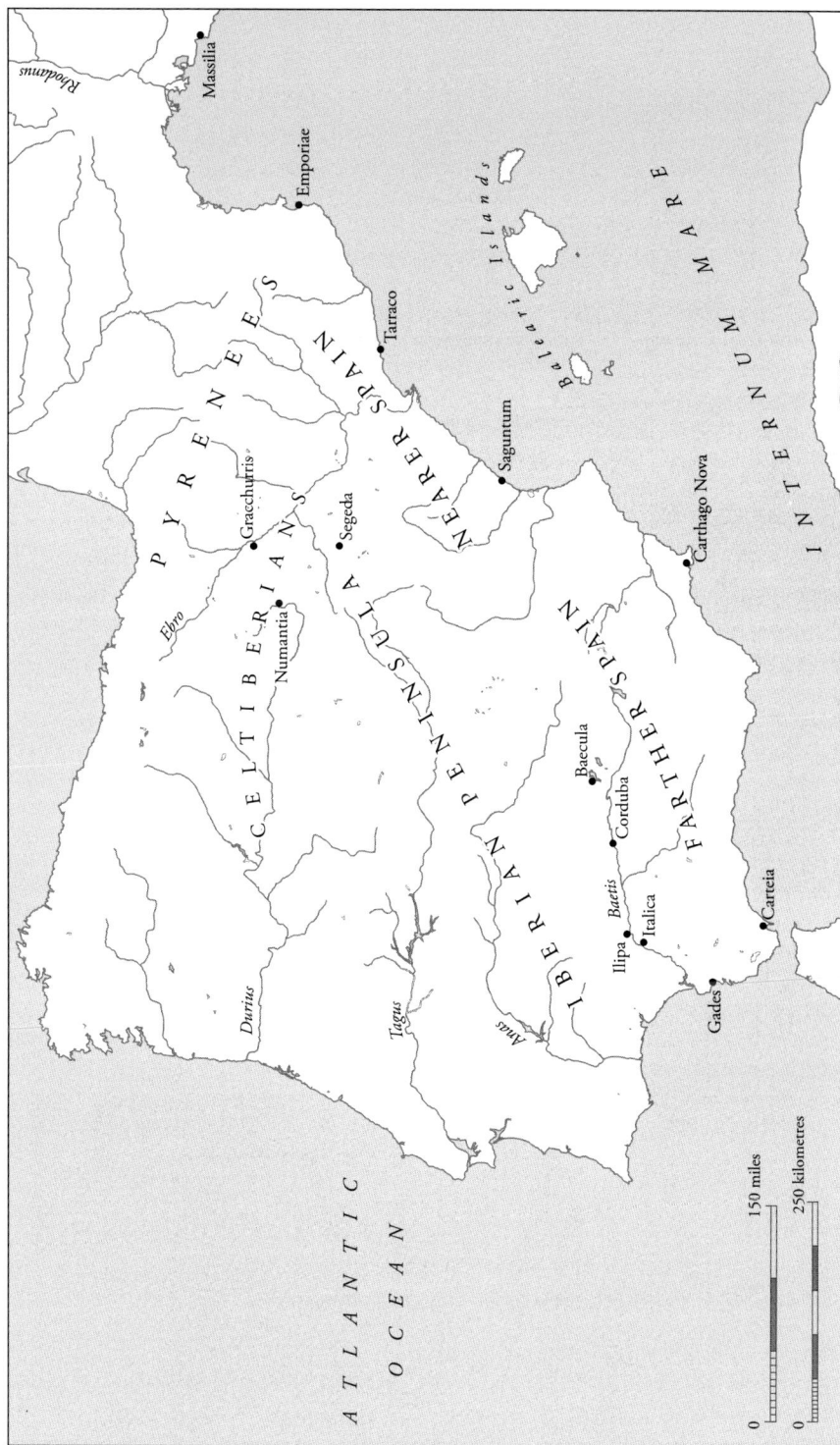

Map 4 Spain

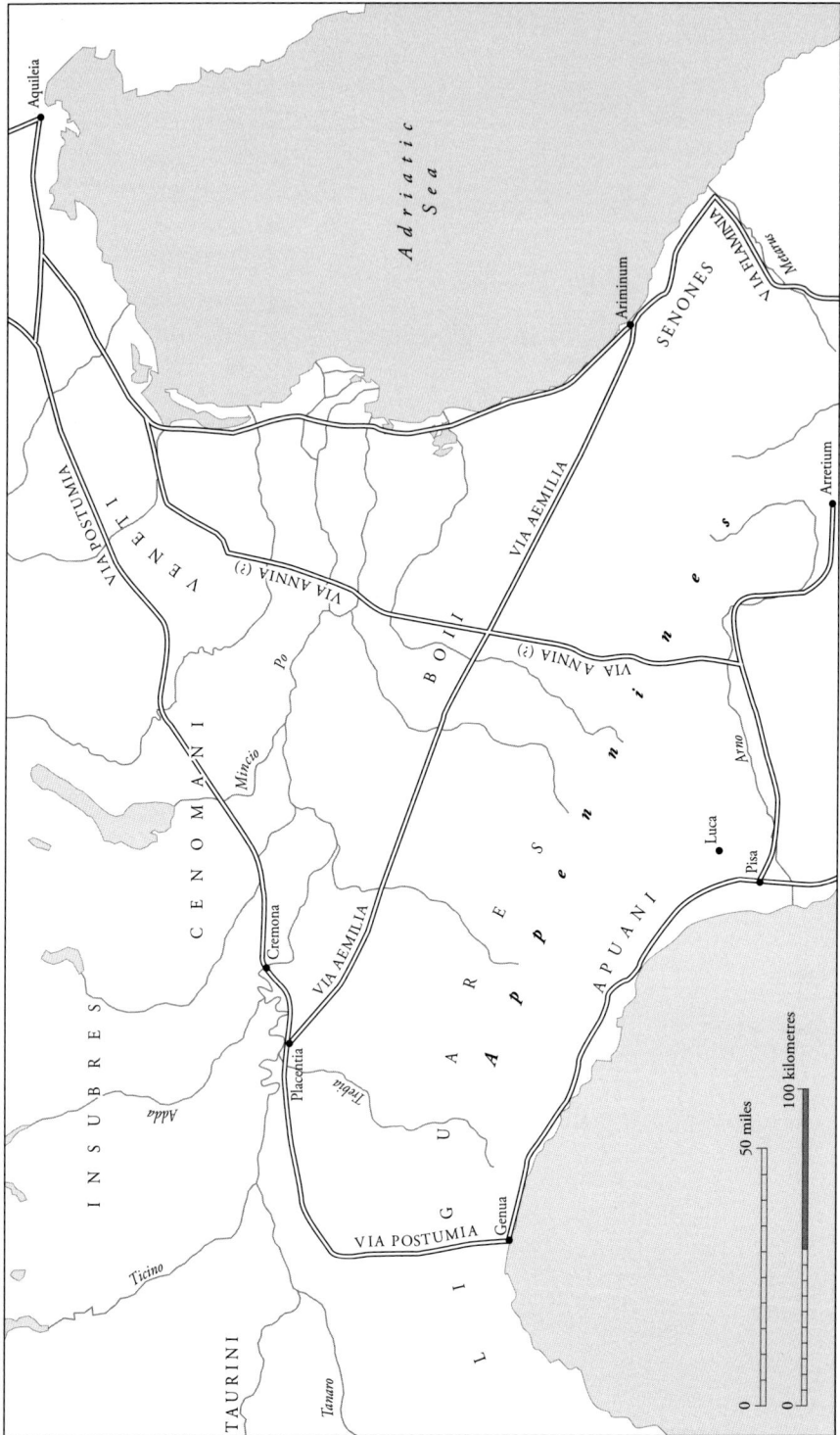

Map 5 Northern Italy

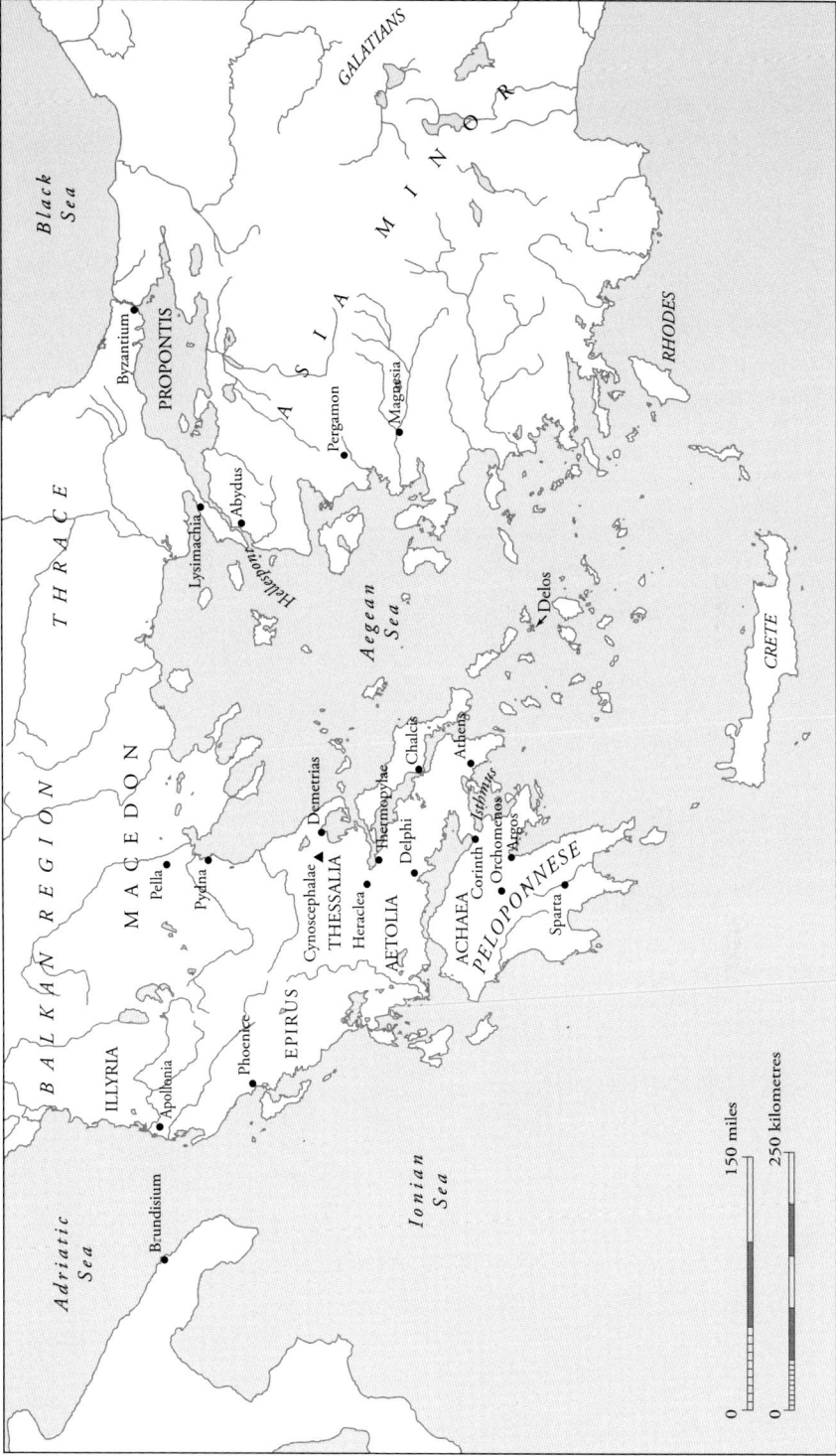

Map 6 Greece and western Asia Minor

CHAPTER 1

Introduction: The aristocracy of the middle Republic

Rome in 290 BC

In the 464th year since the foundation of the city (290 BC) Rome was finally at peace. Over the past decade and more the Romans had warred repeatedly to the north and south against Etruscans, Umbrians, Gauls, Sabines, and Samnites. Conflict with the latter constituted the Third Samnite War, but these struggles often merged into one another as the Republic battled to establish its supremacy across central Italy and its opponents to resist Roman dominion. In 295 the climax came. The Republic sent four legions and allies against a coalition of Samnites and Gauls at Sentinum, in Umbria, while other Roman forces campaigned in Etruria and Samnium. Rome's decisive victory at Sentinum came at the cost of many thousands of lives, including that of one of the consuls, P. Decius Mus, whose solemn offer of his own life as a sacrifice to the gods for victory (*devotio*) later Romans believed turned the tide. The battle shattered the coalition of forces ranged against the Republic (Livy, 10.25.1–30.10). Victories over the next several years against the Etruscans and Samnites ended those peoples' resistance – at least for the time being – and opened the way for the complete conquest of Italy, although wars with Pyrrhus and Carthage caused the Romans to defer a final reckoning with the Gallic menace until late in the century. In the wake of its war with Hannibal, Rome would go on to bring the entire Mediterranean basin under its rule.

That achievement raised a question first addressed over two millennia ago by the historian Polybius (c. 203–118? BC). Polybius was an Achaean Greek from an aristocratic family who, along with many other leading politicians there, suffered deportation to Italy in 167 BC following the Third Macedonian War (see Chapter 6). In the *Histories* he composed during his exile in Rome, Polybius sought to answer for his readers 'by what means, and under what kind of polity, almost the whole of the inhabited world was conquered and brought under the dominion of the single city of Rome' (1.1.5). It is the same question that this book will address, although the explanations it offers will in many cases diverge substantially from Polybius'. Scholars over the past decades have reconstructed a far different picture of how republican government worked from the one Polybius paints. And although his description of the Roman army is the essential starting point for all modern accounts of that critical institution, Polybius says little about the social and economic underpinnings of Rome's military strength. Nor does he describe one of its most vital components, the ways the Republic organised and maintained its control over Italy. However, Polybius was well aware that the conquest of an empire brought profound changes to Italy and Rome itself, and these, too, form a central part of any account of the period. But ultimately, the story of Rome's conquest of an empire in the third and second centuries is mostly the story of its many wars – their origins, courses, and outcomes.

Why the Romans so often went to war in the third and second (and first) centuries has recently aroused considerable dispute. Reacting against an old thesis that held that the wars the Romans fought were mainly defensive and not of their choosing and that they acquired their empire almost by happenstance, W. V. Harris and others have argued that Rome was a society built for war.[1] The aristocracy's value system impelled the Republic's aristocracy to seek glory and prestige through combat and leadership in victorious war and to see in conquest the means to make their personal fortunes. Ordinary citizens, too, gained materially from the Republic's triumphs in the form of land and booty. The combination led the Romans to embrace nearly every opportunity to go to war that came their way and to seek to create opportunities where none existed. In a powerful recent challenge to Harris, however, A. M. Eckstein has sought to shift the focus of analysis from Rome to the international system within which the Republic existed.[2] Bellicosity, he points out, was hardly unique to the leadership at Rome. All ancient states were militarily aggressive because they existed in a harsh, anarchic world. Although for most of us who live in the modern, developed world the threat of war is generally speaking remote to the point of non-existence, things were vastly different in antiquity. No body

1. W. V. Harris, *War and Imperialism in Republican Rome 327–70 B.C.*, Oxford: Oxford University Press, 1979.
2. A. M. Eckstein, *Mediterranean Anarchy, Interstate War, and the Rise of Rome*, Berkeley and Los Angeles: University of California Press, 2006.

of international law backed up by multinational institutions and the threat of diplomatic, economic, or even military sanctions served to restrain aggression between states and repress outbreaks of violence when they occurred. Nor during the third and second centuries BC was there any superpower on the scene to play that role. Instead, a constellation of powerful states in Italy and across the Mediterranean competed for primacy, with little to limit their expansion but their own military capacities measured against those of their opponents. Smaller powers either made their peace with stronger neighbours on whatever terms they could get, submitting to whatever dictates the latter believed they could impose, or they were destroyed. And destruction could be complete, for the horrors visited upon a defeated state were not restricted to the fall of its government, the execution or exile of political leaders, and a military occupation. The slaughter of its soldiers and the sale into slavery of those who survived were common fates visited upon a conquered army. And the sufferings inflicted upon the civilian population could be cruel in the extreme: their movable possessions plundered and carried off, women and young boys raped, expulsion from their ancestral lands and temples, their homes occupied by their conquerors, enslavement, and even the mutilation or execution of adult male captives. Because the consequences of defeat could be so terrible, ancient states did everything in their power to avoid it, and republican Rome was no exception. It built up its military strength in every way it could in the hopes of deterring attacks from ever being launched in the first place and, should deterrence fail, in order to crush any enemy bold enough to march against it.

By the early third century, that accumulation of military power had enabled the city on the Tiber to grow from a small village into a powerful regional hegemon controlling a territory (the *ager Romanus*) of over 15,000 square km embracing the Latin plain and reaching far up the Tiber valley into Etruria. The final year of the Third Samnite War had seen M'. Curius Dentatus complete the conquest of the Sabine lands to the east of Latium, extending Roman territory all the way to the Adriatic. That broad swath of land effectively cut Italy in two and precluded a juncture between the Republic's two principal enemies, the Samnites and the Etruscans. To the south lay the rich agricultural region of Campania and its chief city, Capua, largely incorporated into the *ager Romanus* in the aftermath of the Latin revolt of 340–338. The population that occupied these lands was ethnically diverse: Latins, Oscan speakers in

Campania, Sabines and Praetutti in the east, among others. Their numbers can only be approximated since census figures from this period are unreliable, but a careful estimate puts the total at over 560,000. In addition, the Republic had by 290 planted nineteen colonies at strategic points throughout central Italy encompassing almost 6,000 square km. The colonies served both to defend regions recently conquered and to provide an outlet for some 240,000 land-less Romans and allies. Those allies (*socii*) finally numbered some 725,000 on another 32,500 square km among various towns and tribes in Etruria, Umbria, the central Apennines, Campania, Apulia and elsewhere.[3] This formidable assemblage of citizens, colonists, and *socii* is what enabled Rome to meet the challenges it faced in the 290s, fielding for the campaigns at Sentinum, Etruria, and Samnium in 295 as many as 33,600 citizens and an equal or greater number of Latin and other allies (Livy, 10.26.14, 27.10–11).[4]

The government of Rome

Our most important source of information about the government that built this military powerhouse and oversaw its deployment in the wars Rome waged comes from the *Histories* of Polybius. Through a stroke of luck after his arrival, he was befriended by P. Cornelius Scipio Aemilianus, the younger son of L. Aemilius Paullus, the Roman general who won the Third Macedonian War. So while his compatriots found themselves interned in small towns throughout Italy, Polybius was permitted to remain in Rome for almost twenty years and rub shoulders with members of the Republic's political elite. Therefore when he came to write his lengthy account of how Rome between the outbreak of the war with Hannibal and his own day had come to dominate the Mediter-ranean, he was in an excellent position to explain to his readers 'under what kind of constitution it came about that nearly the whole world fell under the power of Rome' (6.2.3). Polybius' answer, in a nutshell, is that the Republic possessed a mixed constitution in which the consuls, the senate, and the people all shared power, and each required the cooperation of the other two in order to accom-plish anything. The ideal of a mixed or balanced constitution as the

3. A. Afzelius, *Die römische Eroberung Italiens (340–264 v. Chr.)*, Copenhagen: Univer-sitetsforlaget i Aarhus, 1942, 175–81.
4. S. P. Oakley, *A Commentary on Livy, Books VI–X*, 4 vols, Oxford: Oxford Univer-sity Press, 1997–2005, 4.282.

Figure 1 Reverse of a *denarius* issued in 54 BC by M. Iunius Brutus showing a magistrate accompanied by two lictors and an attendant. ANS 1937 158 224. Courtesy of the American Numismatic Society.

basis for good government (which did not originate with Polybius) would go on to enjoy a long and influential history among political theorists. Its distant descendent is the 'checks and balances' system enshrined in the United States Constitution. For our purposes, however, the point to emphasise is that Polybius was wrong about the Roman constitution. An aristocracy governed the Republic from its foundation until Julius Caesar overthrew it.[5]

The magistrates

Polybius was certainly right to see the consuls as a powerful element within the Roman government. They were the Republic's highest magistrates, and two were elected every year. Each possessed *imperium*, the right to issue commands and to enforce them through physical coercion and even execution under certain circumstances. This power was embodied in the *fasces*, bundles of rods bound around an axe carried by each of the dozen attendants, the lictors, who preceded a consul and who used them to scourge or behead

5. A. Lintott, *The Constitution of the Roman Republic*, Oxford: Oxford University Press, 1999.

anyone who disobeyed a consul's command. Consuls' chief responsibility was to administer the Republic's most important affairs. In the third and second centuries, this duty typically meant levying an army and leading it against Rome's enemies. Consuls also performed sacrifices and other religious ceremonies on behalf of the Republic. When in Rome they chaired sessions of the senate (alternating this role monthly when both consuls were present), spoke before the citizens on matters of public importance, presented certain types of bills to the assembly to be voted into law, and conducted elections for their successors and for the next year's praetors, who possessed a lesser *imperium* indicated by their right to only six lictors. Other magistrates lacked *imperium* and so ranked below the consuls and praetors in the hierarchy of offices, including the four aediles, the ten tribunes of the plebs, and the quaestors, whose numbers slowly grew over the years. In addition, two censors were elected every five years to count the citizen population, among other duties. And on rare occasions usually involving a military emergency, the consuls named a dictator, whose *imperium* was superior to that of any other magistrate, indicated by the twenty-four lictors who preceded him. Dictators were the only magistrates who had no colleague, only a second in command, the master of the horse (*magister equitum*). After 290, the appointment of dictators grew increasingly rare, and after the end of the third century the office fell into abeyance until it was revived in 82.

Although the consuls' powers were formidable, various constraints kept the office from developing into an independent arm of government. One-year terms meant that personnel changed frequently and prevented the lengthy tenures that could become the foundation for long-term, institutional power. Even more important was the principle of collegiality. Whenever a magistrate sought to undertake any official action, any colleague of equal rank could prevent it by veto (meaning 'I forbid' in Latin). Any magistrate with superior *imperium* could also veto an initiative by one with lesser or no *imperium*, with the exception of tribunes of the plebs, who could only be vetoed by one another. Since dictators had no colleagues, no one could impede their actions, enabling them to act swiftly and decisively in a crisis. Obstruction could also come from the gods. Many public acts, like holding an assembly, conducting the census, departing from the city for war, or commencing a battle, required divine approval. Magistrates sought this by taking the auspices (on which see below); however, omens such as reports of thunder during the proceedings or the inauspicious behaviour of designated birds could stop the action for that day. And because Roman religious practice emphasised exact performance of ritual actions, errors occurring at the time or even discovered subsequently invalidated the entire undertaking and any public action consequent upon it. Many aristocrats had the power to report such omens to a magistrate or claim irregularities in the ritual, which further enlarged the circle of those able to obstruct magisterial initiatives.[6] Finally and most importantly, the fact that all of the higher magistrates were drawn from the senate while those in the lower grades looked forward to admission to that body created a community of interest between these two parts of the republican government. It would therefore be more accurate to think of the consuls and others holding public office simply as senators exercising a temporary executive authority rather than independent elements of the government.

The Republic's priests constituted another category of public officials.[7] There were many different kinds, but those with the most prominent roles were the members of the three great colleges (*collegia*) of priests: the pontiffs (*pontifices*), the augurs (*augures*), and the ten-man board for ritual actions (*decemviri sacris faciundis*). The pontiffs were nine in number and headed by a chief pontiff (the *pontifex maximus*). They were responsible for supervising various religious rituals, and advised the senate and the public on questions of religious law. The nine augurs' brief comprised the auspices (*auspicia*), rituals that sought, primarily through the observation of birds, divine approval for intended public actions. They also defined sacred space (a *templum*) and controlled the books containing the augural law (*ius augurale*). The ten-man board kept and consulted a collection of oracles known as the Sibylline books. These they examined whenever a prodigy (*prodigium*) revealed that the gods had withdrawn from their alliance with Rome (the *pax deorum*). The books then recommended measures to restore the gods' favour and regain their assistance. Other priests included the six Vestal virgins, who maintained the cult of the goddess Vesta and participated in many other rituals; the *flamines*, priests dedicated to the cult of one particular god, such as Jupiter (the *flamen Dialis*),

6. J. Linderski, 'The augural law', in H. Temporini (ed.), *Aufstieg und Niedergang der römischen Welt: Geschichte und Kultur Roms im Spiegel der neueren Forschung*, Berlin and New York: De Gruyter, 1986, 2146–312.
7. M. Beard, J. North, and S. Price, *Religions of Rome*, 2 vols, Cambridge: Cambridge University Press, 1998.

Mars (the *flamen Martalis*), and Quirinus (the *flamen Quirinalis*) in addition to twelve others; the *fetiales*, who conducted the ritual aspects of declaring war and making peace; and the *haruspices*, Etruscan seers who also advised the senate on prodigies and their remedies.

The priesthood, however, never constituted a separate order at Rome or a caste apart. All priests were senators or drawn from senatorial families, and except in a few cases (mainly the vestals, the *flamen Dialis*, and the *haruspices*) their lives were no different from those of their non-priestly colleagues. Moreover the roles of the most important of them, the three great colleges, were largely reactive and advisory. For the most part, their members did not carry out sacrifices or other rituals but only provided guidance to the senate or the magistrates, and then only when consulted or requested. They were in no position to wield independent power.

The people

In theory the Roman people (the *populus Romanus*) enjoyed sovereign authority in the Republic. It alone could enact laws including those concluding treaties, declaring war, or making peace. The people also in this period served as a high court before which capital trials were held, for only the Roman people could pass a sentence of death upon a Roman citizen. And with the exception of the dictator, assemblies of the citizens elected all magistrates and so possessed the power to deprive them of those offices as well. But here, too, powers considerable in the abstract were sharply limited in their exercise. Roman citizenship was restricted to adult males, so its gender disenfranchised half the adult *populus*. The remainder could only assemble at the invitation of a magistrate, and an assembly could only vote on bills put before it without being able debate them or offer amendments. All bills originated with a magistrate, who formulated them with the advice and approval of the senate. Discussion of proposed legislation was conducted before the people in a different venue, an informal meeting (*contio*), which only a magistrate could summon and at which only the magistrate or those he invited to do so could speak. Speakers typically were supporters of the proposal under consideration or, if a different magistrate opposed the bill, its opponents. *Contiones* were not forums where citizens could hear the pros and cons of a measure debated and then make up their minds accordingly. They were more like campaign rallies, intended to whip up enthusiasm and sway the voters one way or the other.[8]

When the Roman people finally did come together to vote, they did so in three different ways.[9] They could meet as the assembly of the centuries (*comitia centuriata*), a body whose origins went back to the regal period, when it represented the Roman people gathering in their military units, the centuries. By the third century, however, any connection with the contemporary army had vanished. Still, since weapons could not be carried within the city of Rome's religious boundary (the *pomerium*), the *comitia centuriata* met on the Field of Mars (*Campus Martius*). The centuriate assembly elected magistrates with *imperium*, voted on declarations of war and treaties of peace, and conducted capital trials. A magistrate with *imperium*, usually one of the consuls, presided, and the citizens voted by centuries. In the course of conducting the census the censors placed most citizens in one of six classes based on their wealth (a small number were enrolled in the separate class of *equites equo publico*, who were distinguished by both greater wealth and high social status; see below, p. 96). The 193 voting centuries were distributed among these classes and further divided within each class by age: those under the age of 46 (the *iuniores*) in one group; those 46 and older in the *seniores*. Each century cast only one vote based on the votes of a majority of its members no matter how many citizens it contained. As Table 1 indicates, the distribution of centuries was heavily weighted to the wealthiest class of citizens. Prior to 241 BC, the eighteen centuries of *equites equo publico* and the first class between them constituted a majority of the 193 centuries. A reform thereafter shifted a few votes to the second class, but since voting began with the *equites* or, after 241, the first class, and proceeded until a majority was reached and then ceased, it is unclear how often those in the lower census classes ever cast a vote. In addition, it is usually assumed that the distribution of wealth among the citizenry was steeply pyramidal, with many more citizens at the bottom of the pyramid than at the top. Consequently, centuries in the first class will have contained many fewer citizens than the centuries for the lower census classes. Similarly, ordinary mortality ensured that centuries of *seniores* contained significantly fewer citizens than those of the

8. R. Morstein-Marx, *Mass Oratory and Political Power in the Late Roman Republic*, Cambridge: Cambridge University Press, 2004.
9. L. R. Taylor, *The Roman Voting Assemblies from the Hannibalic War to the Dictatorship of Caesar*, Ann Arbor: University of Michigan Press, 1966.

Table 1   *The* comitia centuriata, *after c. 241 BC*

Centuries	Iuniores (men 17–45)	Seniores (men 46+)	Total
Cavalry with the public horse (*equites equo publico*)			18
First class	35	35	70
Second class	15 (?)	15 (?)	30 (?)
Third class	10 (?)	10 (?)	20 (?)
Fourth class	10 (?)	10 (?)	20 (?)
Fifth class	15 (?)	15 (?)	30 (?)
Proletarii, carpenters, musicians (2), and servants			5
Total			193

Order of voting:
1. *centuria praerogativa* (one century selected by lot from the *iuniores* of the first class);
2. the remaining first-class centuries, then 12 cavalry centuries, then the century of the carpenters;
3. the six votes (*sex suffragia:* the six ancient cavalry centuries);
4. the centuries of the second, third, fourth, and fifth classes plus the bottom four.
Voting proceeded until a majority was reached, then ceased. If the votes of the centuries of the cavalry and the first class plus the carpenters were unanimous, a majority would have been reached with the votes of only eight second-class centuries. Therefore sometimes, perhaps often, most citizens in the centuries of the second classes and below would not have cast a vote.

iuniores. In other words, the *comitia centuriata* was far from embodying the principle of 'one man, one vote'. Instead, the old and the well-off predominated in choosing the Republic's higher magistrates, in deciding on war and peace, and in capital trials.

The passage of laws typically took place in two other assemblies, the assembly of the tribes (the *comitia tributa*) or the plebeian assembly (the *concilium plebis*). The major difference between them was that all citizens participated in the tribal assembly while patricians were excluded from the *concilium plebis*. However, since the patricians were by the third century comparatively few in number, membership in each assembly was to all intents and purposes identical. A consul or praetor presided at the tribal assembly; tribunes of the plebs at the *concilium plebis*. In both assemblies the citizens again voted as groups in one of thirty-five tribes, and each tribe cast a single vote. Tribes were defined geographically, and every citizen belonged to one based on where he lived or owned property. Initially, they represented compact regions within the *ager Romanus* or one of four regions of the city itself. As Rome expanded and the *ager Romanus* grew, the boundaries of the tribes were extended. When that became impractical, new tribes were created to accommodate newly incorporated areas and the citizens in them until in 241 it was decided to cap the number of tribes at thirty-five. But since Rome kept expanding and since new territory had somehow to be fitted into the framework of the thirty-five tribes, these additional areas were simply assigned to one of them regardless of location. As a result, a tribe came to resemble a patchwork made up of non-contiguous lands. Although early in the Republic's history voting by tribes may have constituted a more egalitarian form of decision making, by the middle Republic it had become far less so.[10] Roman territory by 241 extended over 26,800 square km, but all assemblies were held at Rome and there was no provision for casting a vote elsewhere. Travel to Rome from out-lying areas could take several days, and at certain times of the year, such as during the harvest or in the winter months, even citizens who wanted to make the journey might face serious obstacles. Such factors made regular attendance impractical for any but those citizens who resided in Rome or within convenient walking or riding distance. But urban residents were mainly restricted to casting their votes in one of the four urban tribes. Those urban residents who voted in the rural tribes were mainly citizens who owned property in the countryside but lived in Rome most of the year. Other rural voters who could attend regularly were those who could afford to leave their farms because slaves remained behind to do the work: in both cases, these were well-to-do men. For important votes, citizens from farther away might be brought in, but they needed to be fed and housed until the assembly met, and again the only people who could afford to bear such an expense were members of the upper classes.

The senate

In contrast with the assemblies and magistrates, the senate possessed few formal powers. It could not enact laws or issue commands; the 300 senators (the fathers or *patres*) could only offer advice to the year's consuls and other magistrates. Yet the senate's influence

10. H. Mouritsen, *Plebs and Politics in the Late Roman Republic*, Cambridge: Cambridge University Press, 2001.

went far beyond a merely advisory role. Its reach extended into nearly every aspect of public affairs, making it the central organ of republican governance. It designated the consular and praetorian provinces every year, which meant determining against which enemies the consuls (and sometimes praetors) would lead Rome's armies. It also allocated the forces that these magistrates would command and decided when to levy new armies and to demobilise old ones. The senate received ambassadors from other countries, dispatched its own emissaries, arbitrated disputes among the Republic's Italian and, later, overseas allies, and generally managed the Republic's foreign affairs. It supervised the treasury, overseeing receipts, examining accounts, and authorising outlays for various public purposes such as military campaigns, construction projects, and religious festivals. These last expenditures constituted only one aspect of the senate's overall management of the Republic's relations with the gods. Reports of any unusual event that might represent a prodigy came before the senators, who decided whether or not the warnings they conveyed concerned the Republic and therefore indicated a rupture in the *pax deorum*. In such cases, the *patres* sought advice from one of the priestly colleges on what steps to take to deal with the problem, and on that basis they authorised measures to placate the gods.

Foreign relations, money, and the gods would have been a potent enough basis for control over the Republic, but there was more. Most magistracies ended after a single year; assemblies met only from time to time and were over in a day. The senate's existence had no temporal limit, and senators served for life. This continuity enabled the *patres* to develop a strong sense of corporate identity along with a consciousness of their common institutional interests and the ability to pursue them over the long term. As noted above, all of the Republic's higher magistrates were senior senators; those in the lower ranks either aspired to membership or had recently been enrolled. A magistrate's loyalty therefore was bound up with the body he would return to or later join when his year in office ended rather than to the magistracy he temporarily occupied. Much the same was true of the Republic's priests, who identified themselves first and foremost as senators. Even the Vestal virgins were drawn from leading senatorial families. Equally important, the senate served as the conduit through which legislation passed on its way to the assemblies, allowing the senate to shape the Republic's laws. Magistrates with bills they wished to propose to the Roman people usually first came before the *patres* for a hearing, where the merits of the measure were debated. Here alterations could be suggested or changes imposed or the initiative crushed altogether, for almost never during the middle Republic did a magistrate dare to bring a bill before an assembly without the senate's sanction. The *patres*' endorsement generally guaranteed passage while its opposition posed an all but insurmountable obstacle to enactment. Likewise deliberations on matters of war and peace and treaties of alliance took place in the senate, and the fathers' recommendation invariably shaped the sentiments of the assembly. Their ability to decide public policy coupled with institutional continuity and a strong loyalty to their class enabled the senators easily to dominate the Republic's government. But that dominance rested on more than simply the senate's centrality within the administration of public business or the collection of competencies it had accumulated over the years. For at the root of its ascendancy was what we might today term 'soft power', an ability to command the assent of both ordinary citizens and the individual senators entrusted with *imperium* despite the senate's lack of any overt means of coercion.

Soft power and coercion

Every government requires some form of coercive power, some way to compel those subject to it to do what the government demands. Otherwise, it cannot govern. In modern states compulsion takes the form of some combination of police and/or military force, penal laws, religious sanctions, economic pressure, bureaucratic regulation, and moral suasion. At Rome, the senate had few of these means at its disposal. No police force existed; the few dozen lictors that attended the higher magistrates were far too few to function as one, save in isolated instances, for a citizen population that numbered several hundred thousand spread across a fifth of Italy. Rome did possess a powerful army, but legions made up of citizen-soldiers constituted a very unreliable instrument with which to coerce other citizens. Religion in the hands of a ruling class can serve as a potent instrument of social and political control, but it is far from apparent that Roman cultic practice was well suited to that role. While the priests, particularly the *pontifices*, often answered questions from ordinary citizens about particular practices or how to interpret specific requirements or prohibitions, Roman religion was not based on an elaborate body of prescriptive rules that could constrain the actions of the population. Nor was there some central cultic place access to which the priests controlled and where they determined when and how the necessary rituals were to be performed. The city of Rome had many temples while hundreds of other temples and cultic places were scattered across the peninsula. Elaborate rules did apply to public sacrifices and other religious ceremonies that magistrates performed on behalf of the Roman people, but these served mainly as a way for senators to control one another (as well as to ensure that the divine requirements had been fulfilled). Secular law was no more effective.[11] The Republic during the third and second centuries did not possess an extensive body of law – penal or civil – the knowledge of which could have allowed the senators to control the rest of the citizens. At an earlier date legal knowledge had been the exclusive preserve of the patricians, who had used it to dominate public life. But Rome's basic law code, the Twelve Tables, had been promulgated in the mid-fifth century. The procedural rules (the *leges actiones*), which defined the specific words and formulas required to bring various types of lawsuits in court, had remained the closely guarded secret of the *pontifices* until 307, when these, too, were revealed. At the same time, the calendar was made public. This divulged the days on which it was proper for the courts to sit and suits to be heard. Polybius claims that the senate investigated crimes throughout Italy – treason, conspiracy, poisoning, and murder (6.13.4). However, what Polybius has in mind are high crimes that endangered state security, not the ordinary criminal activity that local officials dealt with. Senators also served as jurors in civil suits and presided over these trials as magistrates. But such trials mainly concerned the upper classes, for whom the substantial sums of money at stake made coming to Rome and petitioning a praetor to hear the suit worthwhile. Minor magistrates, the *praefecti*, were sent out to some Roman municipalities. They were selected by the praetor in Rome to serve, probably, as legal advisors there (see below, p. 84), but whether these men were senators or only beginning their political careers is uncertain. And it is doubtful that senators travelled out to the countryside to sit as jurors in local lawsuits. Polybius also asserts that the senate's control of public contracts of all sorts represented an important source of economic power since 'almost everyone' (6.17.3) had a stake in them.

11. M. Alexander, 'Law in the Roman Republic', in N. Rosenstein and R. Morstein-Marx (eds), *A Companion to the Roman Republic*, Oxford: Blackwell, 2006, 236–55.

However, Polybius here clearly means 'everyone' in the sense of 'everyone who is anyone', that is, the wealthier citizens or those who worked for them, not the great mass of the citizenry. Yet Polybius' emphasis on the vast number of tasks – building or repairing public buildings, collecting various taxes and dues – that were carried out by the companies (*publicani*) that obtained these contracts points up the dependence of the government on them to function. The Republic had no bureaucracy that the senate could turn to in order to implement its policies and enforce its will like the one its contemporary, the Qin kingdom in China, used to establish a strong, centrally controlled state. That left the *patres* with only moral suasion upon which to found their power at Rome.

Auctoritas

At Rome, moral suasion went by the name of *auctoritas*. The English word 'authority' is obviously derivative, but for an ancient Roman its implications went much farther than what our term conveys. *Auctoritas* was the source of advice so authoritative, so likely to be right, as to carry with it a virtual guarantee that it represented the best course of action available. Such advice all but compelled deference because the *auctoritas* that backed it derived from wisdom far beyond what any ordinary person possessed, wisdom gained through a record of exceptional achievement and offered in a spirit of disinterested benevolence. An incident that occurred early in the first century but completely in keeping with the political culture of the middle Republic aptly illustrates the deference that *auctoritas* commanded in the eyes of ordinary Romans. Late in life M. Aemilius Scaurus, consul in 115, *triumphator* (triumphing general; see below), censor in 109, and *princeps senatus* (the senator whose name the censors placed first in drawing up the list of senators, a position of great honour) in 90, stood accused by one Q. Varus, a tribune of the plebs who had been born in the Spanish town of Sucro, of instigating the allies to revolt. Scaurus, old and ill, came into court and simply said, '"Quintus Varus the Spaniard says that Marcus Scaurus the first senator called the allies to arms; Marcus Scaurus the first senator denies it. There are no witnesses. Which of the two ought you to believe?" Scaurus' response so changed the minds of everyone that the tribune dismissed the charges himself' (Asc. 22C). One can well understand Cicero's characterisation of Scaurus as a man who 'virtually ruled the world with a nod of his head' (*Font.* 24).

Auctoritas was deployed before the assembled populace to advocate for or against legislation in *contiones* or to sway the jurors at a trial. It made itself felt in the senate house (the *curia*) where issues of state were weighed. Debate there proceeded by magisterial rank, and although the voices of even relatively junior senators might be heard, the influence of those called upon to speak first – the *princeps senatus* and then the former consuls (the *consulares*) – was often decisive.

Those who possessed the greatest *auctoritas* were the Republic's leading men, the chief senators (the *principes*). They accumulated it through long and successful service to the affairs of individual citizens and to the public affairs of the entire Roman people (the *res publica populi Romani*). So when the senate exerted its collective *auctoritas*, it was all but irresistible: the *patres*' collective achievements and experience made them far wiser than ordinary Romans, and they had only their best interests at heart. Senators' and would-be senators' willingness to work on behalf of the Republic and their fellow citizens flowed from the vital fact that this represented the principal source of honour at Rome. And winning honour was the all-consuming ambition of every aristocrat at Rome. Yoking honour to service to the Roman people in turn created the dynamic that made senatorial control of the Republic possible, for in their drive to win honour they were led to do those things that continually created, sustained, and enhanced the basis of their individual and collective *auctoritas*.

This intense devotion to the public's and the Republic's welfare was the hallmark of the republican aristocracy, and it could take a variety of forms. Senators regularly provided advice on religious, legal, financial, and family matters to private citizens who consulted them. Cicero has one of the speakers in his dialogue *On the orator*, set in 91 BC, recall how earlier generations of leading men:

> used to make their counsel available to all citizens. In the old days, someone would approach them as they were walking in the forum or at their homes seated on their magisterial chairs not only with questions about the law but even about the marriage of a daughter, about buying a farm, about cultivating a field, in a word about every kind of obligation or business affair … about all sorts of religious and human matters. (*De or.* 3.133–4)

Such men also undertook to further the interests of their friends and those who sought their protection and assistance, especially by acting as their advocates in the law courts and by working on their behalf in any other way they could.

Patronage

Those for whom aristocrats did favours (*beneficia*) were not simply expected to show gratitude (*gratia*) but came under an obligation (*officium*) to reciprocate in whatever way they could. These obligations were a source of social power for the Republic's leading men, a bond often termed a 'patron–client relationship'. The terms *patronus* and *cliens* denoted an unequal relationship between a superior and an inferior party. At one time, scholars believed that patron–client relationships not only structured the social world of republican Rome but defined its politics as well.[12] Because aristocrats knew the law and had the rhetorical skills to argue effectively on behalf of a client in court as well as many other means to aid ordinary citizens, the latter had to attach themselves to one or another powerful aristocrat. And because clients were under an obligation to reciprocate for the protection and other services their patron had offered them and to display loyalty (*fides*) to his interests just as he did to theirs, a patron came to control the votes of his clients (his *clientelae*). The outcomes of elections, therefore, and the results of legislative contests or capital trials came to depend on the will of a small number of aristocratic patrons who formed alliances with one another (*factiones* or *amicitiae*) to pool their political resources for mutual advantage. This system of alliances in turn became the focus of scholarship seeking to understand the workings of republican politics and the basis of aristocratic control of the state.

Patrons and clients certainly existed at Rome during the middle Republic, but scholars have considerably downplayed the political aspect of the relationship in recent years.[13] While poor urban citizens in their struggles to survive might have been highly dependent on small handouts or other favours from wealthy patrons, in this era the votes of such men counted for little in electoral or legislative assemblies. On the other hand, more prosperous Romans whose

12. M. Gelzer, *The Roman Nobility*, trans. R. Seager, Oxford: Blackwell, 1966, 54–136; H. H. Scullard, *Roman Politics, 220–150 BC*[2], Oxford: Oxford University Press, 1973, 12–25.
13. P. A. Brunt, *The Fall of the Roman Republic and Related Essays*, Oxford: Oxford University Press, 1988, 382–442.

votes carried much greater weight in the assemblies, and who often did need the aid of powerful figures to defend their economic or political interests in court or elsewhere, might have several aristocratic patrons whose interests did not always align in the Republic's highly competitive political arena. In such cases, clients could enjoy considerable freedom to decide which obligations to honour. In fact, because of the eagerness of aristocrats to do favours in order to obligate citizens on whose support they might hope to call in future political contests, clients could, ironically, find themselves enjoying considerable leverage in any patron–client relationship. The comic poet Plautus could even parody a patron's helplessness in the face of a client's demands in Menaechmus' lament in the play of the same name:

> What fools we are to cling to this idiotic and supremely boring custom! Yet we do, and the more important we are, the more we cling to it. To have a large following of clients is everybody's ambition. Whether the clients are honest men or worthless is immaterial; nobody bothers about that; a client's wealth is what matters ... Yet look at the trouble a lawless and unscrupulous client can cause his patron. He will deny his debts, and be forever going into court ... When his day of trial comes, it's a day of trial for the patron too (for we have to plead for the malefactors) ... That is the way I have been worried to death by a client today, and prevented from getting on with anything I wanted to do. The man buttonholed me and wouldn't let me go. I had to put up a defence in court of all of his countless crimes ... Gods curse the wretched man, for spoiling my day! Curse me too, for ever going near the forum this morning. (Plaut. *Men.* 571–97)

Aristocratic life

This need to place themselves at the disposal of those who might seek their assistance determined much about aristocratic life. Upperclass residences in Rome typically were located conveniently near the forum, the centre of political life and legal activity. Excavations have uncovered the floor plans of a number of them, and the older houses buried at Pompeii provide further detail about not only how they looked but how they functioned. The homes of wealthy men were constructed around a central, unroofed courtyard, the atrium, which might have a small pool (*impluvium*) in the centre. Rooms surrounded the atrium and opened onto it. They were often without

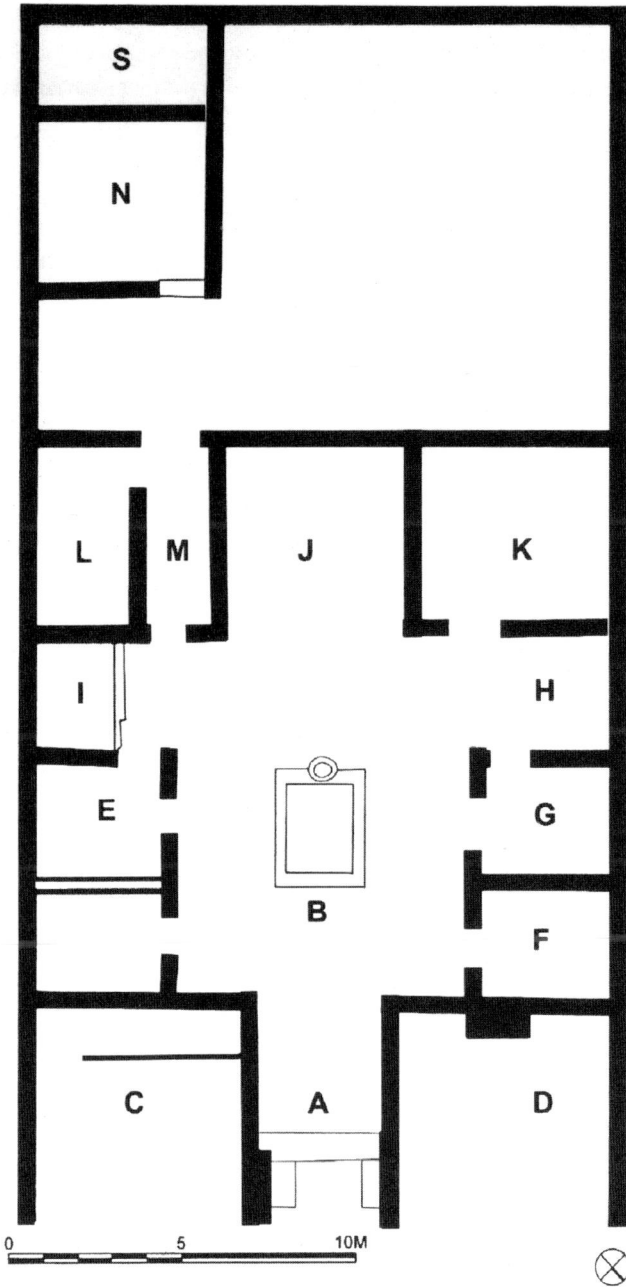

Figure 2 Plan of the House of Diana (Atrium House V), Cosa. From E. Fentress, *Cosa V, an Intermittent Town: Excavations 1991–1997*, Ann Arbor: Published for the American Academy in Rome by the University of Michigan Press, 2003, figure 5.

windows, since exterior side walls typically abutted those of neighbouring houses while the front wall facing the street was either blank or contained small shops without access to the interior of the house. Behind or beside the property there might be a garden (*hortus*), separated from neighbouring properties by high walls. The key feature of such houses was a strong visual axis running from the front door through the entryway (*fauces*), across the atrium and ending at the *tablinum*. This was the most important public room in the house, for it was here that an aristocrat sat in the morning to receive visitors ranging from the humble men who came to pay their respects (*salutatio*) to the more substantial citizens who sought advice or help or to do business of any sort. This axial arrangement placed the master of the house before the eyes of those within as well as of passers-by as he acted the part of a patron, performing those services that both defined him as an aristocrat and advanced his public standing. Placing himself before the public's gaze was critical to an aristocrat's construction of his image, even at home. Some years after our period, an architect offered to build an up-and-coming young senator a house that no one could see into, to which the senator replied, 'If you have that kind of skill, you must build it so that everyone can see whatever I am doing!' (Vell. Pat. 2.14.3).

Two other visual aspects of an aristocratic house also played important roles in establishing its owner's elite status. Anyone approaching such a house might have seen weapons and armour affixed to the exterior walls beside the front door. These were spoils from victorious single combats, trophies stripped from slain enemies. They offered mute testimony to a soldier's willingness to risk his life voluntarily in single combat on behalf of the Republic, when no need had compelled him to run such a risk (for spoils taken in ordinary battles were not displayed in this way). Once hung up, spoils of this sort could not be removed until they fell down though age – even if the house changed owners. They signified a heritage of bravery, perhaps the achievements of the current owner but certainly those of his ancestors, and emphasised the continuity of the family's sacrifices on behalf of Rome. The atrium conveyed the same message once a visitor entered the house. Those waiting in there to speak to a senator would have seen against its walls a succession of small wooden cabinets.[14] Each contained a wax mask (*imago*) representing

---

14. H. Flower, *Ancestor Masks and Aristocratic Power in Roman Culture*, Oxford: Oxford University Press, 1996.

Figure 3 A Roman senator dressed in a toga. The 'Arringatore' (Aulus Metellus). Photo courtesy of the Museo Archeologico Nazionale di Firenze, reproduced by permission.

one of the senator's ancestors, with a label below it to identify him and the offices he had held. There might also be a series of portraits of these ancestors on one wall with cords running between them to show the family relationships among them. And portraits might also adorn the spoils on the exterior, identifying the men whose bravery had earned them. All of this placed before the eyes of the Roman people the long record of the family's service to it, now being carried on by its current representative sitting in his *tablinum* dispensing assistance and advice to all who sought it.

That same devotion to the interests of his clients and friends was again presented to the citizenry when an aristocrat left his home and walked down to the forum (ideally accompanied by a throng of grateful clients and other well-wishers and of course servants) to plead in the courts or intervene on behalf of those who had sought his help. It was crucial not simply that a senator fulfil the obligations of a good patron. He needed to present the right sort of appearance as he did so, to deport himself as befitted a leading citizen.[15] Senators in public wore a toga, a garment that marked all male citizens as Romans. While senators' togas were certainly of better quality than those of commoners, their similarity in dress expressed solidarity with ordinary Romans. They did not use their personal adornment to put themselves above them: they wore no costly jewellery, luxurious fabrics, or elaborate hairstyles. Only a broad purple stripe at the hem of their togas set senators apart, but this mark symbolised precisely their status as servants of the public welfare. The toga itself was a large, semi-circular piece of cloth made of light-coloured wool, about 5.5 × 2.75 m. Worn over a lighter tunic, it was wrapped in such a way as to cover the left arm but leave the right free. Togas were bulky, awkward, and uncomfortable, and ordinary citizens probably did not wear them save for ceremonial occasions. (In Roman legend, when the senators arrived to confer the dictatorship on Cincinnatus as he was ploughing his field, he got his wife to run and fetch his toga so that he could be properly dressed: Livy, 3.26.9–10.) The fact that senators and other members of the elite were expected to present themselves in this formal and constricting garb reflects the Romans' view that the body was the crucial signifier of the inner man, a reflection of his character and habits. For an aristocrat, mastery of the toga was part and parcel of a larger mastery of his body and the self-control that citizens expected in their leaders. A moderate gait, a controlled expression – neither too gay nor too stern – deliberate movements, and a proper style of speaking connoted steadiness (*constantia*) and seriousness (*gravitas*), both of which contributed vitally to senatorial dignity (*dignitas*), a reflection of *auctoritas*. Yet senators also needed to display a certain 'joviality' in public, an attitude of genial condescension that while nominally levelling the differences in status between superior and inferior emphasised the differences in rank and social standing.[16] In canvassing for office, they 'begged' for citizens' vote; in addressing the people, the emphasised their dedication to their welfare. To let the mask of 'joviality' slip could be fatal to one's ambitions. P. Cornelius Scipio Nasica, consul in 167, as a young man seeking the aedileship shook the heavily calloused hand of a farmer and asked as a joke if he usually walked on his hands. The farmer and,

15. A. Corbeill, 'The republican body', in Rosenstein and Morstein-Marx, *Companion*, 439–56.
16. M. Jehne, 'Methods, models, and historiography', in Rosenstein and Morstein-Marx, *Companion*, 19.

Figure 4 A Roman *matrona* dressed in a *stola* and *palla*. Statue of the Empress Livia Augusta as Ceres. Réunion des Musées Nationaux/Art Resource.

once the story got around, the rest of the rural voters took deep offence, thinking that Nasica was mocking their poverty. As a result, Nasica lost that election (Val. Max. 7.5.2).

Their dress also defined elite women. A respectable married woman (*matrona*) was identified by a long, restrictive garment that fell to the feet (a *stola* in later parlance) worn over a long tunic, and a *palla*, a kind of shawl that covered the head. These items came in a variety of colours and styles, but universally were understood to represent the chastity not only of their wearer but of the domestic establishment – children, servants, and even the house itself – over which she presided. Aristocratic women were also freer than their husbands to use their appearance to demonstrate their wealth. Jewellery was appropriate and, following the end of the Hannibalic war, a time when wearing jewellery was outlawed as incompatible with the spirit of public sacrifice the struggle had demanded, women fought hard to have the law repealed (Livy, 34.1.1–8.3; see below, p. 157). They travelled in fine carriages, and when religious ceremonies required them to offer sacrifice at temples, they might use gold or silver utensils borne by a long train of servants (Polyb. 31.26.1–8). Such status markers naturally grew out of competition among elite women for precedence, but they also reflected their husbands' power and prestige.

However, wealth was a tricky issue for aristocrats. Senators and those who aspired to that station naturally had to be fairly wealthy in order to have the leisure to devote themselves to the public's welfare. It was good to be rich: when Q. Caecilius Metellus delivered a speech at the funeral of his father Lucius, consul in 251 and 247, praising him for having 'achieved the ten greatest and best things that wise men spend their lives seeking', prominent among them was 'to acquire great wealth by honourable means' (Pliny *HN* 7.139–40). Those means are usually assumed to have been victorious war, since Roman generals supposedly were free to claim a portion of the booty for themselves. This assumption has lately been questioned, but soldiers and officers were certainly able to keep the spoils they took (see below, p. 110). Unfortunately, we really know very little about senators' finances in the middle Republic. Scholars assume that ordinarily their income came from agriculture – the sale of crops grown on large farms worked by slaves and supervised by bailiffs who were either slaves themselves or former slaves (freedmen) of the owner. Possibly, however, aristocrats undertook other sorts of commercial ventures as well, but indirectly, through freedmen agents who kept their principal's participation discreetly hidden since 'a concern with money-making was considered beneath a senator's dignity', as the historian Livy (21.63.4) puts it in reporting the passage of a law of 219 that forbade senators from owning ocean-going ships suitable for commercial voyages. Yet the fact that such a law was deemed necessary suggests that senators in fact were engaged in overseas trading at that time, and some at least continued to do so thereafter. A generation later M. Porcius Cato, otherwise a paragon of old-fashioned morality, made handsome profits from his investments in maritime loans using a front man (Plut. *Cat. Mai.* 21.6).

But whatever the source of a senator's wealth, it would not do to flash it around. That was fine for aristocratic wives but not for their husbands. Luxuriousness in men signalled effeminacy and a self-indulgence that accorded ill with an ethos of public service. Surprisingly, dining constituted a flash-point for aristocratic concerns over luxury and wealth. Because a senator lived so much of his life in public, peer pressure could be effective in policing many of the boundaries of appropriate deportment. But behind closed doors such strictures were much less easily brought to bear. In 182 the first of a series of sumptuary laws, the *lex Orchia*, was passed limiting the number of guests that could be entertained to dinner. Other laws followed in 161 and 143 imposing restrictions on how much could be spent on meals and what sorts of food could be served as well as on how many guests from outside the family could attend. These regulations proved impossible to enforce, but the fact that the senate had them passed at all attests to the problems dining raised, for commensality lay at the intersection of a senator's public and private lives. The dining room of an aristocratic house (termed a *triclinium* from its three couches, each holding three reclining diners and arranged around a single table) were semi-public spaces, intimate places where private wealth could be exhibited for favoured members of the public in ways that custom otherwise foreclosed to male aristocrats. As such the *patres* struggled to define the limits of the luxury that could be put on display there. The problem was particularly difficult because wealth was spread unevenly within their ranks. Some found themselves at a disadvantage as conspicuous consumption increasingly became an arena of aristocratic competition, and they could appeal to the laws' restrictions and to old-fashioned simplicity in order to excuse their failure to offer lavish entertainments. But other aristocrats had grown rich, and because feasting guests honoured and gratified them, it was simply another type of *beneficium* that a good patron ought to bestow on his friends and clients – the more abundantly and lavishly, the greater the favour shown. The senators never found a satisfactory resolution to the conflict.

Aristocrats and the *res publica*

Through his efforts on behalf of his fellow citizens an aristocrat began to accumulate the store of experience and wisdom that would lay the foundations for his *auctoritas* while at the same time placing the citizens under an obligation to reciprocate. His success in these endeavours brought him prestige and enhanced his reputation in the eyes of the public. His house, his appearance and deportment, the ways he entertained at home, even his wife's dress and accoutrements all helped him fashion an image of himself as someone wholly devoted to serving the interests of the *populus Romanus* and possessing the character and means to do so faithfully and effectively. But all of this was only a means to an end: the chance to gain the highest honours. The first-century historian Sallust summed up succinctly the connection between an aristocratic ethos of service to individuals and the opportunity to win surpassing distinction when he sketched the character and habits of his contemporary, Julius Caesar:

> Caesar was considered great because of his favours and his lavishness ... Caesar gained renown by giving, by supporting, and by forgiving ... Ultimately Caesar determined to labour and be vigilant, to focus on his friends' affairs and ignore his own, to deny nothing that was worthy to give. He was hoping for a great command for himself, an army, and a new war where his excellence could shine. (*Cat.* 54.1–4)

The greatest benefits an aristocrat could confer were those bestowed upon the Roman community as a whole – the *res publica* – by managing its most important business. Outstanding achievements here formed the basis for the kind of *auctoritas* that elicited real deference from his fellow citizens. But opportunities to do so and thereby lay claim to the greatest prestige came only with election to public office. That was what made the magistracies so coveted and the objects of such intense rivalry among senators and those who aspired to that status. Election itself conveyed great honour – public offices were *honores* in Latin – but only because it acknowledged the merit one had already accumulated up to that point through one's efforts on the public's behalf. That acknowledgement in turn evoked immense *gratia* in its recipient for the signal distinction the Roman people had bestowed, leading him to redouble his efforts to serve its interests while in office in order to repay the debt he owed for elevation above his competitors. What he accomplished in that office would constitute further benefits to the *populus Romanus*, whether these came through administering justice as a praetor, supervising festivals to honour the gods as aedile, passing legislation as a tribune of the plebs, or fulfilling the various other tasks that the Republic's welfare depended on. Those benefits then allowed him to lay claim to further *honores* from the public, the granting of which brought forth additional *gratia*, out of which came further services in an endlessly repeating cycle.

As Sallust's depiction of Caesar's ambitions reveals, however, war constituted far and away the Republic's most crucial public business during the third and second centuries. It therefore offered the most abundant scope for services to Rome that would pave the way to honour and *honores*. That fact made martial courage (*virtus*) central to the aristocratic system of values.[17] A willingness to risk one's life in combat constituted the highest form of self-sacrifice on the Roman people's behalf. Courage in battle, according to Polybius, was 'nearly the most important thing in every state but especially in Rome' (31.29.1). The proof of exceptional valour found its physical expression in the spoils stripped from an enemy defeated in single combat and hung on the wall by the doorway of the victor's house. Or it might be manifested in the awards for exceptional gallantry, like the mural crown for being first to mount an enemy's city wall, or the civic crown, a wreath of oak leaves awarded for single-handedly saving a fellow citizen's life by slaying his attacker without giving ground in the fight. Or it could be revealed simply in the scars an aristocratic warrior bore on his breast, mute testimony to his bravery in battle. The men whose deeds in the Republic's wars reflected outstanding courage won renown (*gloria*) and a reputation (*fama*), and these together with the *virtus* they bespoke were indications of the character that the Romans believed fitted a man to lead. These proofs demonstrated in the most graphic terms the selfless devotion to the Republic that the citizens expected of their magistrates. *Virtus* in a very real sense offered a guarantee of that quality, the *auctoritas* that backed it up. Young aristocrats went to war at 17 and served mainly in the cavalry. The freewheeling style of combat that characterised this arm afforded them ample scope for distinguishing themselves by displaying their *virtus*. The payoff from the *fama* and *gloria* they gained here first came when they stood for election as one of the twenty-four junior officers, the military tribunes, for the four consular legions levied each year. Casualties among the military tribunes were often high, attesting to their readiness to lead their men into the thick of the fighting. After ten years of military service young aristocrats embarked on the course of offices that led from the quaestorship, if all went well, to the consulate, with enrolment by the censors in the senate along the way.

A consulship not only conferred enormous honour on the man who reached it; it accorded him the right to lead Rome's armies against its enemies and, the gods willing, to victory. And inasmuch

17. M. McDonnell, *Roman Manliness: Virtus and the Roman Republic*, Cambridge: Cambridge University Press, 2006.

Table 2 *The cursus honorum (course of offices)*

	Military tribunes	Quaestors	Tribunes of the plebs	Aediles	Praetors	Consuls	Censors	Dictator
Offices, following ten years of military service, typically in the cavalry, ages 17–26	(24 annually, 14 with five years of service, 10 with ten years; could be continued in office)	(four annually until 267; six until 227; eight until 197; ten thereafter)	(ten annually; open only to plebeians)	(four annually, two 'plebeian', open only to plebeians, and two 'curule', open to plebeians and patricians in alternate years)	(one annually until c. 242; two until c. 220; four until 197; six thereafter); possess *imperium* inferior to consuls'	(two annually); possess *imperium*	(two every five years; serve 18 months)	(one, rarely and only in emergencies; serves six months); possesses *imperium* superior to consuls'
Functions	Junior military officers, six for each consular legion	Some: financial officers for consuls and praetorian governors; others: administrative duties in Rome and other Italian towns	Legislation in the *concilium plebis*; right to veto magistrates; *intercessio* to protect citizens	Administrative and religious duties in Rome	Judicial and administrative duties in Rome; extra commander when needed; govern overseas provinces	Command armies; preside over senate; conduct assemblies; religious duties	Appoint senate; conduct census; supervise morals; auction public contracts	Supreme military command; master of cavalry (*magister equitum*) second in command
Method of appointment	Elected in *comitia tributa*	Elected in *comitia tributa*	Elected in *concilium plebis*	Elected in *comitia tributa*	Elected in *comitia centuriata*	Elected in *comitia centuriata*	Elected in *comitia centuriata*	Named by consul at senate's direction

Note: Progress through the *cursus* is from left to right in the table.

as war was the most critical issue facing Rome's citizens, winning a signal victory bestowed the greatest of benefits upon the *res publica*. A conquering general demonstrated extraordinary *virtus* and covered himself in glory, and he received his crowning reward in the celebration of a triumph. Nominally ceremonies of thanksgiving honouring Rome's principal guardian, Jupiter Best and Greatest (*Optimus Maximus*), for his aid in securing victory, triumphs celebrated the might and majesty of Rome and the glory of the conquering army's commander while at the same time parading the *beneficium* he had bestowed on the Republic. They brought 'a vivid picture of what their generals had accomplished right before the eyes of the Roman people', as Polybius puts it (6.15.8). At the same time, parades are also rituals in which a community presents an image of itself to itself. Triumphs therefore offered the citizens a flattering picture of themselves as a powerful, conquering people while simultaneously displaying to them in vivid terms those they had vanquished. The triumphing general (the *triumphator*) and his army marched through the city to the temple of Jupiter on the Capitoline Hill in a procession both solemn and boisterous, the only occasions on which soldiers with their weapons were permitted within the *pomerium*.[18] Their spoils and the most important prisoners preceded them, witnessed by admiring civilian throngs. The *triumphator* was conveyed, exceptionally, in a chariot and dressed in special, triumphal robes, perhaps in imitation of Jupiter himself. This was 'the moment when a Roman knew he was first, best, and greatest'.[19] Victory crowned by the celebration of a triumph set the achievements of some men of consular rank apart from the rest and contributed greatly to the record of proven success upon which great personal *auctoritas* was founded.

Aristocratic competition

The road to the consulate, however, was neither easy nor swift. There were always more aspirants to *honores* than offices to satisfy them, and the farther one progressed along the *cursus honorum* the tougher the competition became. Not every quaestor or tribune of

18. M. Beard, *The Roman Triumph*, Cambridge, MA: Harvard University Press, 2007; I. Östenberg, *Staging the World: Spoils, Captives, and Representations in the Roman Triumphal Procession*, Oxford: Oxford University Press, 2009.
19. T. P. Wiseman, 'Competition and co-operation', in T. P. Wiseman (ed.), *Roman Political Life 90 BC–AD 69*, Exeter: University of Exeter Press, 1985, 4.

the plebs would become a praetor; after c. 220, when four praetors began to be elected annually, not every praetor would reach the consulate. And the odds of a consul gaining the censorship were roughly five to one. Yet the pressure on aristocrats to reach high office was urgent and unceasing, particularly for members of the *nobilitas*. They were the cream of the aristocracy, the inner elite. Election to the consulship secured *nobilitas* (notability or celebrity) for a senator, and he passed this informal status down to his descendents.[20] For sons born into these families, their nobility was both a blessing and a burden. Younger nobles were felt to have inherited those personal qualities – signal *virtus*, outstanding dedication to the interests of their fellow citizens and to the welfare of the Republic – that had brought their ancestors to the consulate. *Nobilitas* thereby became the *auctoritas* vouching for their character. In addition, scions of such families entered the political arena with not only their own accomplishments to their credit but the great store of services both to the Republic and to individuals that their ancestors had amassed. Their deeds constituted a strong claim for recompense in the form of honour and *honores* on Rome and its citizens, who were now enjoying the benefits of them. And not surprisingly, the voters acknowledged these debts by repeatedly elevating members of noble families like the Claudii, the Fulvii, the Cornelii, and others to the consulship during the third, second, and first centuries.

Yet elevation to the Republic's highest *honores* was never automatic for a noble. Unlike other aristocracies in Europe and elsewhere, the Roman elite defined itself not by birth but by achievement. Family background was immensely helpful, by providing a head start, but nobles and other aristocrats in each generation had to run their own races and win a place at the top by virtue of their own character and though their own accomplishments. The young men of these families had to measure up to or even surpass the marks their ancestors had set in serving their fellow citizens, displaying valour in battle, winning election to public offices, and then performing outstandingly in them. The pressure was unremitting. As the 18-year-old noble Scipio Aemilianus complained to his friend Polybius, 'in a quiet and subdued voice, and with the blood mounting to his cheeks ... "I am considered by everybody, I hear, to be a mild, effete person, and far removed from the true Roman

20. Gelzer, *Roman Nobility*; P. A. Brunt, '*Nobilitas* and *novitas*', *JRS* 72 (1982), 1–17.

character and ways, because I don't care for pleading in the law courts. And they say that the family I come of requires a different kind of representative, and not the sort that I am. That is what annoys me most"' (Polyb. 31.23.9–12). For as Scipio's lament reveals, it was not just his own fate riding on a young noble but his family's as well. Without members in the Republic's highest offices in every generation, noble families gradually but inexorably slipped into obscurity as more vigorous contenders from families of equal or even lesser stature, but with stronger claims to rewards at the hands of the voters, shouldered them aside. By the same token, republican political culture's emphasis on personal character, services to the public, and their requital through the bestowal of honour and offices meant that Rome's aristocracy could never be a closed caste. It was permeable to talent. Men without consular forebears, even men whose ancestors had never sat in the senate, the so-called 'new men' (novi homines), could aspire to public offices, even the highest, by distinguishing themselves through their exceptional virtus and services to the Republic and its citizens. Such cases were unusual; typically only two or three representatives of noble clans vied for each of the annual consulates because only such men had gained the political capital through their own and their ancestors' achievements to stand a chance of winning. But newcomers gained high offices, even the consulship, frequently enough to underscore the inability of aristocrats to rest on their ancestral laurels.

Also peculiar to the Roman aristocracy was the absence of any fixed hierarchy among them. No formal titles – duke, earl, count, and the like – with an established ranking among them existed to distinguish one aristocrat from another. Precedence in debate and honour stemmed from the offices one had held, but since elections occurred every year, many men enjoyed a similar status at any time, distinguished only by their dates of election. Ancestry too counted for a great deal, but even among noble families none could claim a clear superiority over the rest. The effect of this indeterminacy of an aristocrat's precise place in the pecking order was to exacerbate rivalry as each strove to set himself apart somehow from his peers. Equally unusual was the role of the voters as arbiters in that political competition.[21] Notwithstanding the ways in which the

21. K-J. Hökeskamp, *Reconstructing the Roman Republic: An Ancient Political Culture and Modern Research*, trans. H. Heitmann-Gordon, Princeton: Princeton University Press, 2010, 99–101.

assemblies were skewed in favour of older and wealthier citizens, elections placed the voters in a very powerful position because they controlled the outcomes of these contests, with all the consequences for individual aristocrats' hopes for honour and for the stature of their families that were riding on them. Indeed, the entire system of aristocratic competition could only operate if the determination of winners and losers came from outside of the aristocracy itself. Otherwise, conflicts over honour and offices would tear it apart. That vital role the citizens of Rome played, and the electors at least in theory had wide latitude in making their choices among the candidates who offered themselves for their approval. Aristocratic character could manifest itself in many different ways, and services to the public and Rome could take a variety of forms. In determining which candidate to elevate, the public played a decisive role in establishing the traits that aristocrats ought to display and the sorts of benefits they ought to confer if they hoped for rewards at the hands of the voters. Ordinary citizens, in other words, participated in a very real way in the creation of an aristocratic ideology and consequently in the aristocracy's self-fashioning.

Nobles and other aristocrats responded to the relentless competition for office and honour, the fluid hierarchy within their ranks, and the fact that their fates depended upon the judgement of the citizenry by strenuously advertising their achievements and the benefits they and their families had conferred upon the Roman people. Some of their efforts are still visible, as in the tomb inscription in which the family of the Cornilii Scipiones commemorated one of its most distinguished members, the consul of 298 and the great-great-great-grandfather of Scipio Aemilianus (although the inscription dates from the early second century):

> Lucius Cornelius Scipio Barbatus, son of his father Gnaeus, a strong man and a wise one, whose courage (*virtus*) closely matched his good looks. He was consul, censor, and aedile among you. He captured Taurasia and Cisauna in Samnium, subjugated the whole of Lucania, and brought back hostages. (*CIL* 1.2.7 = *ROL* 4.2–3)

Or in this inscription, for his son, consul in 259:

> This one, Lucius Scipio, most acknowledge was the best man of all the good men at Rome. The son of Barbatus, he was consul, censor, and aedile among you. He captured Corisca and the city of Aleria and gave a temple to the goddesses of the weather in return for the benefits they had bestowed. (*CIL* 1.2.9 = *ROL* 4.4–5)

Figure 5 A mid-republican temple. Temple, probably of Hercules Victor, in the Forum Boarum. Alenari/Art Resource.

Temples like the one the younger Lucius Scipio built placed a solid, emphatic representation of those benefits before the eyes of the Roman people. They attested to the gods' favour in battle, which a general like Lucius often sought to secure by vowing to construct a temple to a god if the deity vouchsafed the Romans victory. But more pointedly the temple underscored the victory that that favour had produced and the general who had won it, as in this temple dedication set up by Lucius Mummius, consul in 146:

> Lucius Mummius, son of Lucius, consul.
> Under his leadership, auspices, and command Achaea was taken and Corinth destroyed. He returned to Rome in triumph. For these achievements, successfully accomplished, he the commander dedicated this temple and statue of the Conquering Hercules, which he had vowed in the war. (*CIL* 1.2.626 = *ROL* 4.84–5)

But the most spectacular and effective advertisements of an aristocratic family's glory and services to the *res publica* were the funeral ceremonies they held for their foremost members. Polybius witnessed them during his stay in Rome and left a vivid description:

> Whenever one of their illustrious men dies, in the course of his funeral, the body with all of its paraphernalia is carried into the forum to the Rostra, as a raised platform there is called ... [H]is son ... or, failing him, one of his relations mounts the Rostra and delivers a speech concerning the virtues of the deceased and the successful exploits performed by him in his lifetime ... After the burial ... they place the likeness of the deceased in the most conspicuous spot in his house ... These likenesses they display at public sacrifices adorned with much care. And when any illustrious member of the family dies, they carry these masks to the funeral, putting them on men ... as like the originals as possible in height and other personal peculiarities. And these substitutes assume clothes according to the rank of the person represented. If he was a consul or praetor, a toga with purple stripes; if a censor, whole purple; if he had also celebrated a triumph or performed any exploit of that kind, a toga embroidered with gold. These representatives also ride themselves in chariots, while the *fasces* and axes and all the other customary insignia of the particular offices lead the way ... On arriving at the Rostra, they all take their seats on ivory chairs in their order. There could not easily be a more inspiring spectacle than this for a young man of noble ambitions and virtuous aspirations ... Besides, the speaker over the body about to be buried, after having finished the panegyric of this particular person, starts upon the others whose representatives are present, beginning with the most ancient, and recounts the successes and achievements of each. By this means the glorious memory of brave men is continually renewed; the fame of those who have performed any noble deed is never allowed to die ... But the chief benefit of the ceremony is that it inspires young men to shrink from no exertion for the general welfare, in the hope of obtaining the glory which awaits the brave. (Polyb. 6.52.11–54.3)

The masks, taken from their cabinets in the atrium of the family's home and worn by the actors along with the regalia appropriate to their offices, brought the family's ancestors themselves physically before the eyes of the Roman people in the forum, the heart of the Republic's civic space. The speech recounting their deeds reminded the public vividly of the *honores* the ancestors had won and the benefits they had bestowed on the *res publica* in them. Equally important, the masks and the eulogy of the deceased and his ancestors reminded young aristocrats of the sorts of men they ought to strive to become if they were to equal or surpass the exploits these funerals commemorated. That character and those exploits would not only ensure their rise to the top of the political hierarchy and secure their family's continued elite status, but would lead them in their turn to strive to serve the *res publica* and its citizens. What the young achieved in that endeavour would thereby become the foundations for their own *auctoritas* and so form the basis for the aristocracy's continued dominance at Rome.

Through their constant struggles to win honour by securing the public's welfare Roman aristocrats created the 'soft power' through which they individually and collectively as the senate controlled the *res publica* of the Roman people. Forging consensus in the latter body was not always easy. Jealousy over precedence and over-sensitivity to personal esteem (*dignitas*) meant competition was inevitable and conflict inescapable. Many senators had held high offices in which they had benefited Rome. Each therefore could believe that his personal *auctoritas* ought to prevail. Once they reached agreement, however, the united *auctoritas* of the *patres* left the Roman people no alternative but to comply with their advice. Yet the strength of senatorial *auctoritas* depended in the last analysis on the public's trust that the course it recommended was all but certain to be the right one, and that trust in turn was founded not only on the memory of past successes but on the expectation of future ones as well. Failure, and especially military failure, threatened to undermine confidence in the senate's *auctoritas* and with it the foundations of senatorial dominance. And because Rome was so often at war in these years, events on the battlefield could entail grave political as well as military risks, as the *patres* would discover in the opening years of the Hannibalic war.

CHAPTER 2

Rome, Pyrrhus, and Carthage

The hard-won victories in the opening years of the third century brought a rare respite to the Republic's warmaking. It did not last long; peace never lasted long for the Romans. In 284 troubles developed on the Republic's northern frontier. Our evidence for these events is very poor.[1] We have only a highly compressed description by Polybius, probably drawing on the earliest Roman who wrote history, Q. Fabius Pictor. Pictor wrote in the late third century BC, half a century after the events that began in 284, and his work exists today only in fragments. Beyond Polybius' account, information about these events comes from writers of the imperial era, whose works also exist only in fragments, and from a summary of the twelfth book of Livy, the great Augustan historian, the surviving books of whose history of Rome *From the foundation of the city* (*Ab urbe condita*) break off after book 10, which covers the year 293, and resume only with the beginning of the Hannibalic war. We know the contents of books 11–20 only through summaries (the *Periochae*). None of our sources, in other words, offers a contemporary narration of these events, and documentary records, if they were kept at all, would have contained only the baldest of accounts. Much therefore is uncertain, but that is typical of our knowledge of this period. What little evidence we have can be put together in more than one way, and no completely definitive account can be written.[2] The most plausible reconstruction has a war band from the Senones, a Gallic tribe living in the far southeastern corner of the northern Italian plain, attacking the Etruscan city of Arretium. The Gauls were probably mercenaries, but in whose employ we do not know. The Romans had subjugated Arretium some time earlier, and so

---

1. Polyb. 2.19.7–13; Dion. Hal. 19.13. 1; App. *Sam.* 6, *Celt.* 11; Dio Cass. frg. 38; Livy, *Per.* 12.
2. T. C. Brennan, 'M.' Curius Dentatus and the praetor's right to triumph', *Historia* 43 (1994), 423–39; M. G. Morgan, 'The defeat of L. Metellus Denter at Arretium', *CQ* n.s. 22 (1972), 309–25.

the Arretines appealed for aid to the senate, which dispatched the consul, L. Caecilius Metellus Denter with an army. Denter was unable to persuade the Gauls, now reinforced by a band of rebellious Etruscans, to lift their siege of the city, and so, probably early in the following year, he brought them to battle. This time the Romans lost, and the consul died in the fighting. The senate quickly raised a new army and sent it north under the command of the veteran general M'. Curius Dentatus. Rome at that time had a treaty with the Senonian Gauls, one that the latter had probably been forced to make following the victory at Sentinum twelve years before. If they were among those the Romans defeated on that occasion, the Senones may also have been forced to cede a portion of their land for the foundation of the Roman colony of Sena Gallica. Be that as it may, their treaty placed the Senones under a variety of obligations to the Romans. This fact explains Dentatus' decision to dispatch envoys to the Senones rather than launch an attack. They demanded the return of the Roman soldiers captured in the recent defeat and ordered the Senones not to allow mercenaries from their tribe to serve among the Etruscan forces that were at that time at war with Rome. The Republic expected no less of its subject allies.

The consul's second demand, if it is reliably reported in our sources, also supplies a key piece of evidence. It reveals that Rome's conflict with the Senones was really a sideshow to the main event, a serious revolt by at least some of the Etruscan cities which were now challenging the settlement that Rome had imposed on them after Sentinum. Rome's conflict with the Senones looms large in our evidence for this period mainly because Polybius is concerned in this part of his history to give a rundown of the Romans' earlier conflicts with the Gauls as a prelude to his description of the massive Gallic invasion of 225 (pp. 71–2), rather than a full account of events in the early third century. The conflict with the Senones, however, became notorious among Roman writers for the sequel. The Senones put Dentatus' envoys to death, hacking them into pieces and scattering their remains, according to one lurid account, and in the process violating the sacred laws that protected ambassadors from harm. The horror of the crime drew the attention of later Roman historians, always eager to portray Roman warmaking as a justified response to the wrongs they or their friends had suffered. In this case, that portrayal may be correct. When news of the outrage reached the consul of 283, P. Cornelius Dolabella, he turned aside from his march into Etruria and invaded the territory of the Senones.

His army defeated their forces, laid waste their lands, killed every man they could find, and sold the women and children they captured into slavery. The rest they drove out of the area, which the senate elected to incorporate into Roman territory, henceforth known as the Gallic lands (*ager Gallicus*). Dolabella then resumed his campaign against the Etruscans.

The expulsion of the surviving Senones from their land alarmed their northern neighbours, the Gallic Boii, a much larger and stronger tribe who feared that a similar fate would soon befall them if they did not take actions to prevent it. They made common cause with those Etruscans then in arms against Rome. Together, they, the Etruscans, and the Senonian mercenaries in their employ advanced towards Rome. This force got to within 45 miles of the city, to Lake Vadimon in the upper Tiber valley, where Dolabella's army met them and won a crushing victory. The few who escaped were unlucky enough to encounter the forces of Dolabella's colleague, who finished them off. Over the three years that ensued, Roman armies campaigned repeatedly in Etruria against those towns that still resisted Rome's dominance, until Rome was forced to suspend operations there to confront more pressing developments in the south.

Rome, Tarentum, and Pyrrhus

Tarentum and Magna Graecia

While Dolabella and his army were winning their victory at Lake Vadimon, the forces under the praetor Dentatus were marching south to deal with threats to the Greek city of Thurii. Once again, our evidence for this episode and its sequel is frustratingly incomplete, but it appears that the Thurians were being harassed by a band of Lucanians from the adjacent highlands and appealed to Rome for aid. A tribune of the plebs, C. Aelius, took up their cause and with or without the senate's blessing had legislation passed to dispatch assistance. For this act the grateful Thurians honoured him with a statue surmounted by a crown of gold (Pliny, *HN* 34.32). Dentatus' mission apparently represented that assistance, which was successful in the short term. He celebrated an *ovatio* (a lesser form of triumph) for his achievements.[3]

---

3. Brennan, 'M.' Curius Dentatus', 432–7.

Behind these small events, however, much larger forces were being brought into play.[4] The Lucanians were a group of Oscan-speaking peoples who occupied the mountains and upland valleys of the southern portion of the Apennine range. They were organised in a loose federation, and ethnically related to the peninsula's other major Oscan-speaking groups, the Samnites, Campanians, and Apulian peoples. The Lucanians had occupied much of southern Italy by the early fourth century, save for the coastal regions controlled by the Greek cities that had been established in Italy at various times beginning in the seventh century. Conflict between the Lucanians and Greeks was endemic, as overpopulation and a need for winter pastures forced the highlanders to move into the fertile valleys and coastal plains that formed the territories of the Greek poleis. A similar conflict between the Samnites and the Greeks and Etruscans of Campania during the later fifth century had led to the conquest of the latter by Samnite migrants. No Greek polis in southern Italy by itself was strong enough to resist the Lucanians' encroachments, and so the poleis formed the Italiot league under the leadership of the strongest of them, Tarentum. Over the course of time, however, Tarentum came to dominate the other members of the league, which the latter naturally resented. In the light of this circumstance, Thurii's decision to call on Rome rather than Tarentum and the Italiot league in 283 represents an effort not simply to defend itself against the highlanders but to establish a counterweight to Tarentum in the form of a relationship with Rome.

Dentatus' mission, although apparently a success, was not the end of the story, for in the following year a Roman army was again in the south under the consul C. Fabricius Luscinus, who broke a siege of Thurii and returned to Rome to celebrate a triumph over the Lucanians, Samnites, and Brutti (Dion. Hal. 19.13.1; Pliny, *HN* 34.32). He also left behind a garrison in Thurii, an act that was viewed by the Tarentines as highly provocative, an attempt to establish a foothold in the south. For the Tarentines certainly understood that the next appeal to Rome that Thurii or some other Greek city in the region made might be for help not against the Lucanians but against themselves. The Tarentines' concerns over Roman encroachment into areas they considered 'theirs' was longstanding by this point. Rome's long struggle to defeat the Samnites had led it to adopt

4. K. Lomas, *Rome and the Western Greeks, 350 BC–AD 200: Conquest and Acculturation in Southern Italy*, London and New York: Routledge, 1993, 36–48.

a two-pronged strategy by seeking to penetrate their enemy's home-land from the east as well as from Campania in the west. That effort had led the Republic to open contacts with some of the towns that dotted the broad grain-lands of Apulia and that were also under threat from the Samnites. However, Apulia was an area that the Tarentines had traditionally dominated, and Rome's growing influence there directly challenged their own. The Republic's victory in the Second Samnite War only strengthened the attraction of its protection to the Apulians, a victory that left no doubt of Rome's far greater military strength compared to what the Tarentines could offer. Having lost ground to Rome in Apulia, the Tarentines could only look upon the Romans' entry into Magna Graecia – that is, southern Italy and Sicily – as a challenge to their dominance within the region. They clearly revealed their determination to resist that challenge soon after Fabricius had left the region. When a squadron of ten Roman warships paid a visit to their city and anchored in their harbour, the Tarentines attacked them, sinking four, capturing another, and putting the rest to flight (App. *Sam.* 7; Livy, *Per.* 12). Although no state of war existed at this point between the Republic and Tarentum, the Tarentines justified the assault on the basis of an old treaty forbidding Roman warships to sail past the Lacinian promontory into the Ionian Gulf. But the Tarentines had not warned the Romans off or sought to resolve the violation through diplomacy and negotiation. They were sending a message to Rome to stay out of their backyard, a message they reinforced soon thereafter by marching to Thurii and expelling its Roman garrison and those Thurian aristocrats who had led the city to seek Rome's protection. And just to make sure that there was no mistaking their meaning, they grossly insulted a high-ranking Roman envoy sent to demand they hand over the Roman captives, return the Thurian exiles to their city, and restore their property to them (Dion. Hal. 19.4.1–5; App. *Sam.* 7: Livy, *Per.* 12). The alternative was war.

Rome's defence of Thurii had involved it once again in hostilities with its longstanding foes, the Samnites, who had joined in the Lucanians' assault of the city. The following year saw one of the new consuls, L. Aemilius Barbula, campaigning against them. When word reached the senate of their ambassador's treatment at the hands of the Tarentines, the *patres* ordered Barbula to suspend operations in Samnium and avenge the insult. The consul presented the same demands to the Tarentines that the ambassador had, but this time an army was there to back them up. Still, the Tarentines refused to knuckle under, and so Barbula ordered his army to devastate Tarentum's territory and seized a number of towns in it. Powerless in the face of this onslaught, the Tarentines understood that they would need help if they were to withstand the might of Rome. And so they did what many Hellenistic states did and what they themselves had done on other occasions when faced with a bigger military challenge than they could handle: they hired themselves a general with an army. Their choice fell upon Pyrrhus, king of the Molossians and the leader of the Epirote league, an area in the western Balkans (he was not, as Roman writers style him, king of Epirus). Tarentum had longstanding ties with the area, and Pyrrhus himself was under obligation to the Tarentines for past favours. And with his arrival in Italy in the winter of 281/280, a new chapter in the Republic's diplomatic history opens, for Rome was being drawn into a web of events that would have repercussions far beyond the confines of Italy.

Pyrrhus

Our own perspective on those events also becomes quite different because of Pyrrhus' fame among contemporary Greeks.[5] He was a formidable warrior as well as a masterful tactician, a general whose personal bravery was able to inspire great loyalty among the men he led. His achievements commanded the attention of a number of contemporary writers, among them the historians Hieronymus of Cardia and Timaeus of Tauromenium. The king himself also composed his memoirs, and his exploits were chronicled by Proxenus, his court historian. Even the Romans themselves recognised in their struggle against Pyrrhus a contest of epic proportions. The earliest Roman poet, Q. Ennius, described the war in the sixth book of his *Annales* in a Homeric vein. The works of these writers have largely perished, but they were extant in antiquity and later authors drew extensively on them, either directly or through intermediaries, in composing their accounts of the conflict. The most important of these was Plutarch of Chaeronea, a first-century AD polymath who included among his collection of biographies of famous Greeks and Romans a *Life of Pyrrhus*. It constitutes our

5. P. R. Franke, 'Pyrrhus', in F. W. Walbank, A. E. Astin, M. W. Frederiksen, and R. M. Ogilvie (eds), *The Rise of Rome to 220 B.C.* Vol. 7, Part 2, of *The Cambridge Ancient History*[2]. Cambridge: Cambridge University Press, 1989, 456–85.

Figure 6 Bust of Pyrrhus found in the Villa dei Papiri at Herculaneum, now in the Museo Archeologico Nazionale (Naples). Photo courtesy of Jona Lendering.

primary source for Rome's Pyrrhic war. The result of this comparative abundance of evidence is both heartening and frustrating. On the one hand, much of what we know about this war derives from relatively reliable, contemporary sources, as opposed to the legendary quality of much of our information about events in earlier periods. On the other, we still do not have as much evidence as we would like to be able to produce a full account of the war. But most unusually, because most of our information derives from Greek sources sympathetic to Pyrrhus, our perspective on the events of the war is often that of the king rather than the Romans.

Pyrrhus' motives in accepting Tarentum's offer to lead their war against Rome went far beyond simply money. The early third century saw the twilight of the age of the Diadochi, the successors of Alexander the Great. Men of hardly lesser stature, they had been Alexander's generals, advisors, and collaborators, who in the wake of his death had warred incessantly against one another as they sought to carve out kingdoms for themselves that would ultimately become the constellation of great powers of the Hellenistic era. Pyrrhus, had he been born half a century earlier, would surely have been one of them, but by the time he came of age, most of the kingdoms had been won and there was little scope for a man of his pedigree (through his mother he had a claim on the throne of Macedon), talents, and ambitions. Still, the western Balkans could not contain their scope. An attempt to wrest the kingdom of Macedon from its ruler had been frustrated, but Magna Graecia offered an open field for his aspirations. He hoped not simply to become a hero to the western Greeks by defending them against the Roman 'barbarians' (as the Greeks saw them) but to win Sicily, where through his wife and son he had a claim to the throne of Syracuse, and perhaps even cross over to Africa and conquer Carthage. Here was a challenge worthy of the successors of Alexander – and perhaps even of Alexander himself.

After a stormy crossing of the Adriatic during the winter of 281/280, Pyrrhus landed in Italy with 22,500 infantry, 2,000 archers, 500 slingers, 3,000 cavalry, and 20 Indian war elephants. The levy of the Epirote league formed the core of his forces, along with mercenaries hired from Greece. This infantry's training and equipment reflected a century of development in Greek and especially Macedonian warfare. They were armed with an 18-foot pike, the *sarissa*, wielded with two hands, and they were protected by a small shield and very light armour. The men formed up in a compact mass, the phalanx, with only about a foot separating one from another. The first three rows of *phalangites* held their spears pointing forward in a dense array, while the rest held theirs upright to avoid wounding the men in the front ranks. The soldiers were carefully drilled to operate with precision in this formation and constituted a powerful force on the battlefield, particularly when supported by an effective cavalry and light forces. Alexander had led such an army to Asia and swept all before him, and forty years of combat among the Diadochi had only served to sharpen this tactical system further. The Romans had never seen anything like it.

After devastating Tarentum's fields, Barbula withdrew his forces north to the territory of the Latin colony at Venusia under orders from the senate as winter set in, intending from there to keep watch on the Samnites and Lucanians. News of Pyrrhus' arrival with a powerful army had greatly alarmed the senate. Rome was at that point not only involved in ongoing hostilities with the highlanders in the south but still attempting to subdue hostile Etruscan cities to the north. The Gallic allies of the latter had been, for the moment, defeated, but no one could say how long they would remain quiescent. No senator could fail to recall the coalition of Samnite,

Etruscan, and Gallic forces that had challenged Rome a generation earlier. The Republic had only with great difficulty broken it at Sentinum and still required several years of hard fighting in the south afterwards to subdue it finally. The Republic now faced the prospect of the revival of that formidable combination, not only renewed by a fresh generation of warriors coming of age, but immeasurably strengthened by the forces of the Epirote league and those of Tarentum and the other Greek cities rallying to Pyrrhus' banner. Accordingly the senate imposed garrisons upon a number of southern Italian towns whose loyalty was in doubt and punished those leading men in them whom they suspected might lead a revolt.

Heraclea

In the spring of 280 Rome sent one of its consuls north to keep the pressure on the Etruscans while the other, P. Valerius Laevinus, marched south to confront Pyrrhus (Livy, *Per.* 13; Dion. Hal. 19.9–12; Plut. *Pyrrh*.16.1–17.5). He found Pyrrhus encamped in the open country between the Greek cities of Heraclea and Panosia along the river Siris. Pyrrhus' arrival had yet to bring forth an outpouring of support from the Greek cities in the region or the Samnites and Lucanians, all of whom were waiting to see what would develop before making any decisions. Nevertheless, the king adopted a posture of superiority by opening talks with Laevinus and proposing to arbitrate the Romans' dispute with the Tarentines. Across the river the consul flatly rejected the offer, which would have been tantamount to admitting that his forces could not prevail against Pyrrhus'. Instead he pressed for battle, worried that the longer he delayed the greater the forces that might rally to Pyrrhus' cause and concerned as well about feeding his army over an extended period so far from Rome.

Laevinus sent his cavalry across the Siris some distance from Epirote forces holding the banks opposite. Once across, the Romans attacked the enemy in the rear and put them to flight, enabling the Roman infantry to ford the river unopposed. Pyrrhus rallied his men as they were falling back, but led them forward again along with the remainder of his army too late to prevent the Romans from crossing. Hard fighting ensued, and the outcome was long in doubt. Pyrrhus himself was in the thick of it, moving along the line of battle, rallying his troops whenever they seemed to waver, and fighting alongside them. At one point, one of the Republic's allied soldiers, a Ferentian cavalryman named Oblax who had been shadowing the king as he rode through the fighting, made a run at him with his spear. He was cut down by one of the king's companions, but not before he had struck Pyrrhus' horse. To foil similar attacks, Pyrrhus gave his cloak and armour to another of his companions and himself fought dressed as an ordinary soldier. But when the companion was killed word quickly spread that Pyrrhus himself was dead, giving heart to the Roman forces and weakening the resolve of the Epirotes. Pyrrhus was compelled to remove his helmet and ride among his men to renew their courage. Finally, with the victory hanging in the balance, Pyrrhus ordered his elephants forward. The animals terrified the Romans and their allies, who had never seen the beasts before, and their unfamiliar odour spooked the cavalry's horses, causing them to panic and flee. Pyrrhus' cavalry then pressed their attack, and at last the Romans broke and fled with the enemy horse in close pursuit. Only the chance wounding of one of the elephants, which threw the rest into disorder and caused Pyrrhus to break off the chase, enabled the Romans to cross the Siris to safety.

Still, their losses were heavy. Greek authors claimed that 7,000 or even 15,000 of the Romans and their Italian allies fell in this defeat, with 1,800 taken prisoner. Figures in ancient authors purporting to number enemy dead are notoriously unreliable – for who would have counted? – but there is no doubt their magnitude reflects what we would in any event expect to have been the case. Somewhat more credence may be placed in a victor's account of his losses, and Pyrrhus', too, were steep according to Hieronymus, who put them at about 4,000 killed, most from the king's best troops.

The king's victory had major repercussions. The Samnites, Lucanians, and Bruttians along with those Greek cities in southern Italy that had been waiting to see the outcome of events now embraced Pyrrhus' cause, which the king represented to the Greek world as nothing short of a great crusade to protect the Hellenes in Italy from the Roman barbarians. He and his Tarentine allies dedicated spoils taken from the enemy and other offerings to the gods at several of the most prestigious sanctuaries around the Greek world. And with his forces now greatly strengthened the king marched north through Lucania. Crossing the Apennines, he entered Campania, the richest agricultural region in the peninsula. The area had enjoyed Roman citizenship for half a century and lay just over 160 km from Latium and Rome itself. Pyrrhus made a grab for Capua, the strongest city in the area, and another for Naples, which with a substantial Greek minority in its population might have been sympathetic to an appeal from the king. Both attempts failed, however, because Laevinus had regrouped and sent forces ahead to occupy these cities as he trailed the king north. Pyrrhus then advanced north up the Liris valley along the *via Latina*, heading for Rome itself. His goal was probably not to capture the city and so end the war. His inability to storm Capua or Naples, much smaller places, cannot have given him any hope of taking Rome, which was heavily fortified, by assault. Instead, he apparently sought to make contact with the Etruscan cities still at war with Rome and rouse others to revolt. The senate at Rome, however, was taking no chances. It ordered the *proletarii* (citizens too poor to equip themselves for war and so exempt from legionary service) to be armed at public expense to defend the city. And fortunately for the Republic, the other consul, Ti. Corucanius, had defeated the Etruscans of Volsinii and Vulci and thereby ended resistance to Rome in the north for the time being. So he was able to bring his forces south to defend the capital. With one consul bearing down on him from the north and the other following to his rear, Pyrrhus feared being caught between them. Having got within 60 km of Rome, he turned back and retired to Tarentum for the winter.

Negotiations

Over the next several months, diplomacy ensued (Dion. Hal. 19.18.1–2; Plut. *Pyrrh.* 18.2–3; App. *Sam.* 10.1). The senate initiated contact by sending a high-level embassy to Pyrrhus seeking to ransom the 1,800 prisoners taken at Heraclea or to exchange them for Tarentines in their custody. The Romans' aim seems simply to have been the recovery of their citizens and allies, but the king and his advisors apparently regarded this request as the opening move in an effort to work out a settlement to the war. Accordingly, he released the prisoners without payment in a gesture of goodwill and also sought to win the support of one of the Roman envoys during their stay. After their return he sent his chief advisor, Cineas, to Rome with proposals for a comprehensive peace on the basis of freedom and self-determination for the Tarentines and the other Italian Greeks, the return of all the lands that Rome had taken from the Samnites, Apulians, Lucanians, and Bruttii, and a formal treaty of peace with Pyrrhus himself. Cineas also endeavoured to gain the favour of influential senators by bringing with him rich gifts for themselves and their wives. In all of this, Pyrrhus was acting in accord with ordinary diplomatic conventions in the Hellenistic world, where a major defeat generally led the losing side to accept the battle's result as definitive – at least in the short run – and agree to terms. And lavish presents to people whose opinions would count in the negotiations were no more than a mark of courtesy and respect for their recipients.

Romans of a later age liked to recall Appius Claudius Caecus' response to the proposals Cineas laid before the senate (Cic. *Brut.* 61, *Sen.* 16; Plut. *Pyrrh.* 18.4–19.3; App. *Sam.* 10.2). As the story goes, the senators were inclining towards accepting Pyrrhus' terms in view of the king's strength and the magnitude of their own losses when Appius rose to speak. He had been one of the architects of Rome's conquest of Samnium during the Second Samnite War as consul, and as censor he had built the great road to the south that bore his name, the *via Appia*. But he was now a very old man, crippled by age, and blind – hence his nickname (*cognomen*), *Caecus* (Blind). He had had to be carried into the senate house so that he could be present at the debate. His speech on that occasion was still read and admired generations later by Cicero and others for its power and passion. It began, 'Until now, senators, I have regarded my blindness as an affliction, but now I wish I was deaf as well, so that I might not even hear the decree you are intending to pass.' And he went on to denounce the peace as unworthy of the very name of Rome, rallying the senators to reject it and continue the war. It is a great story, and the Romans certainly relished telling it because it confirmed them in their image of themselves as men who would settle for nothing short of complete victory over their enemies no matter how dire the situation. And although the version of Appius' speech that Cicero and others read is likely to have been composed by someone else much later, he may truly have spoken against accepting Pyrrhus' offer on that occasion. But if he did, he was only reinforcing a decision the rest of his peers were ready to make.

No senator could accept peace on Pyrrhus' terms. Restoring their lands to the Samnites and others would have rolled back the gains the Republic had made in southern Italy over the previous half century. Agreeing to the freedom and self-determination of the Italiot Greeks would have precluded the Republic from any influence in Magna Graecia, but that would not have prevented Pyrrhus from bringing those cities under his sway. And a treaty with the king would have prevented the Romans from making war upon not only Pyrrhus but any of his new allies, ruling out any attempt to reconquer any part of the south without violating the terms of the pact and bringing Pyrrhus into the war on the side of Rome's opponents. In effect, the king was demanding Rome withdraw from nearly the whole of the peninsula south and east of Campania. Roman dominion would be restricted to Latium, Campania, and Etruria, although how long the Etruscans would be content to remain under the Roman yoke before they sought an alliance with Pyrrhus to aid them in an attempt to break free was anybody's guess. And what was to prevent the cities of Campania or even Latium from following suit? Peace on these terms would have spelled the beginning of the end of any Roman *imperium* in Italy. And Cineas' gifts the senators saw as nothing more than an attempt at bribery.

Ausculum

Once it became clear that a negotiated end to the war was out of the question at Rome, Pyrrhus made preparations to renew the struggle (Dion. Hal. 20.1.1–3.7; Livy, *Per.* 13; Plut. *Pyrrh.* 21.5–10). He recruited additional mercenaries in Greece and records from the temple of Zeus Olympios at Locri reveal that he was making heavy demands for silver to pay them from his Greek allies. Rome, too, raised new legions and made fresh levies upon its allies. The senate sent both consuls of 279, P. Sulpicius Saverrio and P. Decius Mus, south to confront the king. The armies met in Apulia near the town of Ausculum, at the river Aufidus. The battle that ensued raged over two days. In later times, Romans liked to believe that Decius had imitated his father and grandfather by performing the ceremony of *devotio* (see above, p. 1). However, our Greek sources know nothing of this and even report that Pyrrhus, fearing that Decius would attempt a *devotio*, sent word to him that his men had orders to take Decius alive, and that if they did, Pyrrhus would see to it that he was tortured to death. Allegedly, the consuls replied that they had no need of such measures to win (Cic. *Fin.* 61, *Tusc.* 39; Dio Cass. frg. 40.43).

On the first day of fighting, the Romans took up a position in a heavily wooded area that prevented Pyrrhus from deploying his forces effectively, particularly his cavalry, and so more than held their own against him. On the following day Pyrrhus shifted his position to an open plain more favourable to his cavalry and forced the Romans to meet him there. Our Roman sources claim that the battle ended in a draw, but the testimony of Greek authors indicates that the Romans once again got the worst of it. But Pyrrhus' own losses were also heavy: 3,505 men killed according to the king's own memoirs. It was probably in the aftermath of this battle that Pyrrhus, upon being congratulated on his victory, offered his famous response, 'Another victory like this and we'll be ruined.' For it had truly been a 'Pyrrhic victory'. His Epirote phalanx had borne much of the brunt of the fighting over the past two years, and losses among the *phalangites* had been especially heavy. They were not going to be easy to replace. And while Rome's losses had been even heavier, their reserves of manpower were much deeper. In a war of attrition, Pyrrhus was bound to lose, and he knew it. But he also knew that it was not even worth trying to win such a contest.

Pyrrhus in Sicily

The struggle between Rome and Pyrrhus was beginning to have repercussions that extended far beyond the confines of Italy, while developments elsewhere were likewise coming to affect events there. In the autumn of 279 the king was deliberating a return to Greece and an effort to gain the recently vacant throne of Macedon. Pyrrhus had been enticed to come to Italy, after all, not so much by the money the Tarentines were offering as by the prospect of enlarging his domains in the west when further expansion in Greece had been foreclosed. But the death of the Macedonian king and the turmoil in that country following a Gallic invasion offered the prospect of returning east as the kingdom's saviour and staking his claim to the monarchy. Yet Macedon was not the only part of the Greek world that needed a saviour just then. As the king was considering a return to Macedon, Syracusan envoys arrived in Tarentum offering him the command of that city's war against Carthage (Plut. *Pyrrh.* 22.1–3). The latter's longstanding aim of bringing all of Sicily under its power seemed on the verge of realisation. Syracuse, the strongest of the Greek cities in Sicily, was wracked by political strife and at the same time at loggerheads with the other Greeks on the island and the Campanian mercenaries, the Mamertines, in Messana. Carthage stood ready to profit from this disarray and by defeating Syracuse, its principal adversary, reduce the other Greeks to submission. The Syracusans also required salvation, and Pyrrhus was tempted. For as it happened, Pyrrhus' wife, Larissa, was the daughter of Agathocles, the former ruler of Syracuse. Their son therefore could legitimately lay claim to his grandfather's throne. Control of Syracuse could be a stepping stone to rule over Sicily, and Sicily was a rich prize. And the prospect of uniting the Greeks there under his leadership to liberate them once and for all from the threat of Carthage was enormously appealing, particularly when set against the long, difficult, and possibly futile struggle he would face in Italy against Rome.

The possibility that Pyrrhus would take up the cause of the Sicilian Greeks was not lost on the Carthaginians, to judge by the appearance of a Punic fleet in Ostia, the port of Rome, sometime in late 279, following Ausculum (Just. 18.2.1–3). Its commander, Mago, presented to the senate an offer of assistance against Pyrrhus, which the *patres* politely declined. They did, however, agree to a renewal of their treaty with Carthage (Polyb. 3.25.1–5). The terms of the agreement called for either party, should it make a treaty with Pyrrhus, to ensure that the treaty contained a provision allowing either Rome or Carthage to come to the aid of the other if it was attacked. In the event that either party summoned the help of the other, Carthage was to furnish transport for its own or Rome's forces. Carthage's aim in seeking this compact was to encourage Rome to keep Pyrrhus occupied in Italy while Carthage finished its conquest of Sicily. To that end, the Carthaginians held out the prospect of using their ships to launch a sea-borne attack against Pyrrhus' allies in the south or perhaps mounting a blockade of Tarentum to prevent reinforcements from reaching the king. As far as the senators were concerned, it cost Rome nothing to renew the treaty, since it did not commit them to send troops to aid Carthage in Sicily but only laid down that the dispatch of such aid, if it took place, would be permissible under the terms of any treaty they struck with Pyrrhus. The senate could always refuse the Carthaginians' request. The Carthaginian treaty's symbolic value was perhaps more important in the senators' minds, for it represented a clear endorsement of the Republic's continued status as the dominant power in Italy despite its losses at Heraclea and Ausculum. For Carthage, the pact was a card to play in its effort to isolate and defeat Syracuse. It suggested to Pyrrhus that if he were make a treaty with Rome in order to come to the aid of Syracuse against Carthage he could well find himself facing Roman forces there as well. And if the report in a late source is reliable, Mago wasted no time in playing that card. On his way back to Africa, he is said to have visited the king at Tarentum, where he no doubt made known the terms of his city's recent treaty with Rome (Just. 18.2.4).

But Mago's effort was in vain. The glittering prize of Sicily was too enticing and the challenges he faced in Italy too daunting to deter Pyrrhus from accepting the Syracusans' invitation. So early in 278 and without a peace treaty with Rome he departed from Tarentum to fight the Carthaginians (Dion. Hal. 20.8.1–9.3; Plut. *Pyrrh*. 22.4–23.6). Success, however, proved beyond his grasp. He enjoyed some early victories, driving the armies of Carthage west until they held only Lilybaeum on the coast. Yet that city was too strongly fortified to fall to his siege. And between his increasingly heavy demands on his Greek allies for money and men, his interference in their internal affairs, and his high-handed confiscation of lands he claimed had once belonged to his son's ancestor, his coalition partners grew increasingly restive. Some began to desert his cause and side with the Carthaginians, and when Pyrrhus took harsh measures in reprisal, he provoked even more defections to the enemy, who, seeing the tide setting against the king, sent new forces from Africa to the island. In the end, with things in Sicily falling apart around him and his Italian allies urgently summoning him back, Pyrrhus in the late summer of 276 abandoned his dream of a Sicilian empire and returned to Italy.

Maleventum

While the king was chasing that dream, the Romans set about once again subduing the mountain tribes of southern Italy (Dion. Hal. 10.1–12.3; Livy, *Per*. 14; Plut. *Pyrrh*. 24.1–25.5). Between 278 and 276, Roman armies ravaged the lands of the Samnites, Lucanians, and Brutti, campaigns that yielded triumphs for the generals who led them. These were the assaults that provoked the calls for Pyrrhus to return to Italy, but by the time he once again stepped onto Italian soil, he found his resources there considerably depleted. After so many defeats, his allies were unable to offer much support, and in 277, the Greek city of Croton fell to the Romans. Carthage had also given the Republic valuable assistance by attacking the king's fleet as it sailed back to Italy. He lost many of his warships, although most of his troop transports escaped. His bad luck continued once he landed. The Roman garrison in Rhegium repulsed his attack on that important city, and Pyrrhus suffered heavy losses as he retreated. It was a much weakened enemy that faced Rome for the final show-down in 275, therefore. Yet the Republic, too, was labouring under the strain of these wars. Plague had ravaged the countryside, and manpower was in short supply. The consul of 275 who would lead the fight against Pyrrhus, M'. Curius Dentatus, had had to resort to harsh measures to force recruits to come forward as he attempted to levy an army to lead against Pyrrhus.

The senate dispatched both consuls south with their armies, one into Lucania and the other under Dentatus to Maleventum in Samnium to protect the route into Campania. Pyrrhus elected to face the latter first, hoping to win a victory before the consuls could join forces against him. However, the presence of the other consul in Lucania compelled him to divide his forces to keep the enemy in check there. The army he led into Samnium therefore may have been only equal to or even smaller than Dentatus' legions and allied contingents. This imbalance may be the reason that Pyrrhus decided on a risky night march to secure a position on high ground above the Roman camp from which to launch his attack the following morning. Once again, misfortune dogged him. Night operations are notoriously prone to go wrong, and this one proved no exception. His men, marching through heavily wooded terrain along narrow pathways and unable to see their way clearly in the dark, fell into disorder. The dawn revealed them to the Romans, advancing in disarray while the legions formed up in good order and had little difficulty in repelling the attack. This defeat forced the Epirotes down into the plain, where the Romans renewed the fight. As Pyrrhus' elephants pressed the legions back, Dentatus summoned his reserves from his camp, who opposed them with volleys of javelins. They killed two of the animals and trapped the remaining eight, whose drivers surrendered them to grace Dentatus' triumph. The Romans completed their victory with the capture of Pyrrhus' camp. The king himself fled back to Tarentum and thence with a handful of solders to Greece. Having abandoned all hopes of gains in the west, he plunged into wars and intrigues, seeking gains first in Macedon and later in the Peloponnesus. There the king met his end, felled by a roof tile hurled by an enraged housewife whose town he was trying to storm, an inglorious conclusion to a life that had once seemed so full of promise (Plut. *Pyrrh*. 34.1–4).

For the Romans, however, the struggle was far from over. Their victory at Maleventum (which they changed to the more auspicious-sounding 'Beneventum' in commemoration of their victory) had driven Pyrrhus from Italy, but resistance in the southern mountains and among the Italiot Greeks continued. We know nothing of events in 274; presumably campaigning continued in Samnium, Lucania, and Bruttium, for the following year's consuls celebrated triumphs for victories over these peoples, as did the consuls of 272. More importantly, one of the latter, L. Papirius Cursor, negotiated the surrender of Tarentum and the garrison that Pyrrhus had left to guard the city. With the inclusion of the Tarentines in the triumphal procession of Cursor and his colleague, Sp. Carvilius Maximus, the conquest of the south was largely over, save for minor operations, one of which, however, would sow the seeds of Rome's first great contest with Carthage.

The First Punic War

Messana, the Mamertines, and the origins of the conflict

Rome and Carthage had long enjoyed cordial relations. Treaties of friendship attested to that fact, the earliest dating to the Republic's first year, and all engraved on bronze plaques fastened to the wall of the treasury of the quaestors on the Capitoline Hill (Polyb. 3.22.1–26.1). The most recent, struck amid the crisis of the Pyrrhic war, envisioned military cooperation between the two republics against their common enemy. There was little to bring them to blows. Carthage had extensive trading networks across the western Mediterranean and had long cherished hopes of subduing the Greek cities of eastern Sicily, especially the greatest of them, Syracuse. Rome, having completed its conquest of southern Italy in the years following Pyrrhus' withdrawal, might seem to have reached the limits of its territorial ambitions in the south. To the north, however, lay the perpetual menace of the Gallic tribes in the Po valley, and that might have appeared the obvious direction for the Republic to turn its attention in. Yet the northern threat would wait nearly half a century before Rome addressed it. Instead, events unfolding in Sicily's northeastern corner would grow to engulf the western Mediterranean's two most powerful states in a fight that would ultimately be to the death.

It began with the expulsion of a group of Campanian mercenaries from Syracuse in 289, following the death of their employer, Agathocles, the ruler of that city (Polyb. 1.7.2–4, 8.1–12.9).[6] They marched north and found a welcome in the Greek city of Messana, which commanded the western portion of the straits separating

6. The episode is complex and controversial. See recently B. D. Hoyos, *Unplanned Wars: The Origins of the First and Second Punic Wars*, Berlin: De Gruyter, 1998, 33–131, for a careful survey of the events leading to the outbreak of the war.

Sicily from Italy. The mercenaries then turned on their hosts, killing many of the leading men, driving the rest into exile and, we are told, appropriating their houses, their property, and even their wives. Styling themselves *Mamertini* after the god of war, *Mamers* in the Oscan language (the more familiar *Mars* in Latin), they set about raiding their neighbours and establishing a hegemony over their corner of the island during the ensuing quarter century. Meanwhile around 275 Hiero, the son of Hierocles, came to power in Syracuse, ending many years of political turmoil there. The victims of the Mamertines' depredations eventually appealed to him for protection, and after losing to the Mamertines at the river Cyamosorus, Hiero won a decisive victory, probably in 264, at the river Longanus. This he followed up by laying siege to Messana. The surviving Mamertines in desperation appealed for help to both Carthage and Rome. There was nothing surprising in this. Carthage was a long-standing enemy of Syracuse, and the Mamertines and Carthage had cooperated previously when Pyrrhus had crossed to Sicily to champion the Greeks there against both powers. But the Carthaginian presence in the western portion of the island made it very likely that their protection would eventually become domination. The Romans, who were farther away and had evinced little interest in Sicilian affairs, might seem preferable defenders.

The appeal to Carthage quickly bore fruit. A fleet happened to be anchored at the island of Lipara, and when its commander learned of the Mamertines' defeat, he brought a garrison into Messana, forcing Hiero to abandon his siege. At Rome, however, the Mamertine appeal placed the senators in a quandary. Campania had been incorporated into the *ager Romanus* following the end of the Latin revolt in 338, and those who lived there enjoyed Roman citizenship, albeit without the vote (see below, pp. 82–3). Italy's other Oscan-speaking areas contained *socii*. It is not known whether the Mamertines were Roman citizens, but even if they were not their kinship with Rome's allies gave them a moral claim on the Republic's protection. More importantly, developments in Sicily will have raised concerns among the *patres*. Not that they worried greatly about Carthage; relations with that city had always been good. Rather, the rise of Hiero and the growing power of Syracuse gave the senators pause, for they potentially threatened the Republic's recent subjugation of southern Italy. Earlier in the third century Agathocles of Syracuse had brought most of eastern Sicily under his rule and then turned his attention to southern Italy. He captured several cities there and forged alliances with many others. His aim had been to unite and dominate Magna Graecia, and only his assassination in 289 had ended that endeavour. Pyrrhus had cherished similar ambitions when he accepted the Tarentines' invitation in 282. The capture of Messana would put Hiero in a position to exert strong pressure on the southern Italian Greeks by virtue of the city's control over the narrow waterway through which much of their westward shipping had to pass. So the senate had good reason to take the Mamertines, who had surrendered themselves into the protection (*fides*) of Rome, under the Republic's wing in order to safeguard their recent gains in the south.

Still, other concerns complicated their deliberations, foremost among them events of a few years past at Rhegium, a city on the toe of Italy just across the straits from Messana. Our sources for these events and those that followed are particularly poor and contaminated by hindsight. No contemporary Roman or Greek chronicled what happened; the first to do so more than a generation later, relying on the memories of old men or what the young had heard from their elders, wrote when the first war between Rome and Carthage had dramatically altered the significance of the events at Rhegium – strong reason to believe therefore that Roman historians were led to cast Roman motives and actions there in the most favourable light. Even worse, these accounts have not come down to us, but only those of authors like Polybius and later writers who drew on them. Consequently, much remains obscure. It seems, however, that around 282 the citizens of Rhegium sought the Republic's protection against Lucanian raiding parties. Their appeal apparently came at the same time the city of Thurii was seeking similar aid against the same raiders. The commander of the Roman forces in the area, the consul Fabricius, acquiesced and installed a detachment of Campanians and Sidicini under the command of one Decius Vibellius, a member of a prominent Campanian family (Dion. Hal. 20.4.1–2; Val. Max. 2.7.15f). Although some ancient sources call them mercenaries in Roman employ, Campanians were Roman citizens, and the Sidicini were allies. So in all likelihood these were legionaries accompanied by *socii*, an interpretation rendered more likely in view of the similar garrison installed at Thurii in the same year by the same consul and for the same reason (see above, p. 39). With the onset of the war against Pyrrhus, the Rhegium garrison's mission changed, and the troops became a defence against the town's capture by the king. That role may supply the context for the garrison's notorious execution of many of Rhegium's leading citizens and the expulsion of others. Polybius and other authors call this a crime and ascribe it to the soldiers' desire to imitate the Mamertines across the straits (Polyb. 1.7.1–13). But we are told that in preparation for the massacre Decius either had letters forged purporting to be from the consul or a friend warning him that the Rhegians were preparing to open the city gates to Pyrrhus, or, alternately, claimed that the Rhegians themselves were intending to hand the city over to the king (Dion. Hal. 20.4.4–6; App. *Sam.* 9.1). Little credence can be placed in these details, but their appearance in accounts of this affair indicates that later writers found claims in the authors they consulted that the garrison took the measures it did to keep the city out of Pyrrhus' hands. Hence these later authors struggled to accommodate these reports while still insisting that the garrison was guilty of a heinous crime. Those claims, however, may well be closer to the truth of the matter.[7] The Romans had taken steps to secure other allied cities where loyalty was suspect, including the expulsion of leading citizens, while early in the war a Tarentine force had captured Thurii and expelled its Roman garrison. So orders to Decius to take similar measures at Thurii would not have been unparalleled or without point, orders that later Roman tradition sought to disavow in view of the sequel. For the garrison may have gone too far in executing the Rhegian leaders in order to secure the city. Or it may have appeared so once the threat of Pyrrhus was gone and Rome had to win the loyalty of the Greek leadership in the southern Italian cities. Or possibly the garrison went rogue and refused to relinquish the city after the war, intending now that they had got control of it to set themselves up as an independent state in imitation of the Mamertines. Whatever the reason, the Rhegian affair became a profound embarrassment to the senate, which had undertaken to protect the city and its citizens. Once the Pyrrhic war was won, therefore, and Tarentum conquered, the senate resolved to deal with the situation at Rhegium. In 270 a Roman army captured the city. The surviving members of the garrison were brought to Rome, publicly flogged, and beheaded (Dion. Hal. 20.16.1–2).

This business would have remained little more than a curious footnote but for the fact that in 264 the Mamertines' seizure of

---

7. E. Dench, *From Barbarians to New Men: Greek, Roman, and Modern Perceptions of Peoples of the Central Apennines*, Oxford: Oxford University Press, 1995, 78–9.

Messana looked uncomfortably like the crimes alleged against the garrison at Rhegium. A senatorial decision to accept the Mamertines' appeal for protection would appear little short of hypocritical in the light of the punishment meted out to the Campanians and Sidicini, who had betrayed Roman *fides* at Rhegium in much the same way the Mamertines had violated the trust of the citizens of Messana. And then there was Carthage to consider. The senate's concern over the growth of Carthaginian power in Sicily and fears that control of Messana could enable it easily to send armies into Italy loom large in the ancient sources. But this probably reflects hindsight rather than contemporary fears in view of the fact that Rome did eventually go to war with Carthage over Sicily. For writers living a generation or more later and looking back on these events across the experience of the war with Hannibal, the assumption that the prospect of a Punic war was uppermost in the *patres'* minds in 264 would have been easy and obvious. And very probably by the time the senators did debate the Mamertine appeal they knew that a Carthaginian force had occupied the citadel to protect the town. Yet this knowledge will only have increased the senate's uncertainty over how to proceed now that the immediate danger to the Mamertines had receded. The senators were well aware that relations with Carthage had long been friendly – no reason therefore to assume that a contest over who would protect the Mamertines would lead to war. But the Mamertines' preference for a more distant guardian might well put the Carthaginians' nose out of joint, and beyond that how the latter would react to Roman involvement in Sicilian affairs could not be foreseen.

There was every reason to hesitate, therefore, and in the end the senators found the arguments on either side of the question so finely balanced that they could come to no resolution. Instead, and possibly for the only time in memory, they allowed the consuls to bring the question of aiding the Mamertines before the assembly without any recommendation from the senate at all.[8] Speaking to the citizens prior to the vote, the consuls stressed both the strategic advantages of accepting the Mamertines' appeal and the plunder that the soldiers could expect to reap from a war in Sicily (Polyb. 1.11.2–3). Their arguments carried the day, and the assembly voted to dispatch an army south under the command of the consul Ap.

8. So Hoyos, *Unplanned Wars*, 51–66; a different view in A. M. Eckstein, 'Polybius on the rôle of the senate in the crisis of 264 B.C.', *GRBS* 21 (1980), 175–90.

Claudius Caudex. This was not, however, a declaration of war. Claudius' instructions were simply to protect the Mamertines. Still, a consul typically had considerable leeway in deciding what steps to take in carrying out his assignment, especially when military force was involved.[9] Events on the ground could move much too quickly to permit him to send dispatches to Rome and await instructions without detriment to his mission. Deliberations and debate in the senate could delay a reply until whatever decision it reached was no longer relevant to the circumstances a commander faced. That was precisely what happened in 264; by the time Claudius reached Rhegium with his army, he found the situation profoundly changed.

When the news reached Messana that Roman forces were on their way, the Mamertines prevailed upon the commander of the Carthaginian garrison to lead his troops out of the city, a decision for which his superiors later crucified him, angered at having so easily been robbed of their prize. More surprisingly, the Carthaginian general then marshalled his forces outside Messana in order to forestall a Roman occupation of the town. That prospect was deeply troubling to the Carthaginians. It gave the Romans a *point d'appui* on the island and the opportunity to extend their protection to other cities there, not only those threatened by Syracuse and Hiero but others chafing under Carthaginian domination. Eighteen years earlier, the Tarentines had seen the protection Rome offered to Thurii in the form of that garrison nominally installed to ward off threats from the Lucanians as very likely to be directed eventually against themselves, and they had acted accordingly, calling in Pyrrhus and waging war to ward off Roman encroachment in their backyard. The same strategic imperative and the same fears now impelled the Carthaginians to act. Even more surprisingly Hiero, still camped before the city and seeing the prospect of a Roman protectorate over Messana in much the same light, made overtures to his old enemies the Carthaginians. He proposed they join forces against the Mamertines and capture the city before the Romans could enter it, in order to prevent them from gaining a foothold in Sicily.

When Claudius reached Rhegium, therefore, he confronted circumstances much different from what they had been when he left Rome. Messana was now threatened by not one army but two,

9. A. M. Eckstein, *Senate and General: Individual Decision Making and Roman Foreign Relations, 264–194 B.C.*, Berkeley: University of California Press, 1987.

one of which belonged to Rome's old allies the Carthaginians. The consul's initial response reveals that his instructions envisioned something considerably short of war on Syracuse, much less Carthage, at least at the outset. He sought to negotiate an end to the siege, informing both Hiero and Hanno, the Carthaginian commander, that Messana was now under the protection of Rome. When those talks failed to lift the siege, he attempted to bring his forces into Messana, but the Carthaginian squadron thwarted his crossing. Still, matters had not reached the point of open war as far as Hanno and the Carthaginians were concerned. Hanno restored the Roman ships and prisoners he had captured, for he, too, was anxious to avoid a breach in relations with Rome. But he was equally adamant that the Romans should stay out of Sicily. Talks resumed but soon degenerated into acrimony, with the Carthaginians breaking off negotiations by declaring that they would not permit the Romans even to wash their hands in the sea. And Claudius knew they had the power to make good their boast; he possessed no fleet with which he could challenge Hanno's warships. So he resorted to subterfuge. Claudius had the rumour spread around Rhegium that he and his army were returning to Rome since he had no orders to begin a war (another indication that his mandate or at least what was publicly known about it did not envision a war with Carthage), and began sailing north. When the Carthaginians squadron relaxed its patrols, Claudius ordered his ships to turn south and reached the harbour at Messana before the Carthaginians could intercept them (Front. *Str.* 1.4.11). Even at this point, however, Claudius was reluctant to open hostilities. Once again he sought to end the siege through talks. Only when this third attempt had been rebuffed did he finally bring matters to a head, attacking first Hiero's forces and, after putting them to flight, the Carthaginians on the following day with the same result.

The war begins

Yet despite this initial clash of Roman and Carthaginian arms, it is not clear that the First Punic War had begun, at least as far as Claudius was concerned. Hiero had retreated to Syracuse, and Hanno had withdrawn to Carthaginian-controlled towns to the west. Claudius elected to march against Syracuse, although he failed to capture that heavily fortified city. His decision shows that in his mind the main opponent was still Hiero, and in pursuing him Claudius was carrying out his instructions to protect the Mamertines, whose principal enemy had been Hiero all along. Circumstances had forced a battle with Carthaginian forces, unavoidable despite his best efforts, in pursuit of that goal. But although we may see Rome's first war with Carthage as a consequence of that initial clash, escalation into a full-scale war became inevitable only after a number of events had unfolded in the following year. In 263, the senate's initial focus remained Hiero and Syracuse. This time it dispatched both consuls south. Crossing to Sicily without opposition, they moved down the island's eastern coast, receiving the surrender of many towns subject to Syracuse along their march. They also received envoys from Hiero, who by now was eager to open negotiations to end the conflict. He realised not only that continued resistance to Rome would be both costly and probably futile in the end, but also that it was not even advantageous to try. Peace with Rome on acceptable conditions would bring decided benefits. True, he would have to abandon his dreams of bringing all of Greek Sicily under his rule, relinquish control over several towns, and give up some measure of autonomy besides, but he would gain security for his throne and powerful protection from Syracuse's longstanding enemy, Carthage. So Hiero surrendered on the generous terms that the consuls, eager to claim credit for ending the war, were ready to offer. One of them, M'. Valerius Messala, triumphed for his successes in Sicily when he returned to Rome, but not before he had considerably enlarged the scope of his operations. Once Hiero's surrender had been arranged, Messala moved his forces west, capturing several towns within Carthage's domain and accepting the surrender of others. It is not clear, however, that he intended these actions as the opening moves in an all-out offensive against Carthage. For the senate, following Hiero's surrender, had withdrawn Messala's colleague and his legions from Sicily, surprising if the *patres* expected serious fighting to continue on the island. They may instead have intended Messala's campaign as a show of force to deter further Punic opposition to Rome's permanent involvement in Sicily, which had been Carthage's primary aim at Messana in the previous year.

If so, Messala's thrust into Carthage's part of the island had exactly the opposite effect. For the Carthaginian senators undoubtedly now realised not simply that Rome's protection of Messana and now Hiero and Syracuse posed a serious obstacle to their longstanding goal of conquering the entire island. They understood that the dynamic of Roman expansion would in all likelihood lead eventually to conflict and ultimately open war. Towns and peoples under Carthaginian domination would be tempted to break away and turn to Rome for protection, just as a number of towns subject to Syracuse had done the year before. Carthage would then confront a stark choice between watching its hegemony in western Sicily crumble or fighting Rome to preserve it. Determined to meet that challenge before it grew too great, the senators at Carthage began to enlist mercenaries and build up their city's forces at Agrigentum on Sicily's southern coast, hoping perhaps to deter further Roman encroachment or, should deterrence fail, to be ready for war. News of that build-up apparently spurred the *patres* at Rome to respond in kind, for in 262 they again dispatched both consuls with their armies to Sicily, and they made directly for Agrigentum. A five-month siege ensued until a relief force from Africa arrived. After a lengthy stand-off, the two sides met in battle. The Romans emerged from the struggle victorious, and the besieged mercenaries fled the city, which the Romans then entered and plundered. This was the decisive event. Polybius tells us that only with the capture of Agrigentum did the Romans expand their war aims and seek to conquer the whole of Sicily (1.20.1–2). The struggle the Carthaginians foresaw and had tried to forestall had now arrived, and the First Punic War, at least in the minds of the principal contenders, was finally on.

War at sea and on land

That conflict would grind on for twenty more years.[10] The Romans quickly gained mastery of the open country; it would be many years before Punic forces again dared to face the legions and *socii* in a formal battle. The critical struggles instead took place around the island's fortified cities and especially at sea. Although it would be exceeding the facts to say that Rome was unacquainted with naval warfare prior to 264, the conquest of Italy had not required it to develop an extensive navy. Carthage, however, possessed a powerful sea-force and used it early in the war to threaten some of Sicily's coastal towns and retain the loyalty of others. And as long as Carthage controlled the sea lanes around the island and could supply

10. J. F. Lazenby, *The First Punic War: A Military History*, Stanford: Stanford University Press, 1996; A. Goldsworthy, *The Punic Wars*, London: Cassell, 2000, 49–107.

Panormus, Lilybaeum, and Drepana, its principal strongholds, the Romans would have little hope of reducing them by siege. The Republic therefore had to build a war fleet to challenge the Carthaginian superiority at sea.

Polybius explains that the Romans, although lacking familiarity with up-to-date naval architecture, in 261 built a fleet of 120 warships on the model of a Carthaginian quinquereme – a galley powered by five banks of oars – that had run aground and been captured when the Carthaginian squadron pursued Ap. Claudius' ships as they attempted to cross from Rhegium to Messana (1.20.13–16). Still, even though Rome could launch a fleet comparable in size to Carthage's and train its sailors in the rudiments of rowing by having them practice on land, this was not enough to offset the Punic advantage in seamanship. In the era before gunpowder, ships fought one another by ramming. Long, low quinqueremes were weakest in their centres, and a powerful blow amidships could break them in half. Delivering such a blow was the object of combat at sea, and warships were fitted with heavy prows designed for ramming. Manoeuvring a ship into a position where its oarsmen could drive it hard into the side of an enemy vessel put a premium on the skill and discipline of its helmsman and crew. Although Rome had as many ships as the Carthaginians, theirs were slower and heavier and their sailors were inferior to the quality of the men who manned the Punic fleet. To neutralise the enemy's advantages at sea, the Romans created a device they nicknamed the 'crow' (corvus). This device consisted of a tall pole with a pulley on top mounted on a ship's prow and a gangplank roughly 10.5 × 1.25 m. The gangplank had an oblong hole at the rear through which the pole passed and a heavy iron spike with a ring attached to its upper end in the front. A rope ran from the ring up through the pulley and then down to the deck. The rope enabled the front of the corvus to be raised up, the hole permitted it to be swung from side to side, and its length meant it projected well beyond the sides of the ship. As the Romans approached an enemy ship, they raised the corvus, and when they came alongside, they swung the corvus around above the enemy's ship and let go of the rope. The front of the corvus fell onto the other ship, and the spike embedded itself in its deck, holding the two ships fast. Once they were locked together, Roman soldiers swarmed across the gangplank to attack the Carthaginian sailors, turning a sea fight into a land battle, as Polybius characterised it. This device enabled the Romans to win

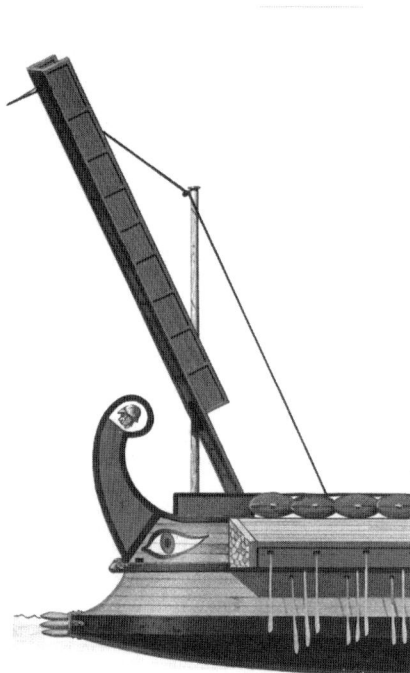

Figure 7 The *corvus*.

the war's first major naval action against the Carthaginians off Mylae in the summer of 260.

Three years of indecisive fighting in and around Sicily followed. Then the senate in 256 elected to embark on a more aggressive strategy. It sought to end the war quickly and decisively by invading Africa and attacking Carthage itself. A massive invasion fleet of about 230 warships in addition to numerous transports for men and horses was assembled and, after battling a Punic fleet intent on stopping it, landed near Aspis in Libya. The Romans quickly gained control of the countryside and plundered widely. As winter approached, one of the consuls returned to Rome with the bulk of the fleet while the other, M. Atilius Regulus, remained in Africa with two legions and their complement of allies. In the following year, Regulus and his troops crushed a major effort by the Carthaginians to drive the invaders from their homeland, then advanced deeper into Carthaginian territory, pillaging and laying waste as they went until the army reached Tunis, where it encamped. The Carthaginian senate at that point sought to negotiate an end to the fighting, but

Regulus, feeling that he was in a commanding position, offered harsh terms that Carthage rejected. Soon thereafter the arrival of a force of mercenaries, including a Spartan named Xanthippus, gave fresh hope to the Carthaginians. Xanthippus convinced the Carthaginian senators that their troops could defeat the Romans in a set-piece battle, and so, relying on his plan of attack, they ordered their forces to march out and confront the enemy. Opening the attack with their elephants, the Carthaginians inflicted heavy losses on the Roman infantry while their cavalry drove off the Roman horse and then attacked the legions on the flanks and rear. At that point, the Carthaginian heavy infantry moved in to finish the job. Their victory was complete. The great majority of the Roman force fell, and most of the rest were captured, including Regulus himself. A very few maniples managed to reach Apsis and safety.

To mitigate the humiliation of this disaster, Roman tradition enveloped it in a thick, protective coating of legend. An enormous snake 120 feet (c. 36 m) long barring the Romans' way at Apsis was overcome only with great difficulty and the loss of many lives (Oros. 4.9.1–4; Zonar. 8.13). Regulus sought to be relieved of his command, on the grounds that his wife and daughter could not keep up his tiny farm by themselves. The senate instead arranged for their upkeep, and he remained in Africa (Val. Max. 4.4.6). And following his capture, the Carthaginians sent him to Rome to urge the senate to accept terms of peace, under oath to return to his captivity should he fail in his mission. When he came before the *patres*, however, Regulus urged them to continue the war. Honour-bound, he then returned to Carthage, where his captors tortured him to death for his patriotism (Cic. *Off.* 3.99–100; Gell. *NA* 7.4.1–2; Livy, *Per.* 18; cf. Hor. *Carm.* 3.5). None of this is likely to be true, but it cast Regulus as a reluctant hero willing to die for his country after waging a campaign that the gods themselves had warned the Romans against pursuing.

Later that same year, the consuls sailed to Africa to evacuate the survivors of Regulus' debacle. As they approached the coast, they found a Carthaginian fleet barring their way. The Romans won the battle that ensued, but a great storm off Cape Pachynus at the south-eastern tip of Sicily soon nullified this success as they sailed home, costing them 170 of their 250 ships. The Carthaginians, encouraged by their victory in Africa and the wreck of the Roman fleet, dispatched new forces to Sicily. Rome responded by building new ships and attacking the stronghold of Panormus, which the consuls of 254 captured and garrisoned. Another storm in the following year resulted in the loss of another fleet and led the senate to abandon operations at sea altogether and concentrate on the land war. By this point, however, the Carthaginians had brought over a large force of elephants to the island, and the Romans, well aware of the part these animals had played in the destruction of Regulus' army, refused to meet the enemy in a pitched battle for several years. Only in early 250 was the stalemate broken when the consul of the previous year, L. Caecilius Metellus, enticed the Carthaginian commander to launch an attack on his position at Panormus. Metellus had readied a large number of soldiers and civilians in the town who hurled javelins at the elephants when the attack began. Their wounds caused the animals to panic, turn, and run back among the Carthaginian forces following them. The elephants' rampage killed many, injured more, and threw the rest into confusion, at which point Metellus ordered his army to attack. He routed the infantry and captured all 100 of the elephants, which graced his triumph when he and his army returned to Rome.

The final phases

Heartened by this success and with their forces now in unchallenged control of the entire island except Drepana and Lilybaeum, the senate resolved that same year to build another fleet and undertake a combined assault on the latter stronghold. The campaign did not go well. Long, bloody, indecisive fighting ensued as the Romans sought to advance their siege engines up to the city walls and batter them down while the defenders tried in every way they could to repel them. Then one day a strong wind arose blowing from the city towards the siege works. The defenders, realising that this was the moment to attack the Romans' wooden siege engines, sallied out and succeeded in setting them on fire in several places. The wind whipped the flames into a conflagration, and the Romans, blinded by the smoke and attacked by missiles, were helpless to prevent the complete destruction of their towers and battering rams. Giving up their plan to take the city by storm, therefore, the Romans dug a trench, erected a stockade, and directed their efforts against Drepana instead.

In 249 the Roman consul at Lilybaeum, P. Claudius Pulcher, sailing north with his ships to Drepana, attempted to surprise the Carthaginian squadron there at dawn while they were still beached.

In this he succeeded, but the Carthaginian commander was nevertheless able to launch his vessels before the Romans could cut them off in the harbour. Sailing out into the open sea, he swung his line of ships south and then turned towards shore, bearing down on the Roman fleet, strung out in a long line hugging the coast. Pulcher now realised that his ships, some of which were just entering the harbour while others were still some way off, were about to be pinned against the shore with little room to manoeuvre, and he desperately tried to turn his forces to face the Carthaginian attack. Despite the initial confusion as the leading ships collided with those behind that were trying to clear the harbour, the Romans managed to form a line of battle, and for a time they held off the Punic assault. Gradually, though, the Carthaginians' advantage in position began to tell. Their ships, if hard pressed, had plenty of sea room to retreat while the Romans, close against the shore, had little room to back water. And the Romans' seamanship was unequal to the challenge of breaking through the Carthaginian line and manoeuvring their ships into a position to ram an enemy vessel. As the Carthaginians began to gain the advantage, Pulcher chose to save himself and flee, followed by about thirty of his fleet. The rest the Carthaginians captured along with most of their crews. The Republic's discomfiture at Drepana was soon made complete by a storm later in the year that destroyed much of the other consul's fleet.

Again, Roman tradition sought to lessen the sting of the defeat at Drepana by heaping the blame on the consul. Legend recounted how Pulcher, as he sailed towards the harbour, ordered the auspices to be consulted. Auspication entailed asking the gods if they approved of the action about to be undertaken.[11] The gods might give the go-ahead or instruct the Romans to wait for another day. Their response could come in a variety of forms, but commonly it was discerned through the actions of birds, and to ensure that birds were handy when an answer was needed, caged chickens and their keepers regularly accompanied Roman armies. There was nothing special or sacred about the chickens; what was important was how they ate when food was scattered in front of them. If they ate when they were released from their cages, and especially if they ate greedily, the signs were deemed propitious. And just to make sure

---

11. J. Linderski, 'The augural law', in H. Temporini (ed.), *Aufstieg und Niedergang der römischen Welt: Geschichte und Kultur Roms im Spiegel der neueren Forschung*, Berlin and New York: De Gruyter, 1986, 2146–2312.

that the birds would cooperate when called upon to eat and furnish the requisite omen, their keepers kept them hungry. Pulcher therefore as he made ready to attack ordered the birds fed, but remarkably they refused to eat. Perhaps they were seasick; perhaps it really was a sign from the heavenly powers that they would not permit an attack that day. In any event, a frustrated Pulcher ordered that the chickens be thrown overboard, with the memorable remark that if they would not eat, perhaps they would drink (Cic. *Nat. D.* 2.7; Livy, frg. 12). For this arrogance, or more likely for fleeing the battle, he was brought to trial at Rome and fined, barely escaping with his life.[12]

Thwarted at sea the Romans once again turned their efforts to the land war. Fighting devolved into a long struggle against a Carthaginian army entrenched in a strong position on Mt Eryx, near Drepana, while the siege of Lilybaeum continued. This stalemate was broken and the war finally brought to an end when the senate in 242 once more elected to build a fleet. Public funds were by this point so limited that the *patres* had to seek loans from private citizens for its construction. Wealthy Romans individually or in small groups advanced the costs of building and fitting out one quinquereme each, the money to be repaid in the event of victory. The consul of 242, C. Lutatius Catulus, and, because his colleague was prevented by religious obligations from leaving the city, the praetor Q. Valerius Falto, sailed south and succeeded in seizing the harbour at Drepana and gaining control of the sea approaches to Lilybaeum. With both cities now cut off and so doomed to fall unless resupplied, the Carthaginian senate readied its own ships. The sea battle that ensued decided the war, for the Romans destroyed the Carthaginian war fleet. By this point in the war the Punic treasury was also empty and private funds to build more ships could not be found. With the fall of their remaining positions on Sicily now inevitable, the Carthaginians had no choice but surrender. The Roman senate required them to evacuate the troops holding Drepana, Lilybaeum, and Mt Eryx and pay heavy war reparations of 3,200 talents of silver (a talent weighed about 26 kg, so over 83 tonnes) in annual instalments over twenty years. All Roman and Italian prisoners of war were be handed over without ransom; the Carthaginians were not to make

12. N. Rosenstein, *Imperatores victi: Military Defeat and Aristocratic Competition in the Middle and Late Republic*, Berkeley: University of California Press, 1990, 77–91, 114–52.

war on Hiero, Syracuse, or any of Syracuse's allies; and they were also to remove their forces from a group of small islands lying between Sicily and Italy. Finally, the allies of either side were to be safe from attack by the other, and neither side was to form an alliance with an ally of the other or enrol troops in its domains. On these terms, the war ended.

Sardinia and Spain

Rome had not finished exacting a full measure of retribution from Carthage, though, and the senate picked a moment a few years later to deliver the blow, when the Carthaginians found themselves in desperate straits. Throughout the struggle with Rome, Carthage had hired mercenaries to do its fighting on Sicily, preferring to spare its own citizens, and the city's financial difficulties in the latter stages of the war had left their pay badly in arrears. When the mercenaries were evacuated from Sicily to Africa, they expected to receive the back pay owing them, but Rome's demands for money reparations had drained what ready cash was available. The mercenaries' disappointment at not being paid for their long years of privation and service was deep and bitter. Negotiations between their representatives and the Carthaginian senate soon broke down, leaving the mercenaries no alternative in their minds but to march on the city and take by force what was owed them. By the latter part of 241, the Carthaginians found themselves besieged by their formers soldiers, joined initially by Numidian and Libyan tribes rebelling against Carthaginian rule and later by the cities of Utica and Hippacra. The conflict, known as the Libyan war, raged fiercely for three years until the Carthaginians at last managed to defeat the mercenaries and reduce their rebellious subjects once again to submission.

Rome largely stayed out of the troubles in Africa. When Utica appealed to Rome for protection after it had broken with Carthage in 239, the *patres* had refused them and in the same year or the year before turned down a similar plea from Carthage's mercenaries on the island of Sardinia, who had also seen in the war in Africa an opportunity to break free of their employers' control. Yet in late 238 or early 237, just after the Carthaginians had gained the upper hand in Africa, the Roman senate suddenly reversed course and, in what can only be described as a calculated act of cynical opportunism, accepted the surrender of the Sardinian mercenaries. They informed the Carthaginians, who were preparing to recover the island, that they would have to surrender Sardinia and pay an additional 1,200 talents or face war with Rome. Exhausted by a war that had come very near to destroying them, the Carthaginians were in no position to resist.

Roman motives are difficult to fathom.[13] The senate claimed that the expedition Carthage was preparing in order to reduce Sardinia once again to submission was actually aimed against themselves, but that smacks of pretext. Carthage at that point was in no position to reignite a war with Rome. The ancient sources offer little help. Modern scholars suggest that the senate feared the Carthaginians could use the island as a staging ground to mount an assault on Italy, or that the Romans were simply eager to expand their empire and seized upon a convenient opportunity to do so. But Rome had twice before been in a position to lay claim to Sardinia, once at the conclusion of its war with Carthage when it presented its peace terms and again during the Libyan war when the mercenaries on the island had appealed to Rome for protection. If Italy's security or greed were uppermost in the *patres*' minds in 238–237, why were they not earlier? Concern over the possibility of a Carthaginian threat to Sicily from Sardinia has also been suggested, but this motive meets the same objection as the others. The demand for an additional 1,200 talents may hold the clue. This was apparently to be paid in a lump sum; there is no mention of annual instalments, which makes it seven and a half times greater than the initial reparations payment required in 241. The goal here was clearly to weaken Carthage financially, and depriving the city of the revenue from Sardinia would contribute to the same goal (while of course enriching the Roman treasury). Carthage had demonstrated an unexpected resilience in its life-or-death struggle in Africa, and that may have surprised and alarmed the senate at Rome, it having imagined that Carthage had been cut down to an acceptable size by its defeat in 241. The Roman senators then may have intended the additional exactions in 238–237 to reduce Carthaginian power to a more comfortable level.

In the years that followed, Carthage sent its general, Hamilcar Barca, to Spain. He had commanded the forces holding out at Mt Eryx during the last stages of the war with Rome, and he was also the father of a soon-to-be famous son, Hannibal, who accompanied him west. Hamilcar's assignment was to enlarge a Carthaginian

13. Hoyos, *Unplanned Wars*, 132–43.

foothold on the lower reaches of the Baetis valley and bring the rest of Spain under Punic control, a charge he executed beginning in 237 with notable success until his accidental death in 229. His achievement there more than offset the losses his city had suffered in its war with Rome and the subsequent seizure of Sardinia. More importantly, it would provide the resources in money and manpower for a new war with Rome, as well as the general who would lead it.

CHAPTER 3

The imperium *and the army*

In the years following the seizure of Sardinia, the Romans undertook the pacification of that island as well as Corsica, which proved no easy tasks. At some point in the 220s, the senate decided that two additional praetorships were needed to govern Sicily and Sardinia. A revolt by the allied city of Falerii was suppressed in 241, and the Republic's armies repeatedly campaigned in Liguria, the northwest corner of Italy south of the Apennines. In 229 Rome also mounted an expedition into Illyria, partly in response to piratical depredations by tribes there against shipping plying the waters between western Greece and southern Italy, and partly in reaction to the murder of a senatorial envoy sent to protest aggression against other states in the region. Another expedition followed a decade later after piracy resumed and the growing power of Demetrius of Pharos threatened the stability of the region.[1] However, the Republic waged its major conflict in the years between the First Punic War and the Second in the north against the Gauls of the Po valley. The Republic had shared a border with one of the strongest tribes, the Boii, since the 280s, when it expelled the Senones from Picenum and confiscated the *ager Gallicus*. In 268 the senate ordered the foundation of a Latin colony at Ariminum to defend the gateway from the Po valley into central Italy, and for the next thirty years there was peace on the frontier. But trouble began to develop in 238 for reasons not easy to discern. Our sources for these events are once again very poor: a brief notice in Polybius and a Byzantine compiler's summation of the account of a late imperial historian. From what we can glean, the Boii appear to have initiated the aggression in hopes of gaining access to the *ager Gallicus* south of Ariminum, possibly in response to population pressures. That required removing the roadblock the colony posed, and after battles with Roman forces on the frontiers the Boii

---

1. D. Dzino, *Illyricum in Roman Politics 229 BC–AD 68*, Cambridge: Cambridge University Press, 2010, 44–52.

launched a major assault on Ariminum. The consul C. Licinius Varus and his army broke their siege in 236, and his victory brought about a cessation of campaigning for a time.

Population was growing in Roman lands as well. By the late 230s the Roman citizen body had recovered from the losses sustained during the war with Carthage, and this may have begun to increase pressure on the farmland available to them. In 232 an ambitious *novus homo*, C. Flaminius, as tribune of the plebs proposed legislation to give Roman citizens individual allotments in the *ager Gallicus*. Apart from the territory of the colony at Ariminum, the senate seems to have allowed these lands to lie fallow after the removal of its previous occupants (Polyb. 2.21.7–8; Cic. *Sen.* 11). Although the measure was firmly resisted by the senate – one story has it that Flaminius' own father dragged him from the speaker's platform as he was putting his law to the vote (Val. Max. 5.4.5) – the bill passed. Not only would it meet the citizens' need for additional land but the new colonists would strengthen the area's ability to act as a bulwark against Gallic penetration into central Italy. Yet the senate's opposition was founded (apart from some members' unwillingness to see the upstart Flaminius gain the credit and win popularity) on fears of further antagonising the Boii and other Gauls. Events soon proved the *patres* right, for war came in 225. A massive Gallic war band surprised the Romans by slipping through the Apennine passes west of Ariminum. Polybius claims the Gallic force numbered 50,000 infantry and 20,000 horsemen and charioteers, comprising warriors from the Boii and other tribes in the Po valley as well as mercenaries from beyond the Alps. While these figures may occasion doubt, the Gallic host was unquestionably huge, causing panic in Rome and throughout Italy (Polyb. 2.23.7–12).

The senate dispatched one consul with his army north to meet the threat and recalled the other with his forces from Sardinia. It stationed additional forces at other strategic points and stockpiled weapons and food. In addition the *patres* ordered the allies to compile lists of their fighting men and dispatch them to Rome. Polybius preserves these totals along with a count of Roman and Campanian manpower, which he found in the work of Fabius Pictor (2.24.1–16). Fabius was a senator active during the later third century, and scholars generally credit at least the individual figures Polybius transmits. However, they debate whether Fabius added them up correctly. Most hold that he did not but double counted the

Table 3   *Men available for military service, 225 BC (Polyb. 2.24.1–17, with Brunt, Italian Manpower, 44–50)*

Ethnic group	Infantry	Cavalry
Romans and Campanians	250,000	23,000
Latins	80,000	5,000
Samnites	70,000	7,000
Apulians	50,000	6,000
Lucanians	30,000	3,000
Abruzzi levies	30,000	4,000
Etuscans	50,000	4,000
Umbrians	20,000	2,000
Totals	580,000	54,000

forces Rome had in the field in 225, so that the proper total is that given in Table 3. A minority argues that he added correctly, so that the total ought to be almost 50 percent higher.[2] Whichever position one accepts, though, this passage in Polybius and the figures it preserves are among the most important for any understanding of Rome's *imperium* and its power during the middle Republic, for they reveal the vast extent of its military manpower.

Rome and its *imperium*

Over the course of the third century the area under the *imperium* of the Roman people (*imperium populi Romani*) grew enormously. In 294, following the Republic's victory at Sentinum, it extended across a thick band of territory running right across the central part of Italy, from northern Etruria to southern Campania, an area of some 38,600 square km. The only exception at that point was Samnium. By 225 its size had more than doubled, to almost 100,000 square km. As Table 3 reveals, it stretched the length of Italy, from Etruria and Umbria in the north to Calabria and Bruttium – the heel and toe of Italy – in the south. By the eve of the Hannibalic war it would encompass the plain of the Po all the way to the Alps.[3] The *imperium* extended beyond the mainland across the straits of Messana to take

2. P. A. Brunt, *Italian Manpower 225 B.C.–A.D. 1*, Oxford: Oxford University Press, 1971, 44–53; E. Lo Cascio, 'Recruitment and the size of the Roman population from the third to the first century BCE', in W. Scheidel (ed.), *Debating Roman Demography*, Leiden: Brill, 2001, 111–37.
3. A. Afzelius, *Die römische Eroberung Italiens (340–264 v. Chr.)*, Copenhagen: Universitetsforlaget i Aarhus, 1942.

in Sicily. Farther north, Sardinia and Corsica fell within its ambit, while to the east it encompassed portions of Illyria's Adriatic coast. Although *imperium* much later came to mean something like its English derivative 'empire', in the third and second centuries the word conveyed something much more akin to 'hegemony' or 'dominion' or even 'sway over' a people or place. This sense derived from the primary meaning of *imperium*, which was the power to give orders and to compel obedience to them. The offices that consuls and praetors held bestowed *imperium* in this sense on them, and the *fasces*, the bundles of rods for flogging bound around an axe for executions that their lictors carried before them, literally embodied that power. Those states or communities that the senate and people of Rome could command and that could be expected to obey or face severe consequences were 'under the dominion of the Roman people' (*sub imperio populi Romani*). The regions these states and communities occupied gave Rome's *imperium* a geographic dimension, but first and foremost the relationship of dominance and subordination between Rome and those who were under its *imperium* captures the essence of the term.

The degree of subordination that those experienced who found themselves under the *imperium* of Rome varied considerably, however, as did the nature of the dominance and the extent to which the Republic exercised it. The tribes that inhabited the Illyrian littoral felt the hand of Rome very little if at all during most of this period. No treaties placed them under any specific obligations that the senate could feel within its rights to enforce should the Illyrians fail to live up to them. At most, the *patres* expected that the Republic's friends there would not act against Rome's interests and would especially refrain from preying on shipping crossing the strait between western Greece and southern Italy. Only when the ruler there failed to prevent piracy in these waters did the senate act, sending a fleet and an army in 219 to bring the Illyrians to heel.[4] Rome's relations with Hiero, the king of Syracuse, were more formal in that they originated in a treaty of peace that ended hostilities with that monarch in 263. But the pact established only a vague 'friendship' between Rome and Hiero and required him only to aid the Republic in its war against Carthage. It did not constitute an open-ended treaty of alliance, although the senate might expect that

4. E. S. Gruen, *The Hellenistic World and the Coming of Rome*, Berkeley and Los Angeles: University of California Press, 1984, 359–73.

Hiero's 'friendship' with Rome would lead him to comply with its requests so long as the *patres* did not overreach. And in the event, Hiero proved a faithful friend to Rome, quick to offer aid whenever the occasion arose. But there was a tacit understanding that although Rome was the dominant partner, the senate would exercise its sway with a light hand and leave Hiero largely free to run his kingdom as he pleased.[5]

The situation on the mainland was different.[6] The senators drew a sharp distinction between the kinds of commitments they were willing to undertake and to expect from states and tribes overseas and their relations with communities in Italy. Here a formal treaty of alliance (*foedus*) was the rule. Unfortunately, we possess not a single example of one of the many *foedera* the Republic struck with its Italian allies (the *socii*). We know in very general terms what these entailed, but as with the informal ties Rome established abroad, there is likely to have been considerable variation in their specifics. Differences will have been due in large part to the circumstances under which these treaties were struck. Some were the fruit of Roman victories. A defeated enemy might be required to cede a considerable portion of its land, surrender any prisoners, and pay an indemnity to reimburse the Republic for the cost of the war as well as enter into alliance as the price of peace. Others came about when a weaker state under threat from a stronger neighbour sought the protection of Rome. And in some cases Rome itself constituted that threat, forcing a community to seek alliance in order to forestall hostilities. In other instances, treaties resulted from the Republic's active courtship of potential allies, as when it sought to open a second front against the Samnites in the late fourth century by winning allies among the cities of Apulia. What the Republic could demand from its allies, in other words, might vary considerably. Still, the Republic remained the dominant partner in all of these arrangements by virtue of its superior military might. And yet it was these very treaties that contributed much to making that superiority possible.

The senate's aim in enlarging Rome's dominion in Italy had not been to rule its allies. The Republic interfered not at all in the internal affairs of the *socii*. Their own elites continued to exercise

---

5. Gruen, *Hellenistic World*, 67–8.
6. M. Fronda, *Between Rome and Carthage: Southern Italy during the Second Punic War*, Cambridge: Cambridge University Press, 2010, 13–37; E. T. Salmon, *The Making of Roman Italy*, London: Thames and Hudson, 1982, 57–72.

power as they had always done, although friendly relations with members of the Roman aristocracy might enhance the stature of particular individuals and provide them with an advantage in competition with rivals for influence and honour. The *patres* levied no money taxes that would have worsened the economic condition of the allies. In those cases where alliance had followed a defeat and the vanquished had had to forfeit land, the terms of their new alliance with Rome offered the prospect of recompense. For what the Republic demanded of its allies was military manpower: infantry and cavalry or in rare instances ships and sailors. The senate fixed the contribution each ally was to make to the Republic's armies according to a formula known as the *formula togatorum*.[7] How this formula worked in detail we do not know. It apparently took into consideration the number of men of military age in an allied community and then established the size of the contingent required of the ally in any year on the basis of a proportion of that figure (e.g. Livy, 34.56.3–7). As a complement to the requirement to supply soldiers, the senate also demanded that an ally 'have the same friends and enemies as the Roman people' (*hostes eosdem habeto quos populus Romanus*: Livy, 38.11.3, in a second-century formulation). The effect of this provision was to place the control of the ally's foreign relations in the senate's hands. The ally was forced to join Rome in military operations against whoever Rome was at war with and similarly make peace at the senate's discretion. Further, allies were precluded from making alliances on their own initiative or going to war against whomever they chose. The treaties Rome struck with its *socii*, in other words, entitled the senate to involve its allies in hostilities against whatever enemy it wished and then to compel them to mobilise their military resources to join Rome's legions in fighting that war.

The Republic typically mobilised four legions every year during the third century down to the Hannibalic war. How many allied soldiers accompanied them we do not know for certain. In the second century the ratio of *socii* to legionaries on foot was typically 3:2, and that was the case in 225, when Polybius provides good data on the size of the forces Rome fielded in that year (on the size of Roman armies, see below, pp. 94–5). If we assume that a similar ratio was the norm over the course of the half century prior to the Hannibalic war, Rome will have demanded about 25,200 infantry

7. V. Ilari, *Gli italici nelle strutture militari romane*, Milan: A. Giuffrè, 1974.

from its allies annually, or somewhat less than 8 per cent of the men of military age. (Polybius, it is true, states that the numbers of *socii* and Romans were equal: 6.26.7. If so, the proportion will have been smaller still.) Allied cavalry numbered three times as many as their Roman counterparts according to Polybius (6.26.7), so 3,600 versus 1,200 for four legions. The latter rate of mobilisation would require about 12 per cent of the allies who presumably qualified for cavalry service by virtue of their wealth as at Rome. However, it is likely, as at Rome, that the allies mainly sent unmarried men in their late teens or twenties off to war (see below). In that case, if each allied soldier served six years between his seventeenth and thirtieth birthdays, about 22 per cent of all allied men will ever have been called to serve in a Roman war until Hannibal appeared in Italy. How this levy worked in practice we do not know. Allies may have been called upon to contribute fairly large contingents every few years, perhaps according to some fixed rotation, or it may be that each ally sent a smaller body of soldiers every year.

The system fed on its own success. Attempts by allies to take themselves out from under the *imperium* of Rome were comparatively rare until Hannibal entered Italy, and they remained so after the end of the Second Punic War down to the great allied revolt in 91. Part of the reason for the allies' willingness to live with this arrangement stemmed from the fact that it offered real benefits to the *socii*. The senate kept its hands off of the allies' internal politics, so locally powerful figures did not see their interests threatened by Roman control of their community's external affairs. Indeed, because these same men often led their local contingents into battle alongside their Roman allies, the Republic's wars afforded them opportunities to win glory, acquire prestige, and so enhance their stature at home. The senate also to some extent lightened the financial burden that the Republic's wars imposed upon its allies and enabled the allies to profit from them alongside their Roman comrades in arms. The Republic supplied the allied contingents' grain rations free of charge, while legionaries had to pay for the food they ate. Although allied states had to tax themselves to pay the soldiers they sent to fight Rome's wars, the stipends could be less than what a legionary required because an allied soldier did not have to buy the bulk of the rations he would consume on campaign. Allies received the same rewards for valour that Roman legionaries did, and when a victorious army returned to Rome to celebrate a triumph, the cash donatives its commander distributed to the allied troops were no different from those his legionaries got (second-century examples: Livy, 40.7.3, 43.7; 45.43.7, and cf. 41.13.7–8). *Socii*, not Romans, formed the army's *extraordinarii*, an elite force attached to the commander and billeted separately (Polyb. 6.26.6). Even better from the allied soldiers' point of view were the opportunities for plunder that warfare afforded. Victory also held the prospect of remediation for those allies that had come under the *imperium* of Rome as a consequence of defeat and been mulcted of a large portion of their lands. Allies were eligible to participate in the colonies Rome founded on lands taken from newly defeated enemies in Italy. The fact that their losses could to some extent be made good by sending landless members of their communities out to colonies gave some allies a tangible incentive to join Rome in future conquests. Finally, some allies at least saw themselves as partners in the Romans' conquests. The Marsi, who lived in the highlands of central Italy and had since the later fourth century enjoyed friendly relations with the Republic, liked to boast, 'No triumph over and no triumph without the Marsi' (App. *B Civ.* 1.46; cf. Strabo, 5.4.2; Livy, 9.45.18). The allied portions of a Roman army probably were organised by ethnicity: units drawn from particular peoples marched, camped, and fought together.[8] In that sense, a Roman army was much more like a large war band than the unified, integrated force that a modern army represents. And ethnic rivalry, a competition among the various groups that went into battle on the Roman side to prove themselves not inferior and even superior warriors to the others, including the Romans themselves, may have contributed not a little to the Republic's military success.

Still, the allure of these carrots needs to be set against the size of the stick that Rome wielded. What kept the Republic's allies and friends in line was the bottom line: the overwhelming military force that could be brought to bear in the event that they refused to honour their obligations to Rome, whether expressed or implied. Table 3 demonstrates incontestably that those resources were stupendous by ancient standards. The Macedonian army, for example, that Alexander the Great had at his disposal on the eve of his expedition against Persia numbered fewer than 35,000 soldiers. Allies and mercenaries might have added 25,000 more. Rome with

8. R. Pfeilschifter, 'The allies in the republican army and the Romanization of Italy', in R. Roth and J. Keller (eds), *Roman by Integration: Dimensions of Group Identity in Material Culture and Text*, Portsmouth, NH : Journal of Roman Archaeology, 2007, 27–42.

its *socii* was in a class by itself, and the manpower it could command made revolt by any ally hopeless.

Suppressing revolts, however, was costly in both money and manpower and only weakened the Republic's military strength. In maintaining their dominance over the rest of Italy, the Romans were aided by the variety of its inhabitants. Before the first century, when the aftermath of the Social war saw the growing integration of the various distinct ethnic groups that heretofore had made up the population of the peninsula, those groups maintained a strong sense of independent ethnic identity. Between the Celts of the Po valley, the Etruscans and Umbrians to the north of Rome, the Samnites, Lucanians, and other highland people of the central Apennine spine, the Apulians living on the Tavoliere (the southeastern plains), the Greeks of southern Italy, the Bruttians, and Calabrians among others, there was little to encourage unity. They spoke different languages, lived according to diverse customs, and worshipped a variety of gods. Some, like the Etruscans and Greeks, had been long urbanised while others, like the Samnites, Ligurians, and other highlanders, lacked poleis-like institutions and were organised tribally. Geography, the economic differences that attended on it, and their demographic consequences often brought the groups into conflict. Poorer mountain regions were from time to time subject to serious population pressures as the number of inhabitants began to bump up against the limits of what the land could support. One solution was migration, reflected in the old custom of the 'Sacred Spring' (*ver sacrum*) in which the children born in a particular year upon reaching their majority would all leave their homeland in search of a new domicile. The extent to which such customs were followed in historical times is uncertain; what is certain is that warriors from Samnium and Lucania repeatedly sought to invade the plains to the east and west of their mountain homes, sometimes as raiders in search of plunder and at others as settlers seeking land. It was through one such movement out of Samnium that Oscan speakers came to displace most of the Etruscans and Greeks in Campania during the late fifth century. And the pressure of a similar flow of migrants on the towns of Apulia a century later opened the way for Rome to forge alliances with them as it waged its own struggle against the Samnites. Similar threats from Lucanians repeatedly menaced the Greek cities of southern Italy, one of which led to Rome's involvement in the region and ultimately its subjugation to the Republic's *imperium*. Rome, in short, did not have to 'divide and conquer' in Italy, for Italy was already divided, and those divisions afforded plenty of opportunity for conquest. However, once Rome had established its hegemony, its power enforced peace between the regions.

But division ran even deeper than Italy's ethnic and geographical fault lines would suggest. These broad categories were in actuality made up of a multiplicity of individual city-states, tribes, and clans. In some cases political structures existed that could facilitate unified action among their constituent parts, but these elements were just as capable of opposition, hostility, and even open warfare against one another. The cities of Etruria, Apulia, Campania, and Magna Graecia had all at one time or another battled among themselves. The threat of one city in these regions growing in power to the point where it could dominate the others especially provoked opposition from the rest. This had happened in the case of Tarentum in the south and Capua in Campania. Incorporation into the Roman *imperium* checked such threats and suppressed conflict between the cities and tribes within a region, but they remained latent. The senate's role as arbiter of disputes within Italy and the protection afforded by Roman military might, in other words, tended to turn weaker powers into supporters of Roman rule out of the simple calculation that it was preferable to be under the remote and lighter domination of the Republic rather than the nearer and more intrusive control of a stronger neighbour. Cross-cutting these intra-regional conflicts were the internal political dynamics within the tribes and cities that Rome dominated. Institutions of government were quite diverse across Italy, but what they all had in common was the fact that each was an arena for rivalry among the rich and well-born (and sometimes others) for influence and prestige. This situation, too, enhanced the prospects for Roman control. Not that the senate interfered in the internal affairs of its allies during the third century (and only to a very limited extent if at all in the first half of the second). This hands-off policy was one of the aspects of the Republic's *imperium* that made it easier for the allies to abide Roman dominion. But because the contingents that composed the allied portion of Rome's armies served under their own officers, the Republic's wars represented a potential source of prestige for them, as did informal ties of marriage or guest-friendship with leading senators at Rome. These could translate into advantages for some allied aristocrats in competition with their rivals, giving them a stake in preserving the diplomatic status quo. Social conflicts, finally, in some cases supplied a further basis for Roman rule. Etruscan society, for example, was sharply divided between a large population of serfs and a smaller body of their masters, the *principes*. The tensions to which this division gave rise afforded Rome a simple means of retaining the loyalty of the latter by supporting their position at the apex of Etruscan society – by military means if necessary, as occurred at Volsinii in 264 (Zonar. 8.7) and on a number of occasions subsequently. And although Etruscan social arrangements were not replicated elsewhere in Italy, Livy occasionally notes that Romans intervened within an allied community on behalf of the well-to-do against insurrections by the poor (e.g. in 296 among the Lucanians: Livy, 10.18.8). Class conflict came to a head in Livy's telling during the Hannibalic war: 'All the states of Italy suffered from a single disease, as it were. The rich and the lower class were at loggerheads, the former favouring the Romans, the latter siding with the Carthaginians' (24.2.8). While Livy's characterisation of the situation after 216 may be overly schematic and mask a more complex reality, to the extent that strife between rich and poor simmered within allied communities it enabled Rome to count on the support of the wealthy and well-born throughout Italy.

Notwithstanding the fact that Italy's geographic diversity, the complexity of its societies, and the potential for conflict among its inhabitants provided the Republic with many ways to 'divide and rule', the one thing that could unite them was resistance to Rome itself. No third-century Roman senator could forget the lesson of Sentinum, where a great coalition of Greeks, Etruscans, and Samnites threatened to crush the Republic's growing power. Roman arms had turned back that threat, and the Republic's leaders were resolved always to maintain the capacity to do so again by increasing citizen numbers in step with the acquisition of new allies so that Roman manpower would always be able to meet any challenge from a coalition of rebellious Italian allies. Natural increase, however, under pre-modern conditions of health and longevity would never be capable of such rapid demographic expansion. Instead, the *patres* relied on a practice first established at the conclusion of the Latin Revolt in 338, namely incorporating entire communities of allies into the Roman citizen body with either full citizenship rights or citizenship without the vote (*civitas sine suffragio*).[9] Decisions

9. A. N. Sherwin-White, *The Roman Citizenship*[2], Oxford: Oxford University Press, 1973.

were made primarily on strategic grounds. Shortly after the consul M'. Curius Dentatus and his army conquered the Sabines in 290, for example, the *patres* made them, or at least a portion of them, citizens *sine suffragio*, thereby extending Roman territory across central Italy all the way to the Adriatic. This step imposed a barrier between the Samnite confederation to the south and the Etruscan cities to the north, making the union of armies from each region such as had faced Rome at Sentinum far more difficult to effect. With the loss of books 11–20 of Livy's *History*, similar measures during the remainder of the third century are obscure to us, but the results are not. The number of Romans grew from around 570,000 c. 290 BC to 967,700 in 225, an astounding increase of almost 70 per cent over 65 years and far beyond the capacity of a pre-industrial population to make through births alone.[10]

Romanising Italy

Enlarging the citizen body by leaps and bounds entailed far more than a simple announcement that this or that group of Italians could now call themselves Romans. The Republic faced the twin challenges of integration and control. The question of the terms on which the new citizens would take their places beside the old ones had critical implications for Roman politics. A great wave of newcomers would swamp the networks of favours and obligations and the stores of prestige in the eyes of the voters that aristocratic families had carefully nurtured over generations and that were in play in any election. And a flood of new contenders for offices and honours would only intensify the competition for them and make the already difficult task that scions of noble families faced in replicating their ancestors' achievements in the political arena that much harder. On the other hand, how was identification with Rome to be fostered among the new citizens, and what would happen to their old ethnic and political identities? At the same time, the slowness of communication and Rome's lack of an extensive cadre of officials posed a significant obstacle to the senate's ability to exercise control over a territory that successive enfranchisements would enlarge from about 15,000 square km c. 290 BC to nearly 27,000 square km by 225.

The institution of citizenship without the vote eliminated the

---

10. Afzelius, *Römische Eroberung*; Brunt, *Italian Manpower*, 44–60.

political problems that a host of new citizens would create.[11] It entailed all the obligations and rights of full citizenship (*civitas optimo iure*) except the right to cast a vote in a legislative or electoral assembly and the privilege of holding public office at Rome. Over the course of the third and second centuries, citizenship without the vote became a stepping-stone to citizenship *optimo iure*. In 268, the Sabines, who initially lacked the vote, became the first citizens in that category to be elevated to full citizenship and enrolled in a tribe. Others followed. However, one cannot lose sight of the initially punitive nature of *civitas sine suffragio*. In the years that followed 338, Rome imposed it as the price of military defeat and forced new citizens to shoulder the twin burdens of taxation and service with the Roman legions. Its recipients certainly could view it as a punishment (e.g. Livy, 9.45.7), but one to which the military power of the Republic forced them to submit.

Still, it was one thing to extend citizenship with or without the vote to a horde of newcomers; it was quite another to rule them. Time and distance progressively diminished the extent of the senate's control, and the *patres* had no intention of creating even a rudimentary bureaucracy to extend their reach beyond the confines of Rome's immediate environs. Instead of modifying the Republic's civic structures to administer a far-flung citizenry, the senate simply availed itself of the structures of governance already in place among those it decided to incorporate into the body of Roman citizens. Their instrument for doing so was the *municipium*.[12] New citizens, with or without the vote, who lived in a self-governing polity prior to the imposition of Roman citizenship became *municipes*. A *municeps* was someone who bore a citizen's burdens (*munera*) but continued to live for the most part under the laws of his former, pre-citizenship community. The same types of local magistrates governed him with their same titles (*dictator*, *octoviri*, *aediles*, *medix*, and *marones*, among others), and his local town, not Rome, remained the focus of his economic life. Even his religious practices seem to have remained largely unchanged. The cults of newly incorporated *civitates* did not automatically become part of the Roman religious establishment but continued to function autonomously. The temple of Juno Sospita at Lanuvium, for instance, was explicitly deemed to

11. M. Humbert, *Municipium et civitas sine suffragio: L'Organisation de la conquête jusqu'à la guerre sociale*, Rome: Ecole Française de Rome, 1978; Salmon, *Making of Roman Italy*, 40–56.
12. Humbert, *Municipium*.

be 'shared' between the citizens of that city and those of Rome, although both groups were Roman citizens (Livy, 8.14.2). Such an arrangement would hardly have been the case if enfranchisement had incorporated the religious practices of Lanuvium into the Republic's civic cult. Even more striking is the fact that cities incorporated without the vote (and probably those granted citizenship *optimo iure*) became Roman by virtue of a treaty (*foedus*) with Rome spelling out the terms and conditions of their new status. *Municipia*, in other words, enjoyed a remarkably wide scope for managing their local political and civic affairs as they always had. While the praetor at Rome did send out *praefecti* annually to (probably) groups of *municipia*, these officials were in no sense governors. Their task seems to have been simply to advise local magistrates on those few areas of Roman law that applied to court cases that came before them and with which the magistrates were unfamiliar.

The degree of autonomy they possessed makes the *municipia* of Roman citizens *sine suffragio* appear strikingly similar to the Republic's *socii*, and it would not be mistaken to think of the former in this respect at least as just another species of Roman ally, particularly in view of the *foedera* that bound the *municipia* to Rome. The key difference lay in the burdens that municipal status imposed, especially the *tributum* (see below, p. 107) and liability to conscription, along with the civic rights that Roman citizenship bestowed. In that sense, the *municipes* might be thought of as enjoying a kind of two-legged citizenship, with one foot in the *civitas* of Rome and the other in that of their local *municipium*. The hybrid character of municipal status was a novelty in the ancient world, but it represented a critical breakthrough for the Republic's *imperium*, for it enabled Rome to expand its citizen population dramatically without having to alter the essentially city-state character of its government and civil administration. The Republic could fold in big groups of new citizens because it did not require them to change very much about the ways in which they had formerly lived, apart from now sending troops to serve in the legions and paying taxes to support them. Neither did their inclusion require the Republic itself to change significantly by creating cadres of new officials to organise and control these new Romans. The *municipia* largely administered themselves. They were a key innovation that enabled a city-state like Rome to enlarge its military potential to the point where it dwarfed its rivals.

Not all Romans, however, lived within the territory that fell within the jurisdiction of a *municipium*. Those whose (or whose ancestors') citizenship predated 338 and who lived within the tenth milestone from Rome were under the charge of officials in the city. Rome was where they pleaded their lawsuits, and the city served as the focus of much of their religious and economic lives. These citizens were comparatively few, however; many times more lived farther afield. This was increasingly the case as the Republic incorporated newly won territories into the *ager Romanus* and then from time to time distributed small parcels of land there to citizens to farm. The senate ordered viritane allotments, as these distributions were termed, to be made in the Sabine territory following its conquest and absorption in 290. Flaminius' tribunician legislation did the same in the *ager Gallicus* south of Ariminum in 232. No preexisting polity was available in these and similar regions to turn into a *municipium* (or the senate elected not to avail itself of those that were in place but instead dismantled them). Instead, the Republic established market towns *(fora)* and meeting places *(conciliabula)* for the new settlers. The principal difference between these two entities seems to have lain in the fact that a *forum* typically was a new foundation created by a Roman magistrate, often in connection with the construction of a road along which the *forum* was situated. *Fora* often took their names from the founding official, for example *Forum Flaminii* along the *via Flaminia*. A *conciliabulum* by contrast was simply a village that had been a recognised place of assembly prior to the region's incorporation into the *ager Romanus*, rather than a new foundation. We know very little about them and only slightly more about the market towns. The latter could be substantial places, boasting public buildings constructed by their founder, as at *Forum Annii* (or *Popillii: ILLRP* 454 = *ROL* 4.150–1, line 15). Both *fora* and *conciliabula* formed the points of contact between non-municipal citizens and their government in Rome. They were the places where recruitment for the legions was conducted, taxes were imposed and collected, edicts published, and public acts of worship ordered by the senate carried out, among other things. Whether such activities were supervised by local officials of some sort is unclear. Possibly there was considerable variation in the ways in which these small settlements were administered. They also constituted important economic and juridical loci for citizens residing in the vicinity. Local market days *(nundinae)* were apparently held there as were courts to try petty lawsuits and criminal cases. M. Porcius Cato as a young man made his mark as a public speaker by pleading cases in these sorts of local courts (Plut. *Cat. Mai.* 1.4). It is not clear, however, whether it was local officials that acted as judges at these trials or officials sent out from Rome, the prefects for declaring the law (*praefecti iure dicundo*). The latter may simply have acted as advisors as the similarly titled officials did for the *municipia*. Yet despite the paucity of details about how precisely the *fora* and *conciliabula* were administered, the lack of close oversight by Rome suggests that these entities, too, were largely self-regulating. The areas that the *praefecti* supervised, the *praefecturae*, were simply too large for a single official to exercise close control over what went on in them. Because the *fora* and *conciliabula*, like the *municipia*, were largely self-contained administrative units, they enabled the Republic to absorb and organise big chunks of new territory and people them with citizens without fundamentally altering its basic city-state structure. And like the *municipia*, the *fora* and *conciliabula* became the building blocks out of which Rome constructed an *ager Romanus* that gradually encompassed most of central Italy and provided the agricultural basis for the large population that provided the Republic with its massive military power.

Amid all this diversity, how was unity possible? What integrated citizens living at such distances from one another and with such differences in religion, language, and customs into one people? How was it possible that they all thought of themselves as 'Romans'? The Republic met this challenge in several ways, the most important of which was the census.[13] Participation was the one single act that every citizen had to perform whether or not he possessed the right to vote, no matter if he lived in Rome, a *municipium*, a small *forum* or *conciliabulum*, or a colony (on which see below), and regardless of whether he travelled to the capital to make his declaration or did so before a local magistrate or an official dispatched by the censors. And because a census was conducted regularly at more or less five-year intervals the message of Romanness that it conveyed was repeatedly reinforced.

The process of making a declaration is outlined in the *Tabula Heracleensis*, a document from the first century BC, but the procedure it spells out is likely to reflect earlier practice.

> Whatever *municipia*, colonies or prefectures of Roman citizens are or shall be in Italy, whoever in those *municipia*, colonies or prefectures

---

13. C. Nicolet, *The World of the Citizen in Republican Rome*, trans. P. S. Falla, Berkeley and Los Angeles: University of California Press, 1980, 48–88.

Figure 8 Citizens registering for the census. The 'Altar of Domitius Ahenobarbus', c. 100 BC. Photo by Erich Lessing, courtesy of Art Resource, NY.

shall there hold the highest magistracy or the highest office, at the time when a censor or any other magistrate shall conduct the census of the people at Rome, within the sixty days next after he shall know that the census of the people is being conducted at Rome, he is to conduct a census of all his fellow *municipes* and colonists and those who shall be of that prefecture, who shall be Roman citizens; and he is to receive from them under oath their *nomina*, their *praenomina*, their fathers or patrons, their tribes, their *cognomina*, and how many years old each of them shall be and an account of their property, according to the schedule of the census, which shall have been published at Rome by whoever is then about to conduct the census of the people; and he is to see that all this is entered in the public records of his *municipium*; and he is to send those books by envoys ... to those who shall conduct the census at Rome. (*CIL* 2.593; Crawford, *RS* 1.337, lines 142–50)

The elements of his declaration integrated the citizen into the body politic in several ways. Giving his name and that of his father first of all identified him as the bearer of the *tria nomina* (three names) that every citizen bore, consisting of his *praenomen* or individual name, his *nomen*, the name of his *gens* (clan), his filiation, which indicated his father (or in the cases of freedmen, the name of his former owner, now his patron), and his *cognomen*, a personal or family nickname; for example, M. (for Marcus) Tullius M. f. (*Marci filius* or son of Marcus) Cor. Cicero. The abbreviation standing between a citizen's filiation and *cognomen* indicated his tribe, in Cicero's case the Cornelia. Membership in one of the thirty-five tribes was the defining criterion for establishing citizenship; every citizen was registered in one. The tribes in turn formed the framework for how one cast a vote in both the tribal and centuriate assemblies, how one's taxes were assessed and collected, and how soldiers were levied for the legions. A citizen's age determined both his liability for military service – those over 46 were exempt – and more importantly whether he voted in one of centuries of *seniories* – comprising again those over 46 – or *iuniores* in the *comitia centuriata*. Stating his property to the censors, including family members and slaves (for those in a father's power – the *patria potestas* – were legally held to be chattel) placed a citizen's wealth at the disposal of the state for purposes of taxation. His property also located him within the hierarchy of census classes and determined in which of the several categories of centuries, based on wealth, he would be enrolled. That determined how much weight his vote would carry in that assembly (see above, pp. 9–10). Finally, what he owned determined how a citizen would serve the Republic in war: in the cavalry, in the infantry, or as an oarsman aboard a warship.

Warfare, too, involved citizens in a common experience of 'Romanness', and not simply because citizens served in the legions while allies were brigaded and fought separately.[14] The legions mixed together citizens who had previously had little if any contact with one another. Men who had lived many miles apart and under different, semi-autonomous civic regimes now ate, slept, marched, and endured the stress of combat together in small groups of tent-mates. Now if not before they were subject to Roman time: when the senate authorised a levy, the consul who was to conduct it proclaimed a date for potential recruits to present themselves at Rome, which meant that citizens had to understand and act in accordance with the Roman calendar, no matter what method of marking the passage of time they had previously employed. Their terms of service were measured by consular years. In addition, military service imposed uniformity of language on the legionaries: they received their orders in Latin (which may be why citizens without the vote, who were often non-Latin speakers, apparently served in separate units until the middle of the third century). Finally, soldiers were paid in Roman coin, which introduced citizens who may in civilian

14. Nicolet, *World of the Citizen*, 89–109; M. Jehne, 'Römer, Latiner und Budesgenossen im Krieg: Zu Formen und Ausmaß der Integration in der republikanischen Armee', in M. Jehne and R. Pfeilschifter (eds), *Herrschaft ohne Integration? Rom und Italien in republicanischer Zeit*, Frankfurt: Antike, 2006, 243–67.

Figure 9 Reverse of a didrachm issued c. 269–266 BC showing a she-wolf suckling Romulus and Remus, with the legend, *Romano[rum]* ('of the Romans'). ANS 1944 100 16. Courtesy of the American Numismatic Society.

life have had little occasion to use coined money in their economic transactions to both the Republic's monetary system and the ideological messages that the coins conveyed. The head of Mars, for example, or the twins or a wolf all alluded to legends of Rome's foundation as well as its bellicose character. Some citizens' earliest exposure to writing may have also come via the same medium, in the legend 'of the Romans' *(Romano[rum])* or Rome *(Roma)* on the coins. Often it will have been through soldiers returning from their service with the legions with their savings that coinage was introduced into circulation among the rural population.

Apart from going to war, citizens – men and women alike – went to Rome to attend the games and festivals. The oldest of them, the Roman or Great games (*ludi Romani* or *Magni*) dated from the mid-fourth century and honoured the Republic's chief deity, Jupiter Best and Greatest (*Optimus Maximus*), the protector of Rome and its people. Over the course of the later third and second centuries, other gods received similar honours: the Plebeian games, also honouring Juipiter, c. 220; games for Apollo in 212; the *ludi Megalenses* in 204, the *Ceriales* in 202, and the *Floralia* in 173. These were annual celebrations lasting several days, great communal acts of worship to honour and propitiate the gods who protected the Republic and its people. But the people partied with their gods. Both enjoyed the entertainments and contests that were held to mark the occasion. These not only renewed and strengthened the bond uniting the divine and human members of the Roman community but also linked the latter as they joined together in honouring the former.

Proximity will have determined frequency: citizens living close to Rome could go often while those domiciled in distant *municipia* or *fora* might make the journey only once or a few times or even never in their lives. But when they did or travelled to Rome for business or to report for military service or any other reason they probably made at least part of the journey on one of the great public highways the Republic had constructed across the peninsula, beginning with the *via Appia* in 312, extending from the capital to Capua and from there through Beneventum, Venusia, and Tarentum to Brundisium by 244.[15] Others followed: the *via Valeria* in 307 running east into the central Apennine highlands; the *via Aurelia* in 241 stretching north from Rome to Cosa along the western coastal plain; and the *via Flaminia* that Flaminus constructed as censor in 220 and that extended the Republic's reach to Ariminum at the southeastern corner of the Po valley. The *via Aemilia* began from that point in 187 and ran northwest to Placentia; from there in 148 the consul of that year, Sp. Postumius Albinus, built the road that bears his name, the *via Postumia*, west to Genua and east to Aquileia, consolidating the Republic's hold on the region. And the *via Cassia*, probably built in 154 by the censor C. Cassius Longinus, ran north from Rome into Etruria as far as Arretium. The primary purpose of many of these roads, particularly the earlier ones like the *via Appia*, was military, to facilitate the movement of troops and supplies into a war zone. Some, such as the *via Flaminia*, enabled armies to move swiftly into a region like the *ager Gallicus* that Rome had recently conquered and where it was now establishing settlers who might need armed support against hostile neighbours. But the impact of these roads went far beyond their effect on the Republic's ability to wage war. They enhanced the civilian transportation network, making the movement of goods, particularly crops, to market much easier and cheaper. In doing so, they often altered the agricultural character of the adjacent areas, shifting production from subsistence farming to growing products for urban markets. But beyond any economic

15. R. Laurence, *The Roads of Roman Italy: Mobility and Cultural Change*, London: Routledge, 1999.

changes the roads' more fundamental effect was to stamp the land-scape around them as unmistakably part of the Republic's *imperium*, even when they did not pass through *ager Romanus*. They were palpable signs of Roman dominion. Citizens and allies alike who travelled along them or only saw them from afar understood the reach of Roman power.

Colonies

The Republic's ability to encompass a variety of Italians within the ambit of Roman citizenship while at the same time allowing for a considerable degree of diversity and self-rule among them enabled it to square the circle of ancient city-states: it could grow to enormous proportions without substantially modifying institutions of govern-ance and administration that were designed for a much smaller, face-to-face community. That achievement in turn was essential to the creation of a manpower base that enabled it to threaten an over-whelming military response to any ally bold or foolhardy enough to contemplate revolt. That capacity coupled with the incentives for cooperation made it possible for the Republic to dominate the rest of Italy and harness its allies into the greatest military power the ancient world had ever seen. Yet the Republic's manpower always remained less than that of the totality of its *socii*, and a massive revolt by a coalition of them remained a nightmarish possibility in the minds of senators who remembered Sentinum. What helped even the odds were the colonies.[16]

The colonies the Republic founded, like its roads, were a means of dominating the regions where they were established. They were of two kinds: Roman and Latin. Roman colonies in the third century were typically small, about 300 families of Roman citizens. The senate usually ordered them created near the coast in order to protect the region around them against raids by pirates. By the time Hannibal invaded Italy, ten had been established. Far more import-ant were the Latin colonies, not only because they were larger, usually 2,000–3,000 families but sometimes numbering 6,000, but because of their far greater strategic importance in sustaining Rome's dominion over Italy. They were the 'empire's ramparts' (*propug-nacula imperii*), in Cicero's famous phrase (*Leg. agr.* 2.73). The

16. E. T. Salmon, *Roman Colonization under the Republic*, London: Thames and Hudson, 1969.

senate established Latin colonies in recently conquered areas that for one reason or another it elected not to absorb into the *ager Romanus* but felt needed a military presence to secure them. The settlers who undertook this role were Latins. By this date, few ethnic Latins remained; most had been absorbed into the Roman citizen body following the end of the Latin revolt in 338. Latin colonists instead were selected from among both Roman citizens and *socii*. Those chosen gave up their original citizenship and in its place were granted a package of rights and privileges analogous to those that citizens of the old Latin league had enjoyed vis-à-vis Rome. These included the right to contract a legally valid marriage with a Roman citizen; the right to have commercial contracts with a Roman citizen enforced by a Roman court of law, which included the right to own property in the *ager Romanus*; and the right to acquire Roman citizenship by migrating to Roman territory provided that a colonist left a son of military age behind to take his place. 'Latin', in other words, was divorced from its ethnic origins and assimilated to a legal status. Anyone could be a Latin just as anyone upon whom the Republic bestowed citizenship could be a Roman.

Latin colonies were independent, self-governing communities (unlike citizen colonies, which were governed from Rome). Colonists included many former Roman citizens, and they were tied to Rome by the legislation establishing them, which spelled out their obligations. Chief among these was the requirement to furnish soldiers for the Republic's armies. At one time scholars believed the communities were virtually 'little Romes' modelled closely on the capital, typically governed by two annual magistrates titled *praetores*, and boasting a forum, a voting place for assemblies styled, as at Rome, the *comitium*, and a temple to Jupiter, Juno, and Minerva, the same triad of deities worshiped at the Capitoline temple in Rome. Public buildings were held to have been constructed in Roman style, and in some colonies the wards bore the names of their counterparts in Rome. Much of this reconstruction has lately been called into question, and it is now unclear to what extent colonies represented the Republic's cultural as opposed to military dominance of the surrounding regions.[17] Still, the connection between Rome and its

17. Salmon, *Roman Colonization*, 55–69, for the older view; E. Bispham, '*Coloniam deducere*: How Roman was Roman colonization during the middle Republic?', in G. Bradley and J-P. Wilson (eds), *Greek and Roman Colonization: Origins, Ideologies and Interactions*, Swansea: Classical Press of Wales, 2006, 73–160, for criticisms.

Latin colonies was extraordinarily close. The senate ensured that the territory a Latin colony controlled was extensive, so that once the colonists had received their generous allotments, many of the earlier inhabitants would continue to live and farm within it. Yet only the colonists had a voice in the colony's government and so enjoyed a privileged political position. They were the Republic's most loyal allies because of the colonists' dependence on Rome for protection. Other allies in the region saw them as interlopers who were occupying land confiscated by Rome from its former possessors, an armed camp in their midst. Without the promise of Roman military aid in the event of attack, the colonists' position would have been untenable. In exchange for Roman support, the colonists for their part not only furnished contingents to the Republic's armies but served as a local defence force to suppress minor troubles and as a forward base of operations for campaigns against Rome's enemies in the region. The 'Latin name' (*nomen Latinum*), as the twenty-eight Latin colonies in place by 225 were collectively termed, were the allies that Rome could most count on in a crisis, and their numbers helped to equalise the disparity between the numbers of Roman citizens and *socii*. Adult male Romans and Latins may have numbered around 252,000 in 290 BC (176,000 of the former and 76,000 of the latter) as against perhaps 226,000 other allies.[18] By 225 the ratio had shifted even further in Rome's favour to about 358,000 Romans and Latins as against 276,000 other allies. The Latins ensured that Rome would prevail if worse came to worst.

This massive accumulation of manpower by itself, however, was not the key to Rome's success in extending its *imperium* across Italy and eventually over the ancient Mediterranean and beyond. Sheer numbers alone never guaranteed victory. Alexander's army, though numerically inferior, repeatedly vanquished Persian forces many times as large. And the Romans themselves, looking back from the late Republic, saw their early history as a time when smaller forces of Romans time and again overcame much larger opponents (Sall. *Cat.* 7.7). To conquer again and again year after year, an army able to win battles even against the odds was essential as was a military system capable of supporting it. During the later fourth and third centuries, the Romans created both.

18. Afzelius, *Römische Eroberung*, 182.

The Roman army

Over the course of the Republic's nearly constant warfare during the fifth and fourth centuries, its legions underwent a long and successful period of refinement, and by the early third century they had evolved into highly flexible formations based on maniples.[19] Thirty of these infantry squadrons, each containing two centuries, made up a legion, and in battle they were arrayed in three lines. In the third century ten maniples of 120 men formed the first line. These were the 'spearmen' (*hastati*). Behind them stood a second line of ten maniples, each also containing 120 legionaries, called the 'chief men' (*principes*). They were followed by a third line of ten maniples of only sixty men each, who were designated the 'third rank men' (*triarii*). In Polybius' day (and it is to him that we owe our fullest description of the Roman army of the middle Republic, in book 6 of his *Histories*), all legionaries carried a heavy wooden shield, the *scutum*, and were protected by a bronze helmet surmounted by a crest of black feathers and a small square of metal held by leather straps on the centre of their chests, although men in the first census class, whatever category of maniple they served in, had the privilege of wearing a coat of mail (the *lorica*). Their weapons were a short, heavy sword, the *gladius*, and two throwing spears, the *pila*, although the *triarii* carried a longer, thrusting spear in place of the *pilum*. While it is not certain that the legions of a century earlier were identically equipped, differences if they existed are likely to have been minor. In addition to the heavily armed legionaries in the three lines of battle, each legion contained both a company of 1,200 skirmishers (the *velites* or 'swift ones'), armed with javelins, a sword, a light shield and helmet, and a force of two or three hundred cavalry. Cavalrymen prior to the Hannibalic war wore no defensive armour, only a tunic, and carried light spears and shields. The absence of armour facilitated mounting and dismounting in battle, for cavalrymen often fought on foot in the era before stirrups, but repeated failures against Hannibal's cavalry led to the adoption of the *lorica*, heavier shields and helmets, and a heavy, slashing sword. A legion's total strength in the third century was normally 4,500 men, but in the second it was raised to 5,500. How the additional legionaries were distributed among the various categories is unclear.

The criteria for assigning recruits to the different categories of maniples partly reflected differences in their ages.[20] The *velites* were the youngest soldiers, around 17 or 18 years old, the age at which citizens became liable for military service. The *hastati* were some-what older, in their early twenties, the *principes* a few years older again, and the *triarii* in their late twenties or early thirties. Only in the direst emergencies did the Romans call up men older than that, although citizens as old as 45 were legally obligated to serve. In addition to age, wealth also determined what type of military service a citizen performed. At Rome as in most ancient city-states, it was believed that the very poorest citizens would not be willing to stand firm in battle but, having nothing to defend, would simply run away. Therefore only those citizens who possessed property beyond a specific minimum amount were considered qualified for service in the legions. These were the *assidui* (meaning 'settled', i.e. on a piece of land); below them were the *proletarii*, those who contributed only their offspring (*proles*). Except in the worst emergencies (as during the Pyrrhic war; see above, p. 46) the latter served only as rowers on warships. One of the censors' principal tasks in conducting the census was to review the property of the citizens in order to place each man among either the *assidui* or the *proletarii*. Among the *assidui* serving with the legions, the *velites* represented not only the youngest but also the poorest soldiers, men who could not afford to equip themselves (at least initially) with anything but the minimal weapons and armour required. The higher census classes served indiscriminately among the *hastati*, *principes*, and *triarii*, the only distinction among them being that citizens in the first census class wore the *lorica*, as noted above. However, the cavalry was drawn from men possessing a level of wealth greater than that of the first census class. How much greater is uncertain. We are nowhere told, and it may be that each pair of censors, who assigned citizens to the cavalry class, determined the amount based on their judgement of how many men the pool of potential cavalry recruits ought to contain over the next few years. Those liable to serve in the cavalry were the horsemen (*equites*). Most supplied their own mounts, generally two or three, and brought along a slave to serve as a groom

20. N. Rosenstein, *Rome at War: Farms, Families, and Death in the Middle Republic*, Chapel Hill: University of North Carolina Press, 2004, 85–6.

in addition. A smaller and much more prestigious class of cavalry-men were the horsemen with a public horse (*equites equo publico*; see above, p. 9), about 1,800 in number and also selected by the censors. They were a survival from the earliest days of the Republic if not the monarchy, a time when it was felt necessary to supply cavalrymen with a horse at public expense. Membership was a signal honour and typically went to senators or members of their families. A legion drew its contingent of 300 cavalrymen, organised in ten squadrons (*turmae*) of thirty men, each with its own officers, from both types of *equites* indiscriminately.

A Roman legion typically began combat by sending its *velites* forward to skirmish with similarly armed troops of the enemy. Their order was loose, and they fought by running forward to hurl their javelins. At a command, they broke off their action and withdrew behind the legions, which then moved forward to engage the enemy. The legionaries began their attack by hurling their *pila*, and then advancing to close quarters. The *pilum* had a long, slender iron tip that was barbed at the end. It was designed to penetrate an enemy's shield and then remain stuck there, so that the shield became awkward to manage in combat and so less effective in protecting its bearer. We are not told much about how the men in each maniple were arranged for combat, but it is possible that the *hastati* and *principes* stood in lines fifteen men across and in files eight men deep, since these maniples were organised for administrative purposes into two centuries of sixty men, each officered by its own centurion, and further subdivided into eight-man squads. Maniples of the *triarii* may have presented a similar front but possessed only half the depth of the others. The legionaries within each maniple stood separated by about three feet from the men in front and behind and on either side of them. This comparatively loose arrangement, less dense than contemporary phalanx formations as Polybius tells us, was dictated by the need for room to wield a sword and to turn from side to side to meet a threat from whichever direction it presented itself (18.30.6–8). However, the greater space between the legionaries also enabled them to move within the maniple itself, and herein lay one of a legion's great tactical advantages. Roman soldiers struck their opponents not only with their swords but with the iron bosses in the centre of their shields, hoping to knock the enemy off balance and so leave them vulnerable to a deadly blow. The short reach of the Roman swords meant that only the soldiers in the first rank could fight at any one time, while perhaps 90 per cent of the maniple's

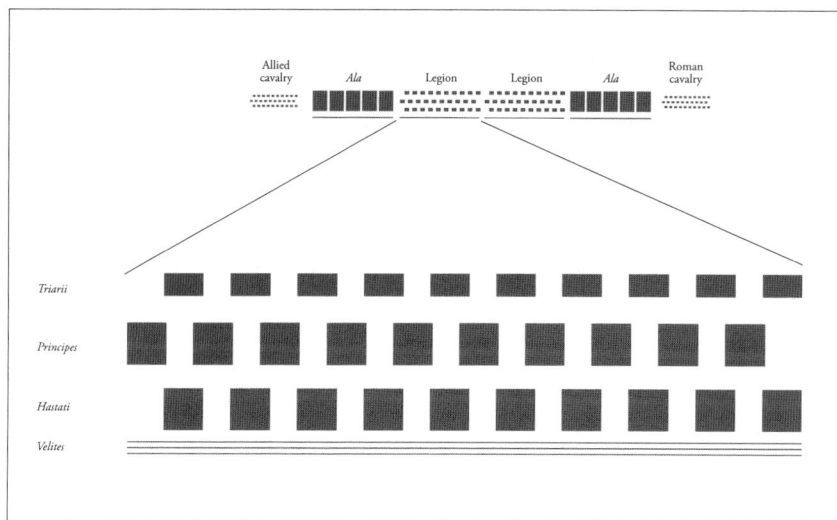

Figure 10 The Roman order of battle (the *quincunx*) in the middle Republic.

strength stood to the rear out of the action. However, because of the gruelling physical effort and emotional stress that hand-to-hand combat demanded, pairs of combatants might, by tacit mutual agreement, step back for a brief time to catch their breaths before renewing their onslaught. But even with these short respites, exhaustion set in quickly for those men fighting in the so-called 'killing zone'. When that happened or when they were wounded, those in the front rank were able to fall back easily to the rear through the spaces between the files while the legionaries in the second line stepped forward to take their places. This alternation of the men actually engaged in combat could be repeated many times during the course of a battle, and much of the effectiveness of a legion in combat can be attributed to the ability of each maniple continually to move fresh troops up to face their opponents. The latter, if they fought – as many did – in a densely packed mass, could far less easily replace fighters who became progressively weakened through exhaustion and wounds.

A similar principle governed how the maniples themselves manoeuvred in battle. A legion's three lines of maniples were deployed in a formation that moderns term the *quincunx* (although the Romans did not use this word to describe it). Each maniple of the *hastati* was separated from its neighbours by a gap equal to its own front. The maniples of the *principes* were similarly spaced, but each stood behind one of the gaps in the line of the *hastati*, and the same held for the *triarii*, so that the formation resembled the arrangements of the black squares on a draughtboard or the five spots of a dice. How the *quincunx* operated in combat is somewhat unclear, but it seems that the gaps in the lines enabled maniples of the first line to fall back and those of the second line to move forward as the situation dictated. In other words, as the battle wore on and the legionaries of the first line of maniples grew increasingly fatigued or greater numbers suffered wounds, the maniples of the *principes*, whose soldiers, having been kept well behind the 'killing zone' up to that point, were entirely fresh, could be moved forward to take the places of the *hastati* while the latter retired to the relative safety of the second line. Or should greater pressure on the enemy be needed, the maniples of the *principes* could simply be brought forward into the front line beside the *hastati*. The third line served as a reserve. In the event that the battle turned against the Romans, the *hastati* and *principes* fell back behind the maniples of the *triarii*, who used their spears to make a last-ditch, defensive stand.

Six military tribunes exercised command of a legion, although precisely how responsibilities were divided up among them in battle is uncertain. When not in combat, charge of the legion rotated among them. A Roman army in this period ordinarily comprised two legions under the command of one of the consuls or a proconsul (usually a former magistrate commanding 'in the place of a consul' – *pro consule*). In addition, a consular or proconsular army was accompanied by an equal or somewhat larger number of troops from Rome's allies (the *socii*). How these forces were armed we do not know, but it is likely that their equipment was similar to that of the legionaries. Allied forces, however, were organised and went into battle in cohorts, larger units than the legions' maniples, perhaps about 600 men strong, and the cohorts in turn were grouped into two wings (*alae*) marshalled to the left and right of the legions in the centre of the battle line. The allied forces were commanded by twelve *praefecti sociorum* (*praefecti* of the allies), who were typically Roman aristocrats. However, each allied contingent also had its own native officers, apparently subordinate to the *praefecti sociorum*. In addition to allied infantry, allied cavalry also served with the legions, usually three times as many as Roman cavalry, so 1,800 in an army of two legions. Thus a full consular army would number at least 18,000 men and perhaps as many as 26,500, depending on the number of soldiers levied from the allies.

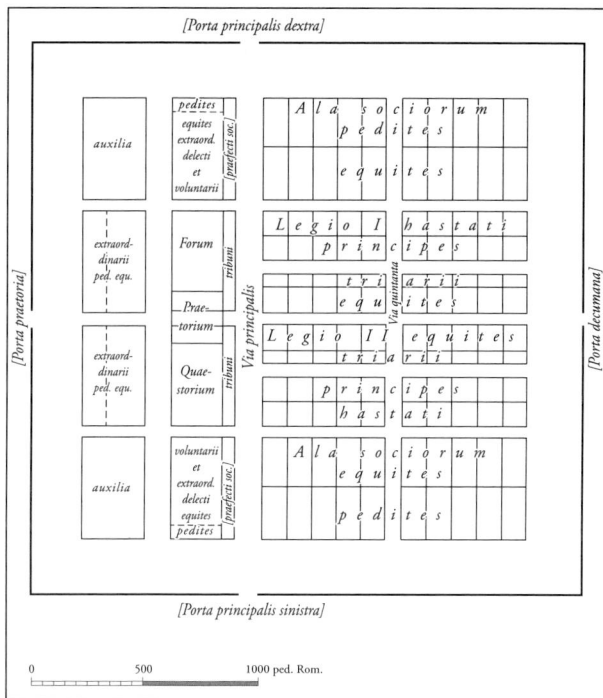

Figure 11 The layout of a Roman army camp according to Polybius. From E. Fabricius, 'Some notes on Polybius's description of Roman camps', *JRS* 22 (1932), 79.

Army encampments

The same high degree of organisation is apparent in republican castrametation, or the laying out of camps.[21] Polybius once again provides a detailed description in book 6 of how Roman armies in his day laid out their encampments, and unusually for this era archaeological evidence enables us to compare his description with the physical remains of a near-contemporary winter encampment at Numantia in Spain. The latter in all probability was occupied by the forces of the consul Q. Fulvius Nobilior during the winter of 153–152 (see below, p. 228). Excavated in the early twentieth century by Adolph Schulten, this camp, which he designated Lager III, along with a number of others in the same region and associated with Rome's long war in eastern Spain between the mid-150s and the

21. M. Dobson, *The Army of the Roman Republic: The Second Century* BC, *Polybius and the Camps at Numantia, Spain*, Oxford: Oxbow Books, 2008.

capture of Numantia in 133, preserve in stone a record of how the tents and other structures in Roman marching camps were organised.[22] Once again, we cannot be certain that castrametation practices remained unchanged between 290 and 150; in all likelihood minor modifications of one sort or another were introduced. However, we know that the Romans were paying careful attention to the organisation of their armies' camps early in the third century. Plutarch, probably drawing on authors contemporary with the Pyrrhic war, reports that Pyrrhus was amazed by the discipline and good order in the Roman camp he saw in 280 (*Pyrrh.* 16.4–5). Latin authors, however, claim that the Romans first learned the arts of castrametation when they captured Pyrrhus' camp following their victory at Maleventum in 275 and were able to observe its layout (Front. *Str.* 4.1.14; cf. Livy, 35.14.8). Whatever the truth of the matter, the evidence at least agrees that the Romans had adopted a sophisticated and rational organisation for their military camps from 275 if not earlier.

The striking feature of both Polybius' ideal camp and Lager III is the way in which the soldiers' living quarters mirror their places within the legion's organisation. Each type of maniple has its own line of tents or huts, and each maniple of that type is housed in its own group of tents or huts. The tents or huts are uniform in size; their arrangement in relation to one another and the areas they occupy are similar; and the blocks of tents and huts are dressed in straight lines along broad streets allowing easy access into and out of each maniple's area. The evidence of the encampments allows us to go even further into the legions' organisational structure, for it reveals that each maniple was subdivided not only into two centuries but into groups of eight tent-mates (*contubernales*) who slept, cooked their meals, and ate together. The fact that the physical arrangement of the living quarters of the maniples of *hastati*, *principes*, and *triarii* mirrored their place within a legion's order of battle further suggests that the groups of *contubernales* may also have fought as a unit within their maniple when the legion saw combat, each group forming one file within it. Be that as it may, what is crucial to note is that once the maniples formed up in the open areas that their tents or huts were grouped around, they could move out into the street in front and then march out of camp

22. A. Schulten, *Numantia: Die Ergebnisse der Ausgrabungen 1905–1912*, 4 vols, Munich: F. Bruckmann, 1914–31.

Lager III

Figure 12 Schulten's reconstruction of the layout of Lager III at Numantia. From A. Schulten, *Numanita: Die Ergebnisse der Ausgrabungen 1905–1912. Band IV. Die Lager bei Renieblas*. München: F. Bruckmann a.-g. 1929. Plan XVII.1.

marshalled for battle with only a minimum of further manoeuvre necessary to form the *quincunx*.

The principal divergence between the camp Polybius sketches and Lager III lies simply in the fact that topography forced modifications to Polybius' ideal plan. Lager III was situated on the top of a hill, and irregularities in its shape made it impossible to align everything along the perfect 90-degree grid that Polybius describes. Adaptations had to be made, but the arrangements of the remains of the barracks reveal quite clearly the efforts the soldiers made to preserve the fundamental structure of the ideal camp, especially in the location of the barracks blocks along the roads transecting it and the position of the commander's quarters (the *praetorium*) and other common spaces (forum and *quaestorium*) in the middle. The main difference lies in the location of the quarters of the *socii* along the western edge of the camp rather than between the legions' tents and the outer wall where Polybius locates them. However, like the maniples' barracks, the huts of each allied cohort are grouped around an open space enabling them to assemble in their ranks and then move into the street ready for battle. Marching camps were fortified with a ditch and a palisade of stakes, which the soldiers carried with them, embedded in the mound of dirt heaped up from the trench in front. Each soldier also carried his own armour and weapons, but a mule was supplied for each group of *contubernales* to transport its tent and other common equipment. The soldiers built camps every time an army halted for the night or established itself for a longer period to undertake operations in a particular area or to pass the winter, as at Lager III, when more permanent structures were constructed to afford the troops better protection from the elements.

The image that emerges from a careful examination of the republican army and its encampments is of an entity constructed out of small, tough, uniform blocks of men – the *contubernales* – that were then combined into progressively larger entities – the centuries, maniples or cohorts, legions, and *alae* – all culminating in a consular army. That gave their forces great staying power in combat, for an enemy had to defeat not a single army but many individual blocks of men, of varying size, in order to win. And the toughness of those blocks was reinforced through being replicated in the ways that the solders lived when they were not fighting, in how they ate, slept, and marched as well as how they undertook various duties like mounting the night guard in and around the camp. All this strengthened the small-unit cohesion – that is, the soldiers' loyalty to their tent-mates and their determination not to let them down in the life-and-death struggle of hand-to-hand fighting – that was essential to their ability to withstand the stress of combat without crumbling into panic and disarray.

Preserving good order in camp and in combat, however, required not simply the maintenance of an extraordinary level of discipline within the ranks but a remarkable degree of organisational skill on the part of the officers. Rome's constant warmaking proved a considerable advantage here, as lessons learned in one campaign could immediately be put into practice in subsequent years. By Polybius' day, too, handbooks existed to instruct officers in their duties, for it is generally thought that Polybius took his description of the ideal army camp and many of the other details he preserves about the Roman army from just such a work. Critical also was continuity of personnel, particularly at the level of centurion. Consuls served for only one year, and while at times, especially during the Hannibalic war and in the second century, the senate might extend a consul's command beyond his year in office so that he became a proconsul, such appointments usually did not last for more than a year or two. The military tribunes of the four consular legions were elected annually and served for a year, although they, too, might continue in their posts if their legions' commander became a proconsul. Stronger continuity, however, lay at the level of the centurions and the enlisted men. Both served over a number of years, probably six for legionaries in the third century and ten beginning with the Hannibalic war, and some centurions may have continued in service even longer, so that techniques developed, knowledge acquired, lessons learned, and discipline instilled were preserved over that time and could be passed on through them to younger recruits.

Waging war

The same organisational sophistication apparent in army encampments is also evident in the logistical arrangements that supported Roman warfare.[23] To operate for any length of time, a Roman army had to be fed as well as furnished with a variety of other supplies, and a force of 20,000–25,000 men required between 600 and 700 tonnes of wheat alone every month. Ancient armies could 'live off the land' for only a very limited period during the year, because grains in the Mediterranean region are ready to harvest only during the early or mid-summer, depending on latitude and elevation. After the harvest, crops were stored behind city walls or hidden, while prior to the harvest unripe grains are inedible. So while an army could sustain itself for a time from the crops its enemy had sown in the summer, if this was its only source of food, this also meant

---

23. P. Erdkamp, *Hunger and the Sword: Warfare and Food Supply in Roman Republican Wars (264–30 B.C.)*, Amsterdam: J. C. Gieben, 1998.

that it could campaign only when the grain was ripe, which imposed serious limitations on the length of its operations and timing. In order to campaign well before and after this window, which the Romans regularly did during the third and second centuries (see below), they needed logistical support. The soldiers themselves could only carry enough food for a few days, so the remainder required some other form of transport. Mules furnished this for short distances, but mules cannot carry more than about 100 kg of weight, and that posed two problems. In the first place, 600 tonnes of wheat would necessitate a pack train of 6,000 mules just for the army's monthly food rations, in addition to the mules carrying the tents and other equipment of each group of *contubernales*. Pack trains that large would have seriously hindered an army's mobility. Moreover employing pack animals to transport the food necessitated feeding them and their drivers as well (horses and mules cannot live exclusively 'off the land' either unless they spend all day grazing), so that the animals had to carry their own food as well as the soldiers' and muleteers'. Because pack animals eat what they are carrying and their loads are limited, over the course of several days of travel the animals consume everything on their backs. The Romans' solution was to organise a more complex network of magazines, generally in friendly towns, where food could be stockpiled. In some cases, grain was requisitioned from Roman allies in the area or other local populations, with the implied threat that they could find themselves treated as enemies if they did not cooperate. Once Rome acquired the provinces of Sicily and Sardinia, subjects there paid their taxes in grain, and these supplies travelled by sea to coastal depots for trans-shipment to magazines closer to the theatres of operations. The same technique was employed to bring supplies from Italy or other regions of the Mediterranean to the coasts. From there supplies moved to the forward magazines, if possible along rivers, and thence were distributed to the soldiers every few days.

The operation of this logistical system was vital to the Republic's military success. It enabled the Romans to project their power over great distances. A Roman army on the march travelled about 20 km per day with a rest day every four or five days of travel, although greater speeds were possible for limited periods, and difficult terrain could slow substantially the rate of march.[24] An army that could

---

24. D. Proctor, *Hannibal's March in History*, Oxford: Oxford University Press, 1971, 26–34.

only feed itself from the food it carried with it might be restricted to a range of only ten days' march, perhaps no more than 200 km, or no farther than Campania in the south or northern Etruria. The ability to stockpile food along the line of march meant that Roman armies could range across the entire length of the Italian peninsula and ultimately as far as the interiors of Spain or Asia Minor, and once there fight the battles that enabled the Republic to conquer its empire.

Equally important, the logistical system that supported them gave Roman armies tremendous staying power. They could and did remain on campaign for months or even years at a time. Encamped in an enemy's territory, the legionaries and allied troops had all the time they required to destroy systematically the enemy's harvest and agricultural infrastructure in the summer and to prevent ploughing and planting next year's crops in the autumn. Their opponents were then faced with a difficult choice between marching out and fighting to stop the devastation and to regain control of their fields, remaining behind their walls to withstand a lengthy siege, or surrendering. Roman logistical strength contributed much to making the first option extremely dangerous. For soldiers to function effectively in a tactical system as complex as the manipular legion they required discipline and training. The Romans fought their wars with civilian conscripts, not with professional soldiers, and civilians in other states typically came to war with little or no military training beyond the rudiments of weapons handling. Rome's conscripts, however, usually served for several years at a stretch, and they often remained with the standards year round. Those months and years under arms furnished the time that was essential if they were to become skilled with their weapons and to imbibe the discipline and training they needed to move forward and back within their maniples in combat and to fall back or advance by maniples in the *quincunx* formation. Repeated drill welded them into a highly effective force in battle, as did the physical endurance that long marches and the often daily labour of constructing a camp instilled in them, and the habituation to teamwork that the constant practice in cooperating together on these and other projects brought about. The military effectiveness that these technical skills produced complemented and enhanced the bonds of mutual loyalty and support among the soldiers that living in close proximity nourished. An enemy force composed of part-time warriors who organised for war only occasionally and often haphazardly faced steep odds against a well-trained, highly disciplined and motivated Roman army. Withstanding a siege, however, was equally risky, for the same staying power that enabled the Republic's armies to reach this degree of effectiveness in combat also made it possible for them to place an enemy under siege for as long as it took to carry their fortifications by assault or starve them into submission, even if this needed years. Surrender therefore often became the best option. It required that an enemy place themselves and their possessions completely in the power of the Roman general, relying on his good faith (an act termed a *deditio in fidem*) to determine their fate. If the enemy sought to surrender before the Romans began their assault on their walls, they could often obtain terms that protected them from the worst consequences that a defeated enemy could suffer, and these, as noted at the outset of this volume, could be horrible.

Paying for war

All of this cost money, and at the most basic level, Rome's military success rested on the financial resources of the Republic and its allies. Legionaries were paid a modest sum (the *stipendium*), about $3\frac{1}{3}$ asses per day in the second century; centurions and cavalrymen received more. From this *stipendium* the price of their grain rations and other stoppages, for example for weapons or clothing, were deducted. In pay alone, therefore, a legion of 4,500 soldiers meant an annual outlay of about six million asses in the third century, seven million in the second, in addition to the cost of other equipment like tents and mules, and the inevitable additional expenses associated with fighting a war. During the third century (when, owing to a reform of the coinage c. 211 that among other things reduced the official metal content of the as by four-fifths, soldiers received fewer asses but asses worth much more than after 211), Rome levied four legions annually while in the second it was not uncommon for six or eight to be in the field. And the Hannibalic war saw as many as twenty-three legions mobilised in a year, although these were seriously undermanned. The sums required to maintain forces of this size therefore could be colossal. A sense of their magnitude can be gleaned from the fact that in the late third century the amount of wealth needed to meet the minimum financial qualification to become a senator was probably a million asses, so that the *stipendium* for one legion for a single year at that point was equal to the minimum total wealth of six senators. The *socii* paid the

stipendium of the soldiers they sent to fight alongside the legionaries, but as noted above the Republic supplied the wheat that these
troops needed free of charge, lightening the economic burden of
Rome's wars on its allies but adding a considerable expense for the
Republic.

War, in Cato's famous phrase, ought to feed itself (*bellum se
ipsum alet*; Livy, 34.9.12), and the senate made sure it did as often
as possible. The senate regularly demanded large sums of money
from those its armies conquered in order to offset the cost of their
subjugation, and in addition generals regularly deposited a portion
of the spoils their troops had taken in the treasury. But these prizes
came only at the end of a campaign; initiating and sustaining a war
for months or years until it was won required cash up front. Unlike
modern governments, the Republic could not simply print money,
while devaluing the coinage by reducing its precious metal content
risked serious economic repercussions. And deficit financing was
almost unheard of. The funds to fight Rome's wars came from an
assessment known as the *tributum* levied on all Roman citizens who
were *assidui* and not serving in the army.[25] The *tributum* was not a
tax in the modern sense but something akin to a compulsory loan
from the *assidui* to the Republic in order to pay the legionaries. The
assidui were assessed at a percentage of the personal wealth that they
had declared before the censors. The exact assessment is not known
but it was probably well under 1 per cent. These funds were
collected not by government officials but by men within each tribe,
the tribunes of the treasury (*tribuni aerarii*). They paid over the sums
required first and then collected (or tried to collect) from each of
their fellow tribesmen that portion of the money he owed.

Financing republican warfare thus depended in the first instance
on those citizens wealthy enough to serve as *tribuni aerarii*, but the
relentlessness of Rome's warfare would quickly have bankrupted
these men if they had not been able to recoup at least most of what
they had advanced to the treasury from the other members of their
tribe. In other words, Rome's military strength required a large
number of at least moderately prosperous *assidui* who could be
tapped to fund the start-up costs of campaigns. This was the case
until the early decades of the second century, when the indemnities
that Carthage and the great Hellenistic kingdoms had to pay following their defeats began to flow into the treasury along with the

25. Nicolet, *World of the Citizen*, 149–206.

extraordinarily rich hauls of booty from the victories over the latter as well as the profits from mines in Spain. The greatest of these came with the conquest and destruction of the kingdom of Macedon in 167, when the capture of the royal treasury enabled the senate to suspend the collection of *tributum* indefinitely. Before that date, creating, maintaining, and enlarging the class of *assidui* was key to sustaining the Republic's military efforts throughout the third and much of the second centuries. This was done in several ways.

In the first place, although throughout the third century the senate repeatedly increased the number of Romans through grants of citizenship until by 225 the number of adult male citizens approached 275,000, until the Hannibalic war the *patres* typically levied only four legions annually, about 18,000 men. In other words, the expansion was not aimed primarily at increasing the size of the army. It was instead a way of increasing the number of taxpayers and so lightening the burden on each: the more *assidui* there were, the less each had to pay in order to furnish the army's *stipendium*. As a corollary, the more *assidui* there were on the rolls, the shorter the time each might have to serve with the legions, although it is not clear that in these years the obligation to perform military service was viewed as a burden by those Rome recruited. The same held true for the *socii*; the more of them there were, the lighter the burdens of conscription and taxation on each. Secondly, because the *tributum* was technically a loan to the treasury rather than a tax, it was repaid to the *assidui* whenever circumstances permitted. In 187, for example, following the defeat of Antiochus, the king of Syria, and the return of the victorious army laden with spoils, the booty was used to pay back arrears in the *tributum* owing to the citizens (Livy, 39.7.4–5). How often the senate could authorise this we do not know, but obviously such a step was very popular among the *assidui*, and given the competitiveness of politics, we might expect individual senators or the *patres* collectively to have returned at least some of the costs of Rome's wars to the citizens whenever possible. This was crucial, for Rome went to war almost every year over the 150 years of the middle Republic, and where we have figures for the sums victorious generals brought to the treasury, they rarely represented more than the cost of the legionaries' *stipendium* alone.[26] Even with

26. N. Rosenstein, 'War, wealth, and consuls', in H. Beck, A. Duplá, M. Jehne, and F. Pina Polo (eds), *Consuls and res publica. Holding High Office in Republican Rome*, Cambridge: Cambridge University Press, 2011.

so many *assidui* to share the burden, had the citizens not been able to recover at least some of what they contributed in *tributum*, its exaction would soon have bled them white.

In other ways, too, the profits from the Republic's conquests found their way into the hands of its citizens. During its wars in Italy, the senate regularly required those it defeated to cede some or even all of their farmlands to Rome. That land became the public property of the Roman people (*ager publicus populi Romani*), and a not inconsiderable portion of it was handed out to citizens and allies who needed farms, either in the form of allotments in officially organised colonies or in individual (viritane) plots. This practice not only enabled poor citizens and *socii* to get a fresh start and establish prosperous, independent farms. It also enabled Rome and its allies to escape the deleterious effects of population growth. Land is a finite resource, and in an economy almost entirely based on farming with pre-industrial agricultural technology, an expanding population sooner or later reaches the point where the productive capacity of the farmland can no longer support the number of people who need to be fed. Had Rome and its allies not been able to acquire additional land, they would have seen most of their people gradually descend into poverty. Roman (and many Italian) families practised partible inheritance, meaning that a family's wealth was divided equally among all its children. Daughters received their portion when they married, as a dowry, while sons usually obtained theirs when their father died. When families had several children who survived to adulthood, as is common in populations that are expanding, they faced the prospect of leaving those children with a share of the family's wealth, typically land, that was less than half of the total. When those children wed partners who brought an equal amount of wealth to the marriage, the resulting household would wind up with less than the household of one or both sets of parents. Repeated over successive generations, the result is a steady decline in the size of many farms and consequently the ability of the family on them, among other things, to pay the *tributum*. Conquest obviated this danger. Families with more sons and daughters than their land could support as adults on independent farms were able to find the additional land they needed in new establishments in colonies or through viritane distributions of *ager publicus*. Even apart from the new farms that the increase of *ager publicus* permitted, this land was available to families to cultivate whose farms were inadequate to support those living on them and so to bring their productive capacities into balance with their economic needs. In these ways, Rome's absorption of much of Italy's best farmland sustained the prosperity of the Republic's ordinary citizens and those of its allies.

Preference in enrolling volunteers for colonial foundations may have gone to citizens and allies who had served as soldiers, forging a direct link between warfare and civilian prosperity. A similar connection obtained where booty was concerned. Polybius has left a detailed account of how Roman armies sacked cities. As he explains, after the civilian population had been thoroughly cowed by a brief but vicious reign of terror, half the soldiers were detailed to stand guard while the other half were sent to plunder. These troops brought the loot back to a central place, where it was equally divided among those who had collected it and those who had protected them (10.15.4–16.9). And perhaps it happened like this, at least sometimes. But plenty of other evidence indicates that despoiling the enemy occurred in a much more disorganised scramble with every man for himself.[27] Nevertheless, the point to stress is that soldiers expected to make money from the victories they won. The consuls of 264 could sway the assembly to approve aid to the Mamertines by pointing out the plunder soldiers could expect to win in the war (see above, p. 57). Almost a century later in 172 volunteers rushed to enrol when the consuls were levying an army for the Third Macedonian War because people had seen those who had gone to fight previous wars in the east come back rich (Livy, 42.33.6). And when those expectations were disappointed, as they were by Aemilius Paullus, the general who gained the victory in that war, the political consequences could be serious. Paullus had not allowed his men to plunder the royal treasury, much to their disappointment, and when they returned to Rome, their anger nearly cost Paullus his triumph (Livy, 45.34.1–7, 35.5–36.7; Plut. *Aem.* 29.1–3, 30.2–31.1; see below, p. 223). Whatever the troops grabbed for themselves or received as a share in camp was separate from the booty and indemnities a general brought back to deposit in the treasury, a portion of which, if he celebrated a triumph, he customarily distributed to each of his men, Romans and allies alike. The sums were often small, but their value in a much less monetised world than ours was probably greater than the figures suggest.[28] Moreover, even

27. A. Ziolkowski, '*Urbs direpta*, or how the Romans sacked cities', in J. Rich and G. Shipley (eds), *War and Society in the Roman World*, London: Routledge, 1993, 61–91.
28. Brunt, *Italian Manpower*, 393–4.

apart from loot, military service put money in soldiers' purses. We do not know how much of a typical legionary's *stipendium* was left over after deductions for food and other items. But over several years of service a recruit ought to have been able to accumulate some savings, and with a bit of capital an enterprising soldier might find additional ways to make money. During the winter of 196–195, Boeotian civilians murdered a considerable number of Roman and allied soldiers stationed in Greece for the money they carried as they travelled around the region on personal business (Livy, 33.29.2–4). It may be that regular access to cash and privileged status as soldiers of a conquering power often afforded opportunities to the men serving with the legions that they were able to exploit for private gain.

In one way or another, at least some of the wealth that the Republic's victories produced found its way back to ordinary Romans and allies and so helped to foster a general prosperity in much of Italy during the third and part of the second centuries. We can glimpse that prosperity as it applied to Rome in a small episode that occurred during the Second Punic War.[29] In 214, the senate determined to build 100 new warships, but it faced a dearth of *proletarii* to serve as oarsmen for the fleet. It therefore decreed that citizens should furnish slaves to row these ships. Romans who had been rated by the censors of 220 BC at 50,000 asses (or had attained this level in the intervening years) were to supply one slave and six months' pay; those worth 100,000 asses provided three sailors and a year's pay; citizens at 300,000 asses were to furnish five slaves; those worth a million, seven; and senators, eight (Livy, 24.11.7–9). The first two sums correspond to wealth that defined citizens of the third and first census classes, and the implications of this fact need to be underscored. The *patres* expected that men squarely in the middle of the Republic's socio-economic hierarchy would own (or be able to purchase) at least one adult male slave while those in the first census class could be called upon to contribute three. Furthermore, the size of the first census class was not small. We know that the number of citizens qualified for cavalry service *equo privato* (with their own horse) stood in 225 at 23,000. These men were part of the first census class, but their wealth was greater than the minimum that qualified a citizen for first-class status. Hence the first census

29. N. Rosenstein, 'Aristocrats and agriculture in the middle and late Republic', *JRS* 98 (2008), 5–8.

class as a whole is likely to have been substantially larger than 23,000. And one might further expect that out of a total adult male citizen population of around 300,000, many more than 23,000 would fall into the second and third census classes. In other words, the senate's decree of 214 reveals that slave ownership was widespread within the Roman population, extending well into its middle reaches. Families that owned a slave or two can hardly be thought of as impoverished; slaves were valuable commodities that represented a substantial portion of a family's capital. Rome by the late third century had become a society with a sizeable component of citizens who could be described as of the 'middling sort' – not rich but certainly not scraping out a bare subsistence for their families on inadequate holdings. And there is every reason to believe that Roman warfare helped to underwrite their prosperity.

War, agriculture, and families

One additional element contributed to the ability of the Republic's citizens and allies to sustain its constant warfare, and that was a solution to the inherent conflict between warfare and agriculture.[30] The Republic conscripted the men who served its legions and fought in the *alae* from Italy's farms. The *stipendium* enabled them to campaign year round for years on end, but while they were burning the enemy's crops in the early summer, their own harvests were ripening. While they were mounting a blockade or preventing their opponents from sowing next year's harvest in the autumn, their own fields needed to be tilled and planted. During the fifth and much of the fourth centuries, the conflict did not occur because Rome fought its wars relatively close to home and during those times of the year, mainly in the summer, when soldiers' labour was not needed on their farms. Armies could be disbanded in the late summer and the soldiers sent home to tend their fields until they reassembled in the late spring if necessary to protect their crops until they were harvested. However, as the Republic's conquest of Italy in the later fourth and third centuries took its armies farther and farther afield and began to require year-round military service, Roman warfare threatened to undermine the viability of the farms that supplied its soldiers.

Rome's ability to mobilise its citizens and allies for year-round

30. Rosenstein, *Rome at War*, 26–106.

warfare and for several years at a stretch now depended on fitting military operations not into the annual crop cycle but into family life-cycles. Roman and Italian men tended to marry later in life, around the age of 30; women wedded earlier, in their late teens or early twenties.[31] Prior to marriage, when the new couple moved away from their parents' homes and established a household on a farm of their own, young men and women lived on their parents' farms. While a substantial number of farms were sizeable, most in this era were fairly modest in size, five or ten hectares, and the challenge facing farms on this scale, even in an age without modern agricultural machinery, is not too little labour but too much. The work that is needed to plant, cultivate, and harvest the wheat and other crops sufficient to feed a family and perhaps provide a bit more to sell or trade is finite. Beyond that point farmers confront the law of diminishing returns at the margin, where the labour expended to produce more food is greater than the pay-off in the yield that it produces. A family consisting of two parents, an 18-year-old son, and two or three other children had more than enough labour at its disposal to meet its needs, since women and children regularly worked in the fields. In these circumstances, conscripting an adult son did not deprive a family of an essential worker but rather removed surplus labour. And for a family whose land barely sufficed to grow enough food to feed itself, conscripting a son removed a hungry mouth from the dinner table and brought the farm's productive capacity more into balance with the needs it had to satisfy.

Viewed from a somewhat different perspective, sending a son off to war was also one among the various strategies of diversification that farming families in the Mediterranean basin long employed to protect themselves from the risks of crop failure. Rainfall there varies greatly from year to year, and in some years not enough falls to yield a harvest large enough to sustain a family until the next year's crops come in. Several dry years in a row could spell disaster for any family that depended almost completely on what it grew for the food it ate, while a range of other calamities – pests, flood, animals, frost, and the like – also threatened ruin. Farmers therefore adopted a range of strategies to ward off the danger of crop failure. They cultivated a variety of crops, so that if one failed the others might get their families through until the next harvest. They stored

31. R. Saller, *Patriarchy, Property and Death in the Roman Family*, Cambridge: Cambridge University Press, 1994, 23–41.

wealth in good years, in the form of jewellery or cattle or anything else that could be traded for food. And when they had a surplus, they lent to neighbours in need with the expectation that the neighbours would reciprocate in kind when the shoe was on the other foot. A son's military service in effect represented one more way of buffering risk. As noted earlier, soldiers hoped and perhaps even expected to profit from their military service, and the loot and savings a son brought back from the wars might constitute one more resource his family could draw on when hard times came.

Conscription, however, might affect a young family, one comprising a recently married couple whose children were only a few years old, quite differently. A mother with small children to care for had far less time to devote to field work than one whose offspring were in their teens or older. In young families, therefore, the father provided the bulk of the labour necessary to feed his wife and children, and one might expect grave hardship to ensue if he were conscripted and served for years on end. Yet the Republic avoided imposing these sorts of burdens on young families for the most part. It limited conscription to men 30 years of age and younger, even though citizens were legally liable for military service up to the age of 46. Moreover, the demands it made on men in their late twenties were considerably diminished by the fact that soldiers in this age group typically served as *triarii*, of whom a legion contained only 600 out of a total complement of 4,200 infantry, 14 per cent of its total strength. In other words, around the time Roman men were getting ready to wed, far fewer of them were being conscripted, and once they had married, the Republic stopped conscripting them at all, leaving them free to devote themselves to the farms that would support their growing families. We have no information about the age structure of allied cohorts, but they probably solved the problem in the same way.

A far more common threat to families from military service arose from the combination of this late marriage age for men and the short life expectancy typical of this era, which is generally estimated to have been around 25 years.[32] This of course does not mean that there were no old or middle-aged people in third- and second-century Italy. The low average life expectancy was caused mainly by very high mortality among the very young. Estimates are that as many as half of all infants born did not survive beyond their fifth year. In

32. Saller, *Patriarchy*, 23–41.

addition, the survivors died at every subsequent age at rates that were significantly higher than we are accustomed to in the modern developed world. These two factors considerably depressed the average life expectancy. For families, this meant that the proportion of them with a father still living and a son in his twenties was very low, from only around a half to as few as a third. In the rest an adult son of conscription age would have represented much if not all of the adult male workforce. During the third century, when four legions were usually levied every year, deferments were awarded to conscripts whose absence would impose a hardship on their families. But when Rome's demand for soldiers skyrocketed in the Hannibalic war, almost every Roman man aged between 18 and 30 had to be called up. The proportion of young men recruited dropped somewhat in the ensuing decades but still remained at least double what it had been prior to 218. Many farms must therefore have been left without men to work the fields after that date.

The consequences, however, are not likely to have been dire. Families with sons in their twenties often also had daughters of marriageable age, and they would have been seeking husbands among those men who were just completing their military service or had already done so. In many cases, therefore, the labour of a son-in-law was able to replace that of a son going off to war. Families in the upper and even the middle of the Roman census classes, as noted earlier, also commonly owned slaves whose labour would have enabled them to carry on in the absence of a son. Less prosperous families, however, will have had to fall back on the labour of those members a son left behind, and in many cases these will have been women. Would they have been capable of undertaking the field work necessary to sow, cultivate, and harvest the grain and other crops they needed to keep themselves alive? Scholars have often supposed they could not, but without good reason. Women in the contemporary third world often make up much of the agricultural workforce, and historically women in Europe and the United States have laboured in the fields when need or circumstances dictated it. Perhaps the most telling instance occurred during the American civil war, when the Confederate States conscripted nearly 75 per cent of the free, white, adult male population, a rate comparable to the mobilisation of Roman citizens during the late third and early second centuries. Southern farms were left with only women and children to work them, and while the hardships they experienced should not be minimised, neither should one ignore the fact that these women and children typically did not starve. They did the farm work they had to do in order to feed themselves, and there is no reason to assume that Roman and Italian women and children in similar circumstances would not have been able to do so as well.

Telamon

More than just a powerful army made Rome strong. Several layers of interlocking support undergirded the Republic's military might. Marriage patterns and the field work of women and children ensured that when the Republic conscripted young men in their late teens and twenties for long service at war, their absences did not undermine the viability of the farms they left behind. Sustaining those soldiers during that time while they were imbued with the training, toughness, discipline, and esprit de corps that welded them into an effective fighting force required money, and the cash came from the *tributum*. That, however, could be a reliable means of funding the commencement and continuation of military operations only because of the financial strength of the Republic's *assidui* who paid it. Creating and maintaining a robust class of at least moderately prosperous citizens was the fruit of several long-term practices: distributing conquered *ager publicus* to poor farmers in need of a fresh start; refunding the *tributum* whenever the profits from victory permitted; enlarging the citizen body to spread the burden of financing warfare widely; and cutting the troops themselves in for a substantial share of the loot. *Tributum* allowed the Republic to pay its legionaries, and savings from their *stipendium* also may have enabled them to return from their time at war with money in their purses. Pay first and foremost, however, enabled Rome's soldiers to buy food while on campaign, but they could do that only when there was food to buy. The armies' commissariat was the product of a sophisticated logistical system that brought grain and other supplies from a variety of sources and moved it through a series of depots and magazines to the front and the soldiers' campfires. The supply chain grew eventually to reach from Italy to the eastern and western ends of the Mediterranean and permitted Rome to project its power into distant theatres of war and sustain campaigns there as long as it took to win. An ability to maintain its armies for many months and years at a stretch in turn enabled their officers and centurions to make successive levies of civilian recruits into skilled soldiers, masters of a complex tactical system, the manipular legion, that made them capable of standing up to and conquering the most formidable foes in pitched battles. Staying power further allowed armies to remain in an enemy's territory devastating their crops and destroying their farm buildings until the Romans compelled their opponents to march out to confront them on the battlefield, where the legions prevailed far more often than not. Or, should an enemy refuse battle and take shelter behind its walls, Roman armies could mount a siege and maintain it until they either carried the fortifications by assault or reduced their enemy to starvation. Against such a powerful combination of threats, surrender was often the best option Rome's opponents had.

Together this system constituted a potent instrument of war – as the Gauls learned to their cost in 225. Near the town of Telamon in western Etruria they confronted one consular army only to discover that the other had landed in their rear. Forming their army to face both threats simultaneously, the Gauls, many of whom fought nude as was their custom, terrified their opponents by their numbers and their war cries. But at the same time the sight of the golden torques and bracelets the Gauls wore fired the Romans and their allies with enthusiasm for the coming battle, spoils to be stripped from the vanquished if they won (Polyb. 2.29.8–9). The fight was long and hard. One consul lost his life in a desperate cavalry mêlée on a nearby hill and had his head brought to the Gallic leaders. But in the end the legions' and their allies' superior discipline, weapons, and staying power prevailed, and when their cavalry, victorious in the fight for the hill, charged the enemy's flank, they utterly destroyed the Gallic army.

Thereafter the senate resolved to eliminate the northern menace once and for all. It sent both consuls with their armies into the Po valley to battle the Boii and their allies the Insubres every year for the next five years. Their campaigns broke the Gauls' resistance and several generals returned to celebrate triumphs, including Flaminius, who as consul in 223 secured his in the teeth of senatorial opposition (Polyb. 2.32.1–33.9; Plut. *Marc.* 4.1–3; Zonar. 8.20). Roman arms advanced as far as the Alps in a show of force to cow the tribes there. The conquest culminated with the foundation in 218 of two potent colonies along the Po, Placentia and Cremona. The six thousand men in each settlement were intended to secure the area and suppress any further outbreaks of trouble there. But trouble would come nevertheless in Gaul, and when it did in that very year, it would prove far beyond the colonists' power to stop. They were barely able to defend themselves, for the trouble arrived in the form of a Punic army led by Hannibal, and before they were finished he and his soldiers would bring not only these colonies but Rome itself to its knees.

CHAPTER 4

Hannibal

Polybius recognised the Romans' war with Hannibal as the turning point: 'For it was their victory over the Carthaginians in this war, and their conviction that thereby the most difficult and most essential step towards universal empire had been taken, which encouraged the Romans for the first time to stretch out their hands upon the rest and to cross with an army into Greece and Asia' (1.3.6). Whether or not they in fact developed a plan for world conquest in the wake of their victory remains controversial; what is indisputable is that within half a century they had become the masters of the Mediterranean. How Rome and Carthage found themselves at war for a second time therefore elicited considerable interest in antiquity and continues to do so to this day. Polybius naturally offers the earliest analysis, although even he was responding to claims put forth by authors a generation earlier (3.8.1–11). Rejecting those explanations, he traced the origins of the war to three causes: the 'wrath of the Barcids'; Rome's seizure of Sardinia; and the Carthaginian conquest of Spain (3.9.6–10.6).

Hamilcar Barca, the father of Hannibal, had commanded the Punic force holding out on Mt Eryx in the final stages of the First Punic War. He had successfully resisted the Romans' assaults and believed that he could have continued to do so if the government at Carthage had not made peace following their defeat at sea in 241. His anger at the Romans (as illogical as it may seem) remained unabated throughout his city's war against its unpaid mercenaries and rebellious subjects and continued during his nine years in command of Carthage's armies in Spain. That anger he passed down to his son. Hannibal himself told the story many years later of how as a youngster of nine he had attended his father as he was sacrificing before setting out for Spain. When the omens proved favourable, Hamilcar asked Hannibal if he wished to go with him. When the boy eagerly replied that he did, Hamilcar led him to the altar and ordered him to lay his hands on the victim and to swear that he would never be a friend to Rome (Polyb. 3.11.1–8). Hamilcar and his son were joined in their hostility by the rest of their countrymen as a consequence of the Republic's seizure of Sardinia and the imposition of an additional war indemnity at the end of the Mercenary war, when Carthage was in no position to resist these new demands. The final cause came into being, in Polybius' view, with Carthage's success in extending its dominion in Spain under Hamilcar, then after his death in 229 under his son-in-law Hasdrubal, and finally under Hannibal when he in his turn succeeded to the command in 221. The money and manpower of Spain furnished the means that enabled Hannibal and his countrymen to requite Rome.

Little of this stands up to scrutiny, however.[1] Hannibal's story of his oath may be true, and very likely he and his family harboured little love for the Romans, but it is a long step from dislike to a decades-long determination to wage war. The Barcids in Spain perhaps were preparing for the possibility that war with Rome would come again, but if so the Romans themselves seem to have been largely oblivious to it. We are told that Roman ambassadors reached Spain around 231, and when they approached Hamilcar and demanded to know what he was up to there, he tartly replied, 'Fighting to get the rest of the money we owe you.' At a loss for how to respond, the envoys departed (Dio Cass. 12.48). The veracity of the episode has been questioned, but whether true or not, it hardly shows that the Romans were worried about the growth of Punic power in Spain. Thereafter Roman interest lapsed (if it had ever arisen in the first place) until 226 or 225, when a delegation (again?) travelled to Spain. These envoys negotiated an agreement with Hasdrubal, now in command, known to scholars as the 'Ebro treaty', although it is very unlikely that this was ever a formal treaty ratified by both governments. Rather, it seems to have been an undertaking on Hasdrubal's part that he would not cross north of the river Ebro in northeastern Spain 'in arms,' that is, to make war (Polyb. 2.13.1–7). What other clauses the agreement contained is uncertain, and nearly everything else about it is mired in controversy. However, one point is beyond dispute and crucial: Hasdrubal had extended Carthaginian sway in the east only as far as the site of New

---

1. B. D. Hoyos, *Unplanned Wars: The Origins of the First and Second Punic Wars*, Berlin: De Gruyter, 1998, 144–259; J. Rich, 'The origins of the Second Punic War', in T. Cornell, B. Rankov, and P. Sabin (eds), *The Second Punic War: A Reappraisal*, London: Institute of Classical Studies, 1996, 1–37, for detailed analyses of the causes and outbreak of the war.

Carthage (modern Cartagena), some 300 km or more south of the Ebro. In other words, by this agreement Rome implicitly or explicitly conceded to Hasdrubal control of a vast swath of as yet unconquered territory in eastern Spain. It is difficult to see how the senate's representatives would have made this concession had the *patres* had the slightest suspicion that Hasdubal was laying the groundwork for a new war against the Republic. The senate had much more immediate worries at this point and much closer to home. Chief among these was the Gallic threat, and Polybius is explicit in linking this to the Ebro accord. Fears about a possible thrust by the Gauls of the Po valley into central Italy had arisen as early as 230, and they were realised in the great Gallic raid of 225 (see above, p. 72). The senate's embassy to Hasdrubal early in 225 or in the prior year finds its context among the several extraordinary measures the *patres* took in anticipation of that crisis. They acted to forestall the prospect of a Punic army marching from Spain to join forces with the Gauls by exacting a promise from Hasdrubal that he would not advance farther north than the Ebro.

Nothing in the years between 236 and 221 therefore suggests that the Republic's leaders saw the Punic enterprise in Spain in and of itself as a growing threat to Rome, and their lack of concern ought to put us on our guard against assuming that Polybius was right, that the Barcid family's conquests there were part of a long-cherished scheme to renew hostilities with Rome. On the other hand, how the senate viewed developments in Spain is complicated by the fact that at some point it extended vague promises of Roman protection to Saguntum, a city in eastern Spain lying well south of the Ebro (Polyb. 3.30.1–2). The date is uncertain and controversial, but the most economical solution to the problem is to assume that the Saguntines surrendered themselves into the protection (*deditio in fidem*) of Rome during the ambassadors' visit to Spain in 226 or 225 (although earlier and later dates have been proposed). Controversy also surrounds the precise nature of the Republic's undertaking to the Saguntines, but it appears that the two parties struck no formal treaty, particularly not one that contained a provision requiring Rome to come to Saguntum's aid if attacked. Even so, it is not easy to see how the senators could square whatever informal, non-binding commitments they made in this case with the implications of the Ebro treaty, which envisioned everything south of the river coming sooner or later under Carthaginian control.

Possibly the senate was well aware of the inconsistency of these two positions, but a growing concern over Punic power in Spain led the *patres* to look upon Saguntum as a potential base of operations should war with Carthage ever come again. Be that as it may, the senators may also have simply expected the Carthaginians to swallow their resentment and submit to Rome carving out an exception to its acquiescence to Punic expansion that the Ebro treaty entailed. In dealing with much of the world, Rome's leaders adopted a position of superiority and took it for granted that lesser states and peoples would acknowledge it. That acknowledgement meant among other things doing Rome's bidding and deferring to its will no matter how unjust it might seem. Insisting that others humble themselves before it was one of the ways in which the Republic projected an image of power that kept other, lesser states and subjects in line and deterred potential challengers from testing its strength. The senators, then, may have expected Carthage, having bowed to Roman arms and surrendered twice already, to bow once again and live with the contradiction between what the Republic appeared to promise in the Ebro treaty and how extending its *fides* to Saguntum violated that understanding. If so, Roman behaviour subsequently at Saguntum only served to drive home that point. For when political discord there threatened to degenerate into violent civil conflict, the two sides agreed to call in the Romans to arbitrate the dispute. And the delegation the senate dispatched certainly did settle the dispute once and for all: they had the leaders of one of the factions, very likely those sympathetic to Carthage, put to death (Polyb. 3.15.7, cf. 30.2).

Still, a display of Roman arrogance, if that is what it was, should not be mistaken for an intent to start a war. Affronts simply served to remind Carthage of its place. Growing Punic power in Spain, however, combined with the accession of a new commander there to stoke a growing anger at such humiliations and to foster a determination to resist further challenges to Carthaginian interests. Yet the events that transformed such sentiments into a decision to go to war originated neither in Rome nor among the Carthaginians but at Saguntum itself. Polybius reports that the Saguntines, relying on the presumption of Roman protection, began attacking neighbouring tribes that were subject to Carthage (3.15.8). This was an intolerable affront. Rome might claim to be Carthage's superior, but Saguntine power was vastly inferior to that of Carthage. On a more pragmatic level, such a challenge could not go unanswered – and unpunished – for if Carthage did not respond forcefully and effectively, there would be little reason for other tribes that had submitted to remain submissive if Carthage would not protect them. And if the Saguntines could attack Carthaginian subjects with impunity, emulators would not be far behind. That prospect posed the threat not only of disaffection and rebellion within Carthage's Spanish empire but of appeals to Rome by other cities and tribes in Spain seeking protection and eventual Roman intervention. Just such appeals had set in motion the Punic response to the Mamertines' *deditio* to Rome in 264 and Tarentum's decision to open hostilities when Rome established a garrison at Thurii in 282. The new Punic commander clearly saw history repeating itself once again and was determined that the outcome would be different this time, for that commander was the son of Hamilcar Barca, Hannibal.

The Spanish army had elevated him to the supreme command in 221 following Hasdrubal's death at an assassin's hands, an outgrowth of a private quarrel, and the assembly at Carthage subsequently ratified the soldiers' choice. Hannibal was about 27 years old at that point and had spent the greater part of his life being schooled in the arts of war and command by his father and brother-in-law. He put those skills immediately to use, leading his forces on two campaigns that extended Carthaginian power as far north as the Ebro. Polybius claims that Hannibal's father had counselled him to avoid conflict with Saguntum in order to deny Rome a pretext for war (3.14.10). It seems unlikely that Hamilcar would have seen an attack on Saguntum as inviting a Roman war declaration since Hamilcar died in 229, long before Saguntum placed itself under Rome's protection, whatever date one prefers for that event. Rather, Hannibal's thrusts north simply continued his father's and Hasdrubal's policy of consolidating Punic power in Spain. However, in the winter of 220, he found that he could no longer ignore Saguntum's attacks upon their neighbours without compromising his country's and his family's achievements in Spain. Nor could he fail to recognise the looming prospect of Roman involvement, for when he and his army returned to their winter quarters at New Carthage, he found a Roman delegation, dispatched by the senate in response to the urgent summons of the Saguntines. For now that Punic arms had subdued everything around them, they foresaw that Hannibal would direct his army against them next.

The envoys' interview with the Punic general did not go well (Polyb. 3.15.1–13). They enjoined him to leave Saguntum alone and to abide by Hasdrubal's agreement to remain south of the Ebro.

An older man might have temporised, but Hannibal was young and flushed with his recent victories. And he was no friend of the Romans. They were dictating commands as if to an inferior, and Hannibal refused to knuckle under. He charged the Romans with bad faith in their recent actions in Saguntum, where instead of impartially arbitrating between the city's factions they had unjustly ordered the leaders of one side put to death. Hannibal asserted that he was the true guardian of the Saguntines and would not overlook the Romans' bad faith, a pointed dig at their claims that the Saguntines had placed themselves under Rome's *fides*. The conference ended on that sour note, and the envoys left convinced, Polybius says, that war was on the way.

If so, their colleagues back in Rome did not agree. Rather than muster their forces for an impending clash with Carthage, the *patres* elected to dispatch both consuls east to deal with a second outbreak of Illyrian piracy in the southern Adriatic. Meanwhile, that same spring Hannibal marched his army north and laid siege to Saguntum. Having stood up to the senate's dictates, in effect announcing that he and Carthage had finished taking orders from Rome, and with his government's blessing, he prepared to back up his words with actions. If a new war with Rome was on the way, Hannibal would see to it that his rear was secure, that Roman armies had no base of operations in Saguntum, and that any tribes or towns contemplating a similar appeal to Rome had a vivid object lesson in just what Roman guarantees of protection were worth in Spain. Yet the city proved a tough nut to crack. The Saguntines heroically withstood eight months of assaults before Hannibal was finally able to storm its defences. Despite tales that the Saguntines elected to destroy their wealth and to die fighting or by suicide rather than surrender (Livy, 21.14.1–4), the spoils from the town, including captives, filled Hannibal's war chest (Polyb. 3.17.9–10).

All during this time the Romans did nothing to help Saguntum. To be sure, their forces were fully occupied in Illyria (in the western Balkans), but there is also reason to suspect that the senators themselves were in some doubt about how to respond to Hannibal's aggression, if the accounts of long deliberations among them that Polybius says he found in some earlier authors took place in 219, while the siege was going on, rather than in the winter of 219–218 after its fall (3.20.1). The Republic's obligations to protect Saguntum had not been sanctified by a treaty. The informal *fides* that the senate had offered left it largely up the senators themselves to

decide just what *fides* entailed in such cases. Some may have felt
that the Saguntines had brought Hannibal down upon them themselves by attacking Carthaginian subjects. The sentaors might
also have considered that by the Ebro accord they in addition had
conceded everything south of the river to Carthaginian control,
which presumably included Saguntum. We get a strong hint of
the discomfort the *patres* may have felt about going to war over
Saguntum in the fact that later Roman writers emphasised
Hannibal's crossing of the Ebro on his march to Italy, thereby
placing the responsibility for starting the war squarely and unequivocally on Hannibal's shoulders. Some authors went so far as to claim
Saguntum was north of the river or that the accord specifically
exempted it, just to leave no doubt that Hannibal was in the wrong
in attacking the town (e.g. Livy, 21.2.7; App. *Hann.* 2–3, *Hisp.* 7;
Zonar. 8.21; even Polyb. 3.30.3!). The *patres* probably also realised
that Spain was a long way from Italy and that a lengthy campaign
there would present serious logistical challenges. The first war with
Carthage had lasted more than twenty years and entailed serious
losses as well as very high costs. So the senate waited, hoping
perhaps as the siege wore on that it would fail and spare them
the necessity of coming to a decision.

When the city finally fell, however, a response could no longer be
avoided. Polybius claims that there was no debate (3.20.1), and he
is certainly correct. A Roman embassy had warned Hannibal
off Saguntum, and he had not only ignored that warning but
brutally sacked the town and enslaved the surviving inhabitants. The
Republic's credibility was on the line. Yet the senate's response still
stopped short of war. In the spring of 218, a high-level delegation
headed by M. Fabius Buteo, consul in 245, censor, and *princeps
senatus*, and including the consuls of the previous year left Rome for
Carthage. When they came before the senate there, they demanded
that Hannibal and his advisors be handed over. Otherwise there
would be war. The Carthaginian senators protested that Hannibal
had been well within his rights in attacking Saguntum since it was
not included among those allies of either side whose security was
guaranteed by the treaty that ended the First Punic War. For the
Romans, however, the time for discussion was long past. They had
laid down an ultimatum regarding Saguntum, and Hannibal had
flagrantly violated it with his capture of the city. The senators at
Carthage would have to choose: they could humble themselves once
again in the face of Rome's demand, a climb-down that was very

likely to entail the loss of much of their empire in Spain since Carthaginian control was closely bound up with the loyalty of the subject tribes to the Barcid family, and surrendering Hannibal meant removing the tribes' ties to Carthage. Or the Carthaginians could fight. The choice was theirs, and the Roman delegation sought to make it unavoidable. In a memorable gesture, Fabius gathered the folds of his toga over his arm and proclaimed that in those folds he brought war or peace, and he would give the Carthaginians whichever of the two they preferred. The Carthaginian spokesman responded that Fabius should let fall whichever he chose. When Fabius released the folds of his toga and announced that he gave them war, the senators shouted, 'We accept!', and the war was on (Polyb. 3.20.6–21.8, 33.1–4; Livy, 21.18.1–14).

Neither side appears to have been eager to start this war, but each faced irresistible imperatives to embrace it when it came rather than accept the alternatives. Carthage had recovered and then surpassed its former strength by 218. It would no longer be dictated to by Rome, especially when those dictates threatened the foundations of that strength, its hard-won empire in Spain. Some may even have anticipated a rematch against Rome sooner or later and viewed the city's Iberian dominions as ensuring that the outcome this time would be different. Hannibal, too, could not ignore the Roman challenge without seeing his country's and his family's achievement begin to slip away. Neither he nor his government was prepared to let Saguntum become another Messana. Rome had staked its credibility, its *fides*, on the fate of Saguntum, and the fall of that city left it no alternative but to exact a fitting retribution in order to vindicate its good faith. Its hegemony in Italy was founded on the twin pillars of fear of swift and terrible retaliation and the credibility of the protection Rome's *fides* offered. If anyone is to blame for starting the war, it is the Saguntines themselves, who attacked neighbouring subjects of Carthage relying on nothing more than vague assurances of Roman protection. But they had no desire to fall under Carthaginian domination, which must have appeared increasingly likely as Hannibal subjugated the regions around them. While their actions set in motion the train of events that ultimately issued in the Second Punic War, they had no intention of starting it. The unforeseen and unintended consequences of short-term decisions in an international system in which honour was paramount, and where the continual need of nations to demonstrate their might in order to keep subjects in line and deflect challenges,

brought about a war that nobody wanted but each side was willing
to accept rather than back down.

The march to Italy

When word reached Hannibal at New Carthage that war had been
declared, his preparations for the invasion of Italy were already well
under way.[2] He certainly understood that his defiance of Rome over
Saguntum would all but inevitably lead to war. The only question
was how to fight it.[3] He had undoubtedly learned from his father
and other, older Carthaginians how his city's previous conflict with
Rome had gone, and especially how despite repeated setbacks –
horrific losses at sea and the destruction of Regulus' army in Africa
– the Romans had fielded new armies and launched new fleets in
order to renew the contest. He understood that the Republic's
enormous reserves of manpower had made these recoveries possible.
For him to remain on the defensive, therefore, and wait for the
Romans to march against him in Spain was out of the question. For
even if he defeated their initial thrust, another army would come,
and another, and another; sooner or later one of them would
defeat him. And a Roman army operating in Spain would have
ample opportunity to sow disaffection and revolt among Carthage's
Spanish subjects, thereby robbing him of strength while augmenting
Rome's. His only hope for victory lay in attacking the core of Roman
military strength, those same manpower reserves. He may also have
understood that that strength consisted of two distinct parts. One
comprised the Roman citizens. Hannibal may not have known their
precise number, but must have known that they numbered many
thousands. The other component consisted of the *socii*. There were
many thousands of these, too, but they were quite heterogeneous.
Some were longstanding partners like the Latin colonies; others like
the Gauls of the Po valley had only recently been subdued and
remained unreconciled to their new status as Roman subjects;
others still like the Samnites and Lucanians were perennially restive
and ready to throw off the Roman yoke if only there were some

2. J. F. Lazenby, *Hannibal's War: A Military History of the Second Punic War*, Warminster: Aris and Phillips, 1978; A. Goldsworthy, *The Punic Wars*, London: Cassell,
2000, 167–309.
3. M. Fronda, *Between Rome and Carthage: Southern Italy during the Second Punic
War*, Cambridge: Cambridge University Press, 2010, 34–50, for a succinct critical survey
of scholarly opinion on Hannibal's strategy.

assurance of success. Rome's Achilles heel lay in the potential
for revolt among these last groups, for rebellion simultaneously
raised up enemies as it diminished the Republic's military resources.
Hannibal could assume that many of the *socii* would prefer freedom
to Roman dominance. What kept them quiescent was Rome's
overwhelming military power and the certainty that any attempt to
break free would fail and that terrible punishment would follow.
Occasional object lessons, such as the destruction of Falerii after its
futile attempt at revolt in 241, drove that point home. As long as
Roman armies appeared invincible, Roman dominance in Italy and
hence Roman military power stood firm.

It is very likely, too, that Hannibal had not only imbibed the
lessons of Carthage's first war with Rome but also learned much
from Pyrrhus' campaigns more than sixty years earlier. Contemporary accounts were available in Greek, including Pyrrhus' own
memoirs, and Hannibal was conversant with that language. There is
every reason to think not only that as a student of war-craft
he would have sought out everything the Hellenistic world had
to teach on that score, but that as someone contemplating a war
against Rome he would have been particularly interested in Pyrrhus'
experiences. For Pyrrhus had beaten the Romans soundly in two
pitched battles, and those victories had provoked revolts in
Samnium, Lucania, and Apulia, while his march north in 280 may
have aimed to rally the Etruscans to his cause. Pyrrhus, in other
words, had been well on his way to assembling a powerful coalition
of rebellious Roman subjects who, joined to the Greek cities of
southern Italy, increased his strength while simultaneously sapping
Rome's. Had he not thrown over his Italian enterprise to pursue
the chimera of conquering Sicily, he might well have succeeded in
destroying the Republic's *imperium*.

Roman power was vulnerable if the *socii* could be induced to
revolt in large enough numbers to offset the great military potential
that Rome's citizen body represented. Pyrrhus had demonstrated
that victory over Roman arms was the key to inciting those revolts,
and Hannibal had what it took to win similar victories. He had
studied war from his youth not only in books but at the feet of
two superb commanders, his father and his brother-in-law. His own
conquests during his first two campaigns in Spain demonstrated
that he had learned well from them. In addition, he had a deeply
loyal army of African and Spanish infantry and cavalry. But most
importantly, he possessed a tactical skill that enabled him to deploy

his forces in novel and unexpected ways that could neutralise superior numbers, capitalise on the element of surprise, and exploit his opponents' weaknesses. Together, these strengths would enable him to bring the Republic to the brink of annihilation.

To do so, however, meant bringing the war to Italy, and so in June of 218, after taking steps to secure Spain and Africa in his absence, Hannibal set out with perhaps 50,000 infantry, 9,000 cavalry, and 37 elephants.[4] Envoys to the Gauls of northern Italy had preceded his march in order to ascertain their willingness to join him in his war against Rome, and these had returned with affirmative answers prior to his setting out. Hannibal had also endeavoured to secure the permission of tribes living between Spain and the Alps to pass through their lands. Many had acquiesced, but upon reaching the Rhone he found his way barred. Battle and subterfuge were required to bring his army across. Even after a crossing point had been secured, the elephants proved a challenge. His men built a number of substantial piers along the left bank and lashed large rafts to their ends. They drove the elephants along the piers and onto the rafts, which were then cut loose. Boats roped to the rafts towed them and the elephants across to the opposite shore. From there the army made its way north up the valley of the Rhone to its confluence with the Isère, then turned east following the Isère towards the Alps. Hannibal's route across those mountains was disputed even in antiquity, and it remains so today despite many investigations. The most likely candidates for the pass that his army followed over the summit and down into northern Italy are the Col du Monte Cenis and the Col du Clapier, although several others have their supporters (Livy, 21.38.6–9). More important is Polybius' statement that the army reached the top of the pass around the time of the setting of the Pleiades (3.51.1), that is, around the time when this constellation appears to be setting at dawn. This occurs on 7 or 9 November, but the phrase may be stretched to indicate a date towards the end of October as well. Such a late ascent meant that Hannibal's army had to struggle against ice and snow as well as fight its way past attacks from hostile tribes along the way. Two weeks of combat and toil brought them across the mountains and down into the plains after a journey that had taken five months altogether (Polyb. 3.54.3–4; Livy, 21.38.1). Their losses had been heavy:

4. D. Proctor, *Hannibal's March in History*, Oxford: Oxford University Press, 1971, 13–80.

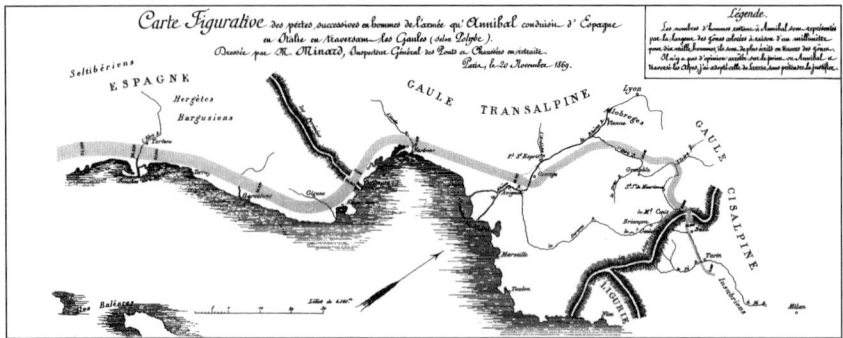

Figure 13 Hannibal's march to Italy. Map drawn by Charles Joseph Minard in 1869 showing the army's route to Italy. The width of the band corresponds to the number of soldiers surviving as the march progressed.

Hannibal reached Italy with only 20,000 infantry and 6,000 cavalry remaining, as he himself recorded on an inscription he erected at Lacinium, which Polybius saw and used as the basis for his report of Hannibal's forces (3.33.18, 56.4). Still, despite losing over half his men, innumerable horses and pack animals, and many of his elephants, he had succeeded in carrying out the first step in his great strategic gamble. He had brought the war to Italy.

And he had brought it just where he needed to. The Gauls of the Po valley, although repeatedly defeated in the years after 225, remained largely unpacified. Two powerful colonies, Placentia and Cremona, containing 6,000 male settlers each, were intended to serve as crucial instruments for effecting that pacification, but the senate had authorised their foundation only towards the end of April 218 out of fear that the Gauls would capitalise on Rome's new war with Carthage to revolt. The colonists arrived on the sites in late May or early June, accompanied by a praetor with a legion and *socii* originally levied for the campaign in Spain to protect them in case of trouble.[5] The senate's precautions were well advised, for the Boii, the Gallic tribe in whose territory the colonies were to be established, attacked soon thereafter, having received word that Hannibal had set out from Spain and would soon arrive to lend them his aid. The onslaught proved too much for both the colonists and the troops, who quickly found themselves besieged. The news impelled the senate to dispatch a second praetor to their relief with another of

5. A. M. Eckstein, 'Two notes on the chronology of the outbreak of the Hannibalic war', *Rh. Mus.*126 (1983), 255–72.

the legions along with 5,000 allies that the consul, P. Cornelius Scipio, was at that time enrolling for service in Spain.

The need to levy two additional legions one after another and muster their complements of *socii* in turn imposed a critical delay in Scipio's getting his campaign off the ground. The senate expected to fight Carthage in North Africa and in Spain, and to that end had ordered the consuls of 218, Scipio and his colleague Ti. Sempronius Longus, to draw lots for these two provinces. Longus got Sicily, the African war, an army, and a fleet while Scipio drew Spain. Both left Rome in late September, but if Scipio had not been burdened with levying additional legions to replace the ones sent to Gaul he would have been able to leave Rome for his province much earlier, and that would have altered the entire course of the war. For after embarking his forces at Pisa and landing them at Massilia (Marseilles), Scipio learned to his amazement that Hannibal was already crossing the Rhone. Scipio expected to find Hannibal still several days' march away and to encounter his forces somewhere west of the Rhone. Had he been able to do so, the Hannibalic war would probably have been fought in southern Gaul rather than Italy and its course would have been very different. Instead, Scipio raced north with his army, but arrived at Hannibal's crossing point three days too late. Realising the pursuit was futile given Hannibal's head start and that a Carthaginian army was now on its way to Italy, Scipio sent his legions on to Spain under the command of his brother, Gnaeus, while he returned in haste to Rome and made his way to the Po valley, where he took command of the two legions already there. His hope was to catch Hannibal and his army as they descended into the plain (Polyb. 3.49.1–4).

Once again the swiftness of Hannibal's march frustrated Scipio's plans. By mid-November Hannibal was already in Italy among the Boii, who had rallied to his cause. The Carthaginian repaid their support by attacking a neighbouring tribe with whom the Boii were at odds and capturing their principal town, the modern Turin. Most of Gaul, however, remained on the sidelines waiting to see how the war progressed. In fact, a large contingent of Gallic cavalry had joined Scipio when he arrived in the north. Hannibal therefore understood that he would have to demonstrate that he could defeat the Romans if he was to succeed in bringing the rest of the Gauls over to his side. He was eager to join battle, as was Scipio in order to crush the incursion before it could provoke further trouble. As the two armies drew near one another, both generals took their cavalry forces and Scipio his light infantry as well and set out to reconnoitre. They encountered one another near the river Ticinus, and in the combat that ensued Hannibal's African cavalry and especially the Numidian contingent proved superior, an early warning of the fatal weakness of Rome's mounted forces. The Romans fled with Scipio himself seriously wounded (Polyb. 3.65.1–66.2). He immediately withdrew his forces south of the Po, fearing the enemy's cavalry. He broke down the bridge his troops had constructed across the river, encamped at Placentia, and awaited the arrival of his colleague, who was marching with his army from Sicily to reinforce him.

Battle at the river Trebia and Lake Trasimene

Sempronius and his legions reached Scipio's camp in late December or early January (Polyb. 3.68.12–75.8). A minor skirmish soon thereafter in which the Roman forces got the better of the enemy encouraged Sempronius to seek a decisive battle as soon as possible, before the new consuls entered office on 15 March and took command of the war, and Hannibal was happy to oblige. He sent out a force of cavalry early one morning with orders to ride up to the Romans' encampment and provoke them to offer battle. Sempronius took the bait despite his colleague's urging him to wait until he was well enough to join Sempronius on the battlefield. On a bitterly cold morning Sempronius quickly marshalled his and Scipio's men and marched them out before breakfast. Their advance towards Hannibal's camp meant fording the chest-high river Trebia, swollen with winter rains and near-freezing, so that they were suffering from cold and hunger as they deployed for battle. Hannibal by contrast kept his men near their tents warming themselves by their fires after their morning meals. He had also hidden his lieutenant Mago and 2,200 infantry and cavalry in a low area screened by woods to the rear of the battlefield. When the battle was fully joined, these troops attacked the Romans in the rear and did great damage. But the battle was really won by Hannibal's cavalry. They quickly drove off the Roman and allied horse on the wings, opening the way for the Carthaginian light-armed troops to attack the flanks of the Roman infantry. This assault prevented the *socii* on either side of the legions from advancing and engaging the heavily armed infantry opposing them. Then the force lying in ambush fell upon the Roman rear, throwing the troops there into confusion. The allies on the flanks turned and fled, pursued by the Carthaginians. In the centre,

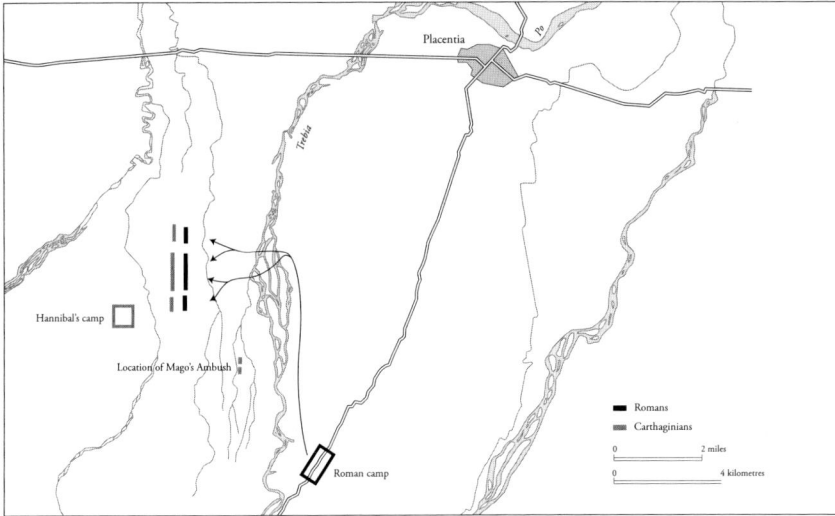

Figure 14 Plan of the battle at the river Trebia.

however, the legions managed to break through the enemy line after a long, hard struggle against their opponents and despite the attack in their rear. Seeing their wings in retreat, realising the battle was lost, and suffering from a severe rainstorm that was now pouring down, they retired in good order to Placentia, about 10,000 in number. Most of the remaining 36,000 died at the hands of the Punic cavalry and elephants as the struggled across the Trebia.

In his dispatch to the senate reporting the results of the battle, Sempronius sought to gloss over the severity of his defeat by claiming that the storm had deprived him of the victory. As other reports reached the *patres*, however, and they realised that their forces had retreated to Placentia, that Hannibal controlled the open country, and that most of the Gauls had joined his cause following the battle, the magnitude of the defeat became apparent. Still, because the legions had broken through the enemy line they remained confident that they could defeat Hannibal in the following year. Accordingly, they made preparations for a show-down then. Meanwhile, the victory enabled Hannibal to secure billets for his weary troops for the winter where they could recover from their wounds and the rigours of their march.

The battle at the Trebia produced another result that would prove enormously helpful to furthering Hannibal's plans, although this was one that he almost certainly did not anticipate. Although

Roman aristocrats competed vigorously with one another for election to public office and for political influence, on a number of key matters they were of one accord, and perhaps none more so than the desirability of restricting high offices and influence with the populace to their own kind. But senatorial authority and the ability of individual aristocrats to attract the voters' support depended very much on the latter's belief that aristocratic leadership benefited the *res publica* and themselves personally. And since in this era those benefits flowed principally from military success, defeat obviously held the potential to undermine that belief, and especially when ambitious outsiders were waiting in the wings to exploit it. Just such a figure was on hand early in 217 in the person of C. Flaminius. As tribune of the plebs in 232 he had forced through the law over the senate's objections that apportioned the *ager Gallicus* south of Ariminum to Roman citizens in individual allotments. On the strength of the popularity that this benefit to the populace had conferred, Flaminius had sought and won the consulship for 223 despite being a *novus homo*. His victory over an army of Gauls in that year had been crowned with a triumph, bestowed exceptionally by a vote of the people once again despite senatorial obstruction (see above, pp. 74 and 117). He had even reached the pinnacle of the *cursus honorum* in 220 with his elevation to the censorship. Yet despite these successes, he persisted in his stance as an opponent of the senatorial nobility, demonstrated as recently as 218 when he alone among the *patres* supported a tribune's bill to forbid senators from owning ocean-going ships (Livy, 21.63.3–4). This stance enabled Flaminius to present himself to the voters at the consular elections for 217, which Sempronius held soon after the defeat at the Trebia, as a critic of aristocratic conduct of the war and the man who could get the job done. The voters agreed and elevated him to a second consulate. However, while members of the *nobilitas* had not only the benefits they had bestowed on the Republic to support their *auctoritas* but in addition those conferred by generations of ancestors, a new man like Flaminius had only his own achievements to rely on. Having proclaimed that he would succeed where the Republic's traditional leaders had failed, he was under great pressure to do so. Fearing that the senate would invent religious flaws in his election in order to deprive him of this second consulate as they had sought to do in his first he left Rome for his army before 15 March, the first day of his consulate. He took up his office exceptionally at Ariminum, without undertaking the vows, sacrifices, and other ceremonies incumbent on a new consul on his first day of office, which could only be carried out at Rome. Naturally, the gods were not pleased. Numerous prodigies were reported to the senate at Rome, and dire omens attended Flaminius' entry into office and again as his army set out in pursuit of Hannibal. The consul ignored them. Disaster was therefore foreordained (Livy, 21.63.5–15, 22.1.5–20, 3.11–13).

Or at least so later Roman writers aver.[6] Modern scholars typically reject these claims as an attempt by Flaminius' colleagues in the senate and the Roman historians who drew on their accounts to saddle Flaminius with the blame for the defeat he suffered.[7] Flaminius' real error, it is now generally held, was over-eagerness to claim the sole credit for ending the war. Flaminius and his colleague, Cn. Servilius Geminus, appear to have been following a coordinated plan in an attempt to confine Hannibal to northern Italy or at least to destroy his forces before he and his Gallic allies could penetrate too far south. Servilius took command of the remnants of Sempronius' forces at Ariminum, guarding that approach into central Italy. Flaminius received Scipio's legions and took up a station at Arretium in order to watch the passes through the Apennines. Both forces were augmented with new levies. Whichever consul made contact with Hannibal first, their plan was probably to shadow the enemy until the other consul arrived with his army, then to coordinate their forces for the attack. Hannibal crossed the mountains as soon as the passes were free of snow, so probably in May, and entered Etruria, where his soldiers began to burn and pillage farms and villages as he marched through the countryside. The sight of this widespread destruction being carried out virtually before the eyes of Flaminius' men following in its wake infuriated them and they clamoured for battle. Flaminius also feared the unpopularity that would arise in Rome when reports of his failure to stop Hannibal's devastation reached the city. He therefore resolved to attack, which was precisely what Hannibal wanted. Flaminius pursued, and Hannibal marched his forces late one afternoon though a defile that led along the shores of Lake Trasimene, where he camped for the night. Flaminius was unwilling to enter the narrows with darkness falling, and so his army made camp outside it. The hills beyond

6. N. Rosenstein, *Imperatores victi: Military Defeat and Aristocratic Competition in the Middle and Late Republic*, Berkeley and Los Angeles: University of California Press, 1990, 77–83.
7. Lazenby, *Hannibal's War*, 65; Goldsworthy, *Punic Wars*, 185–6.

the defile approach the shore closely, leaving only a narrow strip of flat land. Early the following morning Hannibal deployed his light troops and cavalry along those hills with the latter positioned just inside the defile. His Spanish and African infantry he stationed on a hill at the far end of the level ground. Then he waited. At dawn Flaminius led his forces through the defile and along the shore, strung out in a long marching column. The morning was very foggy, which hid the Carthaginians from the Romans until it was too late. Hannibal's light troops attacked the head of the column and forced it to halt, then the main body of his infantry charged down out of the hills while his cavalry closed off any possibility of retreat. The result was annihilation. Flaminius' army could not form up for battle; his men were forced to stand and fight in small groups where they stood. The consul fell fighting as his men were gradually cut down around him, the last of them forced back into the lake itself where the cavalry finished them off. As many as 15,000 Romans and *socii* fell; another 10,000 were made prisoners. A very few escaped to bring news of the disaster to Rome. And this was not all. A few days later the report reached the senate that a force of 4,000 cavalry sent on ahead to augment Flaminius' army by Servilius, who was marching with his infantry to link up with his colleague, had been utterly destroyed by Hannibal.

Fabius takes command

The crisis demanded the appointment of a dictator. The *patres'* choice fell on Q. Fabius Maximus, consul in 233 and again in 228, censor in 230, and an experienced commander who had triumphed in his first consulship. He had also been an augur for many years and so was at the centre of the Roman religious establishment. His appointment arose from the senate's belief that the cause of Rome's defeats lay as much in religious transgressions as in the errors of their generals or the inferiority of their soldiers. The *pax deorum* assured the divine support that was essential to Roman victories, while lost battles demonstrated that that support had been lacking.[8] Religious concerns were particularly acute in the wake of Trasimene because of the allegations that Flaminius had failed to heed the warnings the omens had conveyed. The elevation of Fabius was therefore as much an effort to ensure that the gods' support would

8. Rosenstein, *Imperatores victi*, 54–91.

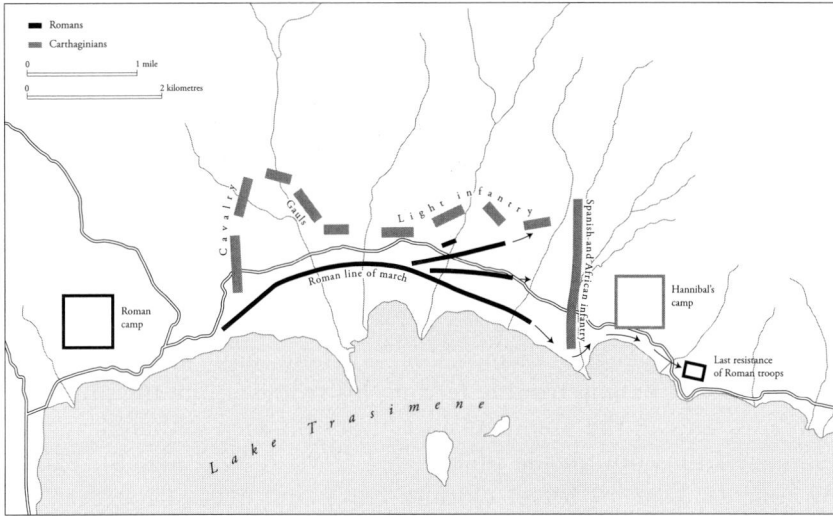

Figure 15 Plan of the battle at Lake Trasimene.

not be lacking in the next battle as to repair the military situation.

Later Romans and many moderns have also viewed Fabius' dictatorship as inaugurating a radically different strategy for fighting Hannibal. This was a strategy of delay, *cunctatio* in Latin, from which Fabius derived his nickname, 'the Delayer' (*Cunctator*). As his contemporary, the poet Ennius, famously wrote, 'One man by delaying set things right for us' (*Unus homo nobis cunctando restituit rem*: *Annales* 370 Vahlens = Cic. *Off.* 1.84). According to this interpretation, Fabius avoided fighting pitched battles and instead sought to wear Hannibal down through attrition. He kept to the high ground, marching parallel to Hannibal and avoiding giving him the opportunity to attack. Meanwhile Fabius pursued a scorched earth policy intended to limit the enemy's ability to gather food, and he attacked Hannibal's foragers wherever he could to the same end. Starvation would whittle down the enemy slowly but inexorably, and the process would be helped along by falling on small detachments whenever an opportunity presented itself. Gradually the Punic forces would be reduced to the point where those that were left could easily be destroyed. Yet popular agitators, impatient of victory, turned the citizenry against Fabius and compelled the abandonment of *cunctatio*, which led inevitably to the decision by one of those agitators, the consul of 216, C. Terentius Varro, to seek a decisive battle against Hannibal and the resulting catastrophe at Cannae.

This analysis fails to convince.[9] Any plan to cut off Hannibal's foragers depended first and foremost on fast-moving cavalry forces that could swiftly find and destroy these small, isolated bands of men as they moved through the countryside before help could arrive. The Roman defeat at the Ticinus, however, and then the destruction of Servilius' 4,000 cavalry following Flaminius' disaster at Lake Trasimene had demonstrated unequivocally the superiority of the Carthaginians' mounted forces both in numbers and in fighting ability. With them Hannibal controlled the open country along his line of march, and there is no evidence that Fabius' cavalry ever effectively challenged them. Nor is there any indication that Hannibal was having trouble feeding his troops; quite the opposite: Polybius stresses the abundance of booty his men gathered as they plundered the countryside unimpeded (3.90.7, 92.2 and 8). Fabius by contrast kept his forces close to camp and massed together. He did not try to wear the enemy down, for his strategy was different. To be sure, Fabius was playing a waiting game, nor was he averse to falling upon small detachments of the enemy in order to reduce their numbers whenever possible. His main objective, however, was to use these small-scale attacks to help restore the spirits of his men, which had been broken by the previous defeats. Indeed as surprising as it may seem the senators appear to have believed that what caused those defeats was the fact that their troops had been newly levied and untrained (Polyb. 3.89.4–7, 90.4, 106.5). And although Fabius was unwilling to fight a pitched battle in the open country against Hannibal, he was waiting for an opportunity to strike a decisive blow under circumstances that all but guaranteed success. One was not long in coming.

Following his destruction of Flaminius' army, Hannibal assembled his captives and then dismissed the *socii* among them to their homes, proclaiming that he had come to Italy not to make war on them but to free them from the Roman yoke. He then directed his course east and down the Adriatic side of the peninsula into Apulia, where the harvest season was earlier and the ripening grain afforded him the means of feeding the 50,000–60,000 men now under his command. And when Fabius and his army would not come down to fight in response to Hannibal's challenge, he marched his forces into Samnium, plundered the region, then descended into Campania and

9. P. Erdkamp, 'Polybius, Livy, and the "Fabian strategy"', *Ancient Society*, 23 (1992), 127–47.

turned his men loose to pillage far and wide. Not only was the area the richest and most fertile in Italy but much of it was *ager Romanus* populated by Roman citizens. For the first time Roman civilians felt directly the ravages of the war as the Carthaginian soldiers burned their homes, laid waste their farms, and carried off their slaves, cattle, and household possessions. Fabius' refusal to stop the destruction only compounded their distress and led to increasingly bitter criticism from his officers, led by M. Minucius Rufus, his master of the horse.

Still Fabius continued to wait for an opportunity to strike, and finally in late summer it arrived. Hannibal now needed to find shelter for his army over the winter, and Apulia offered the most promising prospect. To reach it he would need to re-cross the Apennines, and Fabius, divining his plans, was able to occupy the pass that Hannibal would lead his army through. Fabius placed a detachment of 4,000 men at its summit while he and the rest of the army made camp on the hills nearby. Hannibal meanwhile camped for the night at the foot of the pass. Fabius knew that as the enemy made their way up the grade, they would be strung out in a long column and encumbered by the mass of booty they had collected. An attack from higher ground could scarcely fail, or so Fabius believed. But he had not reckoned with Hannibal's cunning. That night the Carthaginian ordered that some 2,000 oxen captured by his men should be brought to the bottom of the pass and have torches lashed to their horns. He ordered that these should be lit and the oxen driven up the pass. He and his men followed. The sight of the mass of torchlight coming at them and the bellowing of the cattle so terrified the Romans guarding the summit that they fled to a nearby hill. Fabius, too, was uncertain what was happening and so kept his men in camp. The way now clear, Hannibal and his army surmounted the pass unscathed (Polyb. 3.92.8–94.6).

The repercussions from this fiasco quickly made themselves felt both at Rome and in camp. Public anger flared against the dictator, and the senate summoned Fabius to the city, ostensibly to perform certain sacrifices but more probably to explain his conduct of the war. Meanwhile Minucius Rufus was left in command and managed to win a minor skirmish against the Carthaginians. When reports filtering back to Rome exaggerated this exploit into a significant victory, public sentiment turned further against Fabius. This hostility led a tribune to propose the unprecedented step of elevating Minucius to the rank of co-dictator with Fabius. This bill subverted the whole point of the dictatorship, which was to put a single magistrate in charge of all military operations, but it passed easily, and when Fabius returned to the army, he and Minucius divided their forces between them. Hannibal soon learned of the new dispositions of the enemy and saw an opportunity in Minucius' aggressiveness. Hannibal, after he had carefully placed a force in ambush, enticed Minucius to contest a bit of high ground lying between their two camps. Hannibal kept feeding troops into the fray, leading Minucius to do the same until he finally drew up the main body of his army in support. Hannibal then gave the signal for the ambushers to attack, and the trap was sprung. Only the timely intervention of Fabius, who brought his own legions up when he realised what was happening, prevented another disaster and enabled Minucius to withdraw his men without serious loss. The experience tempered Minucius' enthusiasm for tangling with Hannibal, and the two dictators thereafter worked in harmony.

The Roman forces continued to skirmish with Hannibal's army throughout the remainder of 217 and into early 216 after the dictators' six months in office had ended and the consuls Servilius and M. Atilius Regulus, who had been elected to replace Flaminius, resumed command. However, the senate had decided that the new year would at last see the destruction of Hannibal and his army. Abandoning Fabius' 'go-slow' approach the *patres* elected once more to meet Hannibal in pitched battle. Their reasons for doing so were both political and strategic. The devastation of Campania and the public outrage this had provoked had once again provided an opportunity for critics of the senate to voice their complaints at the conduct of the war. Flaminius was dead, but there were others waiting to pick up where he had left off. Any strategy that allowed Hannibal to continue his rampage across Italy unobstructed and especially to devastate the farms of Roman citizens without challenge would only further enflame public outrage, strengthen the senate's critics, and threaten senatorial control. Equally critical was the danger such a strategy posed to Rome's hegemony in Italy. The *socii* had so far stood firm alongside Rome, but if Hannibal's attacks continued to punish them while Rome's armies stood by and did nothing, they were unlikely to remain loyal much longer. Hannibal's challenge to the Republic's empire in Italy and the aristocracy's dominance had to be met. The senators determined to do so in one great battle that would finally crush Hannibal.

Later Roman authors, writing as apologists for the senate, sought to pin the blame for this change of strategy on one of the new consuls for 216, M. Terentius Varro. While the senators and his consular colleague, L. Aemilius Paullus, wanted to continue Fabius' cautious approach to fighting Hannibal, Varro demanded and got a show-down (e.g. Livy, 22.34.2–35.5, 38.6–40.3). Polybius, however, working from Fabius Pictor's contemporary account of the senate's deliberations, locates the responsibility for the decision squarely among the *patres* (3.107.7). What made them believe that their forces could win a pitched battle this time was their analysis of the defeat at the river Trebia. In that battle the legions in the centre had broken through the forces opposing them. Only the flight of the infantry on each wing once the Punic cavalry had driven off the Roman and allied horse, exposing the infantry to an attack on their flanks, had nullified that victory. This analysis suggested that if the Roman centre could achieve a breakthrough quickly enough, the legions could then turn and destroy the remainder of the enemy's forces piecemeal. To ensure success in the coming battle, the senate not only committed both consular armies to the campaign but greatly strengthened each. By how much, the sources differ. Polybius says that the senate doubled the number of legions to eight, each containing 5,000 men and accompanied by 5,000 *socii*. To these 80,000 infantry they added 6,000 cavalry (3.107.9, 113.5). Livy, however, puts the total force lower: only four legions, but strengthened by an additional 10,000 men to a total of 50,000–55,000 infantry and cavalry (22.36.1–4). Whichever figure is preferred, the Roman force was clearly meant to outnumber Hannibal's army of about 40,000 African, Spanish, and Gallic infantry and 10,000 cavalry (Polyb. 3.114.1–5). More critical was the decision to modify the *quincunx* formation by reducing the spaces between the maniples and cohorts within the line of battle and between the files within them. The depth of each maniple was also made much greater than its front, so that the legions and the *socii* would enter the battle as a dense mass, much like a Greek phalanx (Polyb. 3.113.3). The cavalry was stationed as usual on the wings with orders to hold off the enemy as long as possible. The object of these changes was to increase the force of the infantry's advance and so achieve a breakthrough quickly, before the cavalry was driven off and the events of the Trebia repeated. It was a reasonable plan and seemed to offered strong prospects for success. It played to the Romans' superiority in manpower and drew on the lessons learned from their prior defeats. Unhappily for Rome, it could not counter Hannibal's superior generalship.

Cannae

In the summer of 216, Varro and Paullus, who had triumphed in his previous consulship three years earlier and in whom the senate placed great confidence, faced Hannibal near the town of Cannae in northern Apulia.[10] Although the consuls were in accord with the decision that a full-scale battle was to be fought that year, they disagreed on where to fight it. Paullus held that they should move to where the terrain was less suitable for cavalry in view of Hannibal's superiority in that arm so that the outcome of the fight might be determined primarily by the infantry. Varro on the contrary insisted on fighting where they were despite its flat, treeless character, apparently eager for the victory and convinced that they could not lose (Polyb. 3.110.1–3). On 2 August by the Roman calendar, which was close to solar time in this period, and after some preliminary manoeuvres and skirmishing, Varro ordered his forces to cross the river Aufidus and form up for battle. Hannibal countered with one of the greatest tactical feats in the history of warfare. He deployed his troops in a long line with the centre, consisting of his Gallic allies and a portion of his Spanish infantry, advanced well beyond the Africans on either wing and imbricated, so that the centre was crescent-shaped. His Punic and Numidian cavalry he placed on each flank. As the battle opened and the Romans pushed forward, those in the centre were the first to make contact with the apex of Hannibal's line of battle. The power of their advance forced the Gauls opposing them to fall back. The Romans who were on either side of those engaged with the enemy crowded towards the centre to join in the fighting, since the enemy opposite them were still some way off, while the Gauls and the Spanish continued to fall back gradually until the convex shape of Hannibal's line had become concave and the mass of Roman and allied troops converging on the centre found themselves between Hannibal's Africans on either flank. These troops suddenly wheeled to face the Roman flanks on the left and right and attacked. The Roman advance ground to a halt

---

10. The battle is endlessly studied; see recently G. Daly, *Cannae: The Experience of Battle in the Second Punic War*, London: Routledge, 2002; A. Goldsworthy, *Cannae*, London: Cassell, 2001.

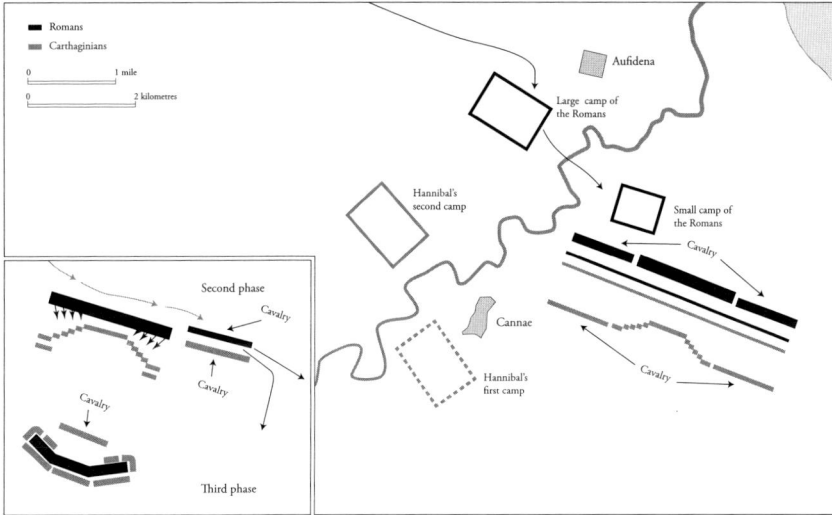

Figure 16 Plan of the battle at Cannae.

as the men on the wings were forced to turn and face this new threat
while the soldiers in the centre could no longer advance without
exposing their own flanks to the enemy. The Romans now found
themselves surrounded on three sides, soon to be four. For while the
infantry battle was unfolding, a furious combat was taking place
between the cavalry contingents on the wings. Despite putting up a
desperate fight, both the Roman and the allied horse were put to
flight. While the Numidians pursued the fugitives, the Punic horse
swung around and attacked the Romans in the rear, cutting off
their escape from what now became a death trap. The result was
slaughter.

How many Roman legionaries and Italian allies died is uncertain.
Polybius claims about 70,000, including Aemilius Paullus, but his
figures may derive from an inflated estimate of the size of the
Romans' forces (3.116.9, 117.3). Livy reduces the total to 48,200,
but even that may be too many in view of his statements elsewhere
that almost 20,000 were captured and 14,550 escaped with Varro
(22.49.13–18, 50.3, 11, 52.4, 54.1–4). The most careful modern
analyses put the total lower still, at about 30,000 killed, wounded,
and missing.[11] But whatever the true numbers there is no gainsaying

11. G. De Sanctis, *Storia dei Romani*, 2nd edn, Florence: Nuova Italia, 1953–, 3.2.128–
30; P. A. Brunt, *Italian Manpower 225 B.C.–A.D. 14*, Oxford: Oxford University Press,
1971, 419 n. 4.

the magnitude of the Roman disaster or the brilliance of Hannibal's achievement. His tactical skills had enabled a significantly smaller force to annihilate a larger one utterly, and he had proved unequivocally that he could defeat the greatest army the Romans had ever put in the field. And that victory had cost him only about 5,700 killed, mostly Gauls (Polyb. 3.117.6).

Legend recounts how in the aftermath of the battle, the commander of Hannibal's cavalry, Maharbal, approached his general and announced that if he would order him and the cavalry on ahead to Rome and follow with the rest of the army, within five days he would hold his victory banquet on the Capitoline. Hannibal, however, overwhelmed with joy at what he had accomplished and unable to comprehend that complete victory lay within his grasp, hesitated, leading Maharbal to proclaim, 'Hannibal, you know how to win victories but not how to use them' (Livy, 22.51.1–4). And some have agreed that at the moment of his greatest triumph Hannibal allowed his best chance to finish the war to slip through his fingers. But only a great commander could have kept the dictates of his grand strategy before his eyes at such a crowning moment. Rome was 400 km away, three weeks' march at least, and so there was plenty of time to organise the defence of a well-fortified city. Hannibal had needed eight months to reduce Saguntum; Rome, much larger and more populous, might take years. Meanwhile, a siege would pin his army down in the heart of enemy territory, making it vulnerable to counterattack and posing serious challenges to keeping his men fed. Much more importantly, decapitation had never been Hannibal's plan for beating Rome; amputation of its limbs was his goal. He sought to incite the allies to revolt by demonstrating that he could beat any army the Romans threw at him. Once the *socii* believed that he could defend them against Roman reprisals, their defections would reduce the Republic's overwhelming advantage in manpower while simultaneously building up his own. Committing his forces to a lengthy siege would rob him of the ability to move around Italy encouraging Rome's subjects to join his cause and punishing those who did not. If Maharbal was in fact urging him to march on Rome after Cannae, Hannibal had every reason not to follow his advice.

All the more so as now, finally, Rome's Italian empire began to crack up. Over the next few years cities in Apulia threw in their lot with Hannibal; the Hirpini and most of the Samnites did as well. The Lucanians and Bruttii went over to his side along with many of the

Greek cities of Magna Graecia, Tarentum most importantly. But by far his greatest coup came with the defection of several Campanian cities, especially Capua. Not only was Capua the second city of Italy after Rome, a wealthy, populous agricultural and manufacturing centre, but its citizens were Romans, albeit without the vote, and several of them could boast marriage connections with the Republic's leading senatorial families. Their decision to break with Rome and embrace Hannibal in 216 sent an unmistakable signal to the rest of Italy that the days of the Republic's *imperium* were numbered. Cannae, in short, represented not the culmination of Hannibal's campaign against Rome but only its beginning.

The *imperium* strikes back

Over the next several years everything seemed to go Hannibal's way. In addition to the gains he was making in Italy, he received an important boost from Philip V, the king of Macedon. In 215 envoys from that monarch approached Hannibal to negotiate a treaty of alliance between the two powers that at least on its face envisioned military cooperation. It is not likely that either side really expected that support to materialise. Hannibal was winning his war at this point; he did not need Philip's assistance, nor would he have welcomed the arrival of a Macedonian army and with it the potential for Philip to interfere in Italian affairs. Instead, the treaty represented an important acknowledgement by one of the leading Hellenistic powers that Rome was finished and that Hannibal was now the man to deal with in Italy. That could only aid in rallying the towns and peoples still sitting on the fence to side with Hannibal, particularly the Greeks of southern Italy. Philip for his part had longstanding ambitions in the western Balkans. This was a region, however, that Rome had twice sent armies into, in 229 and as recently as 219, in an effort to suppress Illyrian piracy. Although the region was not formally incorporated into the Republic's alliance system, these incursions had at the very least established Rome's interest in the area, which might provoke a military response to any attempt by Philip to take control there. From Philip's perspective, then, the treaty simply gave him a green light to do so now that Roman power was on the wane (Polyb. 7.9.1–17, esp. 7.9.13; Livy, 23.33.1–12). Both sides gained by the treaty at little cost to themselves. However, the Romans captured Philip's envoys on their way back to Macedon and discovered the treaty, to the horror of the *patres*. For they could not know that the promises of military co-operation the pact envisioned were empty gestures. Rather they now had to reckon with the prospect of Philip and his army arriving in Italy to fight alongside the Carthaginians.

That same year Hiero, the ruler of Syracuse, died. He had long been a stalwart ally and had readily offered soldiers, money, and grain after each of Rome's defeats. The need for these last two items was especially urgent. Funds in the treasury were running low while the Republic's inability to prevent Hannibal from marching anywhere he wanted meant that all of Italy's cropland was potentially vulnerable to attack. The senate could not be sure of its armies' or its civilians' food supplies. Hiero's passing and the accession of his young grandson, Hieronymus, whose attitude towards Rome was very much in contrast to his grandfather's, deprived the Republic of any hope of additional aid from that quarter. Worse, political turmoil ensued. Factions hatched plots and counter-plots culminating in the assassination of Hieronymus in 214, ushering in more murders and instability until at last a pro-Carthaginian faction took power. The senate now had to confront the possibility that a Punic war fleet would be installed in Syracuse's harbour, from which it could challenge Roman control of the sea-lanes around Italy. Carthaginian naval success would in turn enable the resupply and reinforcement of Hannibal's army from Africa. That nightmare would come a long step closer to reality in 212 when Hannibal, cooperating with sympathisers among the leading citizens of Tarentum, captured that city by surprise. Even though the Roman garrison managed to fortify itself in the citadel, Hannibal now controlled a harbour in Italy capable of receiving not only a convoy from Carthage but military transports from Macedon. And if all this were not enough, early in 215 word reached Rome that a Gallic ambush had killed the consul-elect, L. Postumius Albinus, and wiped out his army. There was now no force in the north to keep the pressure on Hannibal's allies there and prevent Gallic warriors from travelling south to swell the ranks of the enemy.

At Rome, we are told, the news of Cannae brought so great a lamentation among the wives, sisters, and daughters of the slain and captured that the senate could scarcely deliberate about the defence of the city. The sacred rites, even, could not be performed (Livy, 22.55.1–56.5). That the Republic did not collapse under this cascade of disasters and setbacks attests to its leaders' extraordinary determination to fight on. There was never any question among the senators of surrender or negotiation; despite the bleak prospects before them, victory alone would end the war. All political bickering was forgotten now, signalled by their treatment of the surviving consul, Varro, the man whom later tradition would blame for Cannae. In the wake of that debacle he made strenuous efforts to turn the mob of survivors at Canusium into some semblance of an army, constituting two legions out of them. Summoned then to Rome in order to name a dictator, he encountered no hint of criticism, much less retribution. Instead a crowd of citizens of every rank went out from the city as he drew near to thank him for not having despaired of the Republic (Livy, 22.61.14). And for the next several years Varro continued to hold command in various sectors of the war.

This is not to say that aristocratic competition for offices and authority was forgotten.[12] Leading senators came forward out of a mixture of patriotism and self-interest to contend for the glory of rescuing the Republic from the shipwreck of the war's early years. The period after Cannae saw an unprecedented accumulation of honours among a small coterie of men: Fabius Maximus held consulships in 215, 214, and 209 and saw to it that his son was elevated to that post in 213; M. Claudius Marcellus, already consul in 222, was re-elected in 214, 210, and 208; Postumius, the consul-elect for 215 killed in Gaul, was holding that office for the third time; and Q. Fulvius Flaccus had already been twice consul in 212 when he won election to a third consulate and then in 209 to a fourth. Several of the praetorships in the years after Cannae were also held by men of consular rank. These iterations were not the product of a senatorial consensus to rest command of the war in the hands of experienced generals of proven ability. The men who held these offices faced competitors and at times had to elbow them aside to win the posts. Rather, these men appealed to the voters to put their trust in their experience and past achievements. The crisis and the need for solidarity that it imposed forced their colleagues in the senate to accede to the public's will, even though their monopolising of the Republic's highest offices violated an implicit understanding within the aristocracy to observe limits on how much honour any one of them could amass and deprived others of an opportunity to reach the pinnacle of the *cursus honorum*.

12. N. Rosenstein, 'Competition and crisis in mid-republican Rome', *Phoenix* 47 (1993), 313–38.

The *patres'* readiness to stand behind the men the voters chose to lead the war effort notwithstanding any misgivings this might cause was simply a reflection of their determination to stop at nothing to fight on and win the war. Another was their treatment of the survivors of Cannae. When a delegation from the Roman prisoners arrived in Rome bearing Hannibal's offer to free them all in return for ransom and accompanied by a high-ranking Carthaginian prepared to negotiate peace terms if the senators were so inclined, the *patres* not only sent the envoy packing but flatly refused any payment of ransom and returned the delegation to Hannibal (Polyb. 6.58.2–13; Livy, 22.61.1–4, cf. 58.1–61.10). In part, the senators did not want to deplete the treasury's remaining stocks of cash or see that money or the citizens' wealth go to swell Hannibal's war chest. Rome would need to draw on every source of public and private funds in order to continue the war. But more important was the message the senate's refusal sent. The prisoners had surrendered rather than fight to the death as so many of their comrades had done. The senate's stance announced unmistakably what the *patres* expected from the men who would continue the fight against Hannibal. There would be no release from captivity; the Romans had no use for quitters.[13]

Nor did they have much more sympathy for losers. Rather than deploy the two legions that Varro had created out of the survivors of Cannae in Italy, and despite the Republic's desperate shortage of troops during the remainder of 216 and 215, the senate ordered them to Sicily early in 215 and inflicted on them a variety of punishments and petty indignities throughout the remainder of the war: they were to remain in Sicily and not one of them was to receive a discharge until the war was over; they were forbidden winter billets in or within ten miles of any town; no pay or decorations for valour were to be awarded nor any exemption from fatigues; those who had public horses were deprived of them. And just to make sure there was no mistaking what the senators thought about these men, the Cannae legions served as the dumping ground for every weakling or otherwise unfit soldier in the other Roman armies (Livy, 23.25.7–8; 24.18.9; 25.5.5–10, 7.2–4; 26.1.10; 27.14.11).

The gods, too, were not neglected. In the aftermath of the disaster the senators discovered that several dire warnings in the form of prodigies had not been recognised, including the unchastity of two

13. Rosenstein, *Imperatores victi*, 92–113.

Vestal virgins. Ritual errors, also undetected at the time, had likewise disrupted the *pax deorum*. At a loss for how to remedy the situation, the *patres* dispatched Q. Fabius Pictor, the future historian, to Delphi to ask the oracle there by what prayers and offerings the gods could be propitiated. In the meantime, the senators ordered a grisly sacrifice to the deities of the underworld: a Gallic man and woman and a Greek couple were buried alive in the cattle market (Livy, 22.57.2–6).

Still, if the senators were resolved to continue the fight at all costs, they would need something to fight with. The means lay in the Republic's extraordinary human, logistical, and financial resources. Even with the defection of many of its allies, even with the tremendous loss of life in the first three years of the struggle, Rome still had far more potential recruits to draw on than did Hannibal, a large and relatively prosperous citizenry whose wealth it could tap, and many years of practical experience in raising, training, and supplying armies. The senate would have to press these advantages as never before, for in the wake of Cannae the Republic's only hope of victory was to follow a strategy of delay, attempting to limit Hannibal's gains from defections while avoiding direct confrontation with the Carthaginian. Cannae had produced a wave of revolts among the allies, and another serious defeat would only bring another. So no more set-piece battles. Instead, the goal now was to protect those allies that had remained loyal, punish those that had not, and keep the waverers in line by a show of force.

To that end the senate began to field one army after another. Four legions were scraped up in the late summer of 216, two composed of able-bodied young slaves, two of convicts and debtors released from prison. The senate armed them with the only weapons and armour available at short notice, the spoils hung up in the temples by Flaminius following his Gallic triumph. It was not a shortage of *assidui* that compelled recourse to these sorts of men but rather the urgency of the situation. It could take more than a month under ordinary circumstances to levy an army, and Rome needed soldiers at once. Prisoners and slaves were ready to hand, and with the planting season around the corner men suddenly called up from their farms could prove reluctant to report for duty. In 215 only a single additional legion was raised, but in the following year five more were created, then two more in 213, three in 212, another two in 211, four in 210, and two more the next year. At the height of its mobilisation, in 212–211, the Republic was maintaining twenty-five legions in the field, and on average eighteen each year between the second half of 216 and 209. These legions are likely to have been considerably under strength, but even so twenty-five legions probably required some 75,000–80,000 citizens to serve, eighteen legions about 61,000. The senate could reach these totals only by drafting nearly every *assiduus* between the ages of 18 and 30. The demands placed on the Republic's remaining allies to supply the contingents that accompanied these legions were certainly just as heavy if not heavier.[14]

This massive effort enabled Rome to wage war on multiple fronts. No troops could be spared for a major push in the north, but two legions kept watch on the Gauls to prevent a break-out into central Italy. In response to the discovery of the treaty between Hannibal and Philip in 214 the senate dispatched a legion to Brundisium to observe developments in Greece. By 211 Roman diplomatic efforts had stirred up trouble for Philip, and Roman troops soon thereafter were fighting on the Greek mainland. Developments in Sicily, too, demanded action. In addition to the Cannae legions in the west, two more legions arrived on the island as the situation in Syracuse deteriorated in 213, and these soon placed the city under siege. The two legions that had been marching to Spain at the outset of the war remained there to pin down Carthaginian forces and prevent reinforcements from reaching Hannibal. Other armies operated in Apulia and Lucania against rebels in those regions. In addition, the Romans maintained several smaller forces at various critical points in Italy and Sardinia. Nor was the naval war neglected. A fleet based at Lilybaeum in Sicily guarded that island against naval attacks and made several raids on Africa, while in 215 another was stationed at Brundisium and then moved to Greece to carry on the war against Philip. All of this was in addition to the Republic's main effort, carried on by four consular legions every year.

Undertaking warfare on this scale was far beyond anything the Republic had every attempted, and the number of armies involved outstripped the number of the ordinary magistrates available to lead them. The republican administration was geared to manage only two or at most three independent campaigns at a time. The senate therefore met the need for additional commanders by

14. Brunt, *Italian Manpower*, 417–22; N. Rosenstein, *Rome at War: Farms, Families, and Death in the Middle Republic*, Chapel Hill: University of North Carolina Press, 2004, 87, 90.

appointing promagistrates, men acting 'in the place of' magistrates. Usually, these were consuls or sometimes praetors whose commands were simply continued into subsequent years following the close of their year in office, although occasionally men received appointments who had previously held magistracies but not in the preceding year. This practice was not an innovation; the senate had resorted to proconsuls and propraetors before, but never on the scale that waging this multi-front war demanded. The flexibility characteristic of the republican administration in this period proved a critical asset as the senate sought to adapt to the demands of a new style of warfare. Equally important, military operations in so many different theatres required the coordination of the financial, logistical, and manpower resources each needed in order to ensure that every element played its proper role in the execution of Rome's overall strategy. The Republic had no separate military general staff or high command; the senate ordinarily filled that role and did so now as well. But the complex, long-term strategy that the struggle required meant that the senate took on a significantly greater degree of responsibility for managing the *res publica*, coordinating the deployment of armies, appointing their commanders, and issuing the orders that kept all the elements working together towards the ultimate goal of defeating Hannibal.

That goal also required the Romans to go on the offensive wherever possible, to punish defectors but more importantly to demonstrate that the Republic although down was not out, that it was still the power to be reckoned with in Italy. Campania was the first target. The defection of Capua and several other cities there had undermined the confidence of the Republic's remaining allies in its ability to prevail and made them ask themselves whether it was not time to make their peace with Hannibal. So in the second half of 216, the dictator M. Iunius Pera, appointed in the aftermath of Cannae, directed his efforts around the town of Canusium, where the *via Latina* crosses the river Volturus on the route north to Rome. Thereafter in 215 and 214, both consuls and at times a praetorian commander as well ranged across the territory of Capua and the other defectors, ravaging the countryside and driving back the defenders that sallied out to stop them. In 213 the focus shifted to Apulia, where the city of Arpi fell to the Romans, but in 212 the legions were back in Campania. By late that year the Capuan forces had been so thoroughly cowed that they no longer dared to leave the safety of the city's fortifications to challenge the Romans for control of the open country. At that point, the consuls erected a double stockade around Capua and settled in to reduce the city by siege.

The odds even up

While Roman armies were gradually tightening the vice around his chief ally in Campania, Hannibal was elsewhere trying to foment rebellion among the Republic's allies. His frustrations following his triumph at Cannae reveal much about the limitations of his grand strategy and expose what must be considered its fatal flaw.[15] After the initial wave of defections in 216 and 215, few cities abandoned Rome for Hannibal despite his continual efforts to win them over. Roman strategy in large part focused on preventing defections, and the Republic's ability to field multiple armies provided the means to suppress potential revolts. But the armies, while necessary, by themselves were insufficient. There were many more allies than Roman armies, and had they all risen up Roman manpower would have been unable to prevail against them and Hannibal. Two critical factors combined to keep many of them loyal, both of which derived from the underpinnings of Roman dominance in Italy. The first was intra-regional conflict. Rome's establishment of hegemony in Campania, Apulia, Magna Graecia, and elsewhere during the fourth and third centuries had suppressed longstanding local rivalries in these areas and the struggles for regional dominance they had produced. The advent of Hannibal in 218 and the sudden appearance of an alternative to Rome allowed these latent antagonisms to re-emerge and shape local responses to the new possibilities his victories presented. So when one ally revolted from Rome, its traditional rivals in the region generally reacted by remaining loyal to the Republic because a Carthaginian victory would establish or re-establish the dominance of Hannibal's ally over the other cities in the region. The Republic's more distant suzerainty was preferable to the closer control that a regional hegemon could exercise. In effect, therefore, Hannibal found himself trapped in a zero-sum game in which gaining the adherence of one Roman ally placed others out of reach.

Cross-cutting these axes of intra-regional conflict were the internal political dynamics within each city. Rome could dominate allied communities in large measure because its senators maintained

15. Fronda, *Between Rome and Carthage.*

informal connections of friendship and patronage with members of the elite within those communities. Those links helped sustain the local aristocrats' hold on power against their rivals for leadership. The question of whether to break with Rome and support Hannibal therefore often came to be decided less on the basis of the simple desire for the freedom from Rome that Hannibal promised than on the political advantage it might bring to one faction or another. Many allies stuck with Rome because their leading figures understood that to do so was in their immediate self-interest. And where Rome's friends faced serious challenges to their authority, Roman military might was available to keep them in power. Campania illustrates these dynamics perfectly. Although Capua revolted and brought with it several smaller towns that it had traditionally dominated, Naples and Cumae, at odds with Capua during the fourth century, remained steadfastly in the Roman camp despite Hannibal's initial blandishments and then his efforts to take them by storm. And when political agitation at Nola threatened to bring that town into Hannibal's camp, a Roman army took up residence and suppressed the dissidents (Livy, 24.13.8–11).

Hannibal therefore faced serious challenges in winning adherents beyond those that had come to him soon after Cannae, and Roman military operations forced him continually to have to defend those he already had. The tension between these two demands on his resources provided the opening Rome needed to regain the initiative in the struggle. When in 215 it became clear that the Capuan levies were incapable of standing up to the Roman armies opposing them, Hannibal had to come to their rescue. He fortified a permanent camp above Capua, and early each year between 215 and 212 he and his army would descend from there into the plain to dare the consuls to face him in battle. This they refused to do, so rather than waste the remainder of the campaigning season in a futile stand-off with the Romans, Hannibal and his army would depart for Apulia and southern Italy, where he was endeavouring to win over Rome's allies. Once Hannibal was gone, the Romans moved in with their forces to devastate the Capuans' lands and attack their troops when they ventured out of the city to try to stop them. The problem of defending Capua encapsulates the strategic dilemma Hannibal faced. He could not be everywhere at once; the Romans could. His manpower was limited, and an essential element of Roman strategy aimed at keeping it so. He could not easily divide his forces in order to operate on multiple fronts without weakening them, perhaps fatally so. For although most Roman commanders remained wary of tangling with Hannibal himself, they evinced no such reluctance to battle his subordinates. And indeed in 212, when Hannibal sent his lieutenant Hanno with a relief force and a pack train of grain to the aid of the by now starving Capuans, the consuls made short work of him at Beneventum (Livy, 25.13.1–14.14). Hannibal could only hope to make progress on one front at a time, and his opportunities lay primarily in the south, particularly at Tarentum, where he had long been intriguing with dissident aristocrats to betray the city to him. But he had to be nearby for his plots to succeed, which meant that his lines of communication with Campania were long and his ability to respond to developments there slow. That fact left the field open to the Romans once Hannibal and his army had decamped for the south and enabled them to win their first important victory in Italy, the capture of Capua.

The Romans' siege of the city put the entire basis of Hannibal's strategy in jeopardy. He had come to Italy not only offering freedom to Rome's subjects but promising that he would defend those who joined his cause against reprisals. Cannae and the other victories had demonstrated conclusively that those promises were not empty, but what good was Hannibal's prowess on the battlefield if he was nowhere to be found when an ally desperately needed his protection, as the Capuans certainly did by the winter of 212–211? The siege forced Hannibal to respond, and early in 211 he was back in Campania to try to lift it. The Romans were ready for him, however. They had fortified not only the inner line of their siege works but the side facing out as well, and behind that wall they held off his attempts to storm their positions. The blockade also prevented him from communicating with the besieged in order to coordinate a joint attack. Nor could he endeavour to besiege the besiegers, for a long stay in Campania was impossible. Too many Roman armies were available to converge on him. He risked being pinned down and gradually overwhelmed if he settled in for a long siege, to say nothing of the challenges of feeding his army during that time. He was left with only one move. He directed his army against the one objective he knew the enemy had to defend – Rome itself. To conceal his intentions he moved north through the mountains by an indirect route, then suddenly appeared in Latium and advanced on the city. Superior manpower, however, nullified his daring gamble. As it happened, the consuls were just then recruiting two new legions. These they quickly drew up to defend the city, depriving Hannibal of any hope of storming Rome. And although at the news of the city's danger the commanders at Capua had immediately dispatched forces north to counter Hannibal's thrust just as he had anticipated, he learned to his chagrin that they had sent only two of the four legions under their command. The other two stayed to continue the siege. Realising that his gambit had failed, he withdrew from Latium with his plunder and retired south through the mountains, leaving Capua to its fate (Polyb. 9.3.1–7.10; Livy, 26.7.1–11.13).

That fate was not kind. Starvation and despair finally forced the Capuans to capitulate later that year, and the Romans were not inclined to mercy. They beheaded leaders of the revolt, sold many of the citizens into slavery along with their wives and children, and confiscated their property. Others they allowed to remain free but stripped them of their citizenship and ordered them out of the city and its territory, which became the property of the Roman people. The city's civic existence was ended. It was punishment as cruel as the senators could devise against men who had forsaken their Roman citizenship to side with the Republic's enemy. It sent a clear message to the rest of Italy: Hannibal had been powerless to protect those who had relied on his promises. From then on there would be no more defections.

The same year brought good news for Rome on other fronts as well. Ever since 215, when the senate discovered the pact between Hannibal and Philip of Macedon, it had kept M. Valerius Laevinus stationed at Brundisium with a legion and fifty ships to keep an eye on developments to the east. In the following year, Laevinus had crossed to Greece in response to an urgent appeal for aid from the town of Oricum, which was under attack by Philip. Laevinus and his force recaptured Oricum, which had fallen to the Macedonians, who had then moved on to besiege Apollonia. In a night attack, Laevinus' troops surprised the king and his army in their camp, killing many and forcing the rest to flee, including Philip himself, half-dressed. The Macedonians then burned their boats rather than face Laevinus' ships and marched home by land (Livy, 24.40.1–17). The setback kept Philip away from the coast and proximity to Italy for the next two years, but he was still too close for the senate's comfort. During that time Laevinus opened talks with leaders of the Aetolians, a confederation of tribes in central Greece that had long viewed Macedonian power as the chief impediment to their ascendancy in the region. Negotiations and promises of Roman military aid eventually led to the conclusion of an alliance between Rome and the Aetolians in the autumn of 211 with the goal of making war on Philip. The allies opened hostilities at once, and by that winter Laevinus could feel confident that Philip's troubles in Greece would keep him from entertaining thoughts of coming to Italy to join forces with Hannibal (Livy, 25.23.9, 26.24.1–16).

The war at home

Among the proofs of Rome's recovery after its early disasters that Laevinus advanced to persuade the Aetolians that the Republic had now regained its strength were the recent captures of Capua and Syracuse. The latter had fallen in late 212 or 211 to the proconsul M. Claudius Marcellus' army after an arduous siege and much bloodshed (Polyb. 8.37.1–13; Livy, 25.23.1–31.11). Its capitulation obviated the possibility that its harbour would become the base for a Carthaginian naval squadron, and the massive spoils went a long way towards easing the financial pressures of the war. The need to maintain so many armies and the deaths of so many taxpayers had by that point strained the Republic's fiscal resources to breaking point. In 215, the treasury had no funds for food or pay for the soldiers and sailors in Sicily and Sardinia. The senate instructed their commanders to find money wherever they could. A loan from Hiero eased the situation in Sicily, while contributions from allied towns in Sardinia lightened the burden there (Livy, 23.21.1–6). The situation was no better towards the end of the year, when funds were lacking to furnish pay, food, and clothing for the army in Spain. The senate was forced to rely on credit, an extremely unusual step for any government in antiquity. Companies of businessmen (*publicani*) offered to advance the necessary supplies and defer payment until the conclusion of the war, provided that they were exempted from conscription and the Republic assumed responsibility for the cargoes once on board ship (Livy, 23.48.5–49.4). This last provision proved an invitation to fraud, as some put worthless cargoes on leaking hulks. When these ships sank as expected, their owners claimed a much higher value for the lost cargoes from the treasury. Or they claimed shipwrecks where none had occurred. The abuses led to a public outcry and senatorial sanctions when discovered in 212, causing many *publicani* to withdraw into voluntary exile (Livy, 25.3.8–4.11). The condition of the public fisc was so straitened in 214 that companies of *publicani* again announced to the censors that they would undertake public contracts on credit and put off asking for payment until the end of the war. The owners of the slaves who had been conscripted after Cannae likewise agreed to defer reimbursement for their cost until the war's conclusion. Those who held funds in trust for the maintenance of widows, single women, and orphans turned them over to the treasury, which doled out money for the wards' necessary expenses. And the *equites* and centurions serving in the legions announced that they would accept no pay for their military service (Livy, 24.18.10–15). That same year the senate was compelled to ask slave owners to come forward once again, this time to furnish slaves to serve as oarsmen for 100 new warships just launched (Livy, 24.11.5–9; see above, p. 111). So dire was the financial as well as the military situation that in the previous year a tribune, C. Oppius, had passed legislation forbidding women to wear jewellery or costly clothing or ride in carriages in Rome save on religious occasions (Livy, 34.1.3).

The wealth of Syracuse not only eased the financial crisis but more importantly enabled the senate to stabilise and reform the currency. The challenge of meeting so many expenses out of such limited revenues had led the *patres* to authorise progressive debasements of the Republic's coinage until the coins were worth only a fraction of their nominal value. In late 212 or 211, the senate felt the fiscal situation had improved enough to clear away the monetary wreckage and introduce a completely new coinage based on the silver *denarius*, worth ten bronze asses of two ounces each (hence the name *denarius* or 'ten-piece').[16] This new coinage endured without significant alteration throughout the war and down to c. 146, when the silver *sestertius* became the official unit of reckoning for the Republic (although *denarii* continued to be minted). The economic importance of the new coins was great, but perhaps even greater was their psychological effect. They proclaimed that the Republic had recovered its former fiscal strength and was ready to go on to the end against Hannibal.

Not that that claim was altogether true. In 210 the senators once again found the treasury lacked the cash to pay for rowers for a new squadron of warships and once again turned to slave owners to supply oarsmen. This time, however, the slave owners protested vehemently that they were being stripped of their workforce at the same time that taxes to fund the war were crushing them and the

16. M. H. Crawford, *Coinage and Money under the Roman Republic: Italy and the Mediterranean Economy*, London: Methuen, 1985, 52–62.

Figure 17 Reverse of a Roman *denarius* issued in 136 by C. Servilius, showing the Dioscuri on horseback with spears. ANS 1963.31.31. Courtesy of the American Numismatic Society.

enemy was devastating their farms. They flatly refused to comply with the senate's order. The crisis was only resolved when the senators themselves set an example of sacrifice by each handing over all but a small portion of his wealth to the treasury, to be repaid when circumstances permitted. The *patres'* action incited the *equites* and others to rival them in generosity by following suit (Livy, 26.35.1–36.12). Even this, however, did not end the Republic's fiscal troubles. In the following year the senate had to authorise the use of a special reserve of gold kept in the treasury for emergencies to meet the military expenses for the year (Livy, 27.11.11–13). Nevertheless, the financial situation remained tight. Scipio's invasion of Africa in 205 (see below) was financed in part by voluntary contributions from the allies (Livy, 28.45.13–20), while in the same year the lack of money for the war caused the senate to authorise the sale of a portion of the confiscated Campanian land (Livy, 28.46.4–6).

The treasury's difficulties in meeting the expenses of the war mirrored the pressures it imposed on its citizens and allies. The *tributum* was collected every year, and at least once at double the normal rate, in 215 when the Republic's situation looked desperate (Livy, 23.31.1). The need for soldiers drained farms throughout Italy of young men, and the Republic's demands exceeded the ability of some allies to meet them. In 209 delegations from twelve of the thirty Latin colonies came before the senate to announce that they were no longer able to meet their quotas for recruits, nor did they have money to pay them. Spokesmen for the remaining eighteen colonies, however, came forward to promise that they would continue to do what the senate asked of them, much to the relief of the *patres*. No further mention was made of the recalcitrant colonies until 204, when their exemption from furnishing soldiers was brought up in the senate. The *patres* ordered them to supply double the ordinary number of soldiers and imposed a heavy tax on them in addition (Livy, 27.9.7–10, 29.15.2–15).

The strains of the war also found an outlet in heightened religious anxieties among the ordinary citizens and their leaders alike. The expiation of prodigies regularly occupied the senate's attention at the opening of every year, and its authorisation of a number of temples and extraordinary rites sought to regain the favour of the gods. Those steps did not immediately set the citizens' minds at rest, however. In 213 it was brought to the senate's attention that a crowd of women had invaded the forum practising various untraditional rites and sacrifices while prophets were preying on the minds of ordinary citizens. Violence had rebuffed attempts by the aediles to suppress these practices. The senate in response decreed that such rites as did not conform to ancestral practice were forbidden in public and that anyone with books of prophecies, prayers, or rituals should hand them over to the praetor (Livy, 25.1.6–12). The order was apparently obeyed, for one of the books turned in contained prophecies by Marcius, a famous seer. Among them was one that seemed to foretell the disaster at Cannae. That led the senators to take seriously another, which announced that in order to drive out foreign enemies a festival in honour of Apollo should be held every year. The senate accordingly decreed that the festival be celebrated, and the games to Apollo (*ludi Apollinaries*) were soon made a regular part of the religious calendar (Livy, 25.12.2–15; 27.23.5–7). Whether the prophecies were genuine or concocted by the *patres* in order to quiet the public's religious apprehensions cannot be determined at this remove.

By 211 religious innovation, reform of the coinage, increased financial resources, diplomatic success in Greece, and victories at Capua and Syracuse had combined to furnish hope that the Republic had weathered the worst of the crisis. Prospects for the future looked, if not rosy, at least not bleak for the first time since

Cannae. Only Spain clouded that picture. There the two commanders, Publius Cornelius Scipio, the consul of 218, and his brother, Gnaeus, had won allies and campaigned with notable success, pushing Roman arms south of the Ebro. In 211, however, each met defeat, and both lost their lives along with many of their men. The senate urgently needed a commander to go to Spain and renew the war there. Not only would that commander restore the situation there, but he would prove to be a general more than a match for Hannibal, and the man who would finally bring the war to a victorious end.

Scipio and Spain

The war in Spain had been a side-show thus far in the struggle against Hannibal. The senate had been able to spare few resources for it during the war's early years, and the Scipio brothers had been forced to rely mainly on what they could scrape up in the province in order to keep their troops fed and paid. Despite the unequal odds they faced, reinforcements could not be spared either, and that fact made diplomacy with the Spanish tribes crucial. The Scipios had expended considerable effort on winning over local allies in order to mobilise additional forces to meet the enemy on even terms. In this they had been successful; Livy reports that some 20,000 Spanish fighters had accompanied the Scipios on their final campaigns, a number (if we can trust it) equal to the paper strengths of their Roman and Italian troops (although these had undoubtedly been considerably depleted by this stage). Much of Spain in these years was tribal in its social and political structure, organised around petty kings and chieftains. Personal connections between leaders counted for a great deal more than formal links between governments. The Scipios' coalition of allies arose out of the connections and friendships they had forged with the men who commanded the loyalty of fighters they could bring to the battlefield. Although Rome had scored important successes in 212 and 211, the war was far from won. Hannibal was still at large in Italy, able to move about at will. Even if the victories at Capua and Syracuse had blunted his momentum, reinforcements from Spain would put Rome's gains at risk. To prevent that, it was essential to keep the war in Spain going and pin down the Carthaginian forces there while still husbanding resources for the main struggle in Italy. Those personal ties the Scipios had established would have to be renewed in order to find the Spanish allies Rome needed to continue the war. That fact explains the otherwise very surprising decision to appoint P. Cornelius Scipio, the son of the homonymous consul of 218 and nephew of his brother Gnaeus, to take command of the Roman effort in Spain.[17]

The appointment was remarkable in part because Scipio was by Roman standards still relatively young in 210, only 26 years old. The Republic was a place where young men waited a very long time before being entrusted with an army. Equally striking, he had advanced along the *cursus honorum* no farther than the curule aedileship; he had never held an office that entailed *imperium* or exercised an independent military command (although like all young men of his class, he had been to war and served as a military tribune). He was in fact a private citizen at that point, which seems to be why his appointment was subjected to a vote of the *populus*. Other non-magistrates had in unusual circumstances been vested with *imperium*, most recently his uncle Gnaeus, who like his brother had held the rank of proconsul while they commanded in Spain. But promagistrates like Gnaeus had all previously held a consulate or praetorship and might be thought still to possess a kind of latent *imperium* that could simply be reactivated by the senate, somewhat akin to the way the senate could continue a consul's or praetor's *imperium* into a promagistracy after his year in office ended. However, the senate apparently felt that since Scipio had never held an office that conferred *imperium*, he needed a vote of the *comitia centuriata* before he could possess the proconsular *imperium* that would enable him to command in Spain. Still, he was untried in a position of such enormous responsibility, and so an older, experienced commander, M. Junius Silanus, accompanied him in a subordinate position but clearly expected to act as an advisor. Silanus, however, quickly slipped into the background once Scipio took command, for he needed no advice. In Scipio, Rome had discovered a commander of instinctive military genius.

Scipio reached Spain late in 210. The survivors of his father's and uncle's army, some 8,000 men, had been pushed back across the Ebro to the northeastern corner of the peninsula. The fall of Capua had enabled the senate to reinforce these in 211 with another 10,000 troops, to which Scipio added the 10,000 that accompanied him. That gave him roughly four very under-strength legions and

17. H. H. Scullard, *Scipio Africanus, Soldier and Politician*, Ithaca, NY: Cornell University Press, 1970.

contingents of *socii*, and with them he struck the enemy fast and hard. The Carthaginians' main base in eastern Spain was New Carthage, where they had deposited their war chest and the many high-ranking Spanish hostages that they held to ensure the loyalty of their allies. The town lay some 400 km south of the Ebro, well beyond the Romans' reach, or so the Carthaginian generals imagined, for they and their armies were elsewhere when Scipio and his army attacked it in the spring of 209. Strong fortifications protected the city, and it was surrounded by water on three sides: a harbour, a lagoon, and a canal connecting the two. The only approach by land lay across an isthmus, only about 400 m wide, where the walls were naturally formidable. A long siege was out of the question; the enemy would quickly converge and trap Scipio far from his sources of supply. The situation called for a rapid assault, and Scipio was up to the tactical challenge. He knew that wind-action frequently caused the lagoon's water level to drop in the evening, making it fairly easy to wade across. He announced, therefore, that the god Neptune himself would assist them in capturing the city, and ordered his infantry to attack across the isthmus on the following day while his ships kept up a barrage of missiles from the harbour. This attack concentrated the defenders on those two sectors of the wall. Meanwhile towards evening Scipio sent a small force he had kept in reserve with scaling ladders through the lagoon. When, as he had anticipated, the water began to recede, his prophecy seemed to the waders and the rest of the army to have been fulfilled. The soldiers on the isthmus redoubled their efforts, and the force in the lagoon upon reaching the walls found them deserted. They quickly mounted them and moved towards the gates, dispatching the defenders as they went. When the force got to the gates, they broke through the bolts just as those outside were gaining the upper hand against the last of the enemy. The fall of the city was a stunning blow to the Carthaginians. Not only had they lost control of a strategic strongpoint but, far worse, Scipio released the Spanish hostages back to their families, earning their immense gratitude and at the same time weakening his enemies' hold on their allies' loyalty. It was a brilliant opening to what would become a spectacular achievement in Spain (Polyb. 10.7.1–20.9).

That achievement was a product of Scipio's extraordinary tactical abilities, a talent that put him far in advance of his peers. This he demonstrated once again and in striking fashion at the battle that ended Carthaginian control of Spain. Following his capture of New

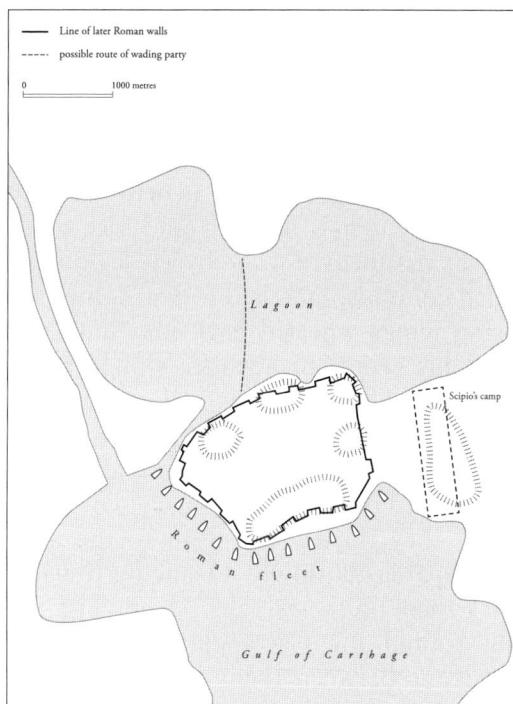

Figure 18 Plan of Scipio's assault on New Carthage.

Carthage, Scipio spent the remainder of the year training his army and rallying many native tribes to his side. In 208 he felt strong enough to go on the offensive. At Baecula in the valley of the upper Baetis (now the Guadalquivir), he met the army of Hannibal's brother, Hasdrubal Barca, and routed it. That victory induced the tribes in the region to join his side. The following year saw little action, but the next would prove decisive. Scipio advanced his forces into the lower Baetis valley, the heart of Punic power, and met the enemy at Ilipa. There he drew up his forces and offered battle on several successive mornings, placing his best troops, his Romans and Italians, in the centre and his Spanish allies on the wings. The enemy commander likewise assembled his army for battle with his best men, the African infantry, in the centre facing the Romans and Italians and his Spanish allies on the wings. However, since Hasdrubal occupied a strong defensive position, he elected not to advance to begin combat but to wait for Scipio to come to him, which Scipio declined to do. When the two armies had stood facing one another for some time, both commanders decided there would

be no battle that day and retired to their camps. Noting his opponent's habit, Scipio marched his men out one morning earlier than
usual, forcing the Carthaginian general to respond quickly and draw
up his own forces. But on this occasion Scipio had marshalled his
Romans and Italians on the wings and his native troops in the centre,
while the Carthaginian formation was as before. Scipio's best troops
were now facing his enemy's weakest and vice versa. Scipio next
executed a complex manoeuvre whereby the legions and *socii* on the
two wings formed columns, marched forward, then when they drew
near the opposing wings wheeled back into lines of battle. Meanwhile he ordered his centre to advance slowly and avoid coming
into contact with the African troops facing them. The manoeuvre
enabled the Roman and Italian troops to put the Carthaginians'
Spanish allies to flight before Scipio's Spanish allies had to engage the
Africans. The latter had remained stationary while all this was going
on, fearful that if they turned and went to the aid of their allies
on the wings the Spaniards slowly advancing towards them would
charge and attack them on their flanks. Meanwhile, the Romans and
Italians, having routed the Carthaginian wings, were preparing
to catch the Africans between them when providentially a severe
thunderstorm broke and enabled the Africans to retreat safely to
their camp. Their few remaining allies, however, now deserted them,
making withdrawal imperative. But before they could get across the
Baetis, Scipio's cavalry caught them, forcing them to stand and fight.
At that point the Roman infantry arrived to finish the job (Polyb.
11.20.1–24.11; Livy, 28.11.10–16.15). When the battle was over, no
organised Carthaginian resistance remained in Spain, and Rome had
finally found a general who could match tactical wits with the victor
of Cannae.

Still, the high level of manoeuvre that Scipio was perfecting
during these years meant that the outcomes of battles were far less
predictable than when two armies simply marched straight at one
another and fought. That had been the case at Baecula two years
before, and the consequences would lead to the crisis of the war
in Italy. At Baecula, Scipio faced the challenge of attacking a
Carthaginian army drawn up on a hill. He began the assault by
sending forward some of his light infantry, to which Hasdrubal
Barca responded in kind. As the struggle grew increasingly heated
and both sides gradually committed the whole of their light-armed
troops, Scipio divided his legions and *socii* into two contingents,
marched each to the left and right sides of the hill and then up to its

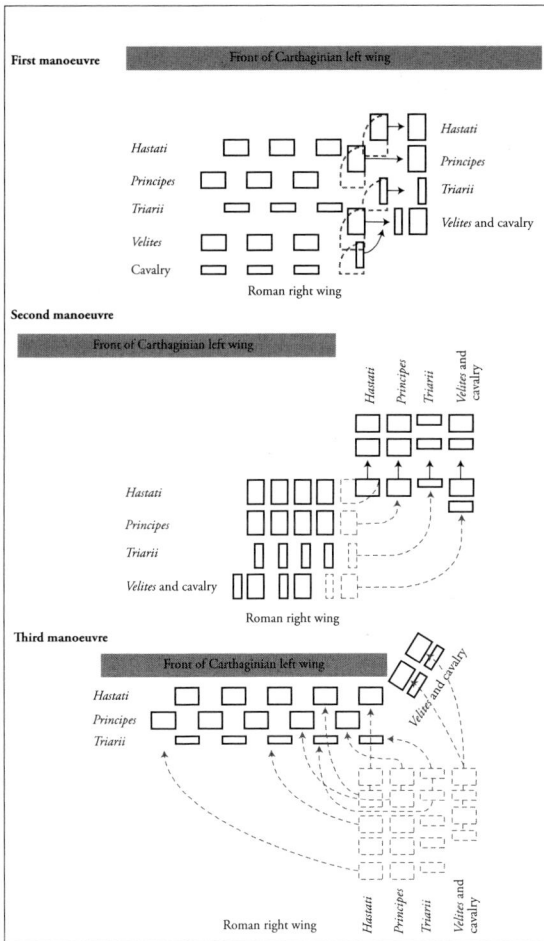

Figure 19 Diagram illustrating one reconstruction of the manoeuvres of the right wing of Scipio's army at the battle of Ilipa.

summit, where he drew them up for battle. However, Hasdrubal had not yet committed his main force to the fight, and when he realised that Scipio was now positioned to attack his flanks, he was able to withdraw the bulk of them intact, although he had to abandon his light infantry to its fate to do so. At that point, rather than retire west down the Baetis valley, Hasdrubal elected to march north, heading for Italy and his brother, Hannibal (Polyb. 10.38.7–39.9; Livy, 27.18.1–19.20).

Whether Scipio should have pursued is an open question. His forces were too few to block all the possible routes across the

Pyrenees even if he could reach them in time. He also feared attack by the remaining Carthaginian armies. And to withdraw would have meant abandoning all the gains he had made in the south including those tribes that had forsaken their alliances with Carthage to rally to Scipio and Rome. Yet the war in Spain had all along been strategically subordinate to the larger struggle in Italy. The only reason the Romans were fighting there was to prevent reinforcements from there from reaching Hannibal. Scipio may have believed that the surest path to that end lay in the complete destruction of Carthaginian power in Spain, and Hasdrubal's departure only made that task easier. At Rome, however, things looked very different, and Scipio seemed to be confusing his own aims in one theatre with the accomplishment of the senate's overall strategy for winning the war. This would not be the last time Scipio's notions of how the war ought to be waged would clash with those of the *patres*.

Miracle at the Metaurus

The prospect of a new Punic army reaching Italy provoked panic at Rome. In the years since the fall of Syracuse and Capua the Romans had made steady progress against Hannibal. They had recaptured several cities and subdued a number of tribes that had gone over to his side; most importantly, Tarentum had fallen in 209 to Q. Fabius Maximus, holding the consulship for the sixth time. Its capture finally ended the threat of reinforcements and supplies reaching Hannibal by sea. In Greece, Roman forces had steadily moved the locus of combat to the east and away from Italy, and they had brought additional allies into the struggle against Philip. At sea, Roman fleets had raided Africa and defeated Carthaginian efforts to challenge the Republic's naval supremacy. An attempt to renew the struggle in Sicily had been turned back. In Italy itself, Roman successes had gradually restricted Hannibal's freedom of movement, although most commanders were still reluctant to challenge him to a pitched battle. Progress had not been entirely smooth; Hannibal was still a force to be reckoned with. He had destroyed two Roman legions and their commander at Herdonia, and an ambush had claimed the lives of both consuls of 208, M. Claudius Marcellus and T. Quinctius Crispinus. Overall, however, Hannibal was now mainly confined to the south, in Bruttium and Lucania, where the Romans hoped to keep him until they could find a way to finish him off at last.

The arrival of Hasdrubal with a new Punic army threatened to undo all that progress. For the first time in the war, however, fortune favoured Rome. Hannibal had had word from his brother that he was on his way, but in the spring of 207 Hannibal was still awaiting a message from Hasdrubal detailing the route he and the army would take south, enabling Hannibal to move north and join forces with him. Happily for Rome, foragers from the army of the consul, C. Claudius Nero, dogging Hannibal in the south, captured the riders carrying the letter. That stroke of luck enabled Nero to pull off one of Rome's greatest logistical feats. Selecting 6,000 infantry and 1,000 horse from his army and leaving the rest in place to make it appear as if his whole force was still encamped opposite Hannibal, Nero ordered a forced march north to Picenum, some 475 km away, to find Hasdrubal before Hasdrubal found his brother. Men and women lined the army's route offering food and drink as the soldiers hurried past so that they could refresh themselves with only the briefest of stops on their march. They volunteered their mules and carts to transport those overcome by exhaustion. Meanwhile the senate, having received Hasdrubal's letter from Nero, instructed his colleague, M. Livius Salinator, to advance with his two legions into Picenum, where he found Hasdrubal's army. The praetor commanding in northern Italy, L. Porcius Licinus, who had shadowed Hasdrubal as he moved through Gaul, joined him there with his two undermanned legions, but the Romans avoided offering battle until Nero and his column arrived. When they did, Livius ordered his men to take Nero's troops into their tents in order to avoid enlarging his camp. Livius and Nero were eager to tempt Hasdrubal to commit his forces to a battle against an enemy army he believed was weaker than his own, so it was vital to conceal the arrival of Nero's reinforcements lest Hasdrubal and his army flee south to join his brother. Nero therefore waited until nightfall to enter Livius' camp; the plan was spoiled, though, when Hasdrubal's scouts reported that two trumpets had sounded in the Romans' camp, a sure sign that two commanders were present (Livy, 27.45.7–47.6).

Hasdrubal now sought to escape. He had collected a host of warriors on his journey through Gaul, so that by the time he reached Picenum his forces probably equalled those of Livius and Porcius combined, about 30,000–35,000 infantry and cavalry in addition to ten elephants. The arrival of Nero's 7,000, however, tipped the odds against him, and he ordered his men to withdraw across the river

Metaurus to his rear. Once again, luck was with the Romans. Hasdrubal's army lost its way in the dark and missed the ford; their Roman pursuers caught them at the river, forcing them to stand and fight. In the battle that followed, Nero, commanding the right wing, found that his forces could not attack the Gauls opposite him since they occupied a strong position on a hill anchoring the left side of the Carthaginians' line of battle. Unwilling to stand idly by while Livius' army on the left was locked in a furious struggle against Hasdrubal's veteran Spanish troops, Nero withdrew several units from his front, assembled them in the rear, and then marched them behind the rest of the army past the left end of the Roman formation. He then charged the right flank and rear of the Spanish, which decided the battle. The Romans annihilated the Spanish forces and their general fell in the thick of the fighting. Next the Romans advanced upon the Gauls and butchered them, many still asleep, drunk in their beds. The victory complete, Nero formed up his men, and they marched south as swiftly as they had come, reaching their camp before Hannibal realised they were gone. They did not neglect to let the Carthaginian know where they had been, however. They had brought his brother's head with them, and they hurled it into Hannibal's camp, at the same time parading several African officers they had captured before the enemy. They released two to Hannibal, to provide a full account of what had happened. He now understood that his last hope was gone and withdrew deep into Bruttium. With Scipio's victory at Ilipa in the following year, no further help would be forthcoming from that quarter. All he could do now was wait while the Romans decided how to finish the war (Polyb. 11.1.2–2.1; Livy, 27.48.1–50.1, 51.11–13).

Scipio and the endgame

News of the victory brought wild rejoicing at Rome. Never before had the Republic decisively beaten the enemy in Italy. Livius and his army returned to march through the city in triumph; Nero, though the real hero of the battle, had to be content with the lesser honour of an ovation since the battle had been fought in his colleague's province. The senate could now look forward at last to a victorious conclusion to the war, a victory that became all the more certain with the arrival of the news of Scipio's conquest at Ilipa in the following year. Just how to go about completing that victory, however, opened the first serious rift within the aristocracy since

Cannae. Scipio returned to Italy late in 206. He, too, was denied a triumph, since he had held no regular magistracy in connection with his command in Spain. There was no denying him a consulship, though, when he stood for that office for the following year. The centuries' vote was unanimous amid confident predictions that Rome had finally found the man who would finish the war. No one was more confident of that than Scipio himself. His plan was to cross to Africa and bring the war home to Carthage itself. When the *patres* met to discuss provincial assignments soon after Scipio and his colleague for 205 entered office, Scipio boldly demanded Sicily, command of a fleet, and permission to lead an army to Africa. Fabius Maximus, however, announced he was opposed. It was too dangerous with Hannibal still at large in Italy; the war should be won there before mounting any invasion of Africa (Livy, 28.38.1–12; 40.1–44.18).

Fabius had a point. The Republic would be risking a great deal in sending an army to Africa, where it could not easily be reinforced. The last one that had fought there, under Regulus during the First Punic War, had been utterly destroyed. Another misfortune like that and the momentum would shift back to Carthage. The fate of the invasion force would rest in the hands of a single man and a young one at that, whose errors of judgement some might argue had allowed Hasdrubal to slip away into Italy, very nearly undoing the hard-won gains of the previous nine years. Rome had once before staked everything on a single campaign, at Cannae, and that defeat had brought the Republic to the brink of destruction. Senatorial strategy ever since had sought to minimise the risk of a similarly catastrophic defeat by waging a multi-front war. Each pair of consuls had done their part against Hannibal, but none had had the fate of the Republic riding on his shoulders. In keeping with that strategy, Scipio and his colleague should do their part in a concerted effort against Hannibal in Italy, directed by the senate.

Behind this clash over how the last stages of the war were to be waged lay personal and political issues. Fabius had been one of the chief architects of the cautious, step-by-step strategy that had enabled Rome to claw its way back from the disasters of the war's early years. He had held four consulships since then, and although after the last one in 209 he had been eased out of active command, he remained a dominant voice in the senate. His idea of how to defeat Hannibal envisioned a continuation of senatorial control of the war, which meant that he and several other like-minded senior figures would continue to exert a decisive influence on its conduct. Moreover, Fabius' personal prestige and his claims to authority on the basis of his services to the *res publica* were inextricably bound up with seeing his incremental strategy carried to its logical conclusion, the destruction of Hannibal and his army in Italy. Scipio had very different ideas. The invasion of Africa was his chance to win the war and lay claim to the immense glory and prestige this would bring. The prospect of placing himself under close senatorial control in Italy for limited gains will have been as unattractive as it was unaccustomed. In Spain he had operated as he saw fit without the senate telling him what to do. Spain was too far away for that kind of supervision; Africa was, too. And once there, with the outcome of the war riding on his conduct of a campaign that could take years, he could involve his army so deeply in critical operations that the senate would not dare to replace him until the job was done.

No surprise, then, that the debate was long and heated, all the more so because Scipio hinted that if he did not get his way he would go before the people and request a law to give him what he wanted. Yet when the *patres* called his bluff, he backed down and entrusted his fate to them. Surprisingly, they gave him the permission he sought. The war had gone on for a dozen years now, and Italy was nearing exhaustion. Invading Africa offered the best hope of a swift conclusion. Perhaps as well, many of the younger senators had had enough of the small group of now elderly men whose repeated consulates during the war had denied that office to other aspirants and whose dominance in the senate had drowned out other voices. Many might feel with justification that it was time for new blood in command.

With Hannibal still a potential threat, the senate refused to reduce its troop strength in Italy in order to provide Scipio with an invasion force. He was instead given command of the disgraced legions from Cannae, which had seen little action since then and had been the repository for the remnants from every legion disgraced by defeat in the intervening years. This assignment may have been Fabius' final revenge. The senators also allowed Scipio to augment this force with volunteers, and 7,000 came forward. He spent the whole of 205 at Syracuse training his army as well as the fleet that would accompany them to Africa. Meanwhile the senate took what steps it could to prepare for the final showdown. It had been gradually reducing its commitment to the war against Philip as the king became increasingly bogged down in indecisive fighting in eastern Greece. In 207, with Hasdrubal's invasion immanent, it withdrew the last of its forces there in order to husband its resources for that struggle. Realising that their allies had abandoned them and unable to resist Philip alone, the Aetolians sued for peace in the following year. The senate made a half-hearted attempt to rekindle the conflict in 205, but their erstwhile allies would have none of it, and with Scipio preparing to take the war to Africa, the *patres* elected to sign on to the peace with Philip and focus all the Republic's energy on the war with Carthage (Livy, 29.12.1–13).

Nor did the senators neglect to do what they could to ensure heavenly support for the invasion. In that same year a prophecy was discovered in the Sibylline books announcing that if ever a foreign enemy made war in Italy, he could be driven out and defeated if the Idean Mother, the goddess Cybele, was brought from her home in Asia Minor to Rome.[18] Ambassadors were sent east, negotiations entered into, and in 204 word arrived that Cybele's arrival was at hand. The honour of receiving her would go to the best man in the state, a distinction that the *patres* conferred on P. Cornelius Scipio Nasica, cousin to the conqueror of Spain. A shrewd choice: it avoided elevating the consul of 205 any higher than he had vaulted already. At the same time, he and his supporters could hardly complain at such a great distinction conferred on his family. Legend quickly surrounded the advent of the Magna Mater. Most famously, the Vestal virgin Claudia Quinta, suspected of unchastity, proved her virtue by pulling the ship carrying the goddess's image off a sandbar with her sash (Ovid, *Fasti* 4.291–344). The *matronae* of Rome passed the statue from hand to hand once it reached the city and installed it appropriately in the temple of Victory on the Palatine hill. With it came Cybele's noisy retinue of exotic, eunuch priests, something the senators had not bargained for. Nevertheless, they decreed an annual festival be held in her honour, the Megalesia, on 4 April, to celebrate her arrival (Livy, 29.10.9–11.8, 14.1–14).

In 205, however, disturbing reports reached Rome of outrages inflicted by one of Scipio's officers, Q. Pleminius, on the population of Locri in southern Italy. The town had revolted to Hannibal early in the war, and when an opportunity arose, Scipio crossed over from Sicily, recaptured it, and drove away Hannibal and a relief

18. E. S. Gruen, *Studies in Greek Culture and Roman Policy*, Leiden: Brill, 1990; reprint Berkeley and Los Angeles: University of California Press, 1996, 5–33; E. Orlin, *Foreign Cults in Rome: Creating a Roman Empire*, Oxford: Oxford University Press, 2010, 76–84.

force. Scipio left Pleminius in charge of the garrison and returned to Syracuse, but Pleminius proceeded to abuse the citizens to such an extent that, after receiving no redress from Scipio, they sent an embassy to the senate to complain (Livy, 29.6.2–9.12). Residual antagonism towards Scipio in the wake of the debate over his request to cross to Africa was fuelled by rumours that the consul was traipsing around Syracuse in Greek clothing and sandals, exercising in the gymnasium, neglecting his duties, and corrupting the discipline of the army. The shocked *patres* dispatched a high-powered delegation to Locri to deal with Pleminius with instructions then to go on to Sicily to investigate the charges levelled against the consul. If the legates judged him guilty, they were to haul him back to Rome to face the senators. At Locri, they found Pleminius and thirty-five others guilty and sent them in chains to Rome. At Syracuse, however, Scipio was ready for them. He assembled his army and fleet, and when the envoys arrived he put on a display of their manoeuvres. That put all doubts to rest. The legates gave him their blessing and urged him to cross to Africa as soon as possible, certain that the hopes reposed in him would be fulfilled (Livy, 29.16.4–22.6).

Scipio did not disappoint. In 204 he embarked his army for Africa and made land near the city of Utica. After establishing a well-defended camp, he spent the remainder of the year ravaging the countryside and fighting a number of minor actions against Carthage's home defence forces. The following spring, the Carthaginians assembled a strong force in anticipation of a decisive action that year. They were joined by their ally, Syphax, the king of Numidia, with a powerful cavalry contingent. Scipio struck first, however, in a daring night attack on their camps. His raiders succeeded in surprising their opponents as they slept and setting their wooden huts on fire, with devastating loss of life. Collecting new forces later that year, Syphax and the Carthaginians met the Romans on the Great Plains south of the city, and once again Scipio and his army prevailed. It was this defeat that finally compelled the Carthaginian senate to recall Hannibal from Italy to defend his homeland, a homeland he had not seen in thirty-five years. The orders to return came as a bitter blow, the culmination of a long series of setbacks. Hannibal's great victories, his fifteen years of war in Italy, had all been for nothing. In the autumn of 203 he and the remnants of his army returned to Africa (Livy, 30.19.12–20.9).

In 202 after preliminary manoeuvring, Scipio and Hannibal finally faced one another at Zama. Their armies were fairly evenly matched in numbers, about 35,000–40,000 men each, but the Romans were far better trained while Carthage was scraping the bottom of the barrel. Mercenaries and citizen levies made up most of its strength. Still, Hannibal had his veterans from Italy, some 12,000 of them, and they had never been vanquished. Their general held them in reserve, as his third line, with the mercenaries and citizens forming the first and second. Carthaginian cavalry and Syphax's Numidian horsemen protected his flanks, and some eighty elephants would open the attack. Scipio adapted his dispositions to meet this initial threat. Abandoning the usual *quincunx* formation, he arranged his maniples one behind another, creating wide lanes between them. When the battle began and the elephants advanced, the Roman and Italian light infantry positioned in front of the legions and *socii* attacked the elephants with missiles. Their wounds caused many of the elephants to escape to the left and right of the armies, while the rest ran forward between the maniples, doing little damage, to the rear of the army where the troops stationed there dispatched them. As this action was under way, the Roman cavalry on one end of the line of battle and the Numidian cavalry under their prince, Masinissa, whose alliance Scipio had secured, on the other charged the enemy's horse and routed them. Then the main bodies of troops closed. The fight was hard and bloody and long, until the Romans despite heavy losses at last overcame Hannibal's first two lines of infantry. At that point, Scipio halted the advance, got his men to dress their ranks, then moved the maniples of *principes* and *triarii* forward and positioned them in the gaps between the maniples of *hastati*. His army now presented a solid front, and Scipio ordered it forward against Hannibal's veterans. The ground was soaked with blood by this point and so covered with bodies, Polybius reports, that the Romans and their allies had difficulty clambering over them. As the two armies met, the Roman and allied Numidian cavalry returned from their pursuit and charged the Carthaginians in the rear. Few of them escaped that slaughter, although Hannibal himself managed to make his way to safety (Polyb. 15.9.1–14.9; Livy, 30.32.1–35.11).

With that, the war was effectively over. The only questions that remained concerned the peace terms Scipio would impose and how long the Carthaginian senate would hold out before bowing to the inevitable and surrendering. Surprisingly, Scipio's terms were relatively mild for an enemy that had brought his country to its knees, ravaged much of Italy, and cost the Republic and its allies

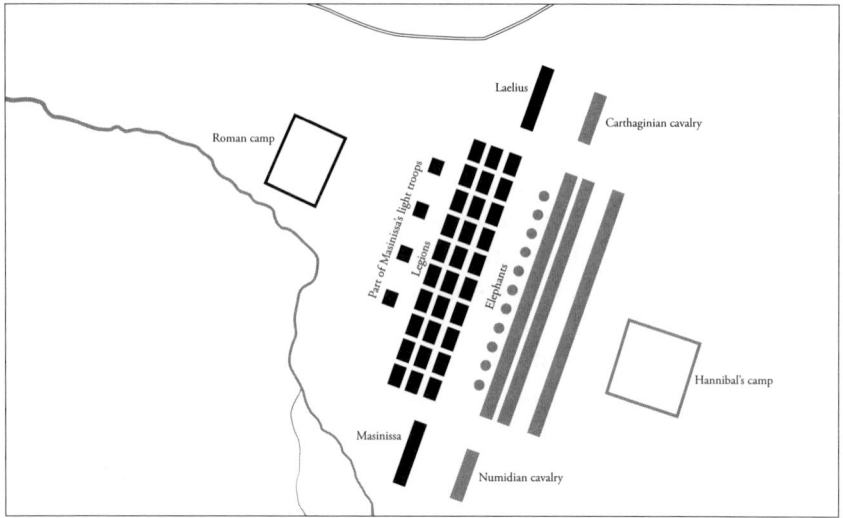

Figure 20 Plan of the battle at Zama.

countless lives and treasure. Severe limits were imposed on Carthage's military forces as well as its ability to wage war without Roman permission. All of his ancestral lands were to be restored to Masinissa. An indemnity of 10,000 talents was imposed, to be paid at the rate of 200 talents per year for fifty years. All deserters and prisoners were to be handed over and a hundred young Carthaginian men besides as hostages. However, the Carthaginians were to retain all of the territory in Africa they ruled at the outset of the war. All of their property was spared. And they were to enjoy their own laws and no garrison was to be imposed (Polyb. 15.18.1–8; Livy, 30.37.1–6). That is to say, Carthage was not to be despoiled, its temples violated, its buildings razed to the ground, the people enslaved, and their goods carried off – a far different fate from what the senate had imposed on Capua. But pressures in Rome were shaping Scipio's terms. He wanted to reap the glory not just of defeating Hannibal but of ending the war. Harsh terms could only provoke continued resistance and possibly the necessity of besieging the city. Now that the unconquerable Hannibal had finally been conquered and the war was all but over, Scipio was no longer indispensable. Others could hope to take his place in Africa and snatch credit for Carthage's capitulation if resistance continued. Consuls in 203 and 202 had had such hopes. They had strenuously demanded that the senate send them, as the Republic's chief magistrates, to fight in Africa. Scipio's allies among the *patres* had had to arrange various compromises to meet their legitimate claims to the right to conduct the city's most critical military affairs. Similar demands would be even harder to resist after Zama. Indeed, one of the consuls of 201 went so far as to veto the senate's decree endorsing the peace in order to prolong the war so that he could lead it. But his was a lone voice of opposition. The veto was overcome, and the assembly joyously ratified the peace. The war was over. Scipio returned bearing the *cognomen* 'Africanus', in commemoration of his exploits there. Rome had conquered half the world, but it and Italy had paid an awful price in suffering, death, and destruction (to say nothing of the Carthaginians, Spanish, Greeks, and Gauls). It would take years for the Republic and its allies to recover. Yet within a year the Romans would embark on a great, new war, one that would begin their conquest of the other half.

CHAPTER 5

The conquest of Gaul, Greece, and Spain

The Second Punic War was the most complex strategic challenge the Roman Republic had ever faced. Defeating Hannibal in Italy demanded coordinated campaigns in several distinct theatres both there and abroad, and Rome's success ranks as one of antiquity's most impressive military achievements. Yet fighting in Gaul, the Greek east, and Spain did not end with Carthage's surrender. By that point those conflicts had taken on lives of their own separate and apart from the supporting roles they had played in the larger struggle. Nowhere was this more true than in northern Italy.

Northern Italy

The Gallic threat had menaced central Italy for generations, and only in the late 220s had Rome gained the upper hand. That conquest was short-lived, however, for Hannibal's arrival and victory at the river Trebia sparked an uprising that overwhelmed the colonies at Placentia and Cremona and the Republic's nascent efforts to secure the region. Cannae and the destruction of the consul L. Postumius Albinus and his army in Gaul a few months later forced the senate to defer any effort to re-subjugate the region. Two legions took up a station at Ariminum. Their task throughout the war was simply to keep reinforcements from reaching Hannibal and prevent incursions by raiding parties. The Gauls for their part seem to have been content to let matters lie. Little is heard of them until 207, when Hasdrubal Barca enticed a sizeable contingent of Gallic troops to join his campaign after he and his army reached Italy. Once that threat had been ended at the river Metaurus the senate returned to the defensive. Even when a third Barcid brother, Mago, landed near Genua in 205 with 17,000 soldiers and thirty warships and seized the town, the senate's response was merely to increase its defences in the north. Only when Mago marched east and entered the Po valley in 203 with a large force of Ligurian and Gallic allies did the Romans move against him. In the hard-fought battle that ensued Mago fell wounded, precipitating the flight of his men (Livy, 30.18.1–19.6). He retreated into Liguria with the remnants of his army, where he received his government's summons to return to Africa at about the same time Hannibal was being recalled to defend the homeland. Mago died of his wounds, however, before he could join his brother for the final showdown at Zama.

From the senate's perspective, victory in Africa altered the situation in Gaul not one whit. The war there (or the rebellion, as the *patres* would have termed it) remained unfinished, and the urgency of that task was brought fully home to them in the following year. One of the largest tribes, the Boii, destroyed a force sent by the consul to check their plundering of Roman allies (Livy, 31.2.5–11). Their victory provoked several of the leading Gallic and Ligurian tribes to stage a massive uprising in 200 to rid themselves of the Romans once and for all. Yet vestiges of the Second Punic War persisted even still. One Hasdrubal, a survivor of Hasdrubal Barca's or Mago's army, led a force that attacked and sacked Placentia then marched against its sister colony, Cremona. The praetor L. Furius Purpurio, temporarily in command of a consular army, marched rapidly from Ariminum to relieve the colony, brought the enemy to battle, and crushed them. Relieved by the consul, who was anything but pleased to have had the victory won by someone else, Furius made his way to Rome and requested a triumph, which the senators, after considerable debate, awarded (Livy, 31.10.1–11.3, 21.1–22.3, 47.4–49.3).[1] Furius' victory was hardly the end of the war. In the following year, the Insubres, who had joined in the attack on the colonies, annihilated a Roman army that had invaded its land to exact revenge. With that disaster, the senate determined that it was time to put an end to Rome's problems in Gaul for good. As a first step, Placentia was re-established and fugitives from there and Cremona returned to the towns. In 197 the senate dispatched both consuls north in a coordinated assault on the region. One, C. Cornelius Cethegus, marched west with his army from Ariminum, just as the coalition of Gallic tribes that had assembled to meet this invasion had anticipated. Unexpectedly, however, the other, Q. Minucius Rufus, crossed the Apennines with his force from

---

1. M. Pittenger, *Contested Triumphs: Politics, Pageantry, and Performance in Livy's Republican Rome*, Berkeley and Los Angeles: University of California Press, 2008, 168–80.

Genua and attacked the territory of the Boii. This sudden threat caused the Boiian contingent to withdraw from the coalition facing Cethegus. The Gauls who remained, the Insubres and the Cenomani, were no match for Cethegus' army, and the Cenomani seem to have realised it. They proved receptive to the consul's overtures and made a separate peace. That isolated the Insubres, and in the ensuing battle many of them fell and Hasdrubal was captured. Cethegus' victory took the fight out of the Boii, and they refused to leave the safety of their towns as Rufus' troops ravaged their lands (Livy, 32.29.5–31.6). Over the course of the following six years one or both consuls continued the assault on the Insubres and the Boii. The former capitulated to L. Valerius Flaccus after a defeat in 194; the latter bowed to P. Cornelius Scipio Nasica in 191 after he won a decisive victory over them.

That left the Ligurians. This collection of tribes occupied a series of rugged, highly defensible valleys nestled between high mountain ridges in the northwest corner of the peninsula. Geography made them difficult to conquer and even harder to pacify, unlike the Gauls in the broad, open plains of the Po. The Romans had warred in the region in the 230s but ignored it thereafter. Once one of the tribes, the Apuani, threw its support behind Mago and joined his incursion into Gaul, the Ligurians, too, became caught up in the late stages of the Hannibalic war. The senate's two-pronged strategy against the Gauls in 197 had necessarily entailed cowing at least temporarily the Ligurian tribes through whose territory Rufus and his legions passed as they marched east from Genua. Still, the senators apparently regarded the Gauls as the more pressing danger and remained content to ignore Liguria for the time being. The Ligurians were not about to ignore Rome, however. In 193 a force said to number 20,000 and drawn from the entire region attacked the town of Luca and then moved against Pisa. In that same year, another large force, some 10,000 strong, marched east to loot the territory of Placentia (Livy, 34.56.1–13). What provoked the Ligurians to go on the offensive now is not clear, but possibly they realised that with the subjugation of the Insubres in the previous year Rome's conquest of Gaul was nearing its end and the senate would be likely to set its sights on them next. They determined to strike first in a show of force hoping to deter a future Roman attack. In this they were sadly mistaken. The assaults on Luca, Pisa, and Placentia made the senate acutely aware of the threat the Ligurians posed, and the dynamics of Roman imperialism ensured that a military response would not be

Figure 21 Obverse of a tetradrachm with the head of Philip V of Macedon. ANS 1937.152.211. Courtesy of the American Numismatic Society.

long in coming. Over the next forty years Roman armies regularly campaigned in Liguria, gradually reducing one stronghold after another. At times, pacification meant the deportation of whole populations to areas elsewhere in Italy (e.g. Livy, 40.37.9–38.9, 41.3–4, 53.1–3). Fighting persisted, at least intermittently, down to the middle of the century in parts of the region. The last Ligurian triumphs were celebrated in 166, 158, and 155.

The origins of the Second Macedonian War

At the same time as the Republic was beginning its reconquest of northern Italy, it was taking the first steps down a path that within a generation would lead to the conquest of the Hellenistic world. Here, too, Roman involvement grew out of the strategic imperatives of the Hannibalic war. The need to obviate the possibility of a Macedonian army augmenting Carthaginian forces in Italy furnished the impetus behind the First Macedonian War. Once Rome had roused the Aetolians and others against Philip in 211 and entangled the king in a protracted struggle in central Greece, the senate gradually withdrew its forces until by 207 none remained active in the conflict. Roman policy here was to fight 'to the last Aetolian', and once the Aetolians realised it they made peace with Philip in 205. Roused to action at last, the senate dispatched a proconsul with 11,000 troops and thirty warships to Greece in hopes of restarting the war. The Aetolians were having none of it, and although Philip offered battle, the proconsul declined. Scipio's invasion of Africa was impending, and without allies in Greece, the senate had little appetite for stirring up major trouble there that would divert resources from the climax of the Carthaginian war. Having made a show of force, the proconsul proved receptive to Philip's offer for talks. At Phoenice he and the king hammered out a treaty, which the senate approved and the people subsequently ratified. It gave Philip most of what he wanted in the western Balkans while protecting Roman interests along the Illyrian coast — a settlement that both sides could live with.[2]

That Rome and Macedon found themselves at war once again only five years later therefore comes as a surprise. Roman ambitions in the east had to that point entailed little more than restricting Illyrian depredations on shipping between western Greece and southern Italy and preventing Philip from joining forces with Hannibal. But by 200 Hannibal was no longer a threat, and Macedon had never been a party to Adriatic piracy. Yet the senate was determined to renew hostilities, so much so that when the war-weary voters in the centuriate assembly rejected the declaration of war – an unprecedented refusal to follow the senate's advice – the *patres* insisted that the consul P. Sulpicius Galba harangue the citizens to urge the necessity of this war. This time the assembly gave in but apparently only after receiving assurances that no one who had fought in Africa would be compelled to serve in this new war against his will (a promise that was ignored: Livy, 31.6.1–8.6; 32.3.2–7). Why the senate was determined to start this war has been much discussed by modern scholars since it began the conquest of the Greek east, with all of the consequences that entailed for Rome and the west.[3] No theory commands universal assent, however, and among 300 senators more than one consideration probably shaped their collective thinking.

Certainly the *patres* can have had little in the way of goodwill towards a monarch who had thrown in his lot with Hannibal in

2. E. S. Gruen, *The Hellenistic World and the Coming of Rome*, Berkeley and Los Angeles: University of California Press, 1984, 379–81.

3. Important recent discussions: W. V. Harris, *War and Imperialism in Republican Rome 327–70 B.C.*, Oxford: Oxford University Press, 1979, 212–18; Gruen, *Hellenistic World*, 382–98; A. M. Eckstein, *Mediterranean Anarchy, Interstate War, and the Rise of Rome*, Berkeley and Los Angeles: University of California Press, 2006, 257–92.

the Republic's darkest hour. The peace of Phoenice had not been the senators' idea. They had been prepared in 205, if not to revive the conflict with Philip at all costs, at least to demonstrate their commitment to continuing hostilities. Hence their agreement to a treaty that on its face might have laid the basis for a stable peace with Macedon may reflect no more than a short-term decision to prioritise finishing the war against Hannibal. For many senators, the treaty left the war against Philip unresolved, and in 200 Rome was simply picking up where it had left off. An element of revenge in the senators' thinking cannot be discounted, therefore. Still, simple vengeance cannot be the whole story for it fails to explain the senate's insistence on undertaking a new war against Macedon so soon after the end of the one against Carthage, particularly in view of the citizens' reluctance as well as the serious conflict looming in northern Italy.

Possibly a desire for the glory of a victory motivated some of the *patres*. Although Rome had emerged victorious from its second war with Carthage, the cautious, incremental strategy the senate had pursued after Cannae had produced few important victories. Until 201, only two men had celebrated triumphs while two others had had to content themselves with the lesser honour of an ovation. And the enormous glory of ending the war belonged to Scipio alone. Some senators in 200 may therefore have seen in a new war against a fabled kingdom an opportunity to win the military laurels that the Hannibalic war had largely withheld. However, only those men who believed themselves likely to win consulships in the near future and so gain a command against Macedon can have cherished such ambitions. These will have played a lesser role in the thinking of others. And with a serious campaign in Gaul in prospect, no one can have doubted that plenty of opportunities to win triumphs would be forthcoming.

Fear may have loomed larger in the thinking of many senators. A generation of men scarred by the Republic's near-death experience in the Hannibalic war may well have worried that Philip would eventually find some opportunity to cross to Italy as Pyrrhus had done eighty years earlier, and Rome would find itself once again fighting for its life. The speech that Livy reports the consul P. Sulpicius Galba gave to the voters urging them to pass a declaration of war adds weight to this line of thinking.[4] While the speech itself is Livy's own composition and not a transcript of what Galba

4. Eckstein, *Mediterranean Anarchy*, 280–8.

actually said, it may well reflect the gist of the consul's argument on that day and so the senate's thinking. Galba, in Livy's telling, made two key points: first, Philip is as great a threat as Hannibal if not greater, and second, if the Romans do not fight him now in Greece, they will eventually have to fight him in Italy (Livy, 31.7.1–15). It was an argument very likely to persuade a group of citizens who had lived through the horrors of fifteen years of Hannibal in Italy, particularly since they probably knew very little about Philip or his military strength and intentions beyond what the consul told them. Yet a cool appraisal of both may have caused less alarm among the *patres* than the voters. Philip had fled ignominiously in 214 rather than face Roman troops, and after 211 he had been able to make little headway against Rome and its allies in Greece. Moreover the king's efforts after 205 had led him away from areas of potential conflict with Rome and into regions where the Republic had no prior interests. He had sought gains among the Aegean islands and in the coastal regions of western Asia Minor. And he had not found the going easy. The kingdom of Pergamon and the Republic of Rhodes joined forces to oppose him, and by the winter of 201/200 the king found himself bottled up along with his fleet at Bargylia. Little of this will have induced a collective shudder of fear among the *patres*.

They may, however, have viewed developments in the broader international situation in the eastern Mediterranean with a far deeper sense of foreboding. In 201 an embassy from Rhodes laid before the senate reports of a pact between Philip and Antiochus the Great, king of Syria, to divide between them the kingdom of Egypt and its territories (App. *Mac.* 4). The old king of Egypt had recently died and been succeeded by a boy, Ptolemy V Epiphanes. His accession had left the kingdom's leadership weak and divided and had opened the way for aggressors to gain at its expense. On the basis of this evidence, some scholars have seen in the senate's rush to war alarm at the overturning of the balance of power that had long existed in the east. The coalition between Macedon and Syria would gain in power at Egypt's expense and sooner or later grow strong enough to threaten Italy and Rome.[5] Although in the event military cooperation between Antiochus and Philip proved anything but smooth after 203 or 202, the probable date of the pact, the senators may not have known this. Indeed, they were dependant on reports brought to them by the various Greek embassies, especially from

5. Eckstein, *Mediterranean Anarchy*, 259–89.

Rhodians, for much of what they knew of developments in the east. The ambassadors of course had every reason not only to report the Syrio-Macedonian alliance but to inflate its potential strength and danger to Rome, since inciting the Republic to declare war on Philip could only help the Rhodians and others in their struggle to resist the monarch. That fact in turn may have led the more sceptical among the *patres* to ask, '*Cui bono?*' ('To whose benefit?'), for it was not obvious that Philip, with or without Antiochus, would move against Rome once he got the chance. The peace he and the Republic had negotiated at Phoenice had been satisfactory to both sides, at least on its surface, and had given rise to no longstanding enmity. Senators versed in the ways of ancient interstate relations may have suspected that if conflict were going to arise anywhere, it would be between Philip and his erstwhile ally, Antiochus, whose proximity greatly increased the likelihood that eventually their interests would clash. Better to wait, they might reason, rather than attack Philip now when he could call upon Antiochus' aid. Still, irrational fears may have played a role in some senators' backing a decision to go to war, fears arising out of a heightened sense of anxiety over Italy's security after the experience of Hannibal's invasion.

What may have brought all of these factors together and led the senators in 200 to confront Philip with an ultimatum was their concern to restore the Republic's reputation in the eyes of the Greeks.[6] Roman behaviour in its first war with Macedon had been anything but honourable. The senate had enticed the Aetolians and others to join it in a war with Philip and then hung them out to dry. The arrival in the autumn of 201 of embassies from Rhodes, Pergamon, Athens, and other Greek cities appealing for aid against Philip offered the *patres* a chance to demonstrate that Roman *fides* could be counted on. That interpretation gains support from the senate's extensive public relations campaign throughout the courts and capitals of the Hellenistic east prior to presenting its demands to Philip. Legations from the senate spent much of the spring and summer of 200 proclaiming that Rome would demand that Philip cease making war on any of the Greeks and submit any disputes to arbitration. Only after making the rounds and drumming up support did the delegation send one of its members to Abydus, which Philip was then besieging, to present Rome's ultimatum to the king.

One may reasonably ask at this point what the senate expected

6. Gruen, *Hellenistic World*, 391–8.

Philip to do. Some have suggested that the *patres* assumed he would bow to Roman demands. He had after all fled in previous encounters with Roman forces, and by the time the legate reached Abydus, he and his colleagues had assembled a powerful coalition of Greek states in support. On the other hand, Philip is supposed to have thought that the ultimatum was all bluff, that the Romans would not back up their high words with deeds. Yet the view that both sides were engaged in what amounted to a game of diplomatic chicken that went horribly wrong fails to convince. Philip had been ready enough for a fight in 205 when the senate attempted to restart the earlier war with Macedon, and the senators cannot have been ignorant of that fact since one of the ambassadors they dispatched east had been the commander of the Roman forces in Greece in that year. Nor by the time the ambassador arrived can Philip have failed to know that the assembly had voted for war and that an advanced force was already in Illyria. It is difficult to believe he did not take the Roman threat of war seriously.

The senate, it is true, had left the king a way out: he *could* submit. But the *patres* certainly understood the position they were placing Philip in. They were demanding, arrogantly through the embassy's most junior member, that a sovereign monarch do what they told him, a monarch who had, as Philip pointed out to the ambassador, a treaty with Rome. It was the Romans who were now ready to violate its spirit if not its letter (Polyb. 16.34.1–7). One side or the other was bound to lose face and more. If he meekly capitulated to the Romans' dictates, Philip would thereafter find his ability to enlarge his kingdom and protect his subjects and allies curtailed. Any state that felt it threatened it could run to Rome in anticipation of a senatorial order to cease and desist. On the other side, if the senators were worried about their credibility in the eyes of the Greeks, a climb-down now would only confirm that they could not be relied on, particularly after they had trumpeted their demands across the Hellenistic world. In the zero-sum game of ancient international relations, the only way out for either side was to fight, and it strains credulity to imagine that neither side expected the other to do so. The senate, it is true, was slow to mobilise. It was autumn before the consul Galba and his army crossed to Greece to begin the war. But the war had been declared, the province assigned, and the legions levied well before that date. The delay was merely tactical, to allow time to rally public opinion in Greece against Philip. If it came to pass that Philip did back down, so much the better. But few in the senate can have held more than a slim hope that in that way war could be averted.

Realists among the *patres* will have expected war. The question remains, however, why in 200 the senators were ready to put Philip in a position where he had no good option but to fight. Trouble was brewing in Gaul; the public's mood was anything but bellicose. The senators themselves were apparently not of one mind. A tribune of the plebs, Q. Baebius, spoke against the declaration of war and helped bring about its initial defeat, suggesting that at least a few of his colleagues saw no reason to push matters to open conflict (Livy, 31.6.4–5). But most were adamant. Some combination of anger at Philip for supporting Hannibal, eagerness for the conquest of a prestigious kingdom, fear of an eventual attack on Italy by Philip, and a desire to vindicate Roman *fides* in the court of Hellenistic public opinion all conspired to lead the senators to seize the opportunity that the pleas of the Greek embassies for aid presented for a confrontation with Philip. Perhaps, too, crushing Carthage had given the senators a new and increased sense of the Republic's power and importance within the broader Mediterranean world.[7] They were now prepared to make the Greeks acknowledge that fact by forcing one of the greatest Hellenistic kingdoms to submit, even at the cost of war. For as Polybius claimed, it was their victory over Hannibal that 'encouraged the Romans for the first time to stretch out their hands upon the rest [of the world] and cross with an army to Greece and Asia' (1.3.6). Perhaps he was right.

Cynoscephalae and the settlement of Greece

Peace negotiations during the war and the terms of Rome's settlement of Greece following Philip's defeat go a long way towards clarifying the nature of the senate's objectives. They reveal as great a concern with image and prestige as with material gains from Rome's victory, if not more so. Galba and his successor accomplished little in 200 and 199. Fighting got bogged down in the mountains of Illyria as Philip blocked the passes into Greece proper and the Romans failed to dislodge his forces. The situation changed with the arrival early in 198 of the energetic, young consul of that year, T. Quinctius Flamininus. He broke through the Macedonian blockades and moved the fighting into Thessaly. By the winter of that year,

7. Harris, *War and Imperialism*, 217.

Figure 22 Gold stater, obverse depicting T. Quinctius Flamininus, reverse Winged Victory with wreath. CM 1954,1009.1. By permission of the British Museum.

Philip was ready to talk peace. He had lost ground and now decided that the wiser course would be a negotiated settlement to the war. He sent a herald to Flamininus seeking a meeting, and the consul agreed.[8] Flamininus was at that point nearing the end of his year in office, and he did not yet know whether the senate would send one of the consuls of 197 to Greece to replace him or would extend his command for another year. If the latter, he certainly did not want to end the war, for he had yet to win a decisive victory that would do so with the king's surrender. However, if a successor was on his way, Flamininus would be better off returning to Rome with a negotiated settlement than empty-handed. So he was prepared to hear the king out and shape his own response and advice to the senate, which would have to approve any settlement, according to his own advantage. That point is worth emphasising. Flamininus believed he could convince his fellow senators to look upon what he had achieved in Greece to date and whatever terms Philip would offer in the negotiations as either fulfilling the senate's aims in the war or not.

Flamininus and his allies met the king in Locris, where after three days of talks Philip made a number of territorial concessions that by no means satisfied Rome's Greek allies. With negotiations at an impasse, Philip asked to send a deputation to Rome to present his

8. A. M. Eckstein, 'T. Quinctius Flamininus and the campaign against Philip in 198 B.C..', *Phoenix* 30 (1976), 119–42.

terms to the senate for its consideration, and Flamininus agreed, dispatching several of his officers along with delegations from the allies. On their arrival, the officers learned that the senate would send both consuls for 197 to fight the Gauls and so would extend Flamininus' command in Greece for another year. The officers therefore worked to sabotage the negotiations by arranging for the allied delegations to speak first, with perhaps some coaching. The Greeks in their speech laid great stress on the so-called Three Fetters of Greece, the cities of Chalkis, Corinth, and Demetrias. These three strongholds, the envoys explained, were the keys to Macedonian control of central and southern Greece, and Philip was not proposing to give them up. Philip's representatives entered next, and when they began to speak, the *patres* cut them short by demanding to know about the Three Fetters. When the envoys replied that they had no instructions about them, the senators declared the discussion at an end (Polyb. 1.1–12.5; Livy, 32.31.1–37.6).

What needs to be underscored here is Flamininus' confidence that he could have arranged for the talks in Rome to achieve a completely different result: a treaty of peace between Rome and Macedon on the terms Philip was proposing. The consul's assurance suggests strongly that what the senators wanted out of the war was a demonstration that Rome would back up its promises to protect its friends in Greece with military force; an acknowledgement from the king of Roman might, which his readiness to seek peace represented; and a show of Roman power to drive any thoughts of westward aggression from Philip's mind. Most of all, the senators wanted to free Greece from Macedonian control, yet they had little concrete notion what that would look like on the ground. They allowed the allied speakers to persuade them – correctly as it turned out – that forcing Philip to relinquish the Three Fetters would achieve that goal. But had the senators decided to send one of the new consuls to Greece, Flamininus' officers would have got Philip's envoys to speak first, then in their own report downplayed the importance of the Three Fetters and emphasised that Philip's concessions would leave Greece 'free'. Peace would have been made then and there with the *patres* believing that all their objectives in the war had been met.

So the war continued for another year, enabling Flamininus to win the crushing victory that was his own goal. On a ridge in Thessaly called Cynoscephalae, the 'Dog's Head', in 197 the two armies stumbled into one another. The encounter represents the last time in this era we can see the inherent flexibility of the manipular legion,

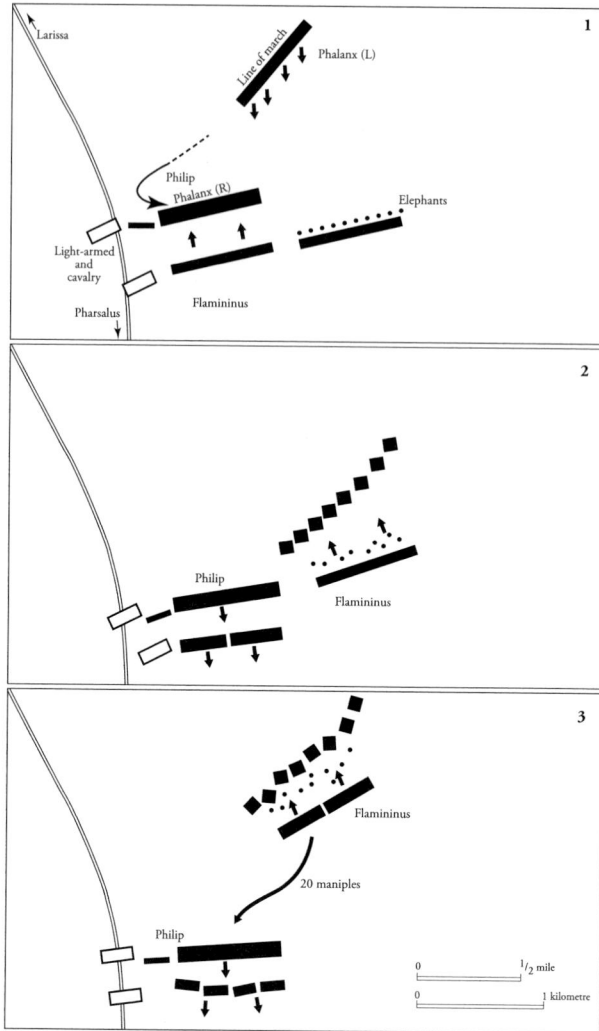

Figure 23 Plan of the battle at Cynoscephalae.

composed of independently manoeuvrable blocks of soldiers, exploited tactically to achieve victory. In the encounter, the Roman right wing prevailed over the Macedonian phalanx opposing it, but the Macedonian charge drove the left wing back. The two wings became separated as one continued to advance up the hill while the other fell back some distance from the summit with the enemy in pursuit. At that point, one of the military tribunes with the right wing sized up the situation on the left and withdrew twenty maniples under his command from the formation. These he led down the hill and with them charged the rear of the phalanx pressing the Roman left. The Macedonians, now caught between two forces, threw away their weapons and ran. Philip, seeing the battle was lost, fled the field along with the remainder of his soldiers (Polyb. 18.18.1–27.6; Livy, 33.5.1–8.10).

His army shattered, Philip was now compelled to sue for peace. Flamininus referred the matter to the senate, which in 196 dispatched a commission of ten men including several of its senior members to oversee the peace and the settlement of Greece. The arrangements these *decem legati* and Flamininus put in place once again demonstrate the senate's concern with image as well as security. Philip retained his throne but was hobbled economically and militarily. He was to pay a war indemnity of 1,000 talents, half at once and half in equal instalments over ten years, and he was to surrender his fleet. The Romans thus left Philip with the means to defend his kingdom but by depriving him of his war fleet and much of his treasure they set to rest whatever fears they might have had of a Macedonian invasion of Italy (Polyb. 18.44.1–7). The senate had taught Philip a lesson he would not soon forget and compelled the ruler of one of the Hellenistic world's great kingdoms to submit to their dictates. That demonstration of the Republic's majesty and power put Rome on a par with the eastern Mediterranean's other great powers. The *decem legati* also required Philip to evacuate all of his possessions in central and southern Greece including the now infamous Three Fetters. Greece was to be free, as the allied envoys had defined this to the senate the year before. To ensure that the Republic derived the maximum public relations benefit from this measure, the commissioners and Flamininus took advantage of the Isthmian games, where a great number of leading men from the Hellenistic world had assembled, to make the announcement that all of the cities formerly occupied by Philip were to be left free, ungarrisoned, subject to no tribute, and in the enjoyment of their own laws. The crowd, Polybius reports, could scarcely believe its ears and demanded that the herald repeat the proclamation. After he did, the cheering was so loud, one author claims, that ravens flying overhead fell out of the sky dead (Polyb. 18.45.7–46.15; Plut. *Flam.* 10.1–6). By this act the *decem legati* and Flamininus made Roman *fides* and magnanimity clear to the world.

Figure 24 Obverse of a gold stater with the head of Antiochus III of Syria. ANS 1967.152.579. Courtesy of the American Numismatic Society.

Rome and Antiochus the Great

Philip's preoccupation with the struggle against Rome presented his erstwhile ally, Antiochus, the king of Syria, with the chance to gain at his expense.[9] Antiochus' ambition during the last decades of the third century had been to recreate the empire of Alexander, and to that end he had attempted to secure the submission of the eastern satrapies as far as the Indus valley. Between 212 and 205 he had undertaken a spectacular expedition to the east, his *anabasis* as he named it, and he returned proclaiming himself 'great king' in imitation of both Alexander and the Persian rulers whose empire Alexander had conquered and then appropriated. Antiochus himself now bore the sobriquet 'the Great,' likening himself unmistakably to Alexander. That the new great king had in reality subdued the vast swath of territory conquered by his illustrious predecessor may be doubted. His *anabasis* garnered more fame than dominion. Yet in the ancient world perception was often power, and his imagined empire made Antiochus appear formidable. After concluding his pact with Philip in 203 or 202, he turned his attention to the newly

9. Important studies on the origins of this war include E. Badian, *Studies in Greek and Roman History*, Oxford: Blackwell, 1964, 112–39; Harris, *War and Imperialism*, 219–23; Gruen, *Hellenistic World*, 612–36; Eckstein, *Mediterranean Anarchy*, 292–306.

weakened Egypt, seeking to gain possession of the area known as Coele-Syria, today the coastal regions of Lebanon, Syria, and Israel, which had been under Egyptian control. Once Philip was fully occupied with the war in Greece, Antiochus turned north and west, gobbling up those Ptolemaic possessions in western Asia Minor that his pact with Philip had conceded to Macedon. He next crossed the Hellespont in 196 and re-established the city of Lysimachia to serve as a military base for further expansion in Thrace. At this point Flamininus and the ten commissioners began to worry about the security of Greece. They feared that a Roman evacuation of Greece might tempt Antiochus to take Philip's place. Soon after their proclamation at the Isthmian games, the *decem legati* demanded via Antiochus' representatives at the festival that the king not attack any of the free cities of Asia Minor, that he relinquish control of those previously subject to Philip or Ptolemy, and that he stay out of Europe (Polyb. 18.47.1–3).

A few months later several of the commissioners journeyed north to Lysimachia to deliver the same demands to the king in person. They were unprepared for Antiochus' response. A canny Hellenistic diplomat, the king had little trouble beating the Romans at their own game. Antiochus wondered what business the Romans had poking their noses into the affairs of Asia since he did not interfere in Italy (where there were, as everyone knew, plenty of Greeks who were anything but free). The Greek cities of Asia would certainly receive their liberty in good time, Antiochus continued, but only through his own act of grace. His crossing into Europe, he claimed, represented merely the recovery of an area formerly conquered by his great-great-grandfather some eighty-five years earlier and subsequently stolen from his family. As for the young Egyptian king, the Romans should not trouble themselves about him. Antiochus would look after Ptolemy's affairs since he was about to become Antiochus' son-in-law! The Romans, by no means pleased at having been out-manoeuvred, attempted to salvage the situation by inviting representatives of Antiochus' victims to air their complaints, but the monarch cut them short and terminated the interview (Polyb. 18.50.1–52.5).

Scholars in the past believed that these negotiations began a gradual but inevitable descent into war. More recent studies, however, have stressed the extent to which both sides here were posturing before the court of Hellenistic public opinion. Nether power at this stage had any interest in pushing their disagreement to the point of military conflict. Each instead pursued its own interests. For the Romans these involved settling affairs in Greece, which occupied Flamininus and the ten commissioners for the remainder of 196 and 195. Their approach was two-pronged. First they eliminated various minor hegemonies in central and southern Greece, leaving many smaller cities free from the domination of their more powerful neighbours. As a corollary they removed from power many of the leading men in the cities that Philip had dominated and established others in their place. The loyalty of the former, having owed their positions to Macedonian support, was now suspect while the new leaders would be beholden to Rome. In the process Flamininus found himself embroiled in a brief war with Nabis, the ruler of Sparta, who had dreamed of reasserting his city's ancient dominance over the Peloponnesus. Roman power cut those dreams short. At the beginning of 194 the senate elected to evacuate all of its forces from Greece, despite the warnings of some at Rome that a war with Antiochus was looming. Nevertheless, the senators found political considerations of more immediate concern than security concerns for Greece (see below, p. 243), and by the end of 194 not a single legionary or *socius* remained east of the Adriatic.

On reflection the senate's decision seems surprising. It had not placed any of the cities Rome liberated under the formal obligations of a treaty, nor had the *patres* established any of the other instruments of imperial control they were employing elsewhere at this time – colonies of citizens and allies in Italy and Gaul or the dispatch of a praetorian governor, as in Sicily and Sardinia and now Spain. In the last of these provinces, troops accompanied the governor to enforce his will and secure Roman rule. The senators apparently believed that Greece was different, that the Greeks, once freed from Macedon and the threat of another hegemon taking its place, were capable of establishing a stable balance of power to keep the peace while gratitude to Rome would ensure their loyalty. These conditions would obviate the need for direct Roman control. Behind these expectations lay more pragmatic considerations. Roman administration of Greece would require enlarging the number of praetors elected annually beyond the current six. The problem here was that each praetor hoped to advance to one of the two consulates elected every year, and political rivalry, already keen, threatened to get out of hand if more contenders entered the lists. The *patres* themselves had no interest in managing the petty conflicts and internal disputes of a multitude of squabbling Greek cities and their citizens.

Hence their hopes that the Greeks could be left largely to run their own affairs. Unfortunately, their optimism proved wildly unrealistic.

The coming of war

Flamininus' military intervention had forced Nabis to give up his ambitions to enlarge Sparta's domains, but Rome's former allies, the Aetolians, had not relinquished theirs. This league of western tribes had dominated central Greece in the third century but then seen its power dramatically curtailed by the revival of Macedon under Antigonus Doson (r. 229–221) and Philip. The Aetolians joined Rome in its first war against Macedon in hopes of using a victory to expand their sway over the region once again, and the same goal lay behind their decision to fight alongside the Romans in the second conflict. Their entry into that war had been hesitant, but they had fought alongside the Romans at Cynoscephalae, and they claimed much of the credit for the victory. They expected the *decem legati* to reward their contribution by placing a number of cities under the league's control. The settlement therefore proved a bitter disappointment. The decision to leave all the cities in Greece independent denied the Aetolians what they believed were their just deserts. Their anger at the Romans coupled with a determination to take for themselves what the commissioners and Flamininus failed to give them set in motion the events that would lead to a new Roman war in Greece. The Aetolians understood that they were not strong enough to win against a Roman army should they attempt to overturn the senate's arrangements in Greece. They would need powerful allies. Nabis was one candidate, but the dispatch of a Roman naval squadron in 192 had once again checked his aggrandisement. Philip at this point had more to gain from cooperation with Rome, for the senate was encouraging him to incorporate cities into his kingdom as a way of limiting the Aetolians' advance (revealing that the senators were willing to trade away Greek freedom in the interests of finding a balance of power in Greece). That left Antiochus.

The king's relations with the Republic down to 192 reveal little to suggest that war was coming. In the previous year, following the senate's evacuation of Greece, he had dispatched envoys to Rome to endeavour to reach an understanding on the basis of the status quo. The senate instructed Flamininus and the ten commissioners to negotiate privately with the envoys. At their meeting, Flamininus offered them a simple trade: if Antiochus would evacuate Europe, the Romans would cease to interest themselves in the king's treatment of the Greek cities in Asia Minor. Once more, the senate was ready to compromise the freedom of the Greeks in the interest of establishing a stable situation in the east. The king's representative rejected the deal. It would have required Antiochus to abandon his gains in Thrace in exchange for nothing more than a treaty of friendship with Rome (Livy, 34.57.1–59.8). Subsequently a Roman legation journeyed east to present the same offer to the king himself, and once again it was rejected (Livy, 35.16.1–17.2). Antiochus' refusal to come to terms with Rome indicates that he had little reason to fear an outbreak of hostilities at that point. At the same time he was well aware that the treaty Philip struck with the Republic in 205 had proved no impediment to a Roman declaration of war when it suited the senate's purposes. He would therefore be giving up a lot in exchange for very little.

One of the enduring mysteries in this period, then, is what induced Antiochus to alter this situation by invading Greece. For in the autumn of 192 the king sailed from Asia Minor to the mainland with 10,000 infantry, 500 cavalry, and six elephants (Livy, 35.43.1–6). Livy and the Roman historical tradition had no doubt on this point; they laid the blame on that perennial republican *bête noire*, Hannibal. At the conclusion of the Second Punic War the senate had, remarkably, not demanded that the government of Carthage hand over Hannibal to be put to death. He remained at Carthage and soon began to take a leading role in public affairs. A political struggle there had led his opponents to denounce him before the Roman senate, which dispatched an embassy to investigate. Hannibal, fearing the worst, made his escape to the only refuge that now remained beyond the reach of Rome, the court of Antiochus the Great. Once there, Livy claims, he began urging Antiochus to go to war with Rome, and, Livy continues, the prospect of having the Republic's greatest adversary at his side to advise him encouraged Antiochus to undertake hostilities (Livy, 34.45.6–60.8; 35.42.1–43.1). But the Carthaginian if anyone ought to have understood that 10,500 soldiers were far too few to win against Rome. An ordinary consular army numbered at least 20,000 infantry, and the senate could call upon many, many more, as it had done against Hannibal himself. Nor is it likely that Antiochus was unaware of the Republic's military power, for he had long experience of war. Rather, the comparatively paltry force that accompanied him holds the key to his thinking, for its size reveals that he did not anticipate a clash with Rome.

The catalysts for his crossing were the Aetolians. They along with others filled Antiochus' ears with exaggerated claims that all of Greece was clamouring for him to come and free them from the Romans. And when an Aetolian force treacherously seized the city of Demetrias, one of the strategic Three Fetters, and then informed Antiochus that the town had spontaneously revolted from the Romans and gone over to his side, the king was convinced that he would everywhere be welcomed as a liberator. His behaviour once he arrived bears this out. He raced from one city to another trying to bestow freedom but meeting with very little success. For while the Aetolians' unhappiness with the Roman settlement along with the discontent of those whom Flamininus and the commissioners had removed from power created an obvious constituency supporting regime change in many Greek cities, those leaders who had gained from the Roman settlement were naturally opposed. And since they controlled the cities, they saw to it that the gates were closed when Antiochus approached. Despite these setbacks, Antiochus remained unconcerned about how his efforts to liberate Greece would play in Rome. If the senate had evacuated Greece, he reasoned, it cannot have cared much what happened there. So rather than prepare for war, Antiochus devoted the winter to parties and the pleasures of the company of a beautiful young woman he met in Greece and soon married (Polyb. 20.8.1–5).

The war with Antiochus

Any distinction between a goodwill tour and a full-scale invasion was lost on the senate. Although the *patres* had sent Flamininus and other envoys to Greece in 192 in an effort to confirm the loyalty of the Greeks, stifle discontent, and prevent an outbreak of hostilities, once the king landed they reacted swiftly. The consul of 191, M'. Acilius Glabrio, crossed to Greece with an army and marched against the king. The senators perhaps feared that Antiochus' operations in Greece were merely the prelude to a full-scale invasion of Italy, but more probably they were angered at the king's challenge to their claim to have liberated Greece in 196. They were not about to let Antiochus give them the lie. And his efforts to foment uprisings everywhere threatened the positions of those Greeks whom

Flamininus and the *decem legati* had put in power. The senate could usually be counted on to defend its friends when they were under attack. Yet even with a Roman army bearing down upon him, Antiochus seems not to have taken the threat seriously. He was more concerned to pose as the champion of Greek freedom against the barbarians from the west than to mount an effective defence. And where better to do that than at Thermopylae, the storied site of Leonidas' and his 300 Spartans' heroic stand against the Persian hordes in 480. The king and his forces took their stand at the pass, casting themselves as the ancient Hellenes and the Romans as the foreign invaders. For Antiochus, it was all about symbols; he expected to do little more than make a grand gesture before beating a hasty retreat, since he was well aware that things had turned out badly for Leonidas and his men. The Persians found a path around the pass, cut off the Spartans' retreat, and slaughtered them to a man. The Romans, too, apparently knew the story: the consul sent a squad of legionaries to execute the same manoeuvre. Once the king and his soldiers realised they were about to be surrounded, they fled in disorder. Most the Roman cavalry hunted down and killed, but Antiochus himself escaped to Asia (Livy, 36.16.1–19.12).

The king seems to have imagined that this would be the end of his little escapade, but he could not have been more mistaken. For if the senators had initially evinced little interest in starting a war in Greece, once it had got going they were determined that nothing short of a total victory would end it. That meant more than simply chasing Antiochus out of Greece. In 190, the consul L. Cornelius Scipio, brother of the great Africanus, who accompanied him in the role of advisor, crossed with an army into Asia Minor. Antiochus now understood that he had a major war on his hands and led out his full army. Still, he was not eager to measure his strength against Rome's. He made several efforts to negotiate a peaceful settlement to the conflict, but the Scipios drove a hard bargain: payment of full costs of the war and evacuation of all the king's possessions in Asia Minor. This was too much, and the king resolved to fight. It was a poor decision. At Magnesia the two armies met, and the legions, joined by contingents from several allied states including Pergamon, had little difficulty in annihilating the Syrian phalanx (Livy, 37.39.1–44.2). The king had no choice now but to bow to whatever terms the victors imposed as did the rest of the Greek world.[10] The Scipios

---

10. Gruen, *Hellenistic World*, 639–43.

ordered Antiochus to withdraw from all lands west of the river Halys and the Taurus mountains and to pay the enormous sum of 15,000 talents, 500 immediately, another 2,500 upon ratification of the peace at Rome, then the balance in twelve annual instalments of 1,000 talents each. He was also to hand over Hannibal and several other advisors who had urged him to undertake the war and provide twenty hostages (Polyb. 21.17.1–7; Hannibal fled and later committed suicide). Antiochus, however, was to retain his throne, for the last thing the Romans wanted was to leave behind a situation that would invite further instability and require another military intervention. This same desire to secure a durable peace also lay at the heart of a number of additional steps the senate took in the wake of its victory over Antiochus.

In the following year both consuls went east. One, M. Fulvius Nobilior, finished the war in Greece by compelling the hapless Aetolians to surrender. The other, Cn. Manlius Vulso, succeeded to Scipio's command in Asia Minor and led the army deep into the interior. His campaign aimed to cow the tribes there, particularly those descended from the Celtic invaders who had entered the area nearly a century before. These tribes had long been accustomed to prey on the Greeks along the coast. This show of force was part of an effort to avoid a permanent military presence east of the Adriatic, in this case one required by the need to protect Greek cities from depredations by their neighbours to the east. Both Fulvius and Manlius returned to Rome in 187 loaded with spoils. Meanwhile, the senate dispatched another ten-man commission to settle affairs in the east. All pretence that the Republic had gone to war to free the Greeks was now cast aside.[11] Leaving behind a gaggle of autonomous little states in the expectation that somehow they would manage to keep the peace among themselves had proved a chimera. Now the *patres* decided to establish four regional hegemons and place the various smaller states in each area under their control. These states had sided with Rome against Antiochus. Pergamon under its king Eumenes was given control over the northwest of Asia Minor, while the island Republic of Rhodes was granted sway in the southwest. The Achaean league would dominate the Peloponnesus, and Philip would exercise suzerainty over central Greece. The senate expected these four to keep control of events within their spheres of influence, keeping the peace by arbitrating whatever disputes arose

11. Gruen, *Hellenistic World*, 545–50.

between the cities and ensuring domestic tranquillity by preventing political conflicts within each town from boiling over into civil war. The *patres* could thus step back from close involvement in eastern affairs. It was a sensible plan and one largely in keeping with contemporary Hellenistic notions of what it meant for a small state to be 'free'. And it worked – for a while.

The beginnings of Roman Spain

The senate's concern to limit the Republic's military commitments in the east needs to be understood in the light of the demands that other theatres were making on Roman and Italian manpower at this time. Although the conquest of Cisalpine Gaul had been more or less finished with Scipio Nasica's victory over the Boii in 191, a long campaign to subjugate Liguria was in prospect by 189 and often required the efforts of both consular armies. Equally important in the senate's calculations was Spain. Here again Roman involvement was a consequence of the Hannibalic war. After 206 and Scipio's victory at Ilipa, the senate maintained a force of two legions in Spain simply to preclude any attempt by the Carthaginians to renew the struggle there. After 202 and Zama, even these forces no longer needed to remain. Down to that point, the senators seem to have been uncertain about how to deal with Spain.[12] Their arrangements for the commands of the armies there had been irregular and improvised. Two generals were sent to succeed Scipio, and like him neither had held one of the senior magistracies; therefore like Scipio each had his command bestowed by a vote of the people. Moreover the senate made no explicit division of territorial responsibilities between the two. In 201 the senate got the plebeian assembly to elect a successor for one of these generals, and the *patres* also ordered the Spanish commanders to reduce their forces by roughly half and send the veterans back to Italy. All of this suggests that the senators had seen their arrangements in Spain during the war as provisional. Now that Zama had eliminated any strategic imperative for remaining there, the senators were intending to reduce Rome's military commitment with a view to eventually eliminating it entirely.

And yet they did not. The *patres* instead found themselves embarked on a course that would lead to a quarter century of

12. J. S. Richardson, *Hispaniae: Spain and the Development of Roman Imperialism, 218–82 BC*, Cambridge: Cambridge University Press, 1986, 62–125.

war and necessitate a permanent military establishment in Spain. What accounts for the change? A definitive answer eludes us, but the best guess seems to be that over the course of a dozen years of combat against the Carthaginians in Spain, Publius and Gnaeus Scipio and after them the future Africanus had established ties with a variety of tribes and cities that had engaged Roman *fides*. These commitments entailed continuing obligations for protection and assistance even after the victory at Zama. The struggle to overthrow Carthaginian power in Spain had subsumed within it a multiplicity of local antagonisms that disposed various tribes and towns on one side or the other of the principal conflict. The defeat of Carthage hardly ended these smaller rivalries, and Rome's *fides* obligated the Republic to defend its allies against their enemies. In this case, too, the Hannibalic war left a legacy of conflict for Rome.

If the Romans were going to remain a presence in Spain, something would have to be done to bring the administrative arrangements there into line with normal practices. If armies were required, they would have to be led by magistrates with *imperium* – praetors, since the consuls would be elsewhere leading the Republic's major wars. That step meant increasing the number of praetors elected from four to six so that two could be sent regularly to govern in Spain. In addition, a more explicit division of territory between them would be required since *imperium* and the auspices that complemented it operated ordinarily within a well-defined *provincia* (province) that limited their exercise. Therefore in 197 the senate designated two Spanish *provinciae*, Nearer Spain (*Hispania Citerior*), which encompassed the Ebro basin and the eastern seaboard of the peninsula, and Farther Spain (*Hispania Ulterior*), comprising the Baetis valley and adjacent regions. Although the senators may have hoped these designations would provide a clear-cut separation between the two praetors' areas of authority, in practice the territorial division remained fuzzy for some time, and occasionally one praetor is found operating in what ought to have been the other's *provincia*. And in at least one instance, the two praetors joined forces and campaigned together. The *patres* apparently also expected the provinces to be at peace or at least to require only the suppression of minor resistance. Each praetor received a mere token force of 8,000 *socii* and no Roman legionaries. Events, however, soon proved the senators greatly mistaken.

To the Spanish, the new arrangements signalled unmistakably Rome's intention to establish a permanent presence and ultimately control of the peninsula. Their response was a massive uprising. Many of the tribes, and especially those that had fought on the Roman side in the recent war, could justifiably feel that they had merely exchanged Carthaginian rule for Roman, and they wanted none of it. The war was too much for the praetors and their limited forces to handle. One of them suffered a serious defeat and later died of his wounds in 196. The senators realised that a much greater military effort would be needed, and so in 195 they dispatched one of the consuls, M. Porcius Cato, with an army along with a new praetor leading additional troops. Cato was one of the outstanding figures of his age, a remarkable politician, soldier, businessman, and polymath. He also founded the Latin historical tradition, being the first to write a history of Rome in that language, the *Origines*.[13] As one of the leading orators of his day, he also composed dozens of speeches, many of which were available to later authors, like Livy and Plutarch, to consult along with his *Origines*. Cato was not a man to hide his glory; modesty was not a trait that Roman aristocrats much admired. He dwelt extensively in his history and in his later speeches on his exploits in Spain. The result is that we know far more about Cato's campaigns there than those of any other commander in those provinces. However, the fact that Cato made himself the hero of his account also means that we must be particularly on guard against his tendency to magnify his own achievements.

His puffery is nowhere more in evidence than in his boast that when he left Spain, the provinces were pacified. In fact, he fought only one major battle, defeating the inhabitants of the town of Emporion in the extreme northeastern corner of the peninsula, a region well north of the centre of opposition to Rome. The rest of what he accomplished he achieved through diplomacy, deception, and simple bribery (Livy, 34.7.4–9.13, 11.1–21.8; Plut. *Cat. Mai.* 10.1–11.3). Cato returned to Rome and a triumph in 194, but the war in Spain was by no means finished. The praetors who arrived in the following year found many areas still in revolt and in fighting to subdue them one suffered a serious defeat. Campaigning continued throughout the years that followed, mostly successful as the many triumphs recorded for commanders there attest, but sometimes not. Combat moved from the coastal regions in the east and the Baetis valley in the west into the interior of both provinces. Finally in

13. A. E. Astin, *Cato the Censor*, Oxford: Oxford University Press, 1978.

179–178 victories under the praetors L. Postumius Albinus and Ti. Sempronius Gracchus broke Spanish resistance. Equally important, the terms of peace that Gracchus imposed proved broadly acceptable to the defeated. Their content is not fully known, but in general the provincials seem to have been required to pay a fixed tax, the *stipendium*, and perhaps one twentieth of their grain harvest as well. The money and grain to a large extent eliminated the need for the treasury at Rome to fund the Republic's military forces in Spain. In addition, Gracchus provided land for a large number of landless Spaniards and established settlements for them, which apparently relieved much of the economic distress that had helped fuel the war. Gracchus' settlement ended most fighting in the peninsula for the next quarter century.

The senate and the *imperium*

If nothing else, the foregoing survey reveals the absence of any grand senatorial scheme for world conquest. The senators mainly reacted to the various situations that confronted them in the wake of the Hannibalic war and thereafter. The Gauls of northern Italy had long threatened the regions to the south, a threat brought terrifyingly home to the *patres* by the aid the region had given to Hannibal. That was a danger the senate could not long ignore once Carthage had been dealt with, all the more so when the Boii's victory over a Roman force sparked a widespread insurrection throughout Gaul and Liguria. In the eastern Mediterranean, however, security concerns were only one element in a complex of factors that led the senate to confront Philip at Abydus. And there is a very real possibility that many in the senate had hopes that the king would back down. Posturing, a desire to triumph in the court of Hellenistic public opinion rather than on the battlefield, may have been the aim here. Warfare in Spain, too, seems not to have been anticipated. Arrangements remained provisional and ad hoc down to 197. The designation of *provinciae* there and their incorporation into the framework of republican governance in that year hardly indicate the senate's intention to undertake an expansionist policy in view of the paltry forces sent there. That limited commitment is not surprising with a major push under way in Gaul and the Macedonian war still unresolved.

The senate also had very different aims in each theatre. As far as the *patres* were concerned, Gauls and Ligurians were savages who could not be trusted to remain at peace until their resistance had been thoroughly broken. The Roman record in northern Italy is one of repeated devastation, enslavement, land confiscation, and whole-sale deportation of populations – what today would be condemned as 'ethnic cleansing'. As the Gallic and Ligurian presence was reduced or eliminated altogether, large-scale in-migration from the rest of the peninsula began either in the form of colonies authorised by the senate or informally as individual settlers migrated in. In Greece and Asia Minor by contrast Roman imperialism assumed a very different aspect. Although the senate was fully intent upon subjugating the states there once it resolved on war, it eschewed the sorts of overt techniques of control it had developed for Italy. No colonists were dispatched. No formal treaties of alliance imposed specific obligations on Greek cities or kingdoms and bound them to serve Roman interests. Instead the senators seem to have been groping for some way to create a situation that was self-administer-ing yet lay under a general Roman suzerainty. Their initial attempt stemmed in part from their belief that because the Greeks possessed governmental structures quite different from those of the Gauls, Ligurians, or Spanish tribesmen the senators could leave them to run their own affairs, relying only on the informal ties of friendship (*amicitia*), patronage, and protection (*fides*) with both prominent individuals and whole communities to ensure that they ran them in ways that accommodated Roman interests. When that settlement proved no longer viable in the aftermath of the Antiochine war, the senators opted for a version of freedom that was in many ways more compatible with contemporary Hellenistic notions of liberty: a limited autonomy for smaller states under the aegis of a larger power. The former enjoyed their own laws and managed their own internal affairs while the latter protected them from aggression from their neighbours and kept political competition from getting out of hand. In both cases, however, the senators' overarching goal was to be able to withdraw Roman forces and to leave behind arrangements that required only minimal attention on their part.

Spain was a different case altogether and in many ways the antithesis of Greece. No commissions went west to supervise a settlement. The *patres* appear to have been largely indifferent to the arrangements that generals there made to keep the peace and administer their provinces. Formal treaties are unknown. Gracchus' agreements with the various tribes he dealt with remained unratified at Rome, and it is doubtful whether he ever presented them to the senate for its inspection and approval or to an assembly for a formal vote. Because Spanish society lacked the sorts of constitutional and administrative forms common in the Greek east, it may be that the senators were reluctant to enter into treaties with the Spanish because they could not be sure who or what they were dealing with. But more germane is the fact that they had determined to establish a permanent magisterial presence in Spain. Praetorian control might therefore have led the senators to believe that there was no need for treaties spelling out the rights and obligations on either side. Their absence enhanced flexibility, which was essential in dealing with a more fluid political and diplomatic situation to which a society based on personal loyalties to petty chieftains and the lack of hard-and-fast tribal identities gave rise.

The Spanish case is also arresting for the ways in which the senate sought to balance its imperial responsibilities with political concerns and aristocratic competition. The hesitancy over what to do about Spain down to 197 stemmed in part from a reluctance to create the two additional praetorships needed to govern the provinces. The senators' lack of comfort with this situation is evident in the *lex Baebia*, passed in 181, which among other things reduced the number of praetors elected annually from six to four in alternate years beginning in 179. Its effect was to create longer terms of command for praetors sent to Spain, regularising a situation that had arisen out of conditions during the 180s, when a series of unusual military needs had required the services of one or more of a year's praetors, taking him away from one of the ordinary praetorian *provinciae*. Several praetors in Spain consequently had their tenures extended by a year, which enhanced their effectiveness in carrying out their duties. The length of time required to travel to Spain also often left a magistrate little time to accomplish anything before a successor arrived. Having a second year enabled him to familiarise himself with local conditions and lay plans for the upcoming campaign. So military effectiveness was certainly one end the *patres* had in view – although not necessarily the primary goal, since the practice of alternating four and six praetors was abandoned by 176 and six regularly elected thereafter.

The law was actually a broad piece of legislation that also aimed at curbing electoral corruption, and that suggests that political concerns played as great if not a greater role in the move to reduce the number of praetors. Electing six praetors every year greatly affected competition for the consulship, for every praetor was a potential contender for that honour, and the more of them there were the more hotly contested elections became. The effect was cumulative since many of the ex-praetors who failed to win election one year were ready to try again in the next or the next after that, further intensifying competition. The senators could hope that reducing the number of praetors to four in alternate years would go some ways towards easing those pressures (see below, pp. 251–2).

What concerned the senators far more than the nuts and bolts of imperial administration was the distribution of honour and standing among themselves. This is particularly clear in the case of triumphs. Senatorial debates on whether a particular consul, praetor, or promagistrate should or should not be awarded a triumph for his victory loom much larger in our sources than deliberations about how those conquests should be administered.[14] With wars often being waged simultaneously in Greece, northern Italy, and Spain, opportunities to win triumphs and the lesser honour of an ovation abounded in this period. Between 200 and the mid-170s, these celebrations averaged a little over one per year. Spain was particularly fruitful. Roughly one of every two men who governed those provinces down to 178 earned one or the other of these laurels. And because Spain was a praetorian command, they went to aristocrats at a stage in their *cursus* where ordinarily they would have had little or no chance of winning them. Such honours in turn gave the praetors who gained them a decided advantage in their struggle to reach the consulate. Military glory and the service to the *res publica* that it reflected always constituted a strong claim to reward in the form of higher office. Nearly every praetor who was awarded a triumph or ovation in the years 200–146 went on to win the consulate. Praetors who had governed the peaceful provinces of Sicily and Sardinia or administered justice in the city had to struggle that much harder to reach the consulship. No wonder, therefore, that many senators were concerned about political competition becoming overheated. But even consular victories were creating invidious distinctions: some were simply more glorious than others. Triumphs for victories in the Greek east stood out for their splendour, the wealth exhibited during their celebrations, and the renown of the vanquished. They elevated the prestige of some senators, like Flamininus, Lucius Scipio, Fulvius, and Glabrio, above many of their peers and overshadowed the achievements of others.

14. Pittenger, *Contested Triumphs*.

The tensions that resulted shaped political rivalry at the highest levels.

The senators' concern with how the growth of the Republic's *imperium* played out in the political arena goes a long way towards explaining the goals of the senate once the wars were won. While the senate as a body did not go to war simply to create opportunities for its members to win military glory, some members certainly had this end in view, and once the Republic had declared war those chosen to command had every incentive to seek a decisive victory in preference to any settlement short of that. No one ever won a triumph for a negotiated peace. By the same token, aristocratic virtues were not displayed to their best advantage in the routine tasks of governing peaceful provinces, so there was little incentive to multiply opportunities to do so as far as furthering individual ambition was concerned. And of course additional provinces would require additional praetors to govern them, which would only intensify political competition, with all of the concerns that raised. Hence the senate's preference for arrangements in conquered regions that would leave them to a large extent self-regulating wherever possible. The main drawback of this reluctance to administer directly the regions Rome dominated was that it left no venue for those in them to voice their complaints or make requests but the senate itself.

This was particularly true for the Greeks.[15] The period following the settlement in 187 saw a steady procession of embassies from various eastern states make their way to Rome to plead their cases before the *patres*. They sought arbitration for disputes with their neighbours or, more commonly, wanted intervention of a diplomatic or military nature against those their state was at odds with. Political factions in various states also sought repeatedly to enlist the *patres'* support against their rivals. Time and again, the fathers listened patiently but did as little as common decency allowed. They sent those requesting adjudication to the regional hegemons or other third parties to obtain decisions. When confronted with petitions for a Roman demonstration of its authority to support one party or another in a dispute the senators typically refrained from taking sides and urged peaceful reconciliation. When a decision had to be rendered, the senate's pronouncements were studies in ambiguity and evasion that masked a profound indifference, even when its best friends' interests were involved, even when the two sides were at

15. Gruen, *Hellenistic World*, 96–131.

open war with one another. When at last a situation demanded something more forceful than anodyne decrees, the senators authorised the dispatch of an embassy to look into the matter. Delegations of senators travelled east year after year and duly investigated the complaints that had been raised. But rarely if ever did they do much about them. For the senate had little incentive to involve itself deeply in the affairs of the Greeks. There was no glory to be gained in running an empire, only in winning one.

This is not to say that the senators were indifferent to what went on in the regions they now dominated, only that there were limits to what they were prepared to do about it. Those limits were on display in their response to complaints brought by delegations from Spain in 171.[16] During the years of relative peace that followed Gracchus' settlement there, some of the praetorian governors had discovered how to work the tax system that Gracchus had put in place. They set an arbitrarily high price on the grain that the Spanish communities were required to supply to the Roman forces stationed in the provinces and then ordered them to pay that price in lieu of the grain itself. The governors then turned around and bought the grain they needed at the lower, market price and pocketed the difference. They had also been in the habit of sending officers around to the various towns to collect the money-tax (the *stipendium*) rather than letting the locals carry out this task, which invited abuse. The delegations accused several senators who had commanded in Spain, and their colleagues took the charges seriously enough to order trials. However, the Spaniards were not allowed to speak for themselves; they were instructed to choose senatorial patrons to plead their cases. The praetor supervising the trial appointed the jurors, all drawn from the senate. The conflict of interest was patent as the results reflect. Of the three men brought to trial one was acquitted while the other two withdrew into voluntary exile, thus terminating the proceedings. It is unlikely that any of the money the defendants had allegedly extorted was recovered. At that point, the praetor supervising the trials suddenly departed for his province, precluding any further hearings and leading to suspicions that a cover-up had been arranged to protect the other guilty parties (Livy, 43.2.1–11). When it came to a choice between protecting the interests of the provincials and those of their peers, the senators opted for the latter. And although the

16. Richardson, *Hispaniae*, 114–15.

senate passed decrees forbidding the abuses for the future, they lacked teeth.

On the other hand, where such conflicts were absent, the *patres* could be generous. In the same year another delegation arrived from Spain, this one representing the children born of Roman soldiers and Spanish women, some 4,000 souls. Their position in their home towns was legally awkward. Because no treaties had been struck between Rome and the Spanish towns providing for a right of inter-marriage between members of the two communities, children born of such unions were illegitimate. They lacked privileges and rights that children of legally sanctioned marriages enjoyed, such as the right to inherit property or hold public office. The delegates appealed to the *patres* to grant them a town of their own where their legal status would be that of full citizens of the new community. And the senators were happy to oblige. They directed that the 4,000 be settled at the town of Carteia along with any slaves they had freed (for a freed slave's citizenship depended on that of his former master). They further decreed that the new settlement have the status of a Latin colony with all the benefits and rights that the *ius Latinum* conferred. The colony marks a milestone in Roman legal develop-ment, for it constitutes the first instance in which this legal status was extended beyond the confines of Italy, a step made possible by its separation in the fourth century from any geographic and ethnic connection with Latium. Of course, the senate's magnanimity came at a price, but not one that Rome was going to have to pay. The current residents of Carteia would have to give up their lands to the new inhabitants of their town. The senate was not wholly heartless, however. The old citizens of the town could by way of compensation become members of the new colony, but they would be entitled to receive only the same allotment of land that the new settlers would obtain. Whatever they had had in excess of that amount was lost (Livy, 43.3.1–4).

By the time the Romans wound up the unfinished business from the Hannibalic war, they were in possession of an *imperium* stretching from the Atlantic to the Taurus mountains in Asia Minor and from North Africa to the Alps. The generation of Romans who came of age in the last years of the third century could look with satisfaction and pride on what they had accomplished in the first thirty years of the second. When the censors offered sacrifice to complete the ceremonial purification of the Roman people that closed the census, they prayed that the gods would make the affairs

of the Romans better and greater (Val. Max. 4.1.10a). By the mid-
170s, the gods had certainly done so. For scholars, the critical
question has long been what, besides the gods, had brought about
this dramatic expansion of Roman power. Was it all just a series of
accidents, or did the senate react aggressively whenever it believed
invasion threatened, even when such fears were unfounded? Did the
patres take the initiative in expanding the Republic's hegemony,
finding opportunities to go to war wherever they could and creating
them when they could not? Or did the Romans simply take the
world as they found it, a harsh, Darwinian place where a state either
became stronger than its rivals or fell victim to them, where the rule
was either dominate or submit?

One-dimensional explanations fail to fit the facts. No senator
could ever dismiss the possibility that Rome would find itself fighting a foreign enemy in Italy, and not only because of Hannibal.
Pyrrhus had landed at Tarentum sixty years before, and the Gauls
repeatedly swept into central Italy both before and after that date.
The Republic's leaders were well aware of what could happen to the
defeated – both soldiers and non-combatants – in the event that one
of those invaders conquered, for the Romans themselves had more
than once visited the very same horrors on those who had fallen
victim to their arms. But to focus only on fear views the emotional
element in senatorial decisions too narrowly. Anger and a desire for
vengeance could play their part as well. So could arrogance born of
a sense of Rome's superiority and an insistence that other powers
bow before it or face the consequences. That posture was bound up
with a broader stance towards the rest of the world. The *patres*
understood that it was essential to deter challenges wherever
possible not only by building up a strong military but also by culti-
vating a reputation for ferocity in battle and an overwhelming
response to provocations even in areas beyond the *ager Romanus* or
Italy itself. Their resolve mapped perfectly onto their understanding
of what Roman *fides* required. Honour and the gods demanded that
the Republic protect those who had entrusted themselves to Rome's
good faith. But *fides* was a flexible concept; the interpretation of
what it required of the Republic permitted the senate a certain
amount of wriggle room. That flexibility should not, however, be
taken as nothing more than a cloak for cynical manipulation that
enabled the *patres* to lead the Republic to war whenever it was
convenient. *Fides* articulated a morality that served the interests of
Roman security by justifying a bellicose response to any challenge

within the broad sphere of Rome's dominion. That response in turn served to deter other challenges from ever arising in the first place. At the same time we should not lose sight of the fact that many at Rome benefited from the victories to which this policy led. Soldiers got booty and sometimes land, officers won renown and *gloria* that enhanced their prestige and often led to success in the competition to win political office, while spoils and war indemnities enriched the treasury and so lightened the tax-burden on the citizens. Once the senate had resolved on war, officers, generals, and ordinary legionaries went at it with gusto.

The moral and material backgrounds to Roman warfare reinforced one another. This had always been true; what was new in the period following the defeat of Carthage was the scale of warfare the combination engendered. The struggle against Hannibal revealed the enormous extent of the Republic's ability to wage war, not simply in the number of soldiers who could be mobilised but in the development of a command structure and an expansion of its logistical system that enabled it to campaign in several theatres simultaneously. The fact that the strategy the senate pursued after Cannae necessitated the deployment of Roman armies in Spain, northern Italy, and Greece, as well as in Sicily and at various points throughout Italy, set the stage for the particular events in each of these regions that led to a renewal or continuation of Roman warfare in them after Zama. Each brought into play the various underlying factors impelling Rome to go to war, but in different combinations and proportions. Anger and fear undoubtedly were foremost in motivating the senate's resolve to subjugate the Gauls once and for all. *Fides* in the end overcame the senate's reluctance to stay in Spain. That decision unleashed a native rebellion which in turn drew the Romans deeper in as they endeavoured to pacify the provinces. Motives in the Greek east were complex: fear, *fides*, and revenge all played a role as did a determination to compel deference and defend Rome's claims to have liberated Greece. And perhaps the senate pushed its brinkmanship too far and brought about a war that some did not really expect to have to fight. What stands out and differentiates the Republic's eastern conquests from those in the north or west is the senate's strong resistance to permanent involvement there. Provincial administration was established in Spain; colonisation and the deracination of the inhabitants imposed Roman control in Gaul and Liguria. However, the senate's belief that the Greeks could be trusted to keep the peace and respect Roman interests shaped its successive settlements. The senate had little interest in governing an empire, only in preserving and extending the Republic's *imperium*. That distinction would unfortunately only lead within a few years to more wars in the west, in the east, and against Carthage once again.

CHAPTER 6

The new brutality

Between 201 and 175 BC Rome had crushed the Gauls of Northern Italy, humbled two great Hellenistic monarchs, and pacified Spain by force of arms (and a wise postwar settlement). These conquests, however, did not put an end to warfare within its newly enlarged *imperium*. Over the next thirty years the Romans would find themselves fighting once again in Greece, North Africa, and Spain. Although a variety of factors contributed, these wars arose principally out of what the senate perceived as challenges to the supremacy that the Republic had established over the preceding quarter century. Not that any of those who now found themselves under Rome's sway were eager for another military confrontation. The defeats they had suffered and the savage brutality they had witnessed had taught them to respect Roman war-craft. What the Republic's military superiority had not made clear were the limits to Roman suzerainty. How much freedom were those Rome now dominated permitted in managing their own affairs and conducting relations with other powers? The senate's reluctance to involve itself more than minimally in their affairs bred uncertainty in the minds of Greeks, Carthaginians, and Spaniards. It encouraged them to assert themselves in a variety of ways that they believed were in keeping with their dignity and autonomy and to equate senatorial inertia with indifference. Unfortunately the senate did care, less about what they did than about what those actions revealed of how they saw themselves in relation to Rome. In the *patres'* view those whom Roman arms had defeated ought to remain properly submissive; gratitude should call forth an appropriate deference from those protected by Rome's *fides*. When instead the senate witnessed acts it deemed incommensurate with those attitudes, when the senators concluded that those over whom Rome held sway were beginning to ignore the senate's wishes and even seek to deal with Rome as an equal, the *patres* took that as a challenge to Roman supremacy and acted with extraordinary savagery to put them in their place.

The preliminaries to the Third Macedonian War offer a case in point.

The origins of the Third Macedonian War

Relations between Rome and Macedon remained cordial for nearly a quarter century after Cynoscephalae.[1] Philip aided the Republic in its war against Antiochus and was rewarded by being made one of the four regional hegemons that were the foundation of Rome's settlement after Magnesia. The senate's willingness to entrust him with such a role indicates its presumption that he could be counted on to continue a friendly collaboration with Rome. As a signal of its confidence, the *patres* had already in 190 returned to Philip his son Demetrius, who had been held in Rome as a hostage under the terms of the peace. Following the end of the war with Antiochus, the senate left Philip largely alone to pursue his kingdom's interests as he saw fit. Despite repeated protests over the years from Macedon's neighbours at the king's aggrandisement at their expense, the *patres* did the minimum they decently could to satisfy them. Meanwhile, Philip rebuilt Macedonian military strength. Polybius, our main source for this period, charges that the king was secretly preparing for a new war against Rome. However, the historian is anticipating the hostilities that in fact broke out in 171, after Philip's death (Polyb. 22.18.1–10). Philip's preparations had nothing to do with Rome. Warlike tribes to the north and west had long threatened Macedon, and a strong army was essential to safeguard the kingdom's borders. The principal drama that consumed the final years of Philip's reign had little to do with Rome or the king's foreign affairs. It was instead a tragedy that played out within his own family.[2]

Demetrius had won the favour of many of the leading senators during his time in Rome, and it paid dividends in 183, when Philip dispatched the young prince to defend him before the senate against a variety of charges brought by the kingdom's neighbours and rivals. The senators' generous treatment of Demetrius on that occasion in turn won him plaudits back home. Unfortunately, his growing popularity in Macedon led his elder brother, Perseus, to fear that

1. E. S. Gruen, *The Hellenistic World and the Coming of Rome*, Berkeley and Los Angeles: University of California Press, 1984, 399–402.
2. E. S. Gruen, 'The last years of Philip V', *GRBS* 15 (1974), 221–46.

Demetrius was plotting to supplant him as their father's successor. And many at court suspected that some in the senate were encouraging Demetrius' ambitions, seeing in him a more congenial and pliant ruler of Macedon than his brother. Scholars debate whether or not Perseus' fears were well founded; the truth cannot be known. But the tensions between the two young princes were all too real and tore the royal family apart. Perseus accused his brother of plotting to have him murdered; allegations were made that Demetrius was secretly planning to flee to the Romans; a letter supposedly from Flamininus appeared to compromise the younger son. The conflict finally forced their father to take sides, and in the winter of 182/181 he ordered Demetrius' assassination to ensure an unchallenged succession for Perseus. Later Philip came to regret his decision bitterly. Little of this, however, explains Rome's decision to go to war with the new king ten years later. Rather, events elsewhere set the stage for the renewal of conflict.

During these years Greece was seething.[3] In the Peloponnesus, the Achaean league struggled to contain secessionist movements among two of its member states, Sparta and Messene. Delegations from all parties repeatedly travelled to Rome seeking the senate's support. After the league suppressed those breakaway attempts and exiled their ringleaders, the latter quickly appealed for Rome's backing for their restoration, provoking Achaean embassies in response. At the same time, the league's stance towards Rome became fodder for political competition. One faction, of which Polybius' family was a prominent member, held that the league should respect the wishes and requests of the senate, but only to the extent that these did not require the Achaeans to contravene their own laws. Their opponents on the contrary argued that the senate's instructions should always take precedence. To the north, in central Greece, a serious debt crisis beset Aetolia, pitting rich against poor. And as in Achaea, conflict over the stance to take towards Rome divided the political elite. Similar problems seem to have arisen elsewhere on the Greek mainland. Further east, territories in Asia Minor that Rome's settlement in 189 had ceded to Rhodes now sought to escape its control. All of this propelled countless emissaries representing the aggrieved parties west towards Rome to lay their complaints and pleas before the

3. Gruen, *Hellenistic World*, 481–505; P. S. Derow, 'Rome, the fall of Macedon, and the sack of Corinth', in A. E. Astin, F. W. Walbank, M. W. Fredericksen, and R. M. Ogilvie (eds), *Rome and the Mediterranean to 133 B.C.* Vol. 8 of *The Cambridge Ancient History*[2], Cambridge: Cambridge University Press, 1989, 290–303.

Figure 25 Obverse of a tetradrachm with the head of Perseus of Macedon. ANS 1997.9.189. Courtesy of the American Numismatic Society.

senate. The *patres* as usual listened politely, dispatched legations to look into the matters, urged the parties involved to work out their differences, but ultimately did nothing beyond making conventional pronouncements and non-committal gestures. Even in 180 when an Achaean envoy, Callicrates, told the senators in no uncertain terms that if they wanted their instructions obeyed they needed to support pro-Roman politicians like himself in Greece, the *patres* neglected to follow up their praise of Callicrates with concrete action (Polyb. 24.8–10.15). The senate's reluctance to involve itself in resolving the problems of the Greeks meant that their conflicts simply festered and impelled them to look elsewhere for solutions. And as fate would have it, in 179 a potential problem-solver appeared in Macedon.

In that year Philip died, and Perseus assumed the throne. The young king quickly signalled the dawn of a new era in the kingdom, freeing political prisoners and those in debt to the crown and recalling exiles. His magnanimity was trumpeted throughout Greece and brought him an abundance of praise. Many there were ready to embrace an alternative to Roman influence, and Perseus was more than willing to supply it. The king responded to Aetolian pleas to help settle its debt troubles, and made overtures to establish friendly relations with Achaea, Thessaly, Boeotia, and Epirus. He contracted a marriage alliance with Syria, and the Rhodians honoured him by transporting his bride, the princess Laodice from the Seleucid royal family, to Macedon. The kingdom's two seats on the Amphictyonic council at Delphi (the league of Greek states that supervised the sanctuary and cult to Apollo there) attest to Macedon's renewed prominence in Greece and Perseus' own popularity there. In all this, Perseus was simply reasserting Macedon's traditional role as patron and protector of Greece. Nothing suggests he was taking a stand against Rome. Quite the reverse: among his first acts following his accession was to renew his father's treaty and friendship with the Republic. And the senate cordially reciprocated, officially recognising him as king of Macedon. Nor did any of Perseus' diplomatic initiatives raise alarms at the time. As late as 174, the senate turned a deaf ear to complaints when Perseus crushed a rebellion among his subjects. Neither did it voice concern when the king travelled with his army peacefully to Delphi to consult the oracle in the same year. Even rumours emanating from Africa of secret negotiations between Perseus and Carthage in 174 and reports in the following year of a Macedonian military build-up failed to move the senate to take decisive action. The catalyst instead came from a completely different source.

Early in 172, Eumenes, the ruler of Pergamon, arrived in Rome to deliver an impassioned denunciation of Perseus, and this finally provoked the senate to act. But what exactly in the king's speech turned the *patres* against Perseus remains a mystery. Eumenes spoke behind closed doors, and the specifics of his accusation were only reported after the fact (Livy, 42.14.1). The speech Livy puts into his mouth contains a laundry list of old charges and exaggerated claims of Macedonian preparations for war. Similarly, a bill of particulars against Perseus that the senate circulated in Greece lists prior acts that the senators had earlier paid little heed to along with wild claims of murders and attempted murders, even of Eumenes himself (*Syll.*[3] 643 cf. Livy, 42.40.3–9)! Little of this seems a sufficient *causa belli* (motive for war). Indeed, the charges suggest the *patres* were scraping up anything they could find in order to justify a war undertaken for less than honourable motives, yet motives that urged them to war. A clue may lie in the senate's oddly dilatory preparations for the conflict. Rather than rush armies to Greece, the senate dispatched high-ranking emissaries to the east who spent much of 172 drumming up support for Rome against Perseus. And although the centuriate assembly duly passed a declaration of war when the new consuls entered office in the spring of 171, even then, months passed before a consul led his legions against Macedon. Indeed, that declaration of war was conditional: there would be war unless Perseus offered satisfaction (Livy, 42.30.11). The senate was clearly leaving the door open to a peaceful resolution of its complaint against Perseus. But the initiative lay with Perseus: he would have to meet the senate's demands. What then did the senators want from him?

Some have seen the senators hell-bent on provoking hostilities simply because they needed a war in which to win glory and riches. And certainly these motives cannot be ignored. But they will have carried weight mainly with those few senators who might have hoped to command a new Macedonian war or serve as officers in it. These men cannot have constituted a majority in the *curia*. Rather, the *auctoritas* that carried the greatest weight belonged to those senators who had already reached the consulship. Repetition of that office was rare in this period. Few of them can have expected to win re-election, while no more than a handful of former praetors were in a position to try for an upcoming consulate. Those who might have anticipated serving as one of the junior officers or in the cavalry typically had not even been elevated to the senate yet. Some did have fathers there, who might have hoped to see their sons return having won wealth and fame, but against that they had to weigh the very real possibility that their sons might not return at all. Still, the *patres* may not have been averse to going to war in this case since it would enable those citizens who would fight in Greece to enrich themselves and perhaps the treasury in the process. On the other hand, fear of an impending Macedonian attack lacks plausibility as the senate's motive. Polybius' claim that Perseus was intent upon realising his father's plan for a new war against Rome has little merit. Others, therefore, have argued that the senate's leisurely diplomatic preliminaries mainly reflect the desire for a public relations victory. Eumenes, so Livy avers, had chided the *patres* that Perseus was gaining popularity at the Republic's expense, helped along by Greek hostility to Rome (Livy, 42.12.2, 13.10). As they had demonstrated in the run-up to the previous war in Macedon, the senators were acutely sensitive to Greek perceptions of Rome. Thus they sought not war but only a reassertion of the Republic's primacy in the east. They never expected Perseus to fight. He had scarcely shown himself antagonistic up to that point, and the senators assumed that he would back down.[4] This gets us closer to the truth. But who at Rome

4. W. V. Harris, *War and Imperialism in Republican Rome 327–70 B.C.*, Oxford: Oxford

will have forgotten that Perseus' father, Philip, when confronted with a similar demand to submit to the senate's dictates, chose to fight instead?

To be sure, the king's transgression lay in offering himself as an arbiter for Greek affairs, threatening thereby to supplant the Republic in that role. But that in and of itself cannot have been the senators' principal concern, for if it had been, there was a much easier solution than going to war. The *patres* could have taken a greater interest in Greece's problems and actually done something about solving them. But neither then nor thereafter did they make much of an effort to do so. Rather the senate saw in Perseus' new prominence in the affairs of Greece an attempt to restore Macedon to its former leading position within the constellation of Mediterranean powers after the eclipse that followed Philip's defeat at Cynoscephalae. This, too, was part of Perseus' fresh beginning. But that was anathema to the *patres*, because in so doing Perseus was seemingly asserting Macedon's equality with Rome and denying its subordination. The senate's stance ought to be familiar by this point. In offering Perseus a stark choice between abasing himself or war, it was demanding that he acknowledge his submission in dramatic and public fashion. Assembling an audience for that degradation had been the goal of the senate's diplomatic missions to the capitals and palaces of the Hellenistic world in the prelude to the war. Having humbled Macedon once, the senators were not about to countenance its escape from that position. And if Perseus and Macedon would not abase themselves before Rome, Roman arms would once again teach them their place.

Perseus certainly did not want a war with Rome. But having begun to restore his kingdom to its ancient glory, he was not about to back down. He would act towards the Republic as a peer rather than an inferior, an attitude reflected in his response to the senate's belligerence. He sought negotiations. He invited one of the senate's envoys to Greece in 172, Q. Marcus Philippus, to meet him to discuss the two sides' differences. When the meeting took place, after considerable delay on the envoy's part, Perseus offered a detailed rebuttal of the charges the senate had levelled against him. Philippus urged him to send representatives to the senate, and they arrived early in 171 (Livy, 42.38.8–43.3). But rather than prostrate

University Press, 1979, 227–33; Gruen, *Hellenistic World*, 408–19; Derow, 'Rome, the fall of Macedon', 303–10.

themselves before the senators, they attempted to head off hostilities and settle the king's differences with Rome by rebutting the accusations brought against him (Polyb. 27.6.1–4; Livy, 42.48.1–4). That was not what the *patres* wanted to hear, any more than the Roman ambassadors to Carthage in 218 had been prepared to listen to the Carthaginian senators cite the terms of the treaty of Lutatius in order to justify Hannibal's treatment of Saguntum. That was the posture of one great power to another, not of a submissive inferior to an acknowledged superior. Their fathers had fought to establish Rome's dominion in the Greek east, and the senators of 172 did not intend to let it slip from their grasp. Perhaps, too, worries over the re-emergence of Macedon as a major military power lay at the root of the senators' decision to break Perseus, even at the cost of war. Although the king's attitude had been anything but threatening down to 172, that could change at some point in the future as his strength increased. Ultimately, there were no guarantees that friendly relations would continue. The senators were hard men – but they lived in a hard world. Better to nip a potential threat in the bud now rather than wait until the challenge grew greater, possibly even too great.

The third war against Macedon

If this is so, then the *patres* had been right to worry. Perseus and Macedon proved a tougher nut to crack than anyone at Rome anticipated. Everyone expected an easy victory and rich booty. Volunteers flocked to the levy to enlist for the new war. Veteran centurions contended for reappointment to their old ranks (Livy, 42.32.6–35.2). Confidence was high. The initial encounter between the Romans and Perseus' forces therefore came as a shock. Macedonian cavalry and light troops met a similar force of Romans and their Greek allies in Thessaly in the autumn of 171 and routed them. Some 2,200 fell on the Roman side and another 600 were captured, we are told, against the loss of a mere sixty of Perseus' men (Livy, 42.60.1), and the consul was forced to withdraw his troops to a position of safety. Yet even at this point, Perseus sought peace. He sent emissaries to the consul offering to renew his father's treaty with Rome, evacuate various towns, and pay reparations for the war. The Romans' reply was uncompromising: Perseus could have peace if he surrendered unconditionally. And they remained steadfast in that position despite several more approaches by Perseus, each time offering to pay a greater sum. (Polyb. 27.8.1–15). Ironically, the king would have been better served if he had lost the battle. As Polybius notes, the Romans, although severe and determined in defeat, could be lenient in victory (27.8.8). The consul and his advisors understood that having failed to beat Perseus in battle, they would appear even weaker if they allowed him to buy them off. It would be tantamount to a confession that they could not defeat him – a humiliation, and all the more so in the light of their invitation to the Hellenistic world to witness them humbling Perseus.

For it was in the court of public opinion that the battle's most serious repercussions were felt. In its wake Greek sympathies swung decisively to Perseus and revealed the depth of the antipathy towards Rome (Polyb. 27.9.1). Fifteen years of senatorial neglect and unresponsiveness were now paying unwelcome dividends, compounded by a general dislike of dominance by western 'barbarians'. Unfortunately, the Roman commanders in Greece did little to improve the Republic's image. Friendly cities were attacked, their leading citizens put to death or driven into exile, and the remainder of the inhabitants sold into slavery. Other cities, marginally more fortunate, were subjected only to extortionate demands for money and grain, and in some cases forced to endure the billeting of sailors in private homes, with all of the indiscipline and abuses that brought in its train. A procession of allied delegations journeyed to Rome to voice their complaints to the senate. The *patres* attempted to mollify the Greeks with kind words, gifts, and assurances that these things had not been done with their knowledge or consent. More concretely, they announced that henceforth any requisitions from the allies would have to be accompanied by a letter of authorisation from the senate. And measures were taken in Rome against the worst offenders. Two tribunes of the plebs in 170 tried the praetor who had commanded the fleet in 171 for abuses against the allies in Greece. He was found guilty and condemned to exile and a hefty fine. The senate censured his successor for similar transgressions and sought to make what amends it could.[5] Delegations were dispatched to mend fences in Greece.

Roman military operations meanwhile met with little success. The consul of 171 won a minor victory later in that year to offset his earlier loss but otherwise accomplished little. His successor proved

5. Recall that the year before the senate had responded to complaints from Spain of mistreatment by praetorian governors of provincial subjects there: see above, p. 206.

similarly inept. Perseus, however, was able to entice the king of Illyria, Genthius, to his side in 169 and elsewhere in the west much of Epirus also threw in its lot with the king in that same year. A growing sense of crisis therefore impelled the senate to get the war back on track. Late in 170 the fathers dispatched a commission to look into the condition of the army in Greece. Its members brought back reports early in 169 of Perseus' successes and of Roman forces reduced by over-many leaves of absence granted to curry the soldiers' favour. Worse, the general run of failures against Macedon had dampened the citizens' enthusiasm for the war. When the consuls of 169 attempted to draft a supplement for the legions in Greece, they claimed that no one would come forward. The praetors of that year, however, asserted that the problem was not lack of recruits but the political ambitions of the consuls, who were too generous in granting exemptions to potential conscripts (which itself reflects the citizens' disinclination to serve in this war). Controversy ensued. The praetors vowed that they would find recruits if the senate gave them the job, the *patres* obliged, and the praetors quickly rounded up the necessary soldiers, much to the consuls' chagrin. The censors also got into the act. In response to reports that many of the legionaries from Macedon who had been given leaves of absence were now in Italy, the censors ordered them to present themselves before them and then return to their legions. The censors also examined the discharges of former soldiers and revoked those they found premature. And in conducting the census they made all citizens of military age swear that they had come forward for the levy and would continue to do so for the term of the current censorship. As a result, Rome was mobbed with men attending the census (Livy, 42.14.2–10, 15.7–8).

A new energy marked events in Greece as well. In the west, the senate opened a second front in Epirus late in the year to pin down Perseus' allies there. The new consul, Q. Marcius Philippus, spent much of 169 on a diplomatic offensive among the Republic's eastern allies, mollifying them and addressing their concerns. He even suggested to the Rhodians that they might serve Rome's interests by offering to mediate the Republic's differences with Perseus (Polyb. 28.17.4–8), advice that would have disastrous consequence for them in the aftermath of the war. Philippus also energised the legions and with them managed to fight his way into Macedon proper, despite Perseus' efforts to block the passes from Thessaly. The year ended with the two armies facing each other in southern Macedon, and the decisive battle looming. L. Aemilius Paullus took command in the next year with additional reinforcements and after some preliminary manoeuvring brought Perseus and his army to battle at Pydna on 22 June. Paullus later used to confess to his friends that he had never been so frightened in his life as when the two sides faced one another and he saw the bristling mass of enemy spear points (Polyb. 29.17.1; Plut. *Aem.* 19.1). Once more, however, the flexibility of the manipular legion met the challenge. Although the 18-feet-long pikes of the Macedonian phalanx initially presented an unbroken wall of iron that kept the legionaries from getting close enough to use their swords, gaps in that wall began to open as the phalanx advanced over the broken ground. Small groups of Romans and *socii* were able to slip in close and cut down the enemy, who had little in the way of defensive armour and inferior short-range weapons. These attacks only enlarged the gaps and brought more legionaries within striking distance to wreak havoc until at last the Macedonians broke ranks and fled with their tormentors in hot pursuit. The Romans later claimed that they had never killed so many of the enemy in a single battle as on that day. They themselves lost fewer than 100 men (Livy, 44.41.1–42.9; Plut. *Aem.* 18.1–22.4). With the victory at Pydna, the Republic's third Macedonian war was over. In Illyria the defeat of King Genthius in the same year brought that contest to a close as well. Now once again the senate had to decide what to do about Greece.

A new harshness

Paullus had not been the only one frightened by Perseus and the Macedonians.[6] The difficulty of winning this war seems to have shaken the senate, too, for the fathers resolved that no challenge should ever arise from that quarter again. After a brief flight Perseus surrendered and was brought to Rome to grace the consul's triumph. He would be Macedon's last monarch. The senatorial commission dispatched to implement a new settlement in Greece ordered the kingdom broken up into four independent republics forbidden to have any dealings with one another. Not only would there be no military or diplomatic cooperation, but citizens of one were not even

---

6. Gruen, *Hellenistic World*, 423–9, 514–19, 569–72; Derow, 'Rome, the fall of Macedon', 317–19. D. Dzino, *Illyricum in Roman Politics 229 BC–AD 68*, Cambridge: Cambridge University Press, 2010, 57–60.

allowed to own property or marry someone in any of the others. The republics would now pay taxes to Rome, half the amount the monarchy had collected. And the senate decreed that Macedon's mines, a major source of revenue for Macedonian kings going back to Philip II and Alexander, would henceforth be closed. The senate's intent here was not simply to punish Macedon but to cripple it, thereby ensuring that it could never again become a major power. Similarly, the *patres* abolished the Illyrian kingdom, dividing that realm into three independent republics labouring in all likelihood under similar handicaps to those imposed on Macedon.

Central and southern Greece suffered as well. On orders from the *patres*, hundreds of allegedly disloyal political leaders were rounded up and deported to Italy, there to languish in exile for decades. A thousand Achaeans alone went west, Polybius among them (see above, p. 1). Callicrates and his friends drew up the list, effectively eliminating all political opposition to their ascendancy in Achaea. Many others politicians whose loyalty to Rome was suspect suffered the same fate. They, however, were more fortunate than 550 leading Aetolians. Their enemies slaughtered them in the council chamber while a detachment of Roman soldiers stood by. Although that may have been going farther than the *patres* intended, their aim was clearly to ensure that only the most pliant, supine leadership remained in Greece. They had been shocked by the groundswell of popular enthusiasm for Perseus after his victory in 171 and clearly now recalled Callicrates' warning of a dozen years earlier: if the senators wanted obedience from the Greeks, they needed to support those politicians who supported Rome. Belatedly, they followed his advice, eliminating any possibility of opposition to Rome's friends in Greece and thereby assuring submission to Roman dominance there.

Farther east, the *patres* resolved to humble Rhodes. The Rhodians had acted on Philippus' suggestion and sent a deputation to Rome in 168 to offer their government's services to mediate between the Republic and Perseus. This embassy had the extraordinary bad luck to be granted a hearing only after the announcement of the victory at Pydna. Obviously, there was no longer any need for mediation. The ambassadors with considerable embarrassment explained to the senate why they had come, acknowledged that their mission was now otiose, and offered congratulations on the victory before departing. The senators were not pleased. Some even advocated declaring war on Rhodes (Polyb. 29.19.1–11; Livy, 45.21.1–8). The Rhodians' fault lay not so much in poor timing as in the very act of proposing a negotiated settlement to the war. To conclude the conflict on any terms other than a complete military victory would have represented in the senators' view an admission of defeat, an acknowledgement of the Republic's inability to prevail on the battlefield. Having spurned Perseus' overtures in 171 for just that reason, the senators looked upon the Rhodians' efforts to bring them to the bargaining table as an act of utter disloyalty, something much more to Perseus' advantage than to Rome's. Who but an enemy would want to see Rome admit defeat? For that perceived treachery, Rhodes would suffer. The senate mulcted the republic of its possessions on the Asian mainland and, far worse, emasculated its economy: the island of Delos henceforth would be a free port. The Rhodian government derived most of its revenues from taxes on goods entering and leaving its five harbours while much of the citizenry made its livelihood from the trade and transshipment that sprang from Rhodes' position as the eastern Aegean's entrepôt. Delos' status as a free port meant no harbour dues, and sea-borne trade naturally gravitated there in short order, leaving Rhodes an impoverished backwater.

The war on the other hand enriched Rome. Macedon's royal treasury became the spoils of victory, and Paullus' handling of the vast wealth it contained was exemplary in its scrupulousness. So great were the riches borne in his triumph and deposited in the treasury at Rome that they enabled the senate to suspend indefinitely the war tax levied on Roman citizens (see below, p. 246). But if the citizens were happy, the soldiers were not. They had signed up for the war expecting to come home rich, and they were angry that Paullus had denied them the opportunity to plunder the royal treasury. To satisfy them and at the same time punish the Epirotes who had supported Perseus, the senate decreed that seventy towns there be handed over to the soldiers to loot. So on the march back to Italy the army paused in Epirus. Messengers were dispatched to the doomed towns, ordering the inhabitants to gather all their gold and silver in their marketplaces. Then on a single day in a simultaneous assault, their officers set the soldiers loose to plunder the towns. Over a hundred and fifty thousand men, women, and children were taken prisoner and sold into slavery (Livy, 45.34.1–7). Yet even this was not enough to satisfy the soldiers' greed. When back in Rome the time came for the assembly to approve the bill authorising a triumph for Paullus' victory, the soldiers in attendance, urged on by one of their junior officers, voted to reject it. In the end, however, Paullus got his triumph. The voting was halted and the soldiers castigated for denying their general the honour unquestionably due to such a victory. Abashed, they and the other citizens dutifully passed the bill. The triumph that followed was memorable for its splendour, for the magnificence of the spoils displayed, and for the pathetic sight of Perseus being led in chains before the chariot of Paullus and the army (Livy, 45.35.5–39.20; Plut. *Aem.* 30.2–32.1). The senate also awarded triumphs to the praetors who had conquered Genthius and commanded the fleet.

The war left the Hellenistic world in no doubt who was now its master. That point was underscored in memorable fashion by an event that had nothing to do with Perseus or those who had lined up for or against him, the so-called 'Day of Eleusis'. While the Romans and Perseus were locked in their struggle, the rulers of Egypt and Syria had gone to war as well. The latter, Antiochus IV, the son of Rome's opponent in 191–189, swept all before him. By 168 he was besieging the Egyptian capital, Alexandria, and seemed on the verge of a complete victory. The Egyptian monarch appealed to Rome for aid, and in response the senate dispatched a legate, C. Popillius Laenas, to settle matters. And settle them he did. Arriving after Pydna at Eleusis, a suburb of Alexandria where he found the king and his army, Popilius approached Antiochus, who offered a friendly greeting – Antiochus after all had been a loyal and friendly ally to Rome. Popillius, however, handed the king a decree from the senate ordering him to end his war with Egypt, and told him to read it first. After Antiochus had read the decree, he asked Popillius to excuse him while he consulted with his advisors about how to respond before giving an answer. Popillius happened to be carrying a short stick. With it, he drew a circle around the king and told him to answer before stepping out of the circle. Shocked at this display of superiority, Antiochus hesitated briefly, then bowed to necessity and yielded to the senate's demands. Popillius thereupon greeted the king warmly (Polyb. 29.27.1–8).

The senate certainly had an interest in preventing a war that might ultimately require Roman intervention. Nor will the senators have been happy to see the ruler of Syria gain control of Egypt and increase his power enormously thereby. The possibility that Perseus might someday become strong enough to challenge Rome had been one of the factors leading the senate to resolve to humble him, and similar concerns may have played a role in the debate over what to do about the situation in Egypt. But most of all, what the *patres* wanted to do was let Antiochus know who was in charge now. Popillius may have chosen a brutally frank way of making that point, but he understood the message his fellow senators wanted to send. Antiochus' independence was at an end. He and the rest of the Greek east would henceforth act only on Roman sufferance.

That did not mean, however, that the senate was now prepared to undertake the burdens of ruling an empire. The senate's position remained what it always had been. In the years that followed Pydna, it evinced little interest in involving itself in the problems and squabbles of the Greeks. It listened to deputations, offered bland pronouncements, and dispatched legates to investigate, but ultimately did as little as it could. The fathers were banking on the effects of the calculated acts of brutality that had followed the war to keep the Greeks properly submissive. And once again for a while it worked.

Illyria, a harbinger

Rome was at peace for most of the decade that followed the defeat of Macedon. Armies campaigned in Liguria and against Gallic tribes in the foothills of the Alps in 167–166, in Corsica and Sardinia in 163, and again in Liguria in 159, but the loss of Livy's history for the years after 167 deprives us of a detailed account of these or any of the other events occurring in this period. It is clear, though, that the consuls who held office in these years often lacked enemies to fight. So in 160 the senate charged one consul with the task of draining the Pomptine Marshes southeast of Rome. That situation changed after 157. In that year, the senate finally dispatched ambassadors to look into matters in Illyria after repeated complaints from the island of Issa and Rome's other friends in the region that Dalmatian tribes from the interior were raiding their territory.[7] The envoys returned later that autumn to report that not only had the Dalmatians refused to make good any of the damage they had inflicted on Issa and the coastal cities, they had not even given the Republic's representatives a hearing and had treated them with utter contempt to boot. In response, the senate sent one of the following year's consuls across the Adriatic with an army. Although the *patres* were outraged at the treatment of their ambassadors, their principal motive according to

7. Harris, *War and Imperialism*, 233–4; Gruen, *Hellenistic World*, 430–1; Dzino, *Illyricum*, 62–4.

Polybius was a desire to keep Italy's soldiers from growing soft from too much time at peace. But there was more to it than that, as Polybius himself realised (32.13.4–8). (Indeed it is difficult to believe that any of the historian's senatorial informants would have proffered so discreditable a reason for the war. More likely it was Polybius' own surmise.)

Over the preceding quarter century the Dalmatians had subdued their neighbours, and the senate by abolishing the Illyrian monarchy in 167 and creating three weak republics in its place had only encouraged Dalmatian ambitions. They had for some time been attempting to extend their sway over parts of the coast, efforts to which the senate had long turned a blind eye despite many complaints from the Republic's friends in the region. Now that the Dalmatians had shown by their treatment of Rome's ambassadors that they would not acknowledge the senate's authority, the *patres* had no choice but to resort to war. To have done otherwise would only have encouraged imitators as well as the Dalmatians them-selves. The senate's laissez-faire approach to managing its *imperium* meant in this case that problems festered until the *patres* were left with few tools other than force to solve them when they finally became too serious to ignore. The senators could hope that the memory of the terror their armies inflicted would teach the Dalmatians and others in the region to comply with the senate's wishes in the future. Still, the *patres* may have had reason for concern about the battle-readiness of their troops. The Dalmatians' initial assault defeated the Romans and drove them from their camp. Regrouping, however, the legions forced the enemy to retreat to the stronghold of Delminium, where Roman torches catapulted over the wall ignited a conflagration that destroyed the town and everyone in it. That ended the war (App. *Ill.* 11).

New fighting in Spain

In Farther Spain at the same time (or possibly a little later; the chronology is confused) similar problems were unfolding.[8] Raiders from Lusitania, the unpacified western region of the peninsula, struck south into the Roman province. The praetors who marched

---

8. J. S. Richardson, *Hispaniae: Spain and the Development of Roman Imperialism, 218–82 BC*, Cambridge: Cambridge University Press, 1986, 126–55; W. V. Harris, 'Roman expansion in the west', in Astin et al., *Rome and the Mediterranean*, 118–42.

against them met defeat, and deeper penetration by Lusitanian war bands soon followed. One even crossed the straits of Gibraltar into Africa. L. Mummius, probably praetor in 155 and prorogued into 154, managed to defeat the raiders in his province, then transported his army to Africa, destroyed the Lusitanian forces there, and returned to Rome to triumph. His victories enabled his successor to carry the war into Lusitania and force the tribes there to surrender. Revolt, however, soon followed and fighting resumed until, in 150, the enemy sent envoys to Ser. Sulpicius Galba seeking terms and pleading poverty as the cause of their raiding. Galba treacherously promised to settle them on good land if they surrendered, to which the Lusitanians agreed. When they had disarmed and committed themselves to the good faith of Rome, he divided them into three groups and, surrounding them with soldiers, killed many and sold the rest into slavery (App. *Hisp.* 59–60). News of this atrocity outraged public opinion at Rome. A tribune proposed a bill to free the Lusitanians Galba had enslaved in wanton violation of Rome's *fides* and to bring Galba himself to trial before a special court. Only Galba's tears and a passionate appeal to the Roman people commending to them the protection of his young sons and nephew moved them to sympathy and defeated the bill (Cic. *Brut.* 89–90; *De or.* 1.227–8; Livy, *Per.* 49). The repercussions of this travesty of justice, however, led the senate to support legislation establishing the Republic's first permanent criminal court, the *quaestio de rebus repetundis*, or the extortion court as it is commonly known.[9] Its purview was abuse of magisterial power, particularly in the provinces and particularly in money matters. Protection of the Republic's provincial subjects is not likely to have been among the senate's paramount concerns here. The senators who sat as jurors on the court failed to convict a single defendant over the ensuing twenty-eight years. Rather the law represented an attempt to exert greater senatorial control over Rome's *imperium* by restricting the heretofore all but untrammelled power of provincial governors to use their offices for financial gain. The threat of prosecution upon their return to Rome would, it might be hoped, deter governors from a refusal to heed senatorial commands and from acts that could lead to discontent among the provincials and ultimately revolt.

Provincial resistance was much on the *patres'* minds in these years,

9. E. S. Gruen, *Roman Politics and the Criminal Courts, 149–78 B.C.*, Cambridge, MA: Harvard University Press, 1968, 12–16.

for in 153 fighting had broken out in Nearer Spain as well, a result of subjects' refusal to obey orders from the senate. The Belli, a Celtiberian tribe, had undertaken to fortify their principal city, Segeda, and to induce smaller tribes in the vicinity to settle in their territory. When the senate demanded that they cease erecting walls around the town, pay tribute, and furnish the soldiers required under the agreement they had struck with Ti. Gracchus in 179, the Belli responded that the *patres* themselves had exempted them from the latter two obligations while the agreement with Gracchus prohibited only the foundation of new cities. It was silent on the fortification of old ones. The senate's response was not negotiation but war: Q. Fulvius Nobilior, the consul of 153, went west with an army. The Belli from Segeda (other Belli remained loyal to Rome) realised that they could not withstand an attack and took refuge with the Arevaci, a powerful neighbour. Fighting shifted to the region around their principal city, Numantia, where Nobilior made little headway during his year in office. His successor, M. Claudius Marcellus, enjoyed greater success, but sought to end the conflict by concluding a negotiated peace. His colleagues in Rome, however, were in no mood to compromise and rejected his treaty out of hand. They wanted an unconditional surrender and intended to prosecute the war until they got it (App. *Hisp.* 44–9). As they had demonstrated repeatedly, the senators expected submission from those under their dominion, and when submission was not forthcoming they were prepared to use force to compel it. Allowing the Belli to create a stronghold at Segeda and bring neighbouring tribes under their control meant that subduing them would only pose a greater challenge should they revolt in the future. More importantly, ending the conflict with them and the Arevaci on any terms other than complete victory suggested that armed resistance might well wring concessions from Rome. Their example of defiance and aggrandisement would only encourage imitation among the other tribes in the region, threatening Roman control of the entire province. The senate's determination to crush the Belli and Arevaci was intended not only to punish them but to cow the rest of the province into remaining peaceful and obedient.

The *patres'* stance here is all the more remarkable in the light of the war's enormous unpopularity among those called upon to fight it. On their return to Rome Nobilior and his officers spread tales of the constant fighting in Spain, the ferocious courage of the enemy, and the heavy losses they had sustained, and their talk led to widespread reluctance among recruits to serve there. In 151, as the consuls were levying troops for the war, those destined for Spain complained that they were being treated unfairly, since others were being assigned to less dangerous theatres because of favouritism. Many claimed exemptions on the grounds of what Polybius termed disgraceful excuses. The tribunes, unable to obtain exemptions for some of the recruits, took the unprecedented step of temporarily imprisoning the consuls. Eventually, a compromise had to be arranged, and soldiers were chosen for Spain by lot. Even more shocking, young aristocrats proved reluctant to come forward to serve as officers for the legions destined for the war there. At that juncture, the young P. Cornelius Scipio Aemilianus took the first step in what would become a meteoric rise by volunteering to serve as one of the military tribunes in Spain. This action shamed the other young men, according to Polybius, and compelled them to follow his example (Polyb. 35.4.1–14; Livy, *Per.* 49; App. *Hisp.* 49). Scipio would go on to win an enormous reputation for valour and leadership in the army of the consul Lucullus in 151–150 during his campaigns in western Spain (see below, p. 267). However, at that point events occurring elsewhere forced the senate to suspend temporarily the Spanish conflicts and concentrate the Republic's military resources on challenges arising in Macedon, Greece, and North Africa.

Revolt in Macedon and disaster in Greece

In 150, a pretender to the Macedonian throne 'fell from the sky', as Polybius put it, endeavouring to describe the sudden appearance of Andriscus (36.10.1).[10] A man of obscure origins, Andriscus claimed to be Perseus' son Philip (who had in fact died in 163 or 160) and so the king's rightful heir and successor. Having gathered an army in Thrace, he invaded Macedon, easily overcame the forces the four republics sent to oppose him, and re-established the monarchy. He met with little resistance. The Macedonians had grown weary of the unaccustomed political strife their new republican governments unleashed and of the restrictions on intercourse among themselves. A sentimental attachment to the monarchy lingered as well as memories of the pride and strength it had represented. His subjects greeted the 'false Philip' with open arms, and with arms they were

10. Gruen, *Hellenistic World*, 431–6.

prepared to defend him. A revived Macedonian phalanx inflicted a humiliating defeat early in 148 upon the legion Rome dispatched to remove the pretender. In response, the *patres* sent a stronger force, two legions with a full complement of *socii*, under the praetor of 148, Q. Caecilius Metellus, soon to take the *cognomen* Macedonicus for making short work of the pretender. Yet just as the situation in the north seemed to be stabilising, troubles long simmering in the Peloponnesus finally boiled over.

The problem lay in Sparta's perennial resistance to incorporation into the Achaean league. Over the preceding years, emissaries from Spartans exiled by the Achaeans for their advocacy of independence had repeatedly travelled to Rome seeking the senate's support for their restoration. And just as often, ambassadors from the league had gone to oppose them, fearing that the return of the exiles would inflame separatist sentiments and open countless disputes over the return of confiscated property. And as usual, the senators did little more than listen politely, issue bland decrees, and send occasional legations to look into matters. But they steadfastly refused to take any steps to resolve the conflict once and for all. So the situation simmered on. As it did so, public opinion in Achaea hardened against efforts to break free at Sparta and among other restive members of the league. A resolve to maintain the integrity of the league coupled with the conviction that the senate was really indifferent to how the Achaeans managed their internal affairs led to a decision to end the Spartan problem definitively. In the winter of 149–148, the Achaeans made ready to crush the latest attempt at Sparta to break free of the league's control. Envoys from Metellus in Macedon urging them to keep the peace were ignored (the campaign against Andriscus was still under way), and the league's forces went on to defeat the Spartan levies that spring. A second campaign in the autumn, once again in spite of Metellus' pleas to suspend hostilities pending the arrival of a delegation from the senate, completed the task of bringing Sparta to heel. The following summer (147), the senate's ambassadors finally arrived, bringing with them a shocking pronouncement: not only Sparta but now Corinth, Argos, Heraclea, and Orchomenus were to be granted their independence. Reaction in Achaea was violent; the ambassadors barely escaped with their lives – or so they claimed later to their colleagues in Rome. The *patres* were indignant as never before, and yet they dispatched a follow-up embassy bearing quite a different message. These legates were to deliver only a mild rebuke to the Achaeans for their treatment of the previous embassy and ask them to punish those responsible. When they arrived in Achaea in the autumn of 147, the envoys said nothing about detaching any member of the league (Polyb. 38.9.1–4, cf. 10.1–5; Livy, *Per.* 51; Paus. 7.14.1).

Modern scholars have long puzzled over the contrast between the tenor of these two embassies, as did contemporaries of the events.[11] Polybius believed that the senate's charge to the second delegation indicated that the senate at that point had no plans to break up the Achaean league. The remarks of the first envoys had been all bluff to cow the Achaeans and check their aggressiveness. And some scholars have found his analysis plausible in view of the senate's longstanding indifference to Peloponnesian affairs. Other Greeks, however, believed that it was the second embassy that was playing the Achaeans false, and many moderns have concurred. According to this view, with the war against Carthage still unresolved (see below), renewed fighting in Spain (where the Lusitanians had recently defeated a Roman force), and the situation in Macedon still unstable, the *patres* wanted to wait before proceeding against the Achaeans (Polyb. 38.9.6–8). It may well be that in reality the senate was undecided what course to take in the matter. The critical fact is that the Achaean leadership's thinking accorded with Polybius' view. In the autumn of 147, they refused to allow the second Roman delegation to address the Achaean assembly, possibly fearing a repeat of the verbal abuse (at most) that their predecessors had suffered. Instead, they prepared for war against Sparta, which in the meantime had once again declared itself independent. Riding a wave of popular antagonism the league's general in the following spring brought a motion to declare war on the Spartans before the assembly, which passed it enthusiastically despite yet another deputation from Metellus urging restraint. But having seen the senate repeatedly fail to follow up its admonitions with action, the Achaeans had good reason to assume that it would be the same in this case. And in any event with wars elsewhere occupying the senate's attention, they could hope that by the time the *patres* finally addressed themselves to the conflict in the Peloponnesus, they would find it ended to the league's advantage. Unfortunately the Achaeans' expectations proved tragically wrong.

The senators had finally had enough. They declared war on

---

11. Harris, *War and Imperialism*, 240–4; E. S. Gruen, 'The origins of the Achaean war', *JHS* 96 (1976), 46–69; Derow, 'Rome, the fall of Macedon', 319–23.

Achaea and ordered Metellus to lead his legions south (Paus. 7.15.1–
16.9). Meanwhile, the consul of 146, L. Mummius, received
command of the war and instructions to take his army to Greece. All
this came as a shock to the Achaeans. Their forces had mobilised,
but not to do battle with Rome. They were marching against
Heraclea, a city in central Greece that had thrown off its allegiance
to the league when it learned that Metellus' army was on its way.
The Achaeans' reaction was to flee in terror, but it did them little
good. The legions caught them near Thermopylae and crushed them.
As Metellus continued to destroy whatever enemy forces he could
find, he also put out feelers to the Achaeans, hoping to negotiate a
surrender and so claim credit for ending the war before Mummius
arrived. However, the Achaeans, having got themselves into a fight
with the Romans, were determined to see it through. They ordered
slaves freed, imposed financial contributions upon themselves, and
mustered their forces for a final stand at the Isthmus. Their resolve
to defy the power of Rome reflects the Achaeans' realisation that
surrender would bring with it the dissolution of the Achaean league.
That they were prepared to defend with their lives. At this juncture,
Mummius arrived and, sending Metellus and his troops back to
Macedon, drew up his army for battle. After a brief fight, Achaean
resistance collapsed, and a panicked flight ensued. Three days later,
the consul capped his victory by seizing and looting the ancient city
of Corinth. Most of the population had fled; the men who remained
were put to the sword, the women and children sold into slavery.
Polybius, arriving to attempt to salvage what he could from the shipwreck that his country had become, was treated to the sight of
Roman legionaries playing dice on priceless paintings they had
thrown on the ground (Polyb. 39.2.1–3). Then acting on senatorial
instructions Mummius razed the city. Leagues like the Achaeans'
throughout Greece were abolished.[12]

The *patres'* determination to declare war on the Achaeans may
surprise in view of their long history of failing to take punitive action
when states ignored their pronouncements and injunctions, even
when they went to war in defiance of the senate's express orders not
to. The Achaeans themselves in 148 are a case in point. Circumstances within the *imperium* at mid-century, however, made the
crucial difference and impelled the senators to make an example
of Achaea. The senate's management of those Rome dominated

---

12. Gruen, *Hellenistic World*, 523–7.

depended mainly on the latter's deference to its wishes, and deference in turn sprang ultimately from a fear of the consequences of disobedience rooted in a healthy respect for Roman military power. There was really very little else in the *patres'* toolkit. So when deference was not forthcoming, the senate had either to overlook it or go to war. And despite the advantages that Rome, its citizens, and individual senators themselves might derive from it, war was not something the *patres* entered upon lightly. Their tendency was to put up with what they could consider minor acts of defiance. Danger, however, lay in the fact that defiance, even minor defiance, gradually eroded deference when no sanctions were forthcoming in response. And since the senators had only the force of arms with which to sanction those who refused to heed their wishes, their laissez-faire approach to managing the Republic's *imperium* was always in tension with the need to cultivate the fear that elicited deference and so sustained the *imperium*. Ordinarily, that tension could be finessed and threats to control avoided, but at mid-century the senate confronted defiance that could not be ignored without worries that in so doing it was inviting replication elsewhere. The Dalmatians insultingly rejected demands to stay away from Rome's friends in the region. Lusitanian raiders began to view Farther Spain as ripe for the plundering. The Belli at Segeda and the Arevaci refused to knuckle under to the senate's demands but stood on their rights and insisted on negotiation. Small wonder, therefore, that the senate responded harshly to the Achaeans' rejection of its repeated insistence that they settle their differences with Sparta without recourse to arms. It might seem to the *patres* that nowhere in the *imperium* did fear of the hard hand of war deter the Republic's subjects and others from acting as they saw fit – above all at Carthage.

The Third Punic War and the destruction of Carthage

The Republic's declaration of war on Carthage in 149 stands as a permanent stain on its honour. The senators, so Polybius avers, had long before determined upon war; they were just waiting for a suitable pretext (36.2.1–4), and when one appeared they grabbed it. Yet the Carthaginians responded to the threat of war by repeatedly dispatching envoys in an attempt to appease the senate and head off hostilities. When the Romans voted to declare war anyway, the Carthaginians quickly surrendered. The senate then demanded 300 hostages from leading families; the Carthaginians handed them over.

The consuls, having arrived in Africa with a fleet and an army, ordered the Carthaginians to surrender all of their arms; 200,000 suits of armour and 2,000 catapults were turned over. At that point, the consuls informed the Carthaginians that they were to take their possessions and move at least ten miles from the sea, for the Romans intended to raze their city to the ground. This last demand proved too much, and the Carthaginians determined to fight rather than abandon their home. They put their fortifications in order, worked day and night to contrive weapons out of whatever materials were to hand (the women, it is said, sacrificed their long hair to make ropes for new catapults), and fought with heroic desperation against repeated assaults for four years until in 146 the city finally fell.

The reasons for the senate's determination to destroy Carthage have long baffled scholars.[13] Many assume that fear animated the *patres*. Carthage in the half century since the end of the Hannibalic war had regained its formidable economic strength. As early as 191, at the inception of the war against Antiochus, Carthaginian ambassadors had come to Rome with promises of assistance including an offer to pay off in one lump sum the balance of the indemnity Rome had imposed on them, 8,000 talents of silver – over 200 tonnes (Livy, 36.4.7). The senate on that occasion refused to let Carthage free itself from its financial obligation to Rome, but in 151 the Carthaginians handed over the final instalment of the indemnity. Clearly Polybius was right to judge the city in his day the richest in the world (18.35.9). That economic strength might have enabled Carthage to rebuild its military power, but would the senators have imagined that its wealth was intended to be the foundation for a renewed assault against Rome? The North Africans' dealings with the Republic over the preceding half century had hardly suggested a growing belligerence. Apart from the deputation in 191, a number of embassies travelled to Rome from Carthage in the interwar years. These missions stemmed from a long-running feud with Carthage's neighbour, Masinissa, the king of Numidia. He had fought alongside the Romans in the final phase of the Hannibalic war, and his cavalry lent invaluable assistance at Zama and elsewhere. For that reason, the peace treaty ending the conflict contained a clause specifying that the king was to receive back all of the Carthaginian lands his ancestors had possessed. This vague provision spawned repeated

13. A. E. Astin, *Cato the Censor*, Oxford: Oxford University Press, 1978, 283–8; Harris, *War and Imperialism*, 234–40; Harris, 'Roman expansion', 142–62.

clashes between him and Carthage as the king, claiming that he was merely recovering territory his ancestors had once held, seized various parts of Carthage's domains. Those conflicts in turn led each party to send delegations to Rome seeking the arbitration of the senate, which as usual dispatched legates to look into the matter. But time and again in these cases, whether judgement was passed by the legates or the senate as a whole, the *patres* sided with the king because, as Polybius reports, they believed that whatever the merits of the case it was always in their interest to decide against Carthage (31.21.5–6). Yet despite clear evidence of the senate's prejudice, the Carthaginians for half a century continued to submit themselves to its adjudication and to accept its decisions.

That changed in 152 when yet another senatorial delegation arrived at Carthage to mediate yet another border dispute with Masinissa. This time the Carthaginians refused to accept Roman arbitration, a striking departure from their past attitude. M. Porcius Cato, who was a member of this embassy, returned convinced that Rome had to impose a final solution to the problem of Carthage. He argued strenuously for war, going so far as to end every speech he gave on any topic whatsoever with the famous phrase, 'Carthage must be destroyed' (*Cartago est delenda*). And indeed something had changed in the Carthaginians' attitude now that the final indemnity payment was impending and with it a sense that they no longer needed to truckle to Rome. They now determined to use force to protect their interests against Masinissa's depredations. In the following year the city raised some 25,000 soldiers and sent them against the king. This act was in stark violation of their treaty with Rome, which had severely limited Carthaginian military capabilities, and it furnished the Roman senate with the *iusta causa belli* (just motive for war) that according to Polybius it had long been seeking. But if reports that a Carthaginian army had once again taken the field alarmed the *patres* with the prospect that it would soon be launched in a war of revenge against Rome, the sequel will have laid those fears to rest. The Carthaginians, having had for the past fifty years no military experience to speak of, were easily defeated and forced to surrender by the Numidians, who after disarming them slaughtered the soldiers almost to a man (App. *Pun.* 70–3). It is difficult to believe that senators could have imagined that the Carthaginians, after such a pathetic showing and after sustaining such a serious defeat, posed much of a threat to Rome. Yet rather than content themselves with the satisfaction that Masinissa had taught the Carthaginians a painful and humiliating lesson, the senators pressed ahead with a declaration of war using this violation of the treaty of 201 as their justification.

Other scholars therefore fall back on the Republic's predatory warrior elite. Naked greed for plunder and glory, in this view, as well as a desire for the longer-term economic gains that the destruction of Carthage would bring impelled the senate to push for war. Yet this analysis, too, fails to furnish a satisfactory solution. As already noted, opportunities for glory and booty would come only to those senators or their sons who commanded the army or served as officers in it. The bulk of the *patres* who voted for the war will not have anticipated gaining personally from it, although they naturally expected that the spoils of victory would benefit the soldiers and treasury. Certainly in the aftermath of victory the field was open for Roman and Italian traders to take over the profitable long-distance trade routes that had furnished much of Carthage's prosperity. Yet the senators rarely if ever sent the legions to war to benefit the Republic's merchant class. Whatever gains the latter made after 146 came as an unintended consequence of the fall of Carthage, not its chief aim. Likewise, the victory over Carthage did indeed turn its territory into the property of the Roman people, *ager publicus*, and eventually one of the Republic's richer provinces. But the senate was not quick to exploit the region's economic potential. The land was solemnly cursed after the destruction of the city, and much if not all of it remained unsettled nearly a quarter century later when Gaius Gracchus passed legislation to establish a colony on the site of Carthage. So it is unlikely that the *patres* had an increase in public revenues or Roman territory in view when they resolved on war. Only after four years of desperate resistance were the survivors of the siege sold into slavery and the territory of Carthage annexed as a Roman province.

In 149 the *patres* seem to have had different aims in view. The consuls ordered the Carthaginians to abandon their city, take their possessions, and resettle anywhere they wished in their territory provided it was no nearer to the sea than ten miles (App. *Pun.* 81; Livy, *Per.* 48, Livy, *Oxy. per.* 48). In other words, the senators seem to have anticipated at the outset of the war that the Carthaginians would remain in occupation of their lands. They were not at that point seeking the extirpation of the Punic race and the appropriation of its lands but only the destruction of Carthage and a limitation on its population's access to the sea. What united these two aims was the same goal the *patres* had had in 237, the desire to cripple the Carthaginians' economic power (see above, p. 69). Their city would no longer be a centre of commerce with harbour dues accruing to its government. Its inhabitants would no longer engage in maritime trade where a successful voyage could generate huge profits. The senators were well aware of the city's commercial prowess. Members of an embassy to Carthage had seen large stockpiles of timber and other materials for shipbuilding in 154 (Livy, *Per.* 47). And the point of Cato's enigmatic remark to a group of his fellow senators that the plump Libyan fig he showed them and whose quality they admired came from a country only three days' sail away was surely to emphasise the extent of Carthaginian trade (Plut. *Cat. Mai.* 27.1). Italy of course grew figs in abundance. Yet Cato was pointing out that the Carthaginians were even able to sell figs at Rome that not only could compete with the domestic product but were superior.

Yet if the senators were concerned about Carthage's resurgent economic power, the question remains against whom did they worry that that power might be directed. Not Rome: the Carthaginians had made not the slightest hostile gesture in the Republic's direction. Rather Masinissa was likely to be its target. The senators' fears centred on the prospect of a rearmed Carthage continuing its war against Numidia and, using its financial resources to expand the conflict, sustaining it for years. If some senators, like the aged Cato, believed the Carthaginians were inveterate enemies of Rome and would sooner or later march against it (*ORF*[4] Cato frg. 195), most will have imagined that this possibility, were it to come to pass, lay in the far distant future. Yet the solution the senators had in mind, the destruction of an ancient and illustrious city and the displacement of its population, was a drastic one and required justification appropriate to its momentousness. And so they hesitated, concerned over how public opinion within the wider Mediterranean world would judge such an awful act, until the Carthaginians' violation of the treaty of 201 afforded the pretext they had been waiting for (Polyb. 36.2.4).

Carthage's determination to go to war to defend its national interests against Masinissa in 151 links developments in North Africa to those in Achaea four years later, when the Achaeans, too, resolved to march against Sparta to protect the integrity of their league. Fear of punishment deterred neither state from acting against the senate's wishes. The threat of reprisals similarly failed to prevent Dalmatian aggression in Illyria or Lusitanian raids into Farther Spain or the Belli's refusal to cease fortifying Segeda. The *patres* expected obedience to their directives, but their longstanding reluctance to punish when these were flouted rendered subsequent pronouncements gradually less effective. At a certain point, when failing to go to war risked a complete loss of credibility, the senate was forced to put up or shut up. The problem was that no one really knew where that point lay, leading the Republic's subjects and neighbours to push farther and farther in the pursuit of their aims until they – and the senators – realised they had crossed a threshold that triggered a Roman decision to go to war.

Complicating matters was the difficulty posed by the military challenges the Republic faced. The Spanish in particular bedevilled Roman efforts at pacification for more than a decade in the west, while the conquest of Numantia in the east was not achieved until 133. An inability to visit swift punishment on those who defied Rome brought forth a determination to make that punishment, when it came, all the more terrible in hopes that its horrors would act as a further deterrent. Numantia, when it fell, was sacked and razed, and its population sold into slavery. But it was Carthage that set the precedent here. The consuls of 149 made little headway against the city's fortifications during the summer despite repeated assaults. A Carthaginian attack on the Roman fleet by fireboats destroyed many ships. And an attempt to destroy a Punic force stationed at Nepheris, some twenty miles away from the city, miscarried when, after an indecisive battle with heavy casualties on both sides, the enemy commander attacked the Romans as they were in disarray fording a river. The following year saw scant progress as well. With the arrival of a new consul in 147, however, the siege entered its decisive phase (see below, p. 268). The blockade was tightened, and the Romans finally destroyed the Carthaginian force at Nepheris, enabling them to gain control of the entire countryside and so eliminate the only source of supplies for the defenders of Carthage. Hunger began to do its work. In the spring of the following year, the Romans at last succeeded in breaching the city's defences. They fought their way through the city streets over the course of six days spreading slaughter, fire, and destruction as they went until they succeeded in compelling the surviving defenders to surrender. These were sold into slavery, the city methodically plundered of its vast wealth, the remaining buildings put to the torch, and the entire site cursed.

The Romans had little love for the Carthaginians, but their awful fate represented much more than just a payback for Italy's suffering during the Hannibalic war. It was a warning to anyone who might someday contemplate defying Rome. The Romans' difficulty in subduing Carthage only strengthened their resolve to increase the effectiveness of its sufferings in preventing future defiance by magnifying their severity. The decision to visit similar horrors on Corinth later that same year underscored the message the senators intended to send. And it seems that those within the Republic's *imperium* heard that message loud and clear. It would be a long time before the Romans again went to war to punish a subject for defying the senate's wishes.

CHAPTER 7

The impact of imperium

Conquest of an empire never leaves its conquerors unaffected, and Rome proved no exception. The acquisition of an *imperium* embracing nearly the whole of the ancient Mediterranean in the years following the victory over Hannibal transformed much about life in Italy, and nowhere more so than among the republican elite. The spectacular victories that won Rome its enlarged empire in these years threatened to disturb the balance of power and status among themselves, and the senators were not slow to appreciate the danger and react against it. Several prominent conquerors were humbled in the years after 201, none more dramatically than Scipio Africanus. This was the era of M. Porcius Cato, nicknamed 'the Censor' for opposing to the rising tide of luxury and moral laxness he saw all around him the old-fashioned self-restraint and stern morality that he believed had won the Republic its *imperium*. His was a losing battle, however. Aristocrats embraced the pleasures and refinements their conquests had made available to them. The new luxuriousness of their lifestyles was bound up with Hellenism at Rome, the growing embrace of customs and practices from the Greek east. But that embrace was never uncritical. Roman aristocrats treated Greek ways as one more among the many spoils their victories had won; they did not forget who had conquered whom. For ordinary Romans the Republic's conquests in these years transformed the city into a world capital. The booty flowing into the treasury funded a construction boom, and a tide of migrants followed, lured from the countryside and beyond by jobs building monuments to Rome's victories and the ever more lavish entertainments and spectacles celebrating them. In the countryside, profound changes were under way, purchased by the heavy cost of lives among the Romans and Italians who fought the Republic's wars, changes that would soon form the backdrop to the political and social turmoil of the late Republic.

The need for limits on aristocratic competition

Despite the intense, continuous competition within its ranks, the Roman aristocracy enjoyed a remarkable stability over the course of the third and second centuries. The fact that it eventually destroyed itself in repeated spasms of civil war should not be allowed to obscure that achievement. The ability of members of the senatorial class and those who sought to join it to contend vigorously with one another for office and influence without their rivalry degenerating into self-destructive partisan strife depended on a broad consensus among them on key values and practices, like the central ethos of service to the Roman people as the only arena within which competition could take place.[1] Another vital element in this consensus was the concern to preserve a rough balance among those at the top of the hierarchy. The concentration of *auctoritas* and of benefits bestowed on the *res publica* in the hands of too few men denied their peers influence and opportunities to cash in on the public's *gratia*. Limits on competition were essential to prevent anyone from winning too often or too much. For that reason, among others, magistracies were collegial and annual, and promagistracies in most cases restricted to one or two years. In addition, steps were taken to limit repetition of the consulate. The first may have come in 342 when a *lex Genucia* forbade holding the same magistracy again within ten years (Livy, 7.42.2; 10.13.8), although scholars have long recognised that the *fasti* for the following years pose serious obstacles to accepting the veracity of this legislation.[2] However, after c. 290 a limit of two consulships at intervals ranging from one to twenty-three years seems to have been in force down to 216, when the crisis of the Hannibalic war led to a measure permitting the people to bestow the consulate on whomever of the ex-consuls they wished as often as they wanted (Livy, 27.6.7). Fabius Maximus and a handful of other senior figures accumulated consulships over the next several years, but with the end of the war a new and more stringent limit was established: no election to a second consulate within ten years of the first.[3] That rule, and the fact that Fabius and

1. K-J. Hökeskamp, *Reconstructing the Roman Republic: An Ancient Political Culture and Modern Research*, trans. H. Heitmann-Gordon, Princeton: Princeton University Press, 2010, 98–106.
2. R. Billows, 'Legal fiction and political reform at Rome in the early second century', *Phoenix* 43 (1989), 112–33; S. P. Oakley, *A Commentary on Livy, Books VI–X*, 4 vols, Oxford: Oxford University Press, 1997–2005, 2.24–5.
3. N. Rosenstein, *Imperatores victi: Military Defeat and Aristocratic Competition in the*

the others had all passed from the scene by 200, took care of the problem that they had posed, but one man remained whose achievements threatened the balance at the top, Scipio Africanus.

The fall of Scipio Africanus

The benefit Scipio had conferred on the *res publica* by conquering Hannibal and ending the Second Punic War placed him head and shoulders above his contemporaries, with everything that entailed in terms of *auctoritas* and the public's *gratia*. He had elected to memorialise his victory not with the usual temple ascribing it to divine support. Instead he built an arch at the top of the road leading up the Capitoline hill. Although not the first victory arch erected in Rome, the form was unusual at the time, and Scipo's was particularly spectacular, featuring gilded bronze statues of seven figures (whether gods or men is unknown) and a pair of horses (Livy, 37.3.7). Its effect was to draw attention to his own rather than a god's contribution to the victory, while at the same time the arch's placement at the top of the *clivus Capitolinus*, the street leading up to the Capitoline, the site of the temple of Jupiter *Optimus Maximus*, recalled stories of Scipio's own supposed communion with Jupiter as a young man (Livy, 26.19.5–9).[4] The date he fixed for the dedication of the arch, 190, was also significant, for his brother Lucius was consul in that year. The senate had given him charge of the war Rome was then waging against Antiochus the Great on the understanding that Africanus would accompany him in the role of advisor (see above, p. 196). The dedication on the eve of his departure for the east reminded the public of his victory over Hannibal as Scipio set out to confront that same enemy who was now with Antiochus aiding him in his war against Rome. It assured the citizens that Africanus would once again return triumphant from this rematch, a prospect that his senatorial colleagues could hardly view with equanimity.

The *patres*' concern over the prospect of Scipio elevating his stature even further had been very much on their minds when they elected to withdraw the army from Greece in 194, despite the fears

Middle and Late Republic, Berkeley and Los Angeles: University of California Press, 1990, 168–70.

4. F. W. Walbank, 'The Scipionic legend', *PCPS* 13 (1967), 54–64 = *Selected Papers: Studies in Greek History and Historiography*, Cambridge: Cambridge University Press, 1985, 120–37.

that Antiochus' expansion into Europe had raised among some of them. But in that year Scipio could again hold the consulate, and once in office he let it be known that he was eager to lead an army east to confront the king (Livy, 34.43.1–8). To see Scipio add to his laurels the conquest of the Hellenistic world's greatest monarch was something few of his peers were prepared to countenance. The desire to check Scipio's ambitions, combined with Flamininus' report that he had pacified Greece and a reluctance to push matters to a confrontation with Antiochus at that stage, led the senators to order the evacuation of Greece. Scipio and his colleague instead spent their year in office chasing Gauls in northern Italy, where they accomplished little. Once war with Antiochus broke out in 191, however, the *patres*' worries about Africanus had to be weighed against the seriousness of the military challenge facing the Republic, and Africanus took full advantage of the situation. When his younger brother, Lucius, won the consulship for 190 and the senate addressed the question of how to assign the provinces for that year, Africanus announced that if command of the war went to Lucius, he would accompany him as his lieutenant. There was no question but that the war at that stage demanded not only the Republic's best general but especially the conqueror of Hannibal, and the senators enthusiastically gave the command to Lucius (Livy, 37.1.7–10). However, the brothers' victory abroad would set the stage for their downfall at home.

The events are not easily disentangled and were confused even in antiquity.[5] Probably in 187 someone in the senate asked about the money for his army's pay that Lucius had received from Antiochus after the victory at Magnesia but prior to the conclusion of peace terms (Polyb. 21.17.4–5, 40.8). Apparently prompting the question was the suspicion that Lucius or Africanus had converted some or all of this money to their personal property, possibly in exchange for offering Antiochus more lenient peace terms. At that point, Africanus intervened. He ordered Lucius' account books brought to him, and when he got them he tore the books into pieces before the startled eyes of the senators, asking them how they could demand an accounting of how this money had been spent but not of how they

5. H. H. Scullard, *Roman Politics, 220–150 BC*[2], Oxford: Oxford University Press, 1973, 290–303; E. S. Gruen, 'The "fall" of the Scipios', in I. Malkin and Z. W. Rubin-sonhn (eds), *Leaders and Masses in the Roman World: Studies in Honor of Ziv Yavetz*, Leiden: Brill, 1995, 59–90; J. Briscoe, *A Commentary on Livy Books 38–40*, Oxford: Oxford University Press, 2008, 170–9.

had acquired the 15,000 talents that Antiochus was paying them and of how they had acquired mastery over Spain, Africa, and Asia. That silenced the critics – for the moment (Polyb. 23.14.7–11; Gell. *NA* 4.18.7–12; Diod. Sic. 29.21; Val. Max. 3.7.1c).

A tribune soon assailed Lucius' conduct in office, however, perhaps shortly after the incident in the senate or perhaps three years later, in 184 – the conflict in our sources over the date is irresolvable. The issue was probably once again the money from Antiochus. Possibly Lucius was charged with theft, put on trial, and fined, but tribunes could also simply impose a fine on someone. Africanus at that point appealed to the other tribunes to veto their colleague's action, only to see eight of them refuse. Ti. Sempronius Gracchus (who married Scipio's daughter after his death and became the father of the homonymous tribune of 133) alone intervened to prevent Lucius from being hauled off to prison when he refused to put up the money for the fine (Gell. *NA* 6.19.1–8; cf. Livy, 38.52.2–60.10). Then it was Africanus' turn. Probably three years later but possibly soon after the prosecution of Lucius, Africanus was brought to trial. What specific crime his accusers alleged is uncertain, but the money received from Antiochus apparently again figured among the charges. Yet when the time came for Africanus to make his defence, he said nothing more than that it was unfitting for any Roman to listen to someone make accusations against P. Cornelius Scipio, thanks to whom his accusers were able to speak at all. And with that remark, the crowd dispersed, leaving his accusers alone (Polyb. 23.14.1–4; cf. Livy, 38.50.1–51.14).

This triumph, however, proved to be Africanus' swan song. He left the city and abandoned any further public role, retiring to his country estate at Liternum where he died, probably in 183 (Livy, 38.52.1). The reasons for his retirement go the heart of the issues at stake in the attacks against him and his brother. For although these nominally involved misappropriation of booty, the money itself was only a stalking horse for a challenge to Africanus' position within the aristocracy and the *res publica*. That position in his view was one unconstrained by the laws and norms that governed the conduct of other aristocrats. So on one occasion when money was needed from the treasury and the quaestor in charge stated that some regulation prevented him from opening it that day, Scipio took the keys and announced that he would do so, saying that it was thanks to him that it was closed (Polyb. 23.14.5). Similarly, his claim at his trial that it was only because of him that his accuser could speak at all asserted that he had preserved the very existence of the Republic and its citizens. *Gratia* for such a *beneficium* demanded nothing less than that the Roman people refuse to countenance any accusation against the person who had bestowed it. It entitled him to ignore whatever rule kept a quaestor from opening the treasury, indeed to supersede a duly elected magistrate in administering the Republic's money. And in the same vein, Scipio's demand to know why his fellow senators were not asking who had brought 15,000 talents into the treasury and added Spain, Africa, and Asia to their *imperium* unmistakably asserted that *gratia* for those achievements and the *auctoritas* he derived from them ought to have kept the senators from asking for an accounting of his or even his brother's conduct of the *res publica*. Tearing up Lucius' account books simply but dramatically gave point to his claim that he occupied a uniquely privileged position within the Republic. But to Scipio's fellow senators, concerned to maintain a balance of prestige and authority, his demand for extraordinary deference was simply unacceptable. No amount of *gratia* or *auctoritas* could put someone above the law or beyond the ability of his peers to control without threatening to undermine the very existence of aristocratic governance of the *res publica*. And so the attacks kept coming in an effort to make Scipio acknowledge that he had to play by the same rules that bound everybody else. To Scipio, however, his peers' failure to accord him the extraordinary deference to which he believed his services to Rome entitled him was deeply insulting. It struck at his *dignitas* and denied him the rewards for his accomplishments that were his due. And in so doing they broke the implicit bargain that underlay the aristocracy's competitive culture: honour and *honores* as the fruit of *gratia* for serving the *res publica*. In Africanus' own mind, it was his fellow senators' refusal to play by the rules that made it impossible any longer for him to participate in public life.

Money and aristocratic competition

The attacks on Africanus and his brother were not isolated events; they occurred within a context of efforts by many senators to impose a greater degree of control over aristocratic competition and especially on the most successful among their number. Nor should it surprise that allegations of misappropriation of booty from the victory over Antiochus provided the flash-point in these cases, for the effects of the new wealth flooding into Rome from the Republic's recent conquests were very much on the *patres'* minds in these years. Some of those hauls, particularly those from the east, had been truly spectacular. Typically triumphs were one-day affairs, but those celebrated for the victories over Philip V and then his son Perseus required three, so rich were the spoils. The Romans recorded them in loving detail: Flamininus brought to Rome 43,270 pounds of silver, 3,714 of gold, 84,000 tetradrachms, 14,514 gold Philippics, and 114 golden crowns in addition to many bronze and marble statues along with wagons piled high with captured weapons and armour (Livy, 34.52.4–8; Plut. *Flam.* 14.1–2). Paullus' haul was even more spectacular: on the first day 250 wagons laden with statues, paintings, and other artwork rolled through the city. On the second came many wagons piled with Macedonian arms followed by 750 large baskets each containing about 75 kg of coined silver and borne by four men. Other men carried a great variety of wrought silver tableware. The final day saw the captured gold paraded, seventy-seven large basketfuls, each again carried by four men while others bore enormous golden mixing bowls for wine. Four hundred golden crowns offered by the various cities in Greece preceded Paullus himself (Plut. *Aem.* 32.2–33.2). The wealth from Macedon enabled the *patres* to suspend indefinitely collection of the *tributum* (Cic. *De off.* 2.76; Plut. *Aem.* 38.1). Similarly eye-popping displays of treasure distinguished the victory parades following Rome's other conquests in the Greek east, and although the spoils from third- and second-century conquests elsewhere never matched them, they, too, filled the Republic's coffers as did the heavy, multi-year indemnities imposed on Philip, Antiochus, Carthage, and the Aetolians.

This enormous influx of wealth transformed the capital. It funded a spate of temple building, twenty-one between the years 200 and 146, most in consequence of vows generals had made for victory. In addition, the censors of 184, 179, and 174 were notable for the number of projects they undertook. They constructed the basilicas Porcia, Fulvia, and Sempronia to provide areas for the administrative business of the city and to house the many shops surrounding the forum. In doing so these censors defined the shape of Rome's central public space for generations to come. They paved streets in the city and many roads outside of it with stone for the first time and constructed a number of bridges. Among the latter was the first stone bridge over the Tiber, the *pons Aemilius*, begun in 179 and finally completed in 142. Other infrastructure improvements included an overhaul of the sewers in 184 at the staggering cost of

Figure 26 The Pons Aemilius. Photo by the author.

1,000 talents and a major increase in the city's water supply. The last new aqueduct had been the *Anio Vetus*, built in 272. A century later the censors of 179 were stymied in their effort to build another by the opposition of an influential senator who refused to let it cross his land. By 144, however, the need was so pressing that the senate ordered the praetor Q. Marcius Rex to build the *Aqua Marcia*, perhaps not coincidentally only two years after the plunder from Carthage and Corinth had brought a fresh infusion of cash into the treasury.

The increasing lavishness and elaboration of every sort of spectacle at Rome likewise marched in step with the expansion of its *imperium*. The 'games' (*ludi*) honouring the gods now extended over several days and included a variety of entertainments: chariot racing in the circus Maximus or Flaminius and on stage musicians, dancers, boxers, jugglers, and other performers as well as comedies and tragedies by early Latin poets like Ennius, Naevius, Caecilius, Plautus, and Terrance. Gladiators did not yet feature in these sorts of festivals, but on the death of a leading senator his sons not uncommonly presented *ludi* in his honour at which fighters contended. Combats at funerals were an Etruscan custom first introduced at Rome in 264, when three pairs fought at the funeral of D. Iunius Pera. In 216, the sons of M. Aemilius Lepidus presented twenty-two, while on the death of P. Licinius Crassus in 183 his sons not only offered sixty pairs to the public but distributed food, feasted the citizens, and put on three days of games as well. By 174, the number had increased to seventy-four pairs along with similarly extravagant largess (Livy, 23.30.15, 39.46.1–2, 41.28.11).

Money to mount the annual *ludi* as well as those generals promised the gods came from the senate, since funding public worship as well as public temples fell within its purview. As the Republic's conquests increasingly enriched the treasury the amounts that could be disbursed for these purposes correspondingly increased. But these were often not enough for the ambitions of those seeking to amuse the public, who were tempted to tap other resources. Lucius Scipio travelled throughout Asia Minor while on an embassy in 184 collecting money and artists from rulers there for games celebrating his victory over Antiochus (Livy, 39.22.8–10). Abuse in exploiting such personal connections grew so excessive that in 182 the senate decreed that givers of *ludi* were not to accept anything from any of the Latins, Italian *socii*, or provincials after Ti. Sempronius Gracchus as aedile had overburdened them with his requests for contributions (Livy, 40.44.12). Private festivities, however, lay under no such restrictions, and their costs could be enormous, even ruinous. Polybius notes that in his day funeral games might cost around thirty talents (about 780 kg of silver) 'if done generously'. The cost of Aemilius Paullus' funeral had threatened to bankrupt one of his two sons, for his entire estate had only amounted to some sixty talents (31.28.5–7). One can well understand why L. Aemilius Lepidus, who had been *pontifex maximus* and *princeps senatus*, enjoined his sons not to spend more than a million asses (roughly twenty talents) on his obsequies (Livy, *Per.* 48).

The growing expense of funeral games was only one aspect of the increasing importance of wealth and its display in aristocratic competition. Of course senators had always been rich; that was a large part of what enabled them to be senators. The aristocratic residence at the so-called 'Auditorium site' dates back to the mid-sixth century. By the early fifth century, it had taken on elements of real grandeur, and it was in continuous occupation for centuries thereafter.[6] Still, Roman writers liked to imagine that the *patres* of long ago had been humble men. Samnite ambassadors supposedly found M'. Curius Dentatus, consul during the Pyrrhic war, at home sitting by the fire cooking turnips for his dinner. When they offered him a mass of gold as a bribe, he scornfully refused claiming that someone satisfied with such a meal had no need of gold (Plut. *Cat. Mai.* 2; cf. Cic. *Sen.* 55; Val. Max. 4.3.5). In trying to gauge the level of wealth among third-century aristocrats we are probably on firmer ground with the report that Dentatus' contemporary, C. Fabricius Luscinus, as censor in 275 BC expelled from the senate an ex-consul for possessing ten pounds weight of silver tableware (Dion. Hal. 13.20; Livy, *Per.* 14). Yet a little more than a century later, the senate decreed that every senator should swear that he would not use more than one hundred pounds of silver tableware at feasts during the Megalesian games (Gell. *NA* 2.24.2), the clear implication of the decree being that some of them possessed considerably more than that.

This exponential rise in the wealth at some senators' disposal seems to have occurred at the same time that the enormous spoils from the Republic's conquests in the first third of the second century were flowing into Rome. There was obviously a connection between these two events, but precisely how the profits of victory found their way into the purses of the aristocracy is unclear. Scholars at one time believed that a victorious general was entitled to help himself from a portion of the booty, the *manubiae*, that had been set aside for him. More recent studies have challenged that claim, and it now seems that *manubiae* were always public monies that remained in the custody of a general pending his use of them for some public purpose – construction of a temple or mounting *ludi*, for example.[7] That does not mean that generals and other officers did not enrich themselves from the spoils of victories, only that a subterfuge of one sort or another was required. Polybius suggests several (18.35.9–11). However, a general's enlarging his personal fortune from the profits of Rome's conquests conflicted with other claims on the loot.[8]

6. N. Terrenato, 'The auditorium site and the origins of the villa', *JRA* 14 (2001), 5–32.
7. I. Shatzman, *Senatorial Wealth and Roman Politics*, Brussels: Latomus, 1975; Shatzman, 'The Roman general's authority over booty', *Historia* 21 (1972), 177–205; J. B. Churchill, '*Ex qua quod vellent facerent*: Roman magistrates' authority over *praeda* and *manubiae*', *TAPA* 129 (1999), 85–116.
8. N. Rosenstein, 'War, wealth, and consuls', in H. Beck, A. Duplá, M. Jehne, and F. Pina Polo (eds), *Consuls and res publica: Holding High Office in Republican Rome*, Cambridge: Cambridge University Press, 2011.

Rome's wars typically did not pay for themselves. Booty and indemnities had to reimburse taxpayers whose *tributum* payments had often funded several years of campaigning before a war culminated in victory. So in 187 the senate decreed that whatever money the citizens had contributed towards military expenses in prior years and was still owing to them should be repaid out of the rich spoils that Cn. Manlius Vulso's triumph had brought into the treasury (Livy, 39.7.4–5). The cost of fulfilling vows to the gods whose aid had enabled the Republic's armies to vanquish their enemies came from the same source. Generals' overt self-enrichment from the spoils was out of the question, therefore.

Equally or perhaps even more important in the minds of the *patres* was their concern to preserve a rough equilibrium among those at the top of the *cursus honorum*. They could all agree that becoming rich was a desirable end in and of itself, but they could also all agree that no one of them should get too much richer than what his peers felt proper, particularly when that wealth affected aristocratic competition. And they were prepared to act decisively when they felt that that might be the case. In 189 two tribunes of the plebs complained that M.' Acilius Glabrio, who had defeated Antiochus at Thermopylae two years before, had neither displayed in his triumph nor deposited in the treasury money and booty seized when his army captured the king's camp. The timing of this challenge to Glabrio's handling of the spoils from his victory was not fortuitous. He was running for the censorship in that year, and popular favour inclined towards him because he had lavished his wealth on the populace. The fact that he was a new man made the prospect of his winning the censorship even more galling to the *nobiles*. It was disturbing enough to them to see a new man win one of the coveted consulships; to see his money raise him to the censorship was clearly intolerable. He was getting above what his fellow senators, and especially the elite among them, thought proper. Criticism and the threat of prosecution in the end forced him to abandon his quest to become censor (Livy, 37.57.9–58.1).

The attack on Glabrio formed the opening salvo in a concerted effort by the *patres* to impose a greater degree of control over aristocratic competition and the most successful within their ranks. The 'fall' of the Scipios likewise entailed an attempt to cut down to size men with outsized achievements to their credit and through whose hands enormous sums of public money had passed. Nor was this the end of it. Other prominent conquerors besides these returned to a rocky reception at Rome. Cn. Manlius Vulso had campaigned extensively in Asia Minor following the peace with Antiochus and the king's withdrawal east of the river Halys. His request for a triumph in 187 encountered stiff opposition, as did that of his colleague, M. Fulvius Nobilior, who had subdued the Aetolians. In Vulso's case, the senators had not authorised him to go triumph-hunting among the Galatians in the interior, an expedition that had turned into a massive looting spree. Hostility was compounded when an ambush in Thrace deprived him of much of the spoils on his journey home. Nobilior suffered in the same year when a personal enemy saw to it that envoys from Ambracia came before the senate to complain of gross abuses at Nobilior's hands after their town had surrendered on terms. Yet despite those assurances, the consul and his army had stripped the place bare, or so it was alleged. Both men got their triumphs in the end. But the difficulties each encountered in obtaining what ought to have been his just deserts emphasised the supremacy of his fellow senators and their power to pass judgement on the merits of his accomplishments. *Gratia* in these cases as in the others did not trump aristocratic control.[9] The lesson seems to have been learned. Following his defeat of Perseus, Aemilius Paullus scrupulously refrained from any action that might have hinted at self-enrichment from the spoils and successfully preserved the royal treasury from plundering by his troops, an action which nearly cost him his triumph (Polyb. 31.22.1–4; Diod. Sic. 31.26; see above, pp. 110, 223–4).

The years following Scipio's withdrawal from Rome also saw a number of reforms aimed at imposing additional constraints on aristocratic rivalry. In 182, following the senatorial decree restricting the amount of silverware to be displayed at certain feasts, a *lex Orchia* established a maximum number of guests who could be entertained at banquets. Both measures sought to set a limit on lavish displays of wealth in private settings. On the heels of this law came another, the *lex Baebia* on *ambitus*. Although the term is usually translated as bribery, *ambitus* refers rather to the use of money in electioneering in ways deemed inappropriate. What the *patres* had in mind was the sort of thing Glabrio had done on his return from his victory in the east, namely use his wealth to shower

9. M. Pittenger, *Contested Triumphs: Politics, Pageantry, and Performance in Livy's Republican Rome*, Berkeley and Los Angeles: University of California Press, 2008, 196–230.

gifts of various sorts on the populace as a means of winning popularity and gaining an advantage in competition for higher office. Both measures responded to the effects on aristocratic rivalry stemming from the enormous sums flowing into Rome (and by various paths into the purses of individual aristocrats). But besides addressing *ambitus*, the *lex Baebia* also enacted that the number of praetors elected annually should be reduced from six to four in alternate years. In part, practicalities dictated this change. As noted previously (see above, p. 203), travel to Spain entailed a lengthy journey, and the magistrates sent there sometimes reached their province with the campaigning season nearly over. Little time remained for them to familiarise themselves with the country and get operations under way for the following year before a successor arrived on the scene. The effect of electing only four praetors every other year, therefore, was to give those who had gone to Spain the year before extra time to get things done. But the addition of two more praetors in 197 had also intensified rivalry for the consulate, which in turn had given rise to electoral practices that the *patres* viewed as corrupt. Cutting down the number of praetors somewhat correspondingly reduced the number of ex-praetors eager to take the next step on the *cursus honorum*, thereby easing pressures to resort to forms of competition that other aristocrats perceived as out of keeping with customary norms, undercutting the role of those virtues on the basis of which voters had traditionally judged the merits of candidates. Then in 180 came the *lex Villia annalis*. This measure for the first time established minimum ages for each of the offices in the *cursus honorum*. It formalised the sequence in which they should be held (although custom and perhaps legislation had already gone some way in this direction) and established a two-year interval between the laying down of one office and entry into the next (Livy, 40.44.1).[10] The effect was to slow the progress of individual aristocrats along the *cursus* and limit how far ahead of their coevals the strongest competitors could get by skipping intervening offices on the way to the consulship. It also complemented the *lex Baebia*: praetors who would now remain in Spain for two years would not return to find themselves outstripped by their colleagues in that office who had been able to win election to a consulate in the year following their praetorship. For senators concerned about the unintended effects on the distribution of status and power within

---

10. A. E. Astin, *The Lex Annalis before Sulla*, Brussels: Latomus, 1958.

their ranks that the recent expansion of the Republic's *imperium* had produced, these laws strengthened the ground rules of political rivalry and were the natural extension of efforts to force men like Nobilior, Vulso, Glabrio, and Africanus to acknowledge that despite their extraordinary services to the Republic they, too, were bound by the rules and by the collective authority of their peers.

Cato the Censor

Among the prime movers behind these events was M. Porcius Cato.[11] It was he who supplied the damning testimony that forced Glabrio to drop his bid for the censorship in 189, an office for which Cato himself was also vying. Although he lost that time, he won when the next elections were held, in 184. If our sources are to be believed, he instigated those who attacked Lucius Scipio and Africanus himself in that same year and earlier, in 187, a claim made more plausible by the fact that as censor he demoted Lucius from the cavalry. Subsequently he opposed the repeal of the *lex Baebia* (ORF⁴ Cato frg. 137, cf. frg. 136). Cato's actions here arose from more than simple animus against the Scipios or a fierce drive to win high office, although these motives are not to be discounted. As a new man from Tusculum, a Latin town that had only received Roman citizenship in 381, Cato had done well to reach the consulship. Winning the censorship was an exceptional achievement. His triumph as consul had certainly helped him prevail over his competitors in 184 as did his oratorical prowess and especially his alliance with L. Valerius Flaccus, the scion of an ancient patrician clan who had been his patron from early days and was his colleague as both consul and censor. But what set Cato apart was his reputation for unbending rectitude and his championing of stern, old-fashioned Roman virtue. His censorship was notorious for its strictness. He expelled several prominent senators from the senate, including Lucius Quinctius Flamininus, whose brother Titus had defeated Philip in the Second Macedonian War. Cato charged that as consul Lucius had murdered in cold blood a Gallic chief who had come before him seeking the protection (*fides*) of Rome while Lucius was at dinner and drunk, all to amuse a young male prostitute who complained that he had never seen a man killed (Livy, 39.42.7–43.5). It was not that Cato was opposed to sex – in his old age following the death of his wife, he

11. A. E. Astin, *Cato the Censor*, Oxford: Oxford University Press, 1978.

sought the comforts of a young female slave. When his son and daughter-in-law disapproved, he married a much younger woman with whom he had a son (Plut. *Cat. Mai* 24.1–6). And the Romans never deemed homosexuality immoral per se, as long as a free-born Roman male was the active rather than the passive partner.[12] What provoked Cato's ire was the lack of self-control Lucius had displayed, particularly while serving as a magistrate. The fact that this had led him to kill an enemy leader who was deserting his countrymen and entrusting himself to the protection of Rome only compounded the crime.

For Cato was all about self-control. It was the essence of the strict moral rectitude that he upheld. And what particularly excited his ire and contempt was the submission to unbridled passions and impulses that he associated with luxury, and especially those refinements that were then being introduced from the Hellenistic world. These accompanied Rome's victorious armies when they returned from their conquests in the Greek east. As Livy writes, drawing on the second-century historian Calpurnius Piso's description of the triumph of Manlius Vulso in 187:

> For the beginnings of foreign luxury were introduced into the city by the army from Asia. They for the first time imported into Rome couches of bronze, valuable robes for coverlets, tapestries and other products of the loom, and what at that time was considered luxurious furniture – tables with one pedestal and sideboards. Then female players of the lute and the harp and other festal delights of entertainments were made adjuncts to banquets; the banquets themselves, moreover, began to be planned with both greater care and greater expense. At that time the cook, to the ancient Romans the most worthless of slaves, both in their judgement of values and in the use they made of him, began to have value, and what had been merely a necessary service came to be regarded as an art. Yet those things which were then looked upon as remarkable were hardly even the germs of the luxury to come. (Livy, 39.6.7–9)

To Polybius, another contemporary observer, the conquest of Macedon only accelerated the decline. In recalling his advice to the young Scipio Aemilianus to cultivate a reputation for self-restraint he notes that:

12. C. Williams, *Roman Homosexuality: Ideologies of Masculinity in Classical Antiquity*, Oxford: Oxford University Press, 1999, 18, cf. 15–61.

This was a glory ... not hard to gain at that period in Rome, owing to the general deterioration of morals. Some had thrown themselves into love affairs with boys; others had dissipated themselves with courtesans; and a great many in banquets enlivened with poetry and wine and all the extravagant expenditure which they entailed, having quickly caught during the war with Perseus the dissoluteness of Greek manners in this respect. And to such lengths had this debauchery gone among young men that many of them had paid a talent for a young male lover and many three hundred drachmas for a jar of Pontic salted fish. (Polyb. 31.25.3–5)

As might be expected, Cato was appalled. He complained in a public speech that one could see the Republic was going to hell when pretty boys were fetching more than farm fields and jars of salted fish more than ploughmen (Polyb. 31.25.5a; cf. Diod. Sic. 31.24).

Cato was a longstanding opponent of luxury. During his consulship, he had opposed the repeal of the *lex Oppia*, a measure passed during the darkest days of the Hannibalic war limiting the amount of gold a woman could own and the finery she could display in public (see above, p. 157). As censor, he laid a heavy tax on luxury items. His own life, by contrast, became a byword for parsimony and self-restraint. He like other aristocrats understood that a family's wealth, built up over long years, had to be carefully preserved for future generations if they were to have the financial resources to maintain and even improve their social standing through political competition. Hence old Lepidus' injunction to his sons to limit what they spent on his funeral. Someone who squandered his inheritance was for that reason an object of deep contempt.[13] Equally important, Cato believed that luxury begat avarice, and the avarice of those who served the *res publica* in turn begat financial misconduct in office. In this, too, his thinking parallels that of his peers, as their concern over the behaviour of their generals in the Greek east and their handling of the spoils of those conquests reveals. The *patres'* backing of the law establishing the extortion court makes the same point. Most importantly, however, excessive luxury aroused in Cato fears for Rome's *imperium*. Military discipline and courage in battle required self-mastery, and allowing oneself to be carried away by the sorts of dissipation that Polybius described represented the antithesis of

---

13. C. Edwards, *The Politics of Immorality in Ancient Rome*, Cambridge: Cambridge University Press, 1993, 173–206.

self-control. Cato worried that luxury was undermining his contemporaries' martial character and so threatened their ability to
maintain their dominance over other peoples and states.

Hellenism

The luxury that excited Cato's anxieties represented only one aspect
of Hellenism, the growing embrace of Greek practices and institutions at Rome during the second century. The adoption of eastern
ways was nothing new; the Romans had long been in contact with
the Greeks of southern Italy. Among the Republic's oldest cults was
that of Apollo, whose temple dated to the fifth century and stood in
a much older precinct dedicated to that same deity. In the second
century, however, as Rome came increasingly to dominate the
Mediterranean and as the wealth from its conquests enriched its
treasury and fattened the purses of many within its upper classes,
a host of Greeks (among others) arrived in Rome to offer their
services. Physicians, architects, artists, poets, sculptors, musicians,
rhetoricians, philosophers, and teachers of one sort or another all
in various ways contributed to a growing sophistication and ease
in aristocrats' lifestyles. Senators collected art. They heard philosophers discourse, rhetors declaim, and poets recite in their homes.
They appreciated the pleasure and relaxation afforded them by the
refinements that Greek architects were adding to traditional atrium
houses. They ate tastier meals. Even that über-Roman Cato was
prepared to acknowledge some value to elements of Greek culture
and kept a learned Greek slave as a tutor in his household (Plut. *Cat.
Mai.* 20.3).[14]

But like Cato, his fellow senators never surrendered themselves
entirely to the allure of Hellenism. They always made it clear who
was boss. Even though nearly every Roman aristocrat could speak
and read Greek in the second century, many with great fluency,
whenever speaking publicly as envoys or military officers to
Greeks abroad, senators pointedly addressed their audience in Latin.
Diplomatic correspondence and treaties were written in that same
language. And naturally when delegations of Greeks came before the
patres in Rome, translators were required unless the emissaries
happened to know Latin, which few did. On the other hand, if

14. E. S. Gruen, *Culture and National Identity in Republican Rome*, Ithaca, NY: Cornell
University Press, 1992, 52–83.

Roman senators were inclined to speak Greek to Greeks, they sought to do so in ways that demonstrated that their command of the language was as good as if not superior to that of native speakers. So when A. Postumius Albinus, a senator steeped in Hellenic culture who became consul in 151, apologised to his readers in the preface to a history he composed in Greek if they found his command of that language less than perfect, his remark drew a stinging rebuke from Cato for its implication that a Roman aristocrat who wrote in that language would do so less than perfectly (Polyb. 39.1.1–7). When Greek entertainers performed before the Roman people, senators stressed that they and the public called the tune. One of the generals in the war against Perseus, L. Anicius Gallus, who commanded the Roman fleet, returned to Rome to celebrate games for his victory, bringing with him a flock of Greek performers to add lustre to the festivities. But he insisted on getting them to perform in novel and awkward ways, with flute-players, dancers, and other musicians confronting one another in a bedlam of mock combat at one point, much to Polybius' disgust but to the great delight of the crowd (30.22.1–12). Finally, like many other non-Hellenic peoples, the Romans were awed by the antiquity and splendour of Greek myths about their past and sought to situate their own legendary history in relation to it. But in doing so they elected to emphasise their Trojan origins – a race firmly embedded in Greek mythology, yet one separate and distinct from contemporary Greeks' Achaean ancestors.[15] Roman aristocrats, in sum, picked and chose from the Hellenistic grab bag, happily incorporating those elements into their lives that gave pleasure or were useful but never surrendering a position of dominance, very much in keeping with the stance they took in dealing with foreign peoples and states. Yet as Cato feared, some aspects of Greek culture could be deeply subversive of Rome's, as the episode of the philosophers' embassy reveals.

In 155, the Athenians, embroiled in a dispute with their neighbours, dispatched a delegation to plead their cause before the senate. To speak for them they sent the heads of the city's three principal philosophical schools, Carneades, representing sceptical tradition, Diogenes, a Stoic, and Critolaus, who led the Peripatetics. As was often the case, the ambassadors had to wait for a hearing, and they passed the time by offering free lectures to the Roman public. These proved wildly popular with the city's young men, particularly

---

15. Gruen, *Culture and National Identity*, 6–51, 223–71.

Carneades' talks, so much so that Cato, who heard them, urged his colleagues to grant them an immediate hearing in order to send them home as soon as possible. The reasons for Cato's concern are revealing. As might be expected, the Republic's martial traditions were prominent among them. He feared, he said, that Roman youth would come to prefer to gain renown by speaking well rather than through valour on the battlefield, very much in keeping with his worries over the enervating effects of luxury. But the threat in his view ran even deeper for, he went on, it was difficult to tell what the truth was when Carneades was speaking. What Cato heard was the philosopher practising a common form of dialectical reasoning, the 'two-sided argument'. Carneades would take up a proposition one day – for example, that justice exists – and argue forcefully for its validity. Then the next day he would maintain the opposite position with equally convincing arguments. The idea that truth was relative rather than absolute, simply a matter of who had the better arguments on that day, was a revelation to young Roman aristocrats, as the popularity of Carneades' and the other ambassadors' lectures reveals. However, it was deeply unsettling to a political culture founded on tradition (the *mos maiorum*) and *auctoritas*, the belief that a man's experience, character, and success in administering the *res publica* accorded his advice so great a likelihood of being right as to amount to a kind of guarantee. Rome was a place where someone like Cato could say, in effect, 'I'm older; I've accomplished more; and I've more self-control than you, so I know better than you what you ought to do' and expect to convince his listeners. The only counter was the *auctoritas* of another leading senator. The assertion that what had been done in the past was the surest guide to what to do in the future moreover empowered those older men whose memories made them the keepers of the *mos maiorum*. In such a world, the realisation that rhetoric could persuade was heady stuff, for if the better arguments could carry the day no matter who advanced them, no matter what had been done previously, where did that leave the authority of the senate's senior figures? No wonder Cato wanted the philosophers gone as soon as possible so that young Romans would heed the laws and the magistrates as before (Plut. *Cat. Mai.* 22.1–5; Pliny, *NH* 7.112).[16]

---

16. J-M. David, 'Rhetoric and public life', in N. Rosenstein and R. Morstein-Marx (eds), *A Companion to the Roman Republic*, Oxford: Blackwell, 2006, 428–9; Astin, *Cato the Censor*, 174–7.

Social and economic changes in Roman and Italy

Hellenism touched the lives of ordinary Romans in ways quite different from those affecting the elite. Many felt it mainly in the form of entertainment. Plautus proudly announces in several of the prologues to his comedies that they are 'translations' of Greek originals, although in fact they are free adaptations rather than word-for-word renderings into Latin, to which Plautus has added his own, distinctively Roman stamp. And as noted earlier performers from the east now began to feature regularly in public spectacles. The impact of eastern practices on the Romans' religious lives was another matter, however. Details of the so-called Bacchanalian Conspiracy seem to come straight out of a Plautine comedy: a naive young lover, a prostitute with a heart of gold, a wicked stepfather, nocturnal orgies, and murder plots. Little of this inspires credulity, yet the upshot was genuine enough. In 186 the consul's report to the senate of Dionysiac worship at Rome provoked the *patres* to stern measures. They ordered the consul to investigate, and the arrest and execution of leaders of the cult along with many devotees ensued. Inquiries in Rome continued throughout the year and in southern Italy during 184 and 182–181. The senators further decreed that in the future worship of the god was to be performed only within the most stringent limits (Livy, 39.8.3–18.9, 41.6–7; 40.19.9–10; *CIL* 1.2.581 = *ROL* 4.254–9).

The reasons for the senate's alarm remain controversial despite much study.[17] Simple antipathy to an alien religion is unlikely, given the Republic's traditional openness to foreign deities, seen most recently in its welcoming of the Magna Mater during the Hannibalic war. Yet while that goddess with her strange rites and eunuch priests took her place within the state pantheon, the Bacchic cult was unacceptable. The *patres* harboured deep suspicion of any organisation that was not subject to some type of aristocratic oversight, particularly one like the worship of Dionysius (Bacchus) that was to some extent secret. Yet little in the evidence suggests it harboured subversive aims or had any political purpose at all. Further, Dionysius had long been worshipped in southern Italy and devotion to him was known at Rome well before 186. So the existence of numerous

17. E. S. Gruen, *Studies in Greek Culture and Roman Policy*, Leiden: Brill, 1990; reprint Berkeley and Los Angeles: University of California Press, 1996, 34–78; M. Beard, J. North, and S. Price, *Religions of Rome*, 2 vols, Cambridge: Cambridge University Press, 1998, 92–8.

adherents to the cult cannot have come as a complete surprise to the senators. Nor on the available testimony does the movement appear to have attracted the poor and dispossessed whose common grievances might have disturbed the status quo. Perhaps, then, it was all a ploy by the senators, an excuse to reassert their control over Italy and possibly over prominent individuals in their own midst. But little indicates a concern among the *patres* that their hold on the *socii* was slipping in these years, and as shown above they had far more effective ways of sending a message to men like Africanus than persecuting adherents of Dionysius. Ultimately, the problem defies a convincing solution because the events leading to the consul's denunciation have been so thoroughly overlaid with melodrama that we cannot know what led him to make the claims that panicked his colleagues. We can only conclude that they were inflammatory enough to provoke the harsh measures that ensued.

One development that may have coloured the senators' thinking was the growth of the city of Rome and the changing character of its population. Much of this was due to the impact of the profits of conquest. Temple construction and other building projects provided jobs that drew great numbers of Romans and Italians from the countryside into the city as well as foreigners from abroad, and the circulation of money within the urban economy coupled with the allure of the festivals and public spectacles made Rome a vibrant, prosperous place by the mid-second century. Migration from the Latin communities was so heavy that twice deputations from some appeared before the senate to ask the *patres* to order their citizens out of Rome and back to their home towns. They feared that the departure of so many men would make it impossible for them to meet their commitment to supply soldiers to the Republic's armies. The senate complied, although probably with little effect (Livy, 39.3.4–6, 41.8.6–12).[18] The attractions of the capital proved too great, and its population swelled. Estimates of growth range from 200,000 around 200 BC to 375,000 or even half a million by the middle of the century (although some scholars put the totals considerably lower).[19] Whatever the correct total, construction of the

18. W. Broadhead, 'Rome and the mobility of the Latins: Problems of control', in C. Moatti (ed.), *La Mobilité des personnes en Méditerranée de l'antiquité à la époque moderne*, Rome: Ecole Française de Rome, 2004, 315–35.

19. P. A. Brunt, *Italian Manpower 225 B.C.–A.D. 14*, Oxford: Oxford University Press, 1971, 384; N. Morley, *Metropolis and Hinterland: The City of Rome and the Italian Economy, 200 B.C.–A.D. 200*, Cambridge: Cambridge University Press, 1996, 39, cf. 113;

Aqua Marcia in 144 clearly attests to a pressing need to slake the thirst of a considerably enlarged population. They came because despite the crowding, the lack of hygiene, and the expense of the city, life was comparatively good in these years for most of those in Rome.

One thing, however, does not seem to have contributed greatly to this urban expansion: the widespread dispossession of small farmers as a consequence of the Republic's acquisition of an empire, long accepted as fact by earlier scholars.[20] They assumed that the conscription of so many men for the Hannibalic war and the second-century conquests that followed deprived great numbers of Roman and Italian farms of the manpower necessary to work them. Poverty and debt ensued, causing many to fail. Their owners were forced to sell or simply abandoned their land. Most, now destitute, remained in the countryside, but a portion flocked to the cities and especially Rome in search of a livelihood, swelling the ranks of the urban poor. Yet at the same time the spoils from those same wars enriched Rome's upper class. Scholars believed that the senators and others, lacking alternative investments for their newly acquired wealth, ploughed their money into land, of which there was now an abundance for sale at knock-down prices owing to the failure of so many small farms. Assembling these into large estates, they bought slaves to work them since these had become cheap owing to the masses of war captives Rome's conquests had also produced, the bulk of whom wound up on the auction block, flooding the market and driving down their price. These slaves in turn produced the food, particularly wine and oil, that their owners sold to a burgeoning urban population made up largely of farmers forced by Rome's wars off the lands that these slaves now tilled and that the rich now owned, growing even richer from the profits they reaped from commercial agriculture.

Or so it was long assumed. Yet as Chapter 3 explained, war and small-scale agriculture were never fundamentally at odds during the middle Republic. The integration of military service into marriage patterns, the widespread ownership of slaves, and the ability of women to do agricultural work if necessary all enabled Rome to win its empire without threatening the viability of the small and medium-

---

lower estimates: P. Garnsey, T. Gallant, and D. Rathbone, 'Thessaly and the grain supply of Rome during the second century B.C.,' *JRS* 74 (1984), 40.
20. N. Rosenstein, *Rome at War: Farms, Families, and Death in the Middle Republic*, Chapel Hill: University of North Carolina Press, 2004, 26–106, on what follows.

sized farms that supported the vast majority of Romans and Italians. Further, although Rome's population was growing in the first half of the second century, its most dramatic expansion along with that of Italy's other cities took place around a hundred years later, in the first half of the first century, when the capital reached approximately a million inhabitants and the number of non-agricultural urban dwellers elsewhere was roughly the same. Likewise the growth of large, slave-based commercial agriculture dates mainly to the late second and especially the first centuries, along with its architectural signature, the great rural villas. Recent research has also yielded a very different picture of the extent of commercial agriculture. Given what can be assumed about urban residents' average consumption of wine and olive oil, Italy's two principal commercial crops, and about average yields of vineyards and olive orchards, only about one half of 1 per cent of the peninsula's arable land was required to supply Rome's population with all of the wine and oil it needed if that population stood at half a million. Even assuming that urban residents elsewhere pushed the total to twice that figure (which is by no means certain) would hardly support the belief that vast swaths of the countryside had been given over to huge, slave-staffed plantations. And the size of the slave workforce that would be needed to cultivate those vineyards and orchards would have been of the order of only 35,000–70,000 workers, scarcely enough to displace much of the free rural farming population.[21] Nor does commercial agriculture appear to have been as profitable as previously thought.[22] Senators and other well-off Romans in the cavalry class might have numbered at least 23,300 in the second century. If each produced wine and oil for sale to (say) a million urban consumers, each producer's share would have been only about 6,900 litres of wine and 1,300 litres of oil, all of which could be grown on about six and a half hectares of land, about sixteen acres. Good data are lacking for the prices that wine and oil fetched in this period, but Cato in his treatise on agriculture at one point suggests that a litre of olive oil might have been worth a little over one third of a *denarius*. At that price, 1,300

21. W. Jongman, 'Slavery and the growth of Rome: The transformation of Italy in the second and first centuries BCE,' in C. Edwards and G. Woolf (eds), *Rome the Cosmopolis*, Cambridge: Cambridge University Press, 2003, 112–16; W. Scheidel, 'Human mobility in Roman Italy, 2: The slave population,' *JRS* 95 (2005), 67–71; L. de Ligt, 'Poverty and demography: The case of the Gracchan land reforms', *Mnemosyne* 57 (2004), 746–7.
22. N. Rosenstein, 'Aristocrats and agriculture in the middle and late Republic', *JRS* 98 (2008), 1–26.

litres of oil might have had a value of only around 450 *denarii*, hardly enough to fund a luxurious lifestyle when a jar of Pontic salted fish cost 300 *denarii*. The wheat necessary to feed a million townspeople would have required considerably more land, perhaps as much as 10 per cent of Italy's arable. But by the mid-second century, imports from Sicily and Sardinia were supplying much of what the urban population ate, greatly reducing the market for wheat producers in Italy. All this makes it very difficult to believe that aristocrats were buying up vast tracts of land from impoverished farmers and populating them with hordes of slaves during the second century in order to support themselves in lavish style and fund the growing expense of a political career from the profits they made growing crops to feed Italy's urban poor.

The effects of Rome's wars on Italian agriculture were rather different and stemmed from the heavy toll those wars took on the lives of the soldiers who fought them.[23] The Republic's armies won nearly every battle they fought in the years between 200 and 146, but casualties were sometimes heavy, and even when they were not, because so many battles were fought by so many armies, even moderate losses of lives added up over time. In the years between the end of the Hannibalic war and the defeat of Perseus, when Livy's text provides us with casualty figures on which to base estimates, something over 100,000 Roman legionaries and Italian *socii* might have died in combat or subsequently of the wounds they received. Equally if not more serious were deaths due to disease arising from poor sanitation or just the effects of contagion among so many men forced to live for long periods in the close quarters of a military camp. Even a conservative estimate of mortality from disease adds between about 75,000 and 100,000 to deaths resulting from combat in the same period, a combined rate of mortality of between 4.75 and 5.45 per cent annually. Put in stark terms, if 116,500 or so citizens and allies were serving with the legions every year between 200 and 168 and each served an average of twelve years, at these rates of mortality between 34 and 40 per cent of the men who went to war might not have returned. Warfare slackened somewhat after 168, yet military mortality is likely to have remained high.

Although tragic for their families, the consequences of the deaths of so many young men were not simply benign but even

23. Rosenstein, *Rome at War*, 107–40.

advantageous for the civilian population in the countryside.[24] A substantial number of the surviving young men among them will have found themselves, contrary to their expectations, able to marry when military service resulted in the demise of an heir and enabled them to succeed to a farm on which to support a wife and children. They and others in their age cohort are also likely to have been able to wed on advantageous terms. Since the men who shouldered the burden of Rome's wars were mostly young and unmarried, the deaths of so many of them will have caused the number of young, marriageable women to outnumber significantly the stock of potential husbands. Dowries ought therefore to have been high compared to the wealth a groom might bring to a marriage. Remarriage, too, would have been easier for widowers so inclined. In economic terms, as war-related deaths reduced the number of young men returning from their stint with the legions and looking for land on which to begin farming, the amount and quality of land that survivors were able to work will have increased. As population pressures ease, marginal land falls out of production as farmers concentrate on the most productive fields. Productivity rises, since the same amount of labour applied to better-quality land yields a higher return. More land can be devoted to cash crops like vines, vegetables, and arboriculture or livestock. Diets become better and more varied as less land needs to be devoted to basic cereals like wheat or barley. Stock rearing in particular boosts productivity since the manure from grazing animals enriches the land, improving yields when it is once again under crops. And to the extent that a demand for free labour existed in the countryside, those in a position to supply it would find themselves in a stronger position when bargaining for wages with prospective employers.

The growth of the city of Rome in the second century will only have augmented these positive effects as migration from the countryside into the city further eased population pressure on the supply of farmland. Because mortality there was considerably higher than the birth rate, it has been estimated that at least 7,000 immigrants will have been needed in order to offset the excess of deaths over births and add 300,000 to the population by the middle of the century.[25] That is a rate of migration as great as – if not greater than – that at which the Republic's wars consumed the lives of its

24. Rosenstein, *Rome at War*, 141–69.
25. Morley, *Metropolis and Hinterland*, 39–46.

soldiers. The effects of colonisation were similar if on a smaller scale. The senate dispatched five or possibly six Latin colonies between 193 and 177 and another in 157, in addition to several smaller colonies of Roman citizens and supplements to colonies whose numbers had been depleted over the course of the war with Hannibal and subsequently – a total of at least 30,000 settlers. In two instances, strikingly large allotments had to be offered, twelve and a half hectares, suggesting that in these cases at least the other options available to potential colonists necessitated substantial benefits to entice them to participate. Conversely, in 189 the senate learned that two Roman colonies, where allotments were typically quite modest, had been abandoned, again indicating that colonists there had more attractive alternatives elsewhere (Livy, 39.23.3). One may suspect that the *patres*' failure to dispatch any colony for twenty years after 177 was not because the Republic had run out of *ager publicus* on which to found one (public land remained plentiful well into the late Republic) but because farmland was available in much more attractive locations, so that potential colonists had little incentive to volunteer.

All these developments point to a generalised prosperity among the rural population in the half century between 200 and 146, and prosperity under conditions of natural fertility tends to raise the birth rate. We know little about birth control in this era, but sexual abstinence and infant exposure are two common methods pre-industrial families used to cope with the problem of too many mouths to feed. These strategies, to the extent that Roman and Italian families practised them, will have declined when times were good. Families are likely to have been willing to have more children and to raise more of those born to them. This trend is reflected in the only demographic evidence we have for these years, the quinquennial counts the censors made of free, adult male Roman citizens. The interpretation of these figures is not easy and has recently become controversial.[26] However, the most plausible reconstruction yields a

---

26. Brunt, *Italian Manpower*, 61–83; contra, E. Lo Cascio, 'Recruitment and the size of the Roman population from the third to the first century BCE', in W. Scheidel (ed.), *Debating Roman Demography*, Leiden: Brill, 2001, 111–38; Lo Cascio, 'The population of Roman Italy in town and country', in J. Bintliff and K. Sbonias (eds), *Reconstructing Past Population Trends in Mediterranean Europe (3000 BC–AD 1800)*, Oxford: Oxbow Books, 1999, 161–71; a possible middle ground in S. Hin, 'Counting Romans', in L. de Ligt and S. Northwood (eds), *People, Land, and Politics: Demographic Developments and the Transformation of Roman Italy 300 BC–AD 14*, Leiden: Brill, 2008, 187–238.

Table 4 *Roman census figures, 203–124 BC*

Year	Census count	Source	'Corrected' count[a]
204/3	214,000	Livy, 29.37	240,000
194/3	143,704	Livy, 35.9	183,000
189/8	258,318	Livy, 38.36	291,000
179/8	258,794	Livy, *Per.* 41	281,000
174/3	269,015	Livy, 42.10	285,500
169/8	312,805	Livy, *Per.* 45	346,000
164/3	337,022	Livy, *Per.* 46	348,000
159/8	328,316	Livy, *Per.* 47	339,000
154/3	324,000	Livy, *Per.* 48	340,500
147/6	322,000	Euseb. Armen. Ol. 158.3[b]	377,000
142/1	327,442	Livy, *Per.* 54	354,500
136/5	317,933	Livy, *Per.* 56	345,500
131/0	318,823	Livy, *Per.* 59	346,500
125/4	394,736	Livy, *Per.* 60	433,500

[a] The 'corrected' count is drawn from Brunt, *Italian Manpower*, 61–74, who adds citizens likely to have been omitted by the censors, including soldiers serving overseas and those Campanians who had been disenfranchised following the suppression of Capua's revolt in 211 until the census of 189/8.

[b] Armenian translation of Eusebius of Caesarea's now lost *Chronicle*, under the third year of the 158th Olympiad.

steadily rising trend from 203 onward (see Table 4), while the dissenting view posits an even greater increase. The census figures in turn are generally held to reflect demographic trends in the population as a whole. More free, adult male citizens indicates a growing number of free Roman women and children as well as, although this is less certain, probably more free Italians. Strong population growth, of the order of about 1 per cent annually, continued throughout the period down to the last decades of the second century. The sharp rise between the censuses of 130 and 124 in the number of citizens counted, confirmed by the census of 115/114 (394,366: Livy, *Per.* 63), suggests that the declines recorded in the censuses conducted after 164 reflect undercounting rather than a drop in the number of citizens. Roman men may have been reluctant to come forward in these years, particularly during the later 150s and up to 134, owing to the unpopularity of military service in Spain and Sicily during these years (see above, p. 229). Failing to register at the census meant a man or his adult sons would not be listed on the roles of *assidui* and so would not become liable for conscription.

The good times in the countryside could not last. In simple

Malthusian terms, an expanding population in a pre-industrial, agrarian economy sooner or later grows beyond the ability of the land's productivity to support it. There is no longer enough farm-land, and at that point serious problems begin. Current thinking among many scholars sees population pressure rather than the growth of slave-based commercial agriculture as the root cause of the economic distress that in turn produced the social and political unrest of the years after 146. Catalysing that unrest, however, was the appearance of aristocrats able to mobilise outpourings of popular support in order to challenge the *auctoritas* of the senate. And the man who pointed the way was Scipio Aemilianus.

Scipio Aemilianus

Scipio's rise to prominence during the Third Punic War would have profound consequences for the late Republic.[27] He made a mark for himself in 151 when he volunteered to serve as military tribune in the army destined for Spain (see above, p. 229). While there he continued to distinguish himself not only as an able officer but for extraordinary courage. At the city of Intercatia he accepted the challenge of an enemy chieftain to single combat, and although the Spaniard was considerably bigger Scipio vanquished him. He was also first to mount the wall during an attempt to storm the city, winning the mural crown (*corona muralis*), and he negotiated the city's surrender (App. *Hisp.* 53–4; Livy, *Per.* 48). Then in 149 he joined the expedition against Carthage, again as a military tribune, where his *virtus* gained him even greater *fama* (reputation). His skilful deployment of the men under his command saved a band of soldiers who had pushed through a breach in the walls and were being driven out again by the Carthaginian defenders. Twice when the enemy assaulted the Roman camp by night his quick thinking put the attackers to flight. His care in guarding foraging parties resulted in his being the only ones not set upon by bands of Punic cavalry. His integrity in keeping his word caused enemy troops in small forts around the countryside to surrender to him and no one else. Following the battle at Nepheris, when the enemy struck the Romans as they were fording a river, Scipio led a troop of cavalry in a counterattack that drove off the Carthaginians and prevented even greater losses. After the army had marched some distance, the

27. A. E. Astin, *Scipio Aemilianus*, Oxford: Oxford University Press, 1967.

officers realised that they had left behind four cohorts that had got separated from the main force, had taken refuge on a hill, and were now surrounded. Scipio led the relief party, earning the very rare award of a siege crown (the *corona obsidionalis*) for rescuing them. Finally, he arranged for the defection of the commander of the Carthaginian cavalry along with many of his men (App. *Pun.* 98–110; Livy, *Per.* 49; Vell. Pat.1.12.4).

Scipio returned to Rome in 148 intending to run for the aedileship, the first curule magistracy on the *cursus honorum*. But on the day of the canvass, a groundswell of popular enthusiasm built to elect him consul (certainly not without encouragement from his political allies). The law forbade it, however. Not only was he too young, but he had held none of the requisite preliminary offices. Nevertheless a tribune of the plebs threatened to veto the consular elections if Scipio was not allowed to run. The senate was forced to order the suspension of the law for that year, and the voters elevated Scipio to the consulate of 147. His achievements had clearly marked him out as a man who could get things done, especially with the war in North Africa seemingly stalled at that point. Even the elderly Cato sang his praises (Polyb. 36.8.7). Moreover, he was by birth the son of Aemilius Paullus, the consul who had taken charge of the war against Perseus at a similar juncture and ended it triumphantly. Still more importantly, as the grandson by adoption of Scipio Africanus he was seen as a man, like his grandfather, fated to conquer Carthage. It was even rumoured that he enjoyed the favour of the same divinity that had aided Africanus. He repaid the voters' trust by taking charge of the war against Carthage and bringing the siege to a victorious conclusion. He returned to Rome as a new 'Africanus'.

Yet Scipio's ascent to the consulate on the wings of popular favour represented an ominous foreshadowing of things to come. The rallying cry of his supporters had been popular sovereignty: the Roman people made the laws, and so the Roman people could transgress them whenever it pleased (App. *Pun.* 112). That claim, however, flew in the face of senatorial *auctoritas*, the belief that the *patres'* advice, based on their collective wisdom and experience, constituted the soundest, most reliable guidance for the people in the administration of their public affairs. This was not the first time that a claim of popular sovereignty had trumped the rules restricting aristocratic competition, but Scipio's manoeuvre at the consular elections for 147 enabled him to go on to perform a great service to the Republic and so reap enormous glory, earn the public's *gratia*, and acquire great personal *auctoritas*. It demonstrated how an ambitious aristocrat could mobilise public support for a measure that would benefit the Roman people and so advance his personal stature in defiance of traditional impediments. Within a few years, tribunes of the plebs would begin to adopt a similar strategy. Capitalising on the economic misery arising from population pressures, and deploying arguments drawn from Greek philosophy in speeches infused with the techniques of Hellenistic rhetoric, they were able to rally public support to pass legislation despite the *patres'* opposition and so threaten the senate's control of the *res publica*. Ironically, just when the senate by the terrifying use of extreme violence had succeeded in cowing those abroad who had ignored its wishes and threatened its control of the Roman *imperium*, events were unfolding at Rome itself that within a generation would lead to similar challenges to its authority in the political arena. And ultimately here, too, the senators would feel themselves forced to resort to extreme violence to reassert control.

Chronology

Political/Military	Religious/Cultural	Events elsewhere
298–290 Third Samnite War 295 Battle of Sentinum		
290 M'. Curius Dentatus conquers Sabinum 289 Mamertines seize Messana		
283(?) Battle of Arretium; annexation of *ager Gallicus* c. 282 Roman garrison in Rhegium		
280–275 Pyrrhic war	c. 280 Rome's first coinage	279 Gauls invade Macedon and Greece; driven out by Aetolians 278–276 Pyrrhus in Sicily
270 Rome captures Rhegium		
264–241 First Punic War		
237 Romans seize Sardinia	239–169 Ennius	241–237 Mercenary war
		238–179 Philip V king of Macedon
227 Sicily and Sardinia-Corsica become provinces 226/225(?) Ebro treaty 225–220 Rome conquers the Gauls of N. Italy 219 Siege and fall of Saguntum; Second Illyrian War	234–149 M. Porcius Cato 220 *Ludi plebeii* established	237–218 Growth of Carthaginian power in Spain
218–201 Second Punic War		

Political/Military	Religious/Cultural	Events elsewhere
216 Cannae 215–205 First Macedonian War 212–211 Capua and Syracuse captured	216 Human sacrifice at Rome 212 *Ludi Apollinares* established c. 211 Silver *denarius* minted	212–205 Antiochus campaigns in the east 203(?) Secret pact between Antiochus and Philip
210–205 Scipio in Spain 207 Roman victory at river Metaurus 204–201 Scipio in Africa 202 Roman victory at Zama	c. 205–c. 184 Plautus composes plays 204 Magna Mater arrives in Rome; *ludi Megalenses* established 202 *Ludi Ceriales* established	202–200 Philip campaigns in Asia Minor
200–196 Second Macedonian War 190s–150s Roman conquest of Celts and Ligurians 197 Senate establishes provinces in Spain; Cynoscephalae 197–178 Spanish wars 196 Isthmian proclamation 194 Rome evacuates Greece 192–189 Syrian war 190 Magnesia	c. 200 Fabius Pictor writes first history of Rome	196 Antiochus moves west, enters Europe
	173 *Ludi Floralia* established	179–167 Perseus king of Macedon
171–168 Third Macedonian War 168 Pydna	168 Polybius brought to Rome, meets Scipio Aemilianus 160s Terence composes plays	171–168 War between Syria and Egypt 168 'Day of Eleusis'
155–132 Renewed fighting in Spain	155 Embassy of the philosophers	151 Carthage declares war on Masinissa
150–148 Macedon revolts		
149–146 Third Punic War 146 Destruction of Carthage; Achaean war; destruction of Corinth		

Guide to further reading

The ancient sources

The most important ancient authors for military, diplomatic and political events of the middle Republic are Polybius and Livy. Polybius, an Achaean Greek brought to Rome as a hostage following the defeat of Perseus (see above, pp. 1 and 22), wrote a history in 40 books covering Roman expansion and events in the Hellenistic East from c. 265 down to 146 to show how the ancient world gradually came under the dominion of Rome. Only books 1 to 5 survive intact. Of the rest we have only fragments of varying size and importance, although among these is the very valuable excerpt from book 6 on the Roman constitution and army. While his judgements are not free from bias, Polybius was an experienced statesman whose intelligent observations and shrewd analyses place his *Histories* among the best historical works the ancient world produced. A Landmark translation is in the works; the Penguin edition of selected passages is a fine alternative. Livy (59 BC–AD 17) composed a history of Rome from the foundation of the city (*Ab urbe condita*) down to his own time in 167 books, of which we have only books 1 to 10 and 21 to 45. Summaries (*Periochae* and the *Oxyrhyncheae periochae*) provide some idea of the contents of the rest. Written in a year-by-year, annalistic format, the work draws heavily on the accounts of earlier historians whose identities and quality are rarely known to us. Livy had no practical experience of politics, war, or diplomacy; he was primarily a literary stylist who sought the moral improvement of his readers through the example of Rome's glorious past. Penguin publishes a good translation of the surviving books in four volumes. Among the other ancient authors who contribute to our knowledge of this period, Dionysius of Halicarnassus, a contemporary of Livy, wrote *Roman Antiquities*, covering the history of the city from its origins down to the First Punic War and, like Livy, drawing on earlier authors of varying quality. We have in full only that portion of the work covering events down to 441, but fragments of the rest often shed important light on events in the first half of the third century. Plutarch (c. AD 50–120) produced among many other works a series of parallel *Lives* of famous Greeks and Romans. Many preserve information not found in other authors and are particularly valuable for that reason. However, since Plutarch's purposes were principally moralistic and didactic rather than strictly historical, his accuracy is sometimes question-able. Again, Penguin offers accessible translations of the relevant Roman biography in *The Makers of Rome* while *The Age of Alexander* contains the *Life of Pyrrhus*. Appian (late first century AD–c. 160) wrote an account of Rome's conquests arranged loosely by geography. Those for the Hannibalic war in Italy, Spain, and North Africa are the most relevant to our period, and provide our only connected narrative of events of fighting in Spain after 155 and the Third Punic War. The quality of his work, however, is inferior to that of Livy or Polybius, and his accounts often leave many questions unanswered. Finally, other authors such as Cicero, Pliny the Elder, Valerius Maximus, and Aulus Gellius sometimes provide evidence not found in other works. The Loeb Classical Library also publishes translations of all of these ancient authors.

Modern works
(See the Bibliography for full publication details.)

Volumes 7 and 8 of the *Cambridge Ancient History* offer a full survey of Rome as well as Italy and the rest of the ancient world in this era. Chapters cover not only political and military/diplomatic events but economic, social, religious, and cultural developments, accompanied by extensive bibliographies. They are not light reading, however, and H. Flower (ed.), *The Cambridge Companion to the Roman Republic*, and N. Rosenstein and R. Morstein-Marx (eds), *A Companion to the Roman Republic*, are likely to be more useful and accessible to students and general readers. A. Lintott, *The Constitution of the Roman Republic*, details the formal structure and functioning of the Republic's government; L. R. Taylor's *The Roman Voting Assemblies* is an older but still important study of that institution. How republican politics really worked has in recent years been much debated. Major contributions include several revisionist articles by F. Millar, now collected in *Rome, the Greek World, and the East*, vol. 1, and the responses of H. Mouritsen, *Plebs and Politics in the Late Roman Republic*, R. Morstein-Marx, *Mass Oratory and Political Power in the Late Roman Republic*, and K-J. Hökeskamp, *Reconstructing the Roman Republic*. Hökeskamp in addition presents a survey and synthesis of much important work done by German scholars on republican political culture since the seminal study by C. Meier, *Res publica amissa*, unfortunately not translated into English. H. Flower, *Ancestor Masks and Aristocratic Power in Roman Culture*, presents an in-depth study of one crucial element of aristocratic self-representation and in so doing offers much insight into republican political competition. Scholarship on high politics has been out of fashion for some time, but A. E. Astin's *Cato the Censor* and *Scipio Aemilianus* remain valuable studies of these two central figures. On cultural changes during this period, E. S. Gruen's *Studies in Greek Culture and*

Roman Policy and *Culture and National Identity in Republican Rome* offer trenchant critiques of earlier scholarship and revisionist analyses. The involvement of ordinary Romans in the civic life of the Republic is well described by C. Nicolet in *The World of the Citizen in Republican Rome*.

There is no good recent work on Pyrrhus in English. By contrast, the current over-production of popularising studies of the Punic wars shows no sign of abating: R. Miles, *Carthage Must be Destroyed*, and R. O'Connell, *The Ghosts of Cannae*, both 2010, are only the latest to appear. Among somewhat older studies, A. Goldsworthy, *The Punic Wars* (2000), perhaps best combines sound scholarship with readability. M. Fronda, *Between Rome and Carthage*, offers the only important advance in our understanding of the war's strategic dimension to appear in many years, while D. Hoyos (ed.), *A Companion to the Punic Wars*, contains a wealth of up-to-date, specialised studies on various aspects of these conflicts. On the army and warfare generally, P. Erdkamp (ed.), *A Companion to the Roman Army*, similarly summarises much current thinking on a variety of topics related to the army of the middle Republic. On the critical question of the forces impelling Roman expansion, W. V. Harris, *War and Imperialism in Republican Rome 327–70 B.C.*, marked the starting point in a fruitful debate among scholars. That debate is reviewed by A. M. Eckstein, *Mediterranean Anarchy, Interstate War, and the Rise of Rome*, by way of setting the stage for his own important critique of Harris and presentation of a system-level analysis of the dynamics of Roman expansion. On the Roman advance in Spain, J. S. Richardson, *Hispaniae*, remains fundamental; on northern Italy, B. D. Hoyos, 'Roman strategy'. J-M. David, *The Roman Conquest of Italy*, and T. Potter, *Roman Italy*, both offer useful although now somewhat dated surveys of developments in Italy generally. However, scholars have recently questioned many long-accepted notions about how 'Romanised' Italy became in the third and second centuries: see H. Mouritsen, *Italian Unification*, and the papers collected in E. Herring and K. Lomas (eds), *The Emergence of State Identities in Italy in the First Millennium BC*, and in G. Bradley and J-P. Wilson (eds), *Greek and Roman Colonization*. Older theories about economic and demographic developments in this period have also come in for considerable criticism: N. Rosenstein, *Rome at War*, and L. de Ligt and S. Northwood (eds), *People, Land, and Politics*, both provide good starting points.

Bibliography

Afzelius, A., *Die römische Eroberung Italiens (340–264 v. Chr.)*, Copenhagen: Universitetsforlaget i Aarhus, 1942.

Alexander, M., 'Law in the Roman Republic', in N. Rosenstein and R. Morstein-Marx (eds), *A Companion to the Roman Republic*, Oxford: Blackwell, 2006, 236–55.

Astin, A. E., *Cato the Censor*, Oxford: Oxford University Press, 1978.

Astin, A. E., *The Lex Annalis before Sulla*, Brussels: Latomus, 1958.

Astin, A. E., *Scipio Aemilianus*, Oxford: Oxford University Press, 1967.

Astin, A. E., F. W. Walbank, M. W. Fredericksen, and R. M. Ogilvie (eds), *Rome and the Mediterranean to 133 B.C.* Vol. 8 of *The Cambridge Ancient History*², Cambridge: Cambridge University Press, 1989.

Badian, E., *Studies in Greek and Roman History*, Oxford: Blackwell, 1964.

Beard, M., *The Roman Triumph*, Cambridge, MA: Harvard University Press, 2007.

Beard, M., J. North, and S. Price, *Religions of Rome*, 2 vols, Cambridge: Cambridge University Press, 1998.

Billows, R., 'Legal fiction and political reform at Rome in the early second century', *Phoenix* 43 (1989), 112–33.

Bispham, E., '*Coloniam deducere*: How Roman was Roman colonization during the middle Republic?', in G. Bradley and J-P. Wilson (eds), *Greek and Roman Colonization: Origins, Ideologies and Interactions*, Swansea: Classical Press of Wales, 2006, 73–160.

Bradley, G., and J-P. Wilson (eds), *Greek and Roman Colonization: Origins, Ideologies and Interactions*, Swansea: Classical Press of Wales, 2006.

Brennan, T. C., 'M.' Curius Dentatus and the praetor's right to triumph', *Historia* 43 (1994), 423–39.

Briscoe, J., *A Commentary on Livy Books 38–40*, Oxford: Oxford University Press, 2008.

Broadhead, W., 'Rome and the mobility of the Latins: Problems of control', in C. Moatti (ed.), *La Mobilité des personnes en Méditerranée de l'antiquité à la époque moderne*, Rome: Ecole Française de Rome, 2004, 315–35.

Brunt, P. A., *The Fall of the Roman Republic and Related Essays*, Oxford: Oxford University Press, 1988.

Brunt, P. A., *Italian Manpower 225 B.C.–A.D. 14*, Oxford: Oxford University Press, 1971.

Brunt, P. A., 'Nobilitas and novitas', *JRS* 72 (1982), 1–17.

Churchill, J. B., 'Ex qua quod vellent facerent: Roman magistrates' authority over praeda and manubiae', *TAPA* 129 (1999), 85–116.

Corbeill, A., 'The republican body', in N. Rosenstein and R. Morstein-Marx (eds), *A Companion to the Roman Republic*, Oxford: Blackwell, 2006, 439–56.

Crawford, M. H., *Coinage and Money under the Roman Republic: Italy and the Mediterranean Economy*, London: Methuen, 1985.

Daly, G., *Cannae: The Experience of Battle in the Second Punic War*, London: Routledge, 2002.

David, J-M., 'Rhetoric and public life', in N. Rosenstein and R. Morstein-Marx (eds), *A Companion to the Roman Republic*, Oxford: Blackwell, 2006, 421–8.

David, J-M., *The Roman Conquest of Italy*, trans. A. Nevill, Oxford: Blackwell, 1997.

de Ligt, L., 'Poverty and demography: The case of the Gracchan land reforms', *Mnemosyne* 57 (2004), 725–57.

de Ligt, L., and S. Northwood (eds), *People, Land, and Politics: Demographic Developments and the Transformation of Roman Italy 300 BC–AD 14*, Leiden: Brill, 2008.

Dench, E., *From Barbarians to New Men: Greek, Roman, and Modern Perceptions of Peoples of the Central Apennines*, Oxford: Oxford University Press, 1995.

Derow, P. S., 'Rome, the fall of Macedon, and the sack of Corinth', in A. E. Astin, F. W. Walbank, M. W. Fredericksen, and R. M. Ogilvie (eds), *Rome and the Mediterranean to 133 B.C.* Vol. 8 of *The Cambridge Ancient History*[2], Cambridge: Cambridge University Press, 1989, 290–323.

De Sanctis, G., *Storia dei Romani*, 2nd edn, Florence: Nuova Italia, 1953–.

Dobson, M., *The Army of the Roman Republic: The Second Century BC, Polybius and the Camps at Numantia, Spain*, Oxford: Oxbow Books, 2008.

Dzino, D., *Illyricum in Roman Politics 229 BC–AD 68*, Cambridge: Cambridge University Press, 2010.

Eckstein, A. M., *Mediterranean Anarchy, Interstate War, and the Rise of Rome*, Berkeley and Los Angeles: University of California Press, 2006.

Eckstein, A. M., 'Polybius on the rôle of the senate in the crisis of 264 B.C.', *GRBS* 21 (1980), 175–90.

Eckstein, A. M., *Senate and General: Individual Decision Making and Roman Foreign Relations, 264–194 B.C.*, Berkeley: University of California Press, 1987.

Eckstein, A. M., 'T. Quinctius Flamininus and the campaign against Philip in 198 B.C.', *Phoenix* 30 (1976), 119–42.

Eckstein, A. M., 'Two notes on the chronology of the outbreak of the Hannibalic war', *Rh. Mus.* 126 (1983), 255–72.

Edwards, C., *The Politics of Immorality in Ancient Rome*, Cambridge: Cambridge University Press, 1993.

Erdkamp, P. (ed.), *A Companion to the Roman Army*, Oxford: Wiley-Blackwell, 2007.

Erdkamp, P., *Hunger and the Sword: Warfare and Food Supply in Roman Republican Wars (264–30 B.C.)*, Amsterdam: J. C. Gieben, 1998.

Erdkamp, P., 'Polybius, Livy, and the "Fabian strategy"', *Ancient Society*, 23 (1992), 127–47.

Fabricius, E., 'Some notes on Polybius's description of Roman camps', *JRS* 22 (1932), 78–87.

Fentress, E. *Cosa V, an Intermittent Town: Excavations 1991–1997*, Ann Arbor: Published for the American Academy in Rome by the University of Michigan Press, 2003.

Flower, H., *Ancestor Masks and Aristocratic Power in Roman Culture*, Oxford: Oxford University Press, 1996.

Flower, H. (ed.), *The Cambridge Companion to the Roman Republic*, Cambridge: Cambridge University Press, 2004.

Franke, P. R. 'Pyrrhus', in F. W. Walbank, A. E. Astin, M. W. Frederiksen, and R. M. Ogilvie (eds), *The Rise of Rome to 220 B.C.* Vol. 7, Part 2, of *The Cambridge Ancient History*[2], Cambridge: Cambridge University Press, 1989, 456–85.

Fronda, M., *Between Rome and Carthage: Southern Italy during the Second Punic War*, Cambridge: Cambridge University Press, 2010.

Garnsey, P., T. Gallant, and D. Rathbone, 'Thessaly and the grain supply of Rome during the second century B.C.', *JRS* 74 (1984), 30–44.

Gelzer, M., *The Roman Nobility*, trans. R. Seager, Oxford: Blackwell, 1966.

Goldsworthy, A., *Cannae*, London: Cassell, 2001.

Goldsworthy, A., *The Punic Wars*, London: Cassell, 2000 (also published as *The Fall of Carthage: The Punic Wars, 265–146 BC*, London: Phoenix, 2006).

Gruen, E. S., *Culture and National Identity in Republican Rome*, Ithaca, NY: Cornell University Press, 1992.

Gruen, E. S., 'The "fall" of the Scipios', in I. Malkin and Z. W. Rubinsonhn (eds), *Leaders and Masses in the Roman World: Studies in Honor of Ziv Yavetz*, Leiden: Brill, 1995, 59–90.

Gruen, E. S., *The Hellenistic World and the Coming of Rome*, Berkeley and Los Angeles: University of California Press, 1984.

Gruen, E. S., 'The last years of Philip V', *GRBS* 15 (1974), 221–46.

Gruen, E. S., 'The origins of the Achaean war', *JHS* 96 (1976), 46–69.

Gruen, E. S., *Roman Politics and the Criminal Courts, 149–78 B.C.*, Cambridge, MA: Harvard University Press, 1968.

Gruen, E. S., *Studies in Greek Culture and Roman Policy*, Leiden: Brill, 1990; reprint Berkeley and Los Angeles: University of California Press, 1996.

Harris, W. V., 'Roman expansion in the west', in A. E. Astin, F. W. Walbank, M. W. Fredericksen, and R. M. Ogilvie (eds), *Rome and the Mediterranean to 133 B.C.* Vol. 8 of *The Cambridge Ancient History*², Cambridge: Cambridge University Press, 1989, 118–42.

Harris, W. V., *War and Imperialism in Republican Rome 327–70 B.C.*, Oxford: Oxford University Press, 1979.

Herring, E., and K. Lomas (eds), *The Emergence of State Identities in Italy in the First Millennium BC*, London: Accordia Research Institute, University of London, 2000.

Hin, S., 'Counting Romans', in L. de Ligt and S. Northwood (eds), *People, Land, and Politics: Demographic Developments and the Transformation of Roman Italy 300 BC–AD 14*, Leiden: Brill, 2008, 187–238.

Hökeskamp, K-J., *Reconstructing the Roman Republic: An Ancient Political Culture and Modern Research*, trans. H. Heitmann-Gordon, Princeton: Princeton University Press, 2010.

Hoyos, B. D., *Unplanned Wars: The Origins of the First and Second Punic Wars*, Berlin: De Gruyter, 1998.

Hoyos, D., 'The age of overseas expansion (264–146 BC)', in P. Erdkamp (ed.), *A Companion to the Roman Army*, Oxford: Wiley-Blackwell, 2007, 68–73.

Hoyos, B. D., 'Roman strategy in the Cisalpina, 224–222 and 203–191 B.C.', *Antichthon* 10 (1976), 44–55.

Hoyos, D. (ed.), *A Companion to the Punic Wars*, Oxford: Wiley-Blackwell, 2011.

Humbert, M., *Municipium et civitas sine suffragio: L'Organisation de la conquête jusqu'à la guerre sociale*, Rome: Ecole Française de Rome, 1978.

Ilari, V., *Gli italici nelle strutture militari romane*, Milan: A. Giuffrè, 1974.

Jehne, M., 'Methods, models, and historiography', in N. Rosenstein and R. Morstein-Marx (eds), *A Companion to the Roman Republic*, Oxford: Blackwell, 2006, 3–28.

Jehne, M., 'Römer, Latiner und Budesgenossen im Krieg: Zu Formen und Ausmaß der Integration in der republickanischen Armee', in M. Jehne and R. Pfeilschifter (eds), *Herrschaft ohne Integration? Rom und Italien in republicanischer Zeit*, Frankfurt: Antike, 2006, 243–67.

Jongman, W., 'Slavery and the growth of Rome: The transformation of Italy in the second and first centuries BCE,' in C. Edwards and G. Woolf (eds), *Rome the Cosmopolis*, Cambridge: Cambridge University Press, 2003, 100–22.

Laurence, R., *The Roads of Roman Italy: Mobility and Cultural Change*, London: Routledge, 1999.

Lazenby, J. F., *The First Punic War: A Military History*, Stanford: Stanford University Press, 1996.

Lazenby, J. F, *Hannibal's War: A Military History of the Second Punic War*, Warminster: Aris and Phillips, 1978.

Linderski, J., 'The augural law', in H. Temporini (ed.), *Aufstieg und Niedergang der römischen Welt: Geschichte und Kultur Roms im Spiegel der neueren Forschung*, Berlin and New York: De Gruyter, 1986, 2146–312.

Lintott, A., *The Constitution of the Roman Republic*, Oxford: Oxford University Press, 1999.

Lo Cascio, E., 'The population of Roman Italy in town and country', in J. Bintliff and K. Sbonias (eds), *Reconstructing Past Population Trends in Mediterranean Europe (3000 BC–AD 1800)*, Oxford: Oxbow Books, 1999, 161–71.

Lo Cascio, E., 'Recruitment and the size of the Roman population from the third to the first century BCE', in W. Scheidel (ed.), *Debating Roman Demography*, Leiden: Brill, 2001, 111–37.

Lomas, K., *Rome and the Western Greeks, 350 BC–AD 200: Conquest and Acculturation in Southern Italy*, London and New York: Routledge, 1993.

McDonnell, M., *Roman Manliness: Virtus and the Roman Republic*, Cambridge: Cambridge University Press, 2006.

Meier, C., *Res publica amissa: Eine Studie zu Verfassung und Geschichte der späten römischen Republik*, Wiesbaden: Steiner, 1966.

Miles, R., *Carthage Must be Destroyed: The Rise and Fall of an Ancient Civilization*, London: Allen Lane, 2010.

Millar, F., *Rome, the Greek World, and the East*, Chapel Hill: University of North Carolina Press, 2002.

Morgan, M. G., 'The defeat of L. Metellus Denter at Arretium', *CQ* n.s. 22 (1972), 309–25.

Morley, N., *Metropolis and Hinterland: The City of Rome and the Italian Economy, 200 B.C.–A.D. 200*, Cambridge: Cambridge University Press, 1996.

Morstein-Marx, R. M., *Mass Oratory and Political Power in the Late Roman Republic*, Cambridge: Cambridge University Press, 2004.

Mouritsen, H., *Italian Unification: A Study in Ancient and Modern Historiography*, London: Institute of Classical Studies, School of Advanced Study, University of London, 1998.

Mouritsen, H., *Plebs and Politics in the Late Roman Republic*, Cambridge: Cambridge University Press, 2001.

Nicolet, C., *The World of the Citizen in Republican Rome*, trans. P. S. Falla, Berkeley and Los Angeles: University of California Press, 1980.

Oakley, S. P., *A Commentary on Livy, Books VI–X*, 4 vols, Oxford: Oxford University Press, 1997-2005.

O'Connell, R., *The Ghosts of Cannae: Hannibal and the Darkest Hour of the Roman Republic*, New York: Random House, 2010.

Orlin, E., *Foreign Cults in Rome: Creating a Roman Empire*, Oxford: Oxford University Press, 2010.

Östenberg, I., *Staging the World: Spoils, Captives, and Representations in the Roman Triumphal Procession*, Oxford: Oxford University Press, 2009.

Pfeilschifter, R., 'The allies in the republican army and the Romanization of Italy', in R. Roth and J. Keller (eds), *Roman by Integration: Dimensions of Group Identity in Material Culture and Text*, Portsmouth, NH: Journal of Roman Archaeology, 2007, 27–42.

Pittenger, M., *Contested Triumphs: Politics, Pageantry, and Performance in Livy's Republican Rome*, Berkeley and Los Angeles: University of California Press, 2008.

Potter, T., *Roman Italy*, London: British Museum Publications, 1987.

Proctor, D., *Hannibal's March in History*, Oxford: Oxford University Press, 1971.

Rawlings, L., 'Army and battle during the conquest of Italy (350–264 BC)', in P. Erdkamp (ed.), *A Companion to the Roman Army*, Oxford: Wiley-Blackwell, 2007, 55–9.

Rich, J., 'The origins of the Second Punic War', in T. Cornell, B. Rankov, and P. Sabin (eds), *The Second Punic War: A Reappraisal*, London: Institute of Classical Studies, 1996, 1–37.

Richardson, J. S., *Hispaniae: Spain and the Development of Roman Imperialism, 218–82 BC*, Cambridge: Cambridge University Press, 1986.

Rosenstein, N., 'Aristocrats and agriculture in the middle and late Republic', *JRS* 98 (2008), 1–26.

Rosenstein, N., 'Competition and crisis in mid-republican Rome', *Phoenix* 47 (1993), 313–38.

Rosenstein, N., *Imperatores victi: Military Defeat and Aristocratic Competition in the Middle and Late Republic*, Berkeley and Los Angeles: University of California Press, 1990.

Rosenstein, N., *Rome at War: Farms, Families, and Death in the Middle Republic*, Chapel Hill: University of North Carolina Press, 2004.

Rosenstein, N., 'War, wealth, and consuls', in H. Beck, A. Duplá, M. Jehne, and F. Pina Polo (eds), *Consuls and res publica: Holding High Office in Republican Rome*, Cambridge: Cambridge University Press, 2011.

Rosenstein, N., and R. Morstein-Marx (eds), *A Companion to the Roman Republic*, Oxford: Blackwell, 2006.

Saller, R., *Patriarchy, Property and Death in the Roman Family*, Cambridge: Cambridge University Press, 1994.

Salmon, E. T., *The Making of Roman Italy*, London: Thames and Hudson, 1982.

Salmon, E. T., *Roman Colonization under the Republic*, London: Thames and Hudson, 1969.

Scheidel, W., 'Human mobility in Roman Italy, 2: The slave population,' *JRS* 95 (2005), 64–79.

Schulten, A., *Numantia: Die Ergebnisse der Ausgrabungen 1905–1912*, 4 vols, Munich: F. Bruckmann, 1914–31.

Scullard, H. H., *Roman Politics, 220–150 BC*[2], Oxford: Oxford University Press, 1973.

Scullard, H. H., *Scipio Africanus, Soldier and Politician*, Ithaca, NY: Cornell University Press, 1970.

Shatzman, I., 'The Roman general's authority over booty', *Historia* 21 (1972), 177–205.

Shatzman, I., *Senatorial Wealth and Roman Politics*, Brussels: Latomus, 1975.

Sherwin-White, A. N. *The Roman Citizenship*[2], Oxford: Oxford University Press, 1973.

Taylor, L. R., *The Roman Voting Assemblies from the Hannibalic War to the Dictatorship of Caesar*, Ann Arbor: University of Michigan Press, 1966.

Terrenato, N., 'The auditorium site and the origins of the villa', *JRA* 14 (2001), 5–32.

Walbank, F. W., 'The Scipionic legend', *PCPS* 13 (1967), 54–64 = *Selected Papers: Studies in Greek History and Historiography*, Cambridge: Cambridge University Press, 1985, 120–37.

Williams, C., *Roman Homosexuality: Ideologies of Masculinity in Classical Antiquity*, Oxford: Oxford University Press, 1999.

Wiseman, T. P., 'Competition and co-operation', in T. P. Wiseman (ed.), *Roman Political Life 90 BC–AD 69*, Exeter: University of Exeter Press, 1985.

Ziolkowski, A., '*Urbs direpta*, or how the Romans sacked cities', in J. Rich and G. Shipley (eds), *War and Society in the Roman World*, London: Routledge, 1993, 61–91.

Index